W9-BXB-157

Vietnam
a country study

Federal Research Division
Library of Congress
Edited by Ronald J. Cima
Research Completed
December 1987

On the cover: Viet Minh soldier waves the flag of the
Democratic Republic of Vietnam over General Christian de
Castries's bunker following the French defeat at Dien Bien
Phu, May 7, 1954.

First Edition, 1989; First Printing, 1989.

Library of Congress Cataloging-in-Publication Data

Vietnam: A Country Study

  (Area handbook series) (DA Pam; 550-32)
  Research completed December 1987.
  Bibliography: pp. 335-361.
  Includes index.
  Supt. of Docs. no.: D 101.22:550-32
  1. Vietnam. I. Cima, Ronald J., 1943-
II. Library of Congress. Federal Research Division. III. Series.
IV. Series: DA Pam; 550-32.

DS556.3.V54   1989   959.7   88-600482

Headquarters, Department of the Army
DA Pam 550-32

For sale by the Superintendent of Documents, U.S. Government Printing Office
Washington, D.C. 20402

Foreword

This volume is one in a continuing series of books now being prepared by the Federal Research Division of the Library of Congress under the Country Studies—Area Handbook Program. The last page of this book lists the other published studies.

Most books in the series deal with a particular foreign country, describing and analyzing its political, economic, social, and national security systems and institutions, and examining the interrelationships of those systems and the ways they are shaped by cultural factors. Each study is written by a multidisciplinary team of social scientists. The authors seek to provide a basic understanding of the observed society, striving for a dynamic rather than a static portrayal. Particular attention is devoted to the people who make up the society, their origins, dominant beliefs and values, their common interests and the issues on which they are divided, the nature and extent of their involvement with national institutions, and their attitudes toward each other and toward their social system and political order.

The books represent the analysis of the authors and should not be construed as an expression of an official United States government position, policy, or decision. The authors have sought to adhere to accepted standards of scholarly objectivity. Corrections, additions, and suggestions for changes from readers will be welcomed for use in future editions.

Louis R. Mortimer
Acting Chief
Federal Research Division
Library of Congress
Washington, D.C. 20540

Acknowledgments

The authors are indebted to a number of individuals who contributed their time and specialized knowledge to this volume: Dorothy Avery of the Department of State for her insights into the Vietnamese political process; William Newcomb of the Department of State for his contribution to the discussion on Vietnam's economy; Nguyen Phuong Khanh of the Far Eastern Law Division of the Library of Congress for sharing her knowledge of Vietnamese law; and Bill Herod of the Indochina Project and Douglas Pike of the Indochina Archives, Institute of East Asian Studies, University of California at Berkeley, for making a number of rare photographs available for publication.

The authors also wish to express their appreciation to members of the Federal Research Division of the Library of Congress, whose high standards and dedication helped shape this volume. These include Sharon Costello, Barbara L. Dash, Marilyn L. Majeska, and Ruth Nieland for editing the manuscript; David P. Cabitto, Sandra K. Cotugno, and Kimberly A. Lord for their numerous contributions to the book's graphics; Susan M. Lender for her assistance in preparing maps; Russell G. Swenson for his review of textual references to Vietnam's geography; and Arvies J. Staton for his contribution to the charts on military ranks and insignia. Thanks are also extended to Teresa E. Kamp for her artwork, and Harriett R. Blood for preparing the map on Vietnam's topography.

The following organization and individuals are gratefully acknowledged as well: Shirley Kessel for preparing the index; Carolyn Hinton for performing the prepublication review; Marilyn L. Majeska for managing production; and Diann Johnson of the Library of Congress Composing Unit for preparing the camera-ready copy, under the supervision of Peggy Pixley.

Finally, the editor wishes to acknowledge Ly H. Burnham and Tuyet L. Cosslett for providing an invaluable native Vietnamese perspective and language capability; Elizabeth E. Green-Revier for her insights into Chinese foreign policy; Elizabeth A. Park and Kim E. Colson for their knowledge of telecommunications; Barbara Edgerton, Izella Watson, Tracy M. Henry, and Meridel M. Jackson for untold hours of word processing; and Russell R. Ross, Robert L. Worden, Richard F. Nyrop, and Martha E. Hopkins for reviewing all parts of the book.

Contents

Chapter 5. National Security 237
Douglas Pike

List of Figures

Preface

The Socialist Republic of Vietnam, created from the former Republic of Vietnam (South Vietnam) and the Democratic Republic of Vietnam (North Vietnam), was established as a new nation in July 1976. Previous editions in this series discussed the North and South separately under the respective titles *Area Handbook for North Vietnam*, published in 1967 and reprinted in 1981 as *North Vietnam: A Country Study*, and *Area Handbook for South Vietnam*, published in 1967. Written at the height of the Second Indochina War, these books described a divided Vietnam that ceased to exist in 1975 when Saigon fell to communist forces.

The current study focuses on the years between 1975 and the mid-1980s, when a nascent and newly reunified nation struggled to develop a postwar identity. It was a period marked by a change in leadership, as Vietnam's first generation of communist leaders began to retire in favor of younger technocrats; by the introduction of significant economic reforms, including the preservation of private enterprise in the South; and by major foreign policy developments, particularly the Treaty of Friendship and Cooperation signed with the Soviet Union, the invasion and occupation of Cambodia, and the 1979 border war with China.

A multidisciplinary team, assisted by a support staff, researched and wrote this book. Information came from a variety of sources, including scholarly studies, governmental and international organization reports, and foreign and domestic newspapers and periodicals.

For the reader's reference, a brief commentary on source material is provided at the end of each chapter; complete citations appear in the Bibliography. Foreign and technical terms are defined when they first appear in the text, and other terms that require further definition are included in the Glossary. Appendixes provide tabular data (see Appendix A) and information on Vietnam's leaders in the 1980s (see Appendix B). Use of contemporary place names is in accordance with the standards of the United States Board of Geographic Names. When place names vary historically, the name consistent with the historical period under discussion is used. All measurements are metric (see Appendix A, table 1).

Table A. Chronology of Important Events

Date	Events
2879 B.C.	Legendary founding of the Van Lang Kingdom by the first Hung Vuong
2879–258 B.C.	Hung Dynasty
257–208 B.C.	Thuc Dynasty
207–111 B.C.	Trieu Dynasty
1800–1400 B.C.	Phung Nguyen culture (Early Bronze Age)
850–300 B.C.	Dong Son culture (Late Bronze Age)
210 B.C.	Kingdom of Au Lac established.
207 B.C.	Chinese general Chao Tuo (Trieu Da) founds Nan Yueh (Nam Viet).
111 B.C.	Nan Yueh conquered by Han.
A.D. 39	Trung sisters lead a rebellion against Chinese rule.
43	Trung sisters' rebellion crushed by Chinese general Ma Yuan, and Viet people placed under direct Chinese administration for the first time.
542–544	Ly Bi leads uprising against China's Liang Dynasty and establishes the independent kingdom of Van Xuan.
544–602	Early Ly Dynasty
938	Ngo Quyen defeats a Chinese invading force at the first battle of the Bach Dang River.
939–968	Ngo Dynasty
939–44	Ngo Quyen rules independent Nam Viet.
968–980	Dinh Dynasty
970–975	Dinh Bo Linh gains Chinese recognition of Nam Viet's independence by establishing a tributary relationship with China's Song Dynasty.
980–1009	Early Le Dynasty
981	Le Hoan defeats a Chinese invasion.
982	Viet armies invade Champa and destroy its capital, Indrapura.

Table A.—Continued

Date	Events
1009–1225	Ly Dynasty
1075	Minor officials chosen by examination for the first time.
1225–1400	Tran Dynasty
1257–58	Mongols attack Dai Viet and are defeated.
1284–85	Second Mongol invasion and defeat. Resistance led by Tran Hung Dao.
1287	Third Mongol invasion repelled.
1360–90	Champa wars. Champa ruled by Che Bong Nga.
1400–1407	Ho Dynasty
1407–27	Chinese invasion and occupation
1428	Le Loi's armies defeat the Chinese.
1428–1527	Le Dynasty
1428	Le Loi proclaims himself emperor. The country once again named Dai Viet.
1471	Champa capital of Vijaya falls, ending the Champa kingdom.
1483	Hong Duc legal code promulgated.
1527–92	Mac Dynasty. Mac rulers control Thang Long and the Red River Delta.
1558–1772	Period of opposition between the Trinh and Nguyen clans
1627	Alexandre de Rhodes, Jesuit missionary, arrives in Hanoi.
1771	Tay Son Rebellion
1778	Most of Nguyen clan annihilated by the Tay Son.
1787	French missionary Pigneau de Behaine persuades French court to assist in restoration of the Nguyen.
1788	Last Le emperor flees to China. Nguyen Hue proclaims himself emperor.

Table A. — Continued

Date	Events
1789	Chinese invasion in support of the Le defeated.
1802	The Nguyen defeat last of Tay Son forces. Nguyen Anh accedes to throne as Gia Long and establishes his capital at Hue.
1802–1945	Nguyen Dynasty
1820	Death of Gia Long. Succeeded by his highly sinicized son, Minh Mang.
1847	French vessels bombard Da Nang.
September 1858	French forces seize Da Nang.
February 1859	French forces capture Saigon.
February 1861	The French defeat the Vietnamese army and gain control of Gia Dinh and surrounding provinces.
June 5, 1862	Treaty of Saigon, which ceded three southern provinces—Bien Hoa, Gia Dinh, and Dinh Tuong—to the French.
1863	Admiral la Grandiére imposes French protectorate on Cambodia.
March 1874	A Franco-Vietnamese treaty confirms French sovereignty over Cochinchina and opens the Red River to trade.
August 1883	Treaty of Protectorate, signed at the Harmond Convention, establishes French protectorate over Annam and Tonkin.
June 1884	Treaty of Hue confirms the Harmond convention agreement.
1885	Can Vuong movement, calling upon the Vietnamese to drive out the French, established.
1887	Indochinese Union formally established.
May 19, 1890	Ho Chi Minh's birth
1897–1902	Paul Doumer is Governor-General.
1904	Phan Boi Chau founds Viet Nam Duy Tan Hoi (Vietnam Reformation Society).
October 1911	Ho Chi Minh departs Vietnam for Europe.

Table A.—Continued

Date	Events
1912	Phan Boi Chau founds Viet Nam Quang Phuc Hoi (Vietnam Restoration Society), replacing Duy Tan Hoi.
1919	Nguyen Ai Quoc (Ho Chi Minh) attempts to meet with President Woodrow Wilson at the Versailles Peace Conference to present a program for Vietnamese rights and sovereignty, but is turned away.
1920	Ho Chi Minh participates in founding of the French Communist Party.
1923	Ho Chi Minh's first visit to Moscow
June–July 1924	Ho Chi Minh attends Fifth Comintern Congress.
1925	Viet Nam Thanh Nien Cach Menh Dong Chi Hoi (Revolutionary Youth League) formed in Guangzhou under Ho Chi Minh's leadership.
1926	Ho Chi Minh forms Thanh Nien Cong San Doan (Communist Youth League) within the larger Thanh Nien organization.
1927	Nguyen Thai Hoc founds the Vietnam Quoc Dan Dang (VNQDD, Vietnam Nationalist Party).
February 1930	Vietnamese Communist Party (VCP, Viet Nam Cong San Dang) founded in Hong Kong (name changed to Indochinese Communist Party, Dong Duong Cong San Dang, in October).
September 1939	World War II begins.
August 1940	Franco-Japanese treaty, recognizing Japan's pre-eminence in Indochina in return for nominal recognition of French sovereignty, signed.
February 1941	Ho Chi Minh returns to Vietnam.
May 1941	ICP Eighth Plenum at Pac Bo establishes the Viet Minh (Vietnam Doc Lap Dong Minh Hoi, or League for the Independence of Vietnam).
1942–43	Ho Chi Minh imprisoned in China.
1944–45	Famine in Tonkin and Annam causes between 1.5 and 2 million deaths.

Table A.—Continued

Date	Events
August 1945	Japan surrenders and the Viet Minh commences the August Revolution, gaining effective control over much of Vietnam.
September 1945	Ho Chi Minh declares Vietnam's independence in Hanoi.
1946	Ho Chi Minh visits Paris during negotiations with France; hostilities begin following violation of agreements.
1946–54	First Indochina War (see Glossary—also known as Viet Minh War)
1951	Dang Lao Dong Viet Nam (Vietnamese Workers Party—VWP) is founded, succeeding the Indochinese Communist Party.
May 7, 1954	French surrender at Dien Bien Phu
May 8, 1954	Geneva Conference on Indochina opens.
July 21, 1954	Geneva Agreements adopted, Vietnam provisionally divided at the 17th parallel, and Ngo Dinh Diem appointed South Vietnam's premier by Emperor Bao Dai.
January 1, 1955	Direct United States aid to South Vietnam begins.
February 12, 1955	United States advisers begin training South Vietnamese army troops.
October 26, 1955	Republic of Vietnam established with Diem its first president.
December 20, 1960	The National Front for the Liberation of South Vietnam (NLF) formed in the South under the direction of the Political Bureau.
December 31, 1961	United States military personnel in Vietnam total about 3,200.
February 8, 1962	United States Military Assistance Command-Vietnam (MACV) formed under the command of General Paul D. Harkins.
November 1–2, 1963	Ngo Dinh Diem overthrown and assassinated.
August 7, 1964	United States Congress passes the "Gulf of Tonkin Resolution," authorizing the president of the United States to use force in Vietnam to repel attacks on American installations.

Date	Events
February 7, 1965	United States begins bombing military targets in North Vietnam.
March 9, 1965	First United States ground combat troops land in Vietnam at Da Nang.
December 31, 1965	United States military personnel in Vietnam total 180,000.
January 30–31, 1968	"Tet Offensive," employing coordinated attacks on the South's major cities by North Vietnamese and National Liberation Front troops, fails to achieve its military objectives but erodes American support for the war.
January 25, 1969	Four-party peace talks open in Paris.
May 14, 1969	United States troop strength in Vietnam peaks at 543,000.
June 10, 1969	Provisional Revolutionary Government of South Vietnam (PRG) formed.
September 3, 1969	Ho Chi Minh's death
April 28, 1970	Joint United States-Army of the Republic of Vietnam force attacks Vietnamese communist sanctuaries in Cambodia.
March 24, 1971	Operation Lam Son 719, a South Vietnamese attack on the Ho Chi Minh Trail in Laos, ends in defeat.
March 30, 1972	People's Army of Vietnam (PAVN) troops launch the largest offensive of the war since 1968.
January 27, 1973	Agreement on Ending the War and Restoring Peace in Vietnam signed in Paris.
March 29, 1973	Last United States troops in Vietnam depart.
March 9, 1975	PAVN offensive in the South begins.
April 30, 1975	Saigon surrenders.
July 2, 1976	The National Assembly proclaims official unification of Vietnam as the Socialist Republic of Vietnam.
December 14–20, 1976	Fourth National Party Congress. The Vietnamese Workers Party renamed the Vietnam Communist Party.

Table A.—Continued

Date	Events
September 20, 1977	Vietnam admitted to United Nations.
June 29, 1978	Vietnam admitted to membership in the Council for Mutual Economic Assistance (Comecon).
July 3, 1978	China announces termination of all economic assistance to Vietnam.
November 3, 1978	Vietnam and the Soviet Union sign a 25-year "Treaty of Friendship and Cooperation."
December 21, 1978	PAVN forces initiate invasion of Cambodia.
January 7, 1979	The Cambodian government of Pol Pot overthrown when Phnom Penh, the capital of Cambodia, falls to Vietnamese forces.
February 17, 1979	China launches invasion of Vietnam.
March 5, 1979	Chinese forces withdrawn from Vietnam
March 1982	Fifth National Party Congress
December 1986	Sixth National Party Congress

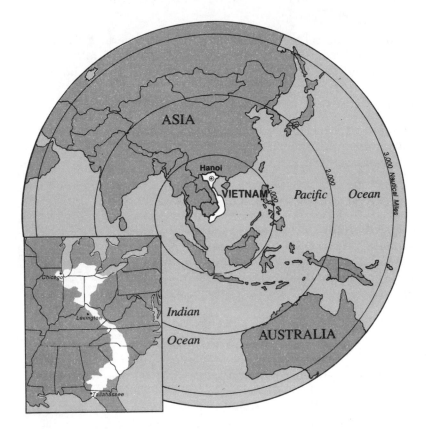

Country

Formal Name: Socialist Republic of Vietnam.

Short Form: Vietnam.

Term for Citizens: Vietnamese.

Capital: Hanoi.

Geography

Size: Approximately 331,688 square kilometers.

Topography: Hills and densely forested mountains, with level land covering no more than 20 percent. Mountains account for 40 percent, hills 40 percent, and forests 75 percent. North consists of highlands and the Red River Delta; south divided into coastal lowlands, Giai Truong Son (central mountains) with high plateaus, and Mekong River Delta.

Climate: Tropical and monsoonal; humidity averages 84 percent throughout year. Annual rainfall ranges from 120 to 300 centimeters, and annual temperatures vary between 5°C and 37°C.

Society

Population: 64,411,668 (1989 census); 2.1 percent average annual population growth rate. Nineteen percent urban; 81 percent rural. Population centers Hanoi and Ho Chi Minh City (formerly Saigon).

Languages: Vietnamese official language; also French, various Chinese dialects, tribal languages, and English.

Ethnic Groups: Vietnamese account for 87.5 percent of population (1979 figures). Fifty-three minorities account for remainder, including Hoa (Chinese, comprising approximately 1.8 percent), Tay, Thai, Khmer, Muong, Nung, Hmong, and numerous mountain tribes.

Religion: Mahayana Buddhism, Theravada Buddhism, Cao Dai, Hoa Hao, Roman Catholicism, Protestantism, Islam, Hinduism, and animism.

Education and Literacy: Nine years of primary and junior high school, three years of secondary school. First nine years compulsory. Manual labor comprises 15 percent of primary curriculum and 17 percent of secondary. Ninety-three colleges and universities, with close to 130,000 students enrolled, able to admit only 10 percent of applicants. Education emphasizes training of skilled workers, technicians, and managers. Students, nevertheless, tend to avoid vocational schools and specialized middle schools because they are believed to preclude entry to high-status occupations. Literacy 78 percent (for all age groups).

Health: Total of approximately 11,000 hospitals, medical aid stations, public health stations, and village maternity clinics, staffed by 240,000 medical personnel. Approximately 1 physician per 1,000 persons. Life expectancy sixty-three years. Malaria, tuberculosis, and other communicable diseases prevalent. Government undertaken a campaign to improve cleanliness by launching "Three Cleans Movement" (clean food, water, and living conditions) and "Three Exterminations Movement" (exterminate flies, mosquitos, and rats).

Economy

Salient Features: In 1984 gross domestic product (GDP—see Glossary) stood at US$18.1 billion, US$300 per capita at official exchange rate of 12.1 dong to US$1 (actual per capita income is closer to US$200). Produced National Income (PNI—see Glossary) grew by 2.1 percent in 1987, down from 3.3 percent in 1986.

Agriculture: Major agricultural products produced in 1985: grain (18.2 million tons), sugar (434,000 tons), tea (26,000 tons), coffee (6,000 tons), and rubber (52,000 tons). Agriculture represented 51 percent of PNI.

Industry: Thirty-two percent of PNI in 1985; major industries included electricity (5.4 billion kilowatt hours), coal (60 million tons), steel (57,000 tons), cement (1.4 million tons), cloth (80 million square meters), paper (75,000 tons), fish sauce (174 million liters), and processed sea fish (550,000 tons). Mineral resources included iron ore, tin, copper, lead, zinc, nickel, manganese, titanium, chromite, tungsten, bauxite, apatite, graphite, mica, silica sand, and limestone.

Energy Sources: Timber, coal, offshore oil deposits.

Foreign Trade: Exports totaled US$739.5 million in 1986. Principal exports consisted of coal, rubber, rice, tea, coffee, wood, and marine products. Imports totaled US$2.5 billion in 1986. Principal imports consisted of petroleum products, fertilizers, rice, and steel. In 1986 total debt estimated at nearly US$7.7 billion. According to figures given to International Monetary Fund by Hanoi, from 1981–85 Vietnam's debt to communist bloc countries rose from US$3 billion to more than US$6 billion. Trade deficit with the Soviet Union grew from US$224 million in 1976 to US$1.5 billion in 1986.

Transportation and Communications

Railroads: Total of 4,250 kilometers of track. Most important section connects Hanoi and Ho Chi Minh City.

Roads: Some 85,000 kilometers of road; of which 9,400 kilometers paved, 48,700 kilometers gravel or improved earth, and 26,900 kilometers unimproved.

Maritime Shipping: 125 vessels, including 80 coastal freighters, 12 oil tankers, and 15 ocean-going freighters. Total of thirty-two ports, of which nine major ports. Three largest located at Da Nang, Haiphong, and Ho Chi Minh City.

Civil Aviation: Controlled by military. Domestic air service connects Hanoi with Ho Chi Minh City, Da Nang, Pleiku, Da Lat, Buon Me Thuot, Phu Bai, and Nha Trang. Ho Chi Minh City also connected to Rach Gia, Phu Quoc, and Con Son Island. International air service connects Hanoi with Vientiane, Phnom Penh, Moscow, and Bangkok. Total of 128 usable airfields, 46 with surfaced runways.

Telecommunications: Two satellite-ground communications stations linking Hanoi, Ho Chi Minh City, and Moscow, and integrating Vietnam into Soviet Intersputnik Communication Satellite Organization.

Government and Politics

Party and Government: Democratic Republic of (North) and former Republic of (South) Vietnam united to form Socialist Republic of Vietnam on July 2, 1976. Constitution adopted in 1980 stipulates National Assembly as highest governing body. Members serve five-year terms and nominally directly elected by electorate. Council of State, which serves as collective presidency, and Council of Ministers, which manages governmental activities, nominally accountable to, and elected by, National Assembly. Political power effectively in hands of Vietnamese Communist Party (VCP, Viet Nam Cong San Dang). Most government positions filled by party members, who act at direction of party. Party led by National Party Congress, which meets infrequently. Congress elects Central Committee, which in turn elects Political Bureau, party's highest policy-making body.

Administrative Divisions: Country divided into thirty-six provinces, three autonomous municipalities, and one special zone. Provinces divided into districts, towns, and capitals.

Judicial System: Supreme People's Court; local People's Courts at provincial, district, and city levels; military tribunals; and People's Supreme Organ of Control. National Assembly elects Procurator General, who heads People's Supreme Organ of Control and performs overall administration of justice.

Foreign Affairs: Vietnam dominated Laos through numerous Hanoi-dictated cooperation agreements; most important—Treaty of Friendship and Cooperation signed in 1977. Occupied Cambodia as result of military conquest in January 1979 and subsequently negotiated Treaty of Friendship and Cooperation. Relations with China marked by China's limited invasion in 1979 and frequent border skirmishes. Formally aligned with Soviet Union through Treaty of Friendship and Cooperation signed in November 1978. Both countries shared membership in Council for Mutual Economic Assistance (Comecon—see Glossary); Soviet Union largest donor of economic and military aid. Limited governmental and commercial ties established with all Association for Southeast Asian Nations (ASEAN) members but prevented from developing further by ASEAN's opposition to Vietnam's Cambodia policy. In 1988 no diplomatic relations with United States, which maintained economic boycott against Vietnam and stressed Vietnam's cooperation in accounting for servicemen missing in action as prerequisite to normal relations. Admitted to membership in United Nations in 1977.

National Security

Armed Forces: Largest military force in Southeast Asia and third largest force in the world after China and the Soviet Union. Estimated in 1987 to total over 5 million: army, 1.2 million; navy, 15,000; air force, 20,000; Regional Force, 500,000; Militia-Self Defense Force, 1.2 million; Armed Youth Assault Force, 1,500,000; and Tactical Rear Force, 500,000.

Combat Units and Major Equipment: Command structure divided geographically into military theaters and military regions or zones. Tactically divided into corps, divisions, brigades, regiments, and battalions, companies, platoons, and squads. Army comprised eight corps (each numbering 30,000 to 50,000 troops). In 1986 total of thirty-eight regular infantry divisions: nineteen in Cambodia, ten in northern Vietnam, six in central and southern Vietnam, and three in Laos. Thirteen economic construction divisions, which carried burden of 1979 war with China, deployed in China border region. Army equipped with 1,600 Soviet-made T–34/–54/–55/–62, Type-59 tanks and 450 PT–76 and type 60/63 light tanks; 2,700 reconnaissance vehicles; some 600 artillery guns and howitzers, unspecified number of multiple rocket launchers, mortars, and antitank weapons; and 3,000 air defense weapons. Navy, with Soviet assistance, largest naval force in Southeast Asia in 1986. Five naval regions, headquartered at Da Nang, Haiphong, Vinh, Vung Tau, and Rach Gia. Navy equipped with 2 principal combat vessels, 192 patrol boats, 51 amphibious warfare ships, 104 landing ships, and 133 auxiliary craft. Approximately 1,300 ex-United States, South Vietnamese naval vessels, naval and civilian junks and coasters augment this force. Air Force divided into seventeen air regiments, (seven attack fighter plane regiments, four basic and advanced training regiments, three cargo transport regiments, three helicopter regiments, and one light bomber force), headquartered at Noi Bai (Hanoi), Da Nang, Tho Xuan, and Tan Son Nhut (Ho Chi Minh City). Air Force equipped with some 450 combat aircraft (including 225 MiG-21s), 225 trainers, 350 cargo-transport planes, 600 helicopters, and 60 light bombers.

Military Budget: No expenditure estimates available. Military aid from Soviet Union estimated about US$1.5 billion annually beginning in 1986.

Police Agencies and Paramilitary: Police functions vested in People's Security Force (PSF), People's Public Security Force (PPSF), and People's Armed Security Force (PASF). PSF strictly law enforcement agency operating chiefly in urban rather than rural areas. PASF composed of party security cadres and PAVN personnel concerned with illegal political acts and insurgency movements as well as criminal activity.

Foreign Military Alliances: Friendship and cooperation treaties signed with Laos in 1977, Soviet Union in 1978, and Cambodia in 1979.

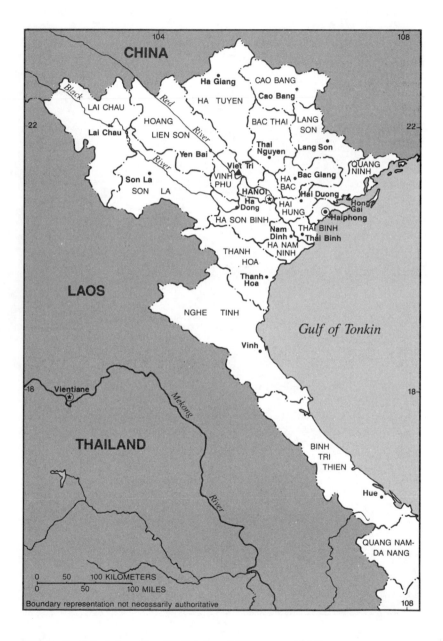

Figure 1. Administrative Divisions of Vietnam, 1985

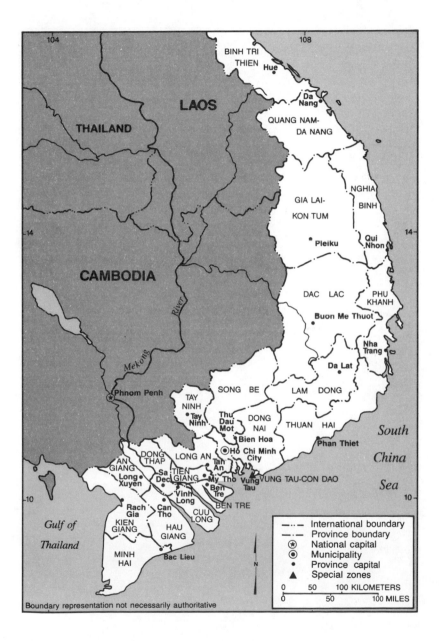

104   108

BINH TRI
THIEN Hue

LAOS   Da
Nang

THAILAND   QUANG NAM-
DA NANG

NGHIA

GIA LAI-   BINH
KON TUM

-14   14-

Pleiku   Qui
Nhon

CAMBODIA

DAC   LAC   PHU
KHANH

Buon Me Thuot

Nha
Trang

Da Lat

Phnom Penh   SONG BE   LAM   DONG

TAY
NINH

Tay   Thu   DONG   THUAN HAI   South
Ninh   Dau   NAI
Mot   China

Bien Hoa
Phan Thiet   Sea
Ho Chi Minh
DONG LONG AN   City
AN   THAP   Tan
GIANG   An
Long   Sa   TIEN   My Tho Vung VUNG TAU-CON DAO
Xuyen   Dec GIANG   Tau
Ben
Vinh   Tre
Long
BEN TRE
Rach Can
Gia   Tho   CUU
KIEN   LONG
GIANG HAU   -10
GIANG

Gulf of

Thailand   --- International boundary
MINH   --- Province boundary
HAI   Bac Lieu   National capital
Municipality
N   Province capital
Special zones

0   50   100 KILOMETERS

0   50   100 MILES
Boundary representation not necessarily authoritative

Figure 1. (continued)

xxxi

Introduction

The victory of communist forces in Vietnam in April 1975 ranks as one of the most politically significant occurrences of the post-World War II era in Asia. The speed with which the North finally seized the South, and the almost simultaneous communist victories in Laos and Cambodia, were stunning achievements. The collapse of the three Indochinese noncommunist governments brought under communist control a region that, over the course of four decades of war, had become the focus of United States policy for the containment of communism in Asia. The achievement was even more phenomenal for having been accomplished in the face of determined United States opposition and for having called into question the very policy of containing communism.

The events of April 1975 prepared the way for the official reunification of North and South in 1976, some three decades after Ho Chi Minh first proclaimed Vietnam's independence under one government in September 1945 and more than a century after France divided Vietnam in order to rule its regions separately. The departure of defeated Japanese troops, who had occupied Vietnam during World War II, had created the opportunity for Vietnamese communists to seize power in August 1945, before French authorities were able to return to reclaim control of the government. Communist rule was cut short, however, by Nationalist Chinese and British occupation forces whose presence tended to support the Communist Party's political opponents. Between 1945 and 1975, the generation of communists responsible for victory in the South pursued a lengthy war for independence from the French, acquiesced temporarily to division of the country into a communist North and noncommunist South, and engaged in a subsequent war for control of the South against a southern regime supported by the United States. Reunification and independence, however, were goals that predated the communists. They were the long-established objectives of Ho Chi Minh's nationalist and anticolonialist predecessors, who had resisted Chinese rule for 1,000 years and French domination for a century.

Indeed, Vietnam's unrelenting resistance to foreign intervention remains a dominant Vietnamese historical theme, manifested in the repeated waging of *dau tranh,* or struggle to gain a long-term objective through total effort, and motivated by *chinh nghia,* or just cause. Vietnam's communist leaders claim that every Vietnamese has been a soldier in this struggle. Paradoxically, Vietnam's fierce determination to remain free of foreign domination has often been combined with an equally strong willingness to accept foreign influence. Historically, the pattern has been to adapt foreign ideas to indigenous conditions whenever they applied.

China was the chief source of Vietnam's foreign ideas and the earliest threat to its national sovereignty. Beginning in the first century B.C., China's Han dynasty (206 B.C.-A.D. 220) imposed Chinese rule that endured for ten centuries despite repeated Vietnamese uprisings and acts of rebellion. Only the collapse of the Tang dynasty (A.D. 618–907) in the early tenth century enabled Vietnamese national hero Ngo Quyen to re-establish Vietnam's independence a generation later. The Vietnamese subsequently were able to fend off further invasion attempts for 900 years (see The Chinese Millennium and Nine Centuries of Independence, ch. 1).

Whether ruled by China or independent, the Vietnamese elite consistently modeled Vietnamese cultural institutions on those of the Chinese. Foremost among such Chinese institutions was Confucianism, after which Vietnamese family, bureaucratic, and social structures were patterned. The Vietnamese upper classes tended also to study Chinese classical literature and to use the Chinese system of ideographs in writing. Emperor Gia Long, in a particularly obvious act of imitation in the early nineteenth century, even modeled his new capital at Hue after the Chinese capital at Beijing. The process of sinicization, however, tended to coexist with, rather than to replace, traditional Vietnamese culture and language. Imitation of the Chinese was largely confined to the elite classes. Traditional Vietnamese society, on the other hand, was sustained by the large peasant class, which was less exposed to Chinese influence.

Vietnam's lengthy period of independence ended in 1862, when Emperor Tu Duc, agreeing to French demands, ceded three provinces surrounding Saigon to France. During the colonial period, from 1862 to 1954, resistance to French rule was led by members of the scholar-official class, whose political activities did not involve the peasantry and hence failed. The success of the communists, on the other hand, was derived from their ability to organize and retain the peasantry's support. The Vietnamese Communist Party (VCP, Viet Nam Cong San Dang) and its various communist antecedents presented Marxism-Leninism as an effective means of recovering the independence that was Vietnam's tradition. Belief in this ideal was instrumental in sustaining Northern and Southern peasant-based communist forces during the lengthy Second Indochina War, which lasted from 1954 to 1975.

In the post-1975 period, however, it was immediately apparent that the popularity and effectiveness of the communist party's wartime policies did not necessarily extend to its peacetime nation-building plans. Having unified the North and South politically, the VCP still had to integrate them socially and economically. In this task, VCP policy-makers were confronted with Southern resistance to change, as well as traditional animosities arising from cultural and historical differences between the North and South. The situation was further complicated by a deterioration in economic conditions that ignited an unprecedented level of discontent among low-level VCP members and open criticism of VCP policies. The party appeared to be in a state of transition, wavering over the pace and manner of the South's integration with the North and debating the place of reform in development strategy. The first generation communist leaders, co-founders of the party together with Ho Chi Minh, were aging and were beginning to step down in favor of younger, often reform-minded technocrats. The Sixth National Party Congress held in December 1986 was a milestone; it marked the end of the party's revolutionary period, when social welfare and modernization were subordinate to security concerns, and the beginning of a time when experimentation and reform were encouraged to stimulate development (see Party Organization, ch. 4).

In the 1980s, Vietnam ranked third in population—60 million—and first in population density—an average of 182 persons per square kilometer—among the world's communist nations. A 2-percent annual population growth rate and uneven population distribution adversely affected resource allocation, work force composition, and land use. Population projections indicated a population of 80 million by the year 2000, if the growth rate remained unchanged. The Fourth National Party Congress in December 1976 stressed the need to curtail the population growth rate and introduced a plan to relocate 54 million people to 1 million hectares of previously uncultivated land, now organized into "new economic zones," by the mid-1990s. As of 1988, however, progress toward the plan's fulfillment was considerably behind schedule (see Population, ch. 2).

A predominantly rural society with more than half of its work force committed to agriculture, Vietnam had a standard of living that remained one of the poorest in the world. A series of harvest shortfalls that reduced food supplies and a scarcity of foreign exchange that made it difficult to replenish food reserves contributed to this condition. Shortages of raw materials and energy forced production facilities to operate at considerably less than full capacity, and the party bureaucracy remained incapable of acting quickly enough to reduce shortages (see Economic Setting, ch. 3).

Economic development prospects for the 1980s and 1990s were tied to party economic policy in critical ways. Party leaders, in establishing economic policy at the Fourth National Party Congress, envisioned Vietnam's post-reunification economy to be in a "period of transition to socialism." The plan, or series of plans, called for the economy to evolve through three phases: The first, outlining the objectives of the Second Five-Year Plan (1976–80), set extremely high goals for industrial and agricultural production while also giving high priority to construction, reconstruction, and the integration of the North and the South. The second, entitled "socialist industrialization," was divided into two stages—from 1981 to 1990 and from 1991 to 2005. During these stages, the material and technical foundations of communism were to be constructed, and development plans were to focus equally on agriculture and industry. The third and final phase, covering the years from 2006 to 2010, was to be a time set aside to "perfect the transitional period."

By 1979, however, it was obvious to Vietnam's leaders that the Second Five-Year Plan would fail to meet its goals and that the long-range goals established for the transition period were unrealistic. The economy continued to be dominated by small-scale production, low productivity, high unemployment, material and technological shortages, and insufficient food and consumer goods.

The Fifth National Party Congress, held in March 1982, approved the economic goals of the Third Five-Year Plan (1981–85). The policies introduced were comparatively liberal and called for the temporary retention of private capitalist activities in the South, in order to spur economic growth. By sanctioning free enterprise, the congress ended the nationalization of small business concerns and reversed former policies that sought the immediate transformation of the South to communism. The July 1984 Sixth Plenum of the Fifth National Party Congress' Central Committee confirmed the party's earlier decision, recognizing that the private sector's domination over wholesale and retail trade in the South could not be eliminated until the state was capable of assuming that responsibility. Proposals subsequently were made to upgrade the state's economic sophistication by decentralizing planning procedures and improving the managerial skills of government and party officials. To attract foreign currency and expertise, the government approved a new foreign investment code in December 1987 (see Economic Roles of the Party and the Government, ch. 3).

Vietnam's security considerations in the 1980s also represented a new set of challenges to the party. Until the fall of the South

Vietnamese government in 1975, the party had relegated foreign policy to a secondary position behind the more immediate concerns of national liberation and reunification. Once the Second Indochina War had ended, however, the party needed to look outward and re-evaluate foreign policy, particularly as it applied to Cambodia, China, the Soviet Union, member nations of the Association of Southeast Asian Nations (ASEAN), and the United States and other Western nations (see Foreign Relations, ch. 4).

By the end of the 1970s, the Vietnamese were threatened on two fronts, a condition which Vietnam had not faced previously, even at the height of the Second Indochina War. Conflict between Vietnamese and Cambodian communists on their common border began almost immediately after their respective victories in 1975. To neutralize the threat, Vietnam invaded Cambodia in December 1978 and overran Phnom Penh, the Cambodian capital, driving out the incumbent Khmer Rouge communist regime and initiating a prolonged military occupation of the country. Vietnam's relations with China, a seemingly staunch ally during the Second Indochina War, subsequently reached their nadir, when China retaliated against Vietnam's incursion into Cambodia by launching a limited invasion of Vietnam in February and March 1979. Relations between the two countries had actually been deteriorating for some time. Territorial disagreements, which had remained dormant during the war against the South, were revived at the war's end, and a postwar campaign engineered by Hanoi to limit the role of Vietnam's ethnic Chinese (Hoa) community in domestic commerce elicited a strong Chinese protest. China was displeased with Vietnam primarily, however, because of its rapidly improving relationship with the Soviet Union.

A new era in Vietnamese foreign relations began in 1978, when Hanoi joined the Soviet-led Council for Mutual Economic Assistance (Comecon) and signed the Soviet-Vietnamese Treaty of Friendship and Cooperation with Moscow. The agreement called for mutual assistance and consultation in the event either was threatened by a third country. A secret protocol accompanying the treaty also permitted Soviet use of Vietnamese airport and harbor facilities, particularly the former United States military complex at Cam Ranh Bay. In return, Vietnam acquired military and economic aid needed to undertake an invasion of Cambodia and was able to exploit Soviet influence as a deterrent to Chinese intervention (see Foreign Relations, ch. 4).

During the 1980s, after China had cut off military assistance to Vietnam, such aid—amounting to US$200 to $300 million annually—was almost exclusively Soviet in origin. As Vietnam's primary source of economic aid as well, the Soviet Union during this period provided close to US$1 billion annually in balance-of-payments aid, project assistance, and oil price subsidies.

Vietnam's growing dependence on the Soviet Union concerned Hanoi's Southeast Asian neighbors. As did China, the ASEAN nations thought that the relationship provided a springboard for Soviet influence in the region and that Soviet support provided a critical underpinning for Vietnam's Cambodia policy. The ASEAN nations assumed a key role in rallying United Nations (UN) General Assembly opposition to Vietnam's interference in Cambodia and led the UN in preventing the Vietnamese-supported regime in Phnom Penh from assuming Cambodia's General Assembly seat. ASEAN members were instrumental in combining—at least on paper—the various Cambodian communist and noncommunist factions opposing the Vietnamese into a single resistance coalition.

The decision to intervene militarily in Cambodia further isolated Vietnam from the international community. The United States, in addition to citing Vietnam's minimal cooperation in accounting for Americans who were missing in action (MIAs) as an obstacle to normal relations, barred normal ties as long as Vietnamese troops occupied Cambodia. In 1987 Washington also continued to enforce the trade embargo imposed on Hanoi at the conclusion of the war in 1975.

Normalization of diplomatic relations with the United States, however, was not a primary Vietnamese foreign policy objective in 1987. The sizable economic benefits it would yield, plus its strategic value, remained secondary to other more immediate security concerns, although the potential economic benefits were judged sizable. Instead, Vietnam prepared to enter the 1990s with foreign relations priorities that stressed extrication from the military stalemate in Cambodia in a manner consistent with security needs, repair of ties with China to alleviate Chinese military pressure on Vietnam's northern border, and reduction of military and economic dependence on the Soviet Union.

Domestic and foreign policy in 1987 reflected changes initiated by the elevation of reformer Nguyen Van Linh to VCP general secretary at the Sixth National Party Congress. Policies were characterized by a program of political and economic experimentation that was similar to contemporary reform agendas undertaken in China and the Soviet Union. The goal of all three nations was to pursue economic development at the cost of some compromise of communist ideological orthodoxy. In the case of Vietnam, however, the conservative members of the leadership continued to view orthodoxy as an ultimate goal. According to their plan, the stress on economic development was only a momentary emphasis; the real goal remained the perfection of Vietnam's communist society.

* * *

In 1988 and 1989, the years immediately following completion of research and writing of this book, Vietnam's foreign and domestic policies were increasingly determined by economic considerations. The mood of dramatic economic and political reform, inspired by the Sixth National Party Congress and Linh's appointment to party leadership, however, appeared to have dissipated, and the mood of confidence that had prevailed in 1987 gradually evaporated as disagreement among Political Bureau members over the pace of change stymied the implementation of many policy innovations.

A campaign for political and economic renewal (*doi moi*) was launched by Linh immediately following the congress, but the progress of change, particularly economic change, failed to meet expectations. Linh was strongly opposed within the party's leadership, and his economic reforms were initially stalled or blocked by the resistance efforts of a strong conservative coalition of party leaders, made up of ideological conservatives, bureaucrats, and members of the military establishment.

Linh's initiatives for dealing with the country's economic problems were bold, but the coalition of conservative party leaders opposing his policies effectively denied him the consensus he needed to implement his plans. Consequently, his powers to effect change appeared to wane as the severity of the country's economic crisis deepened.

Despite their opposition to reform policy, reform, per se, was viewed as "correct" by most, if not all, members of Vietnam's Political Bureau. A member's position on the subject, however, was probably determined less by his view of the process in the abstract than by his willingness to undertake risk, and in 1988 and 1989 the non-risk takers appeared to have the upper hand.

In March 1988 Prime Minister Pham Hung died, and Linh's choice of conservative Do Muoi over fellow reformer Vo Van Kiet to replace him was viewed as a clear concession to the non-risk takers. National Assembly members, however, for the first time challenged the central committee's nominee for a key government post by demanding that two candidates be permitted to run. Muoi, the party's choice, was required to face Vo Van Kiet, the nominee of delegates from the south.

The dissent displayed in the debate leading to Muoi's selection was not isolated, but mirrored a dramatic increase in all political debate and discussion in 1988. The October 1988 meeting of the Congress of National Trade Unions, for example, was extremely critical of the government's economic failures. Similarly, the Fourth Session of the Eighth National Assembly, held in December 1988, heatedly debated the issues. It was conducted without the customary Central Committee meeting beforehand and, on the surface, appeared to be acting without Central Committee guidance.

Lastly, a campaign against corruption, initiated by Nguyen Van Linh in 1987, invited private and official criticism of public policy and encouraged the press to take the lead in uncovering corruption. By early 1988, the campaign had resulted in the replacement of almost all of the country's 40 province secretaries and 80 percent of the 400 or so district party chiefs. Eleven hundred party cadres were tried for corruption in the first six months of the year, and the press was credited with the party's removal of Ha Truong Hoa, the party Provincial Secretary of Thanh Hoa, whose position had widely been regarded as impregnable despite his well publicized abuses of office. The policy of encouraging criticism, however, was mysteriously reversed in early 1989 when the press was urged to moderate its criticism of the Party. It was speculated that the reversal was meant to appease conservatives within the Political Bureau who were concerned about the erosion of party authority caused by public criticism.

Party leaders themselves, however, continued to be critical of party policy. Nguyen The Phan, the head of the theoretical department of the Marxist-Leninist Institute, for example, told a January 1989 meeting of high-ranking officials that by following the Soviet economic model, Vietnam had developed a centralized and subsidized economic system "inferior to capitalism," and "had abolished motivation in people and society." He called on party leaders to learn about marketplace competition from capitalist countries.

Goals established and reinforced at the December 1988 meeting of the Eighth National Assembly were consistent with this theme. The primary goal was described as development of an economy that was less controlled by the government and more subject to the rules of the marketplace. This was to be achieved by subjecting all economic transactions to the standards of basic business accountability and by expanding the private sector. Centralized bureaucratism was to be abolished, and some state-run economic establishments were to be guaranteed autonomy in their business practices. Lastly, the system of state subsidies for food, import-export operations, or for losses incurred by state-run enterprises was scheduled to be eliminated.

Beginning in 1988, individual farmers were given more responsibility for the rice growing process in order to increase their incentive to produce higher yields. Land tenure laws were modified to guarantee farmers a ten-year tenure on the land, and the contract system between peasants and the government was revised to permit peasants to keep 45 to 50 percent of their output rather than the 25 percent previously allowed. Other reforms removed restrictions on private-production enterprises in Hanoi and introduced the concept of developing industry outside the state-run sector. A law passed in January 1989 helped free the economy from central control by granting entrepreneurs the right to pool their capital and set up their own business organizations. Such concessions were of particular assistance to entrepreneurs in the South, where the economy in 1988 and 1989 was more or less directed by its own momentum, and where it had become increasingly evident that Vietnam's economic planners had opted to exploit the region's economic potential rather than stifle it by employing rigid controls.

The sixth plenum of the party Central Committee (Sixth Party Congress), held in late March 1989, concluded, however, that despite the establishment of goals and the introduction of some new policies, little was actually being accomplished because local cadres were failing to implement reform plans or institutionalize party resolutions in a timely manner. The plenum, therefore, resolved to emphasize the implementation and institutionalization of reforms and resolutions already introduced in order to accelerate the process.

Chinese student pro-democracy demonstrations in Beijing a few months later were watched very closely by Vietnam's leaders. In their view, the disaffection demonstrated by Chinese students had resulted directly from China's experimentation with political and economic reforms. Having undertaken similar changes, they were concerned that Vietnam was equally vulnerable to displays of unrest. To avoid China's experience, the government reportedly dealt with student protesters in Hanoi in May 1989 by acceding to their demands for improved conditions. Progress toward greater political liberalization, however, was subsequently checked.

Vietnam's world view noticeably altered in the closing years of the 1980s, moving from an ideologically dominated perspective, stressing Vietnam's independence and the division of the world into communist and noncommunist camps, to a nonideological view emphasizing Vietnam's role in a complex world of economic interdependence. The most significant example of a foreign policy initiative motivated by this view was the decision, announced in early 1989, to remove all Vietnamese troops from Cambodia by the end of September 1989. By disengaging from Cambodia,

Vietnam hoped to remove the single largest obstacle to gaining admission to the regional and world economic community and to convince its noncommunist neighbors, the West, and China, that it was ready to end its diplomatic and economic isolation.

Ending the Cambodian conflict itself, however, was another matter, and as events unfolded in 1988 and 1989 it was not clear whether Vietnam's withdrawal would expedite or prolong a resolution. Initially, the possibility of ending the stalemate appeared to improve. Acting entirely on his own initiative, resistance leader Prince Norodom Sihanouk, in December 1987, arranged unprecedented direct dialogues between himself and Hun Sen, the premier of the People's Republic of Kampuchea. Although they failed to yield major results, the talks nevertheless initiated valuable face-to-face discussions between representatives of both sides and introduced diplomacy as a means of ending the conflict.

In May 1988, eleven days after the Soviets began their troop withdrawal from Afghanistan and three days before a Moscow summit between President Reagan and Soviet Secretary Gorbachev was to convene, Vietnam announced plans to withdraw 50,000 troops by the end of the year. The withdrawal, commencing in June and ending in December as promised, involved not only the removal of troops, but also the dismantling of Vietnam's military high command in Cambodia and the reassignment of remaining troops to Cambodian commands.

In July 1988, Hanoi participated in the first meeting of all parties in the Cambodia conflict. The "cocktail party" meeting, or Jakarta Informal Meeting (JIM), convened in Bogor, Indonesia, was termed a limited success because, if nothing more, it established a negotiating framework and set the agenda for future discussion. However, it also shifted the emphasis of the search for a conflict resolution away from Vietnam and to the question of how to prevent the Khmer Rouge from seizing power once a political agreement was reached. At the meeting, Vietnam linked a total withdrawal of its troops to the elimination of the Khmer Rouge and won the support of the ASEAN nations and the noncommunist factions of the Cambodian resistance coalition, who also feared that Pol Pot would return to power in the absence of Vietnamese forces.

A second "informal" meeting of the four Cambodian factions, held in February 1989, ended inconclusively, deadlocked on fundamental issues such as the shape of the international force that was to supervise an agreement and the manner in which a quadripartite authority to rule in Phnom Penh would be established. The February meeting was followed by a month-long international conference, held in Paris in August 1989 and attended by twenty nations, which also ended short of a comprehensive agreement. Although the conference had been called to help mediate a settlement between the Vietnamese-backed government in Phnom Penh and the three-member resistance coalition, it foundered over finding an appropriate place for the Khmer Rouge once Vietnam's troop withdrawal was complete. Thus in September 1989, on the eve of the withdrawal, the promise of an impending political settlement in Cambodia remained unfulfilled. Instead, the inability of the four factions to arrive at a compromise renewed prospects for an escalation of conflict on the battlefield.

In 1988 one of Vietnam's top foreign policy priorities was finding a way to cut China's support for the Khmer Rouge. China, Hanoi argued, was the key to a Cambodian resolution because, as Pol Pot's chief source of supply, Beijing alone had the power to defuse the Khmer Rouge threat. As the year progressed, it became increasingly evident that Beijing was more interested in a settlement than in prolonging the conflict and that its position on Cambodia was shifting to facilitate settlement. This fact was evidenced in July 1988 when a Chinese proposal, repeating long-standing demands for a complete withdrawal of all Vietnamese troops and a quadripartite government led by Sihanouk, surprisingly ruled out a personal role for Pol Pot in any post-settlement government. The proposal was also novel because it intimated that Beijing, for the first time, was willing to discuss a provisional coalition government before the departure of all Vietnamese troops. At the International Conference on the conflict held in August 1989, the Chinese appeared to be undercutting their support for the Khmer Rouge by arguing that civil war was to be avoided at all costs and promising to cut off military aid once a settlement was reached. China's position on the Khmer Rouge nevertheless remained ambiguous.

In a 1988 incident, possibly related to Cambodia because it potentially strengthened China's position at a future bargaining table, the ongoing dispute between China and Vietnam over sovereignty to the Spratly Islands erupted into an unprecedented exchange of hostilities. The situation was reduced to an exchange of accusations following the armed encounter. Vietnam's repeated calls for China to settle the dispute diplomatically won rare support for Vietnam from the international community, but elicited little response from Beijing.

A conciliatory mood developed on both sides of the Sino-Vietnamese border in 1989, partly because Vietnam's proposal to withdraw completely from Cambodia responded to a basic Chinese condition for improved relations. Formal talks at the deputy foreign minister level were initiated, and a cross-border trade in Chinese and Vietnamese goods flourished in the Vietnamese border town of Lang Son. The internal turmoil experienced by China in May and June 1989 may have actually benefited the relationship from Vietnam's point of view. Historically, whenever Beijing had been forced to turn its attention inward to quell internal dissension, Vietnam's security situation had correspondingly improved.

Beijing's interest in improving ties with Moscow in 1988 and 1989, however, complicated the situation and put Vietnam increasingly at odds with the Soviet Union. As the reality of an eventual Sino-Soviet reconciliation approached, it became increasingly clear that Vietnamese and Soviet strategic interests did not always coincide. The presence of Vietnamese troops in Cambodia, for example, was the leading obstacle to Sino-Soviet reconciliation. Accordingly, the most significant development to occur in Soviet-Vietnamese relations in 1988 and 1989 was the application of increased Soviet pressure on Vietnam to resolve the Cambodian situation, a pressure that undoubtedly helped prompt Vietnam's policy of withdrawal.

Hanoi was naturally wary of any talks between the Soviet Union and China, fearing that a deal would be made on Cambodia at Vietnam's expense. The two powers convened bilateral discussions in Beijing in August 1988 and proceeded to normalize relations at a summit meeting in Beijing in May 1989. Very little with regard to Cambodia was actually accomplished, however, and the summit resulted simply in the two sides agreeing to "disagree" on the mechanics of a political solution.

By actively pursuing an end to the Cambodian conflict, Vietnam acted also to further the chances of normalizing its relations with the United States. Both sides in 1988 appeared particularly receptive to improving relations, and Vietnam's troop withdrawal as well as its participation in the JIM were interpreted by the United States as positive gestures directed toward Vietnam's disengagement from Cambodia, a requirement imposed by Washington for diplomatic recognition. Hanoi also acted, in the early part of the year, to remove other obstacles to recognition by agreeing in principle to resettlement in the United States of thousands of former political prisoners and by consenting to cooperate in joint excavations of United States military aircraft crash sites in an attempt to locate the remains of Americans missing in action (MIAs). Some remains were returned. In 1989, additional sets of MIA remains were returned, and an accord was reached between Vietnam and the United States granting re-education camp inmates who had worked for the United States permission to emigrate.

Finally, Vietnam sought to improve its regional relations in 1988 and 1989 by extending a conciliatory gesture to its Asian neighbors. In response to a rise in the number of Vietnamese refugees, Vietnam assured its neighbors that it would ease their burdens as countries of first asylum by reversing a policy that forbade refugees to return home. Hanoi also proposed to open discussions with Southeast Asian officials on ending the refugee exodus. In 1989, however, Vietnam permitted only those refugees who "voluntarily" sought repatriation to return to Vietnam. Because genuine volunteers were few in number, the policy was regarded as inadequate by countries with Vietnamese refugee populations. More boat people departed Vietnam in 1989 than in any single year since the beginning of the decade, and their numbers were no longer limited to southerners fleeing political persecution but included northerners seeking economic opportunity. The willingness of countries of first asylum to accept Vietnamese refugees had lessened considerably since 1979, however, and many were seriously considering policies advocating forced repatriation.

Vietnam's relationship with the Association of Southeast Asian Nations (ASEAN), nevertheless, showed dramatic improvement during this two-year period, and Thailand, in particular, was singled out by Hanoi as critically important to Vietnam's economic future. The success of a January 1989 official visit to Hanoi by Thai Foreign Minister Sitthi Sawetsila surpassed all expectations and led Thai Prime Minister Chatichai Choonhavan to encourage Thai businessmen to expand trade relations with the Indochinese countries. According to the Thai Prime Minister, the Thai goal was to turn the Southeast Asian peninsula into an economic "Golden Land" (*Suwannaphume* in Thai) with Thailand as its center and Indochina, transformed from "a battlefield into a trading market," as its cornerstone. Although the plan was controversial, it appeared to reflect the shift of regional priorities from security to economic concerns.

Vietnam still lacked an adequate foreign investment structure in 1989, although a Foreign Trade Office and a Central Office to Supervise Foreign Investment, along with a State Commission for Cooperation and Investment, had been established to draft investment policies. The Ministry of Foreign Economic Relations convened a three-day conference in February 1989, attended by 500 delegates associated with foreign trade, to discuss modifying Vietnam's existing foreign economic policies and mechanisms in order to more effectively attract foreign investors. Ho Chi Minh City also authorized the establishment of a "Zone of Fabrication and Exportation" where foreign companies would be free to import commodities, assemble products, use low cost local labor, and re-export final products. Ho Chi Minh City, followed by the Vung Tau-Con Dao Special Zone, led all other localities in the number of foreign investment projects and joint ventures initiated, and a large proportion of the investors were identified as overseas Vietnamese.

Although changes introduced in the closing years of the 1980s stopped short of systemic reform, they demonstrated a new level of commitment on the part of Vietnam's leaders to resolve the country's peacetime economic problems. Having known great success in warfare, the government appeared to have accepted that yet another struggle was underway that would require the kind of focused resolve previously displayed in war. The process was marked both by the possibility for change and by inertia. Political and foreign policy agendas were opened to redefinition, and strategic goals were re-evaluated to emphasize economic rather than military strength. The momentum of change, however, was slowed considerably by party conservatives, who stressed the danger of political liberalization and questioned the pace of economic reform. Change, nevertheless, was evident. In foreign policy, Vietnam moved to attract foreign investment and to end its international isolation by disengaging from Cambodia. Likewise, in the economic sphere at home, where the need for change was determined to be particularly critical, market forces assumed a larger role in Vietnam's controlled economy than they had previously. In undertaking such changes, Vietnam seemed on the verge of joining the geopolitical trend observed in the late 1980s, in which the behavior of socialist and capitalist systems alike appeared to favor economic over military development. The Vietnamese leadership, however, was not prepared to move quickly. Although it was committed to the process of change, the Political Bureau's ability to act was constricted by internal differences over how to proceed and how much to risk. As the country approached the 1990s, the question of whether the need to develop economically was worth the political risk had yet to be fully resolved.

September 21, 1989   Ronald J. Cima

Chapter 1. Historical Setting

Hanoi temple dedicated to King An Duong Vuong (ruler of Kingdom of Au Lac, third century B.C.)

THE VIETNAMESE TRACE the origins of their culture and nation to the fertile plains of the Red River Delta in northern Vietnam. After centuries of developing a civilization and economy based on the cultivation of irrigated rice, the Vietnamese began expanding southward in search of new ricelands. Moving down the narrow coastal plain of the Indochina Peninsula, through conquest and pioneering settlement they eventually reached and occupied the broad Mekong River Delta. Vietnamese history is the story of the struggle to develop a sense of nationhood throughout this narrow 1,500-kilometer stretch of land and to maintain it against internal and external pressures.

The first major threat to Vietnam's existence as a separate people and nation was the conquest of the Red River Delta by the Chinese, under the mighty Han dynasty (206 B.C.–A.D. 220), in the second century B.C. At that time, and in later centuries, the expanding Chinese empire assimilated a number of small bordering nations politically and culturally. Although Vietnam spent 1,000 years under Chinese rule, it succeeded in throwing off the yoke of its powerful neighbor in the tenth century.

The Vietnamese did not, however, emerge unchanged by their millennium under Chinese rule. Although they were unsuccessful in assimilating the Vietnamese totally, the Chinese did exert a permanent influence on Vietnamese administration, law, education, literature, language, and culture. Their greatest impact was on the Vietnamese elite, with whom the Chinese administrators had the most contact. The effects of this Sinicization (*Han-hwa*) were much less intensive among the common people, who retained a large part of their pre-Han culture and language.

China's cultural influence increased in the centuries following the expulsion of its officials, as Vietnamese monarchs and aristocrats strove to emulate the cultural ideal established by the Middle Kingdom. Even for the Vietnamese elite, however, admiration for Chinese culture did not include any desire for Chinese political control. In the almost uninterrupted 900 years of independence that followed China's domination, the Vietnamese thwarted a number of Chinese attempts at military reconquest, accepting a tributary relationship instead. During this period, learning and literature flourished as the Vietnamese expressed themselves both in classical Chinese written in Chinese characters and in Vietnamese written in *chu nom,* a script derived from Chinese ideographs.

3

During the Chinese millennium, other cultural influences also reached the shores of the Red River Delta. A thriving maritime trade among China, India, and Indonesia used the delta as a convenient stopover. Among the array of goods and ideas thus brought to Vietnam was Buddhism from India. While the Vietnamese aristocracy clung to Chinese Confucianism during most periods, the common people embraced Buddhism, adapting it to fit their own indigenous religions and world view.

As the Red River Delta prospered, its population began expanding southward along the narrow coastal plains. The period from the twelfth century to the eighteenth century was marked by warfare with both the Cham and Khmer, the peoples of the Indianized kingdoms of Champa and Cambodia, who controlled lands in the Vietnamese line of march to the south. The Cham were finally defeated in 1471, and the Khmer were forced out of the Mekong Delta by 1749. Vietnamese settlers flooded into the largely untilled lands, turning them to rice cultivation. The southward expansion severely taxed the ability of the Vietnamese monarchy, ruling from the Red River Delta, to maintain control over a people spread over such a distance.

The inability of the ruling Le dynasty to deal with this and other problems led to the partition of the country by the nobility in the sixteenth century. After two hundred years of warfare between competing noble families, a peasant rebellion reunified the country in the late eighteenth century. The rebels, however, were unable to solve the problems of a country ravaged by war, famine, and natural disasters and lost control to a surviving member of the Nguyen noble family. Nguyen Anh took the reign name Gia Long (a composite derived from the Vietnamese names for the northern and southern capitals of the country during partition) and established a new centrally located capital at Hue in 1802.

Gia Long and his successors also were unable or unwilling to solve the persisting problems of the country, particularly the age-old dilemma of land alienation, the concentration of large tracts of land in the hands of a few and the resulting creation of vast numbers of landless peasants. The monarchy and aristocracy grew more and more removed from the people by the mid-nineteenth century. This period also climaxed the growth of European expansionism, as Western nations sought to carve out colonies in Asia and other parts of the non-Western world. Between 1858 and 1873, the French conquered Vietnam, dividing it into three parts—Cochinchina, Annam, and Tonkin—roughly corresponding to the areas referred to by the Vietnamese as Nam Bo (southern Vietnam), Trung Bo (central Vietnam), and Bac Bo (northern Vietnam). To the

Vietnamese, however, these were geographical terms, and the use of them to imply a political division of their homeland was as odious as the loss of their independence.

French colonial rule was, for the most part, politically repressive and economically exploitative. Vietnamese resistance in the early years was led by members of the scholar-official class, many of whom refused to cooperate with the French and left their positions in the bureaucracy. The early nationalists involved themselves in study groups, demonstrations, production and dissemination of anticolonialist literature, and acts of terrorism. Differences in approach among the groups were exemplified by Phan Boi Chau, who favored using the Vietnamese monarchy as a rallying point for driving out the French, and Phan Chu Trinh, who favored abolishing the monarchy and using Western democratic ideas as a force for gradual reform and independence. The success of these early nationalists was limited both by their inability to agree on a strategy and their failure to involve the Vietnamese peasantry, who made up the vast majority of the population. After World War I, another Vietnamese independence leader arose who understood the need to involve the masses in order to stage a successful anticolonial revolt. Ho Chi Minh, schooled in Confucianism, Vietnamese nationalism, and Marxism-Leninism, patiently set about organizing the Vietnamese peasantry according to communist theories, particularly those of Chinese leader Mao Zedong.

The defeat of the Japanese, who had occupied Vietnam during World War II, left a power vacuum, which the communists rushed to fill. Their initial success in staging uprisings and in seizing control of most of the country by September 1945 was partially undone, however, by the return of the French a few months later. Only after nine years of armed struggle was France finally persuaded to relinquish its colonies in Indochina. The 1954 Geneva Conference left Vietnam a divided nation, however, with Ho Chi Minh's communist government ruling the northern half from Hanoi and Ngo Dinh Diem's regime, supported by the United States, ruling the south from Saigon (later Ho Chi Minh City). Another two decades of bitter conflict ensued before Vietnam was again reunified as one independent nation.

Early History

The Vietnamese people represent a fusion of races, languages, and cultures, the elements of which are still being sorted out by ethnologists, linguists, and archaeologists. As was true for most areas of Southeast Asia, the Indochina Peninsula was a crossroads for many migrations of peoples, including speakers of Austronesian,

5

Figure 2. Location of Vietnam in Asia, 1987

Mon-Khmer, and Tai languages (see fig. 2). The Vietnamese language provides some clues to the cultural mixture of the Vietnamese people. Although a separate and distinct language, Vietnamese borrows much of its basic vocabulary from Mon-Khmer, tonality from the Tai languages, and some grammatical features from both Mon-Khmer and Tai. Vietnamese also exhibits some influence from Austronesian languages, as well as large infusions of Chinese literary, political, and philosophical terminology of a later period.

The area now known as Vietnam has been inhabited since Paleolithic times, with some archaeological sites in Thanh Hoa Province reportedly dating back several thousand years. Archaeologists link the beginnings of Vietnamese civilization to the late Neolithic, early Bronze Age, Phung Nguyen culture, which was centered in Vinh Phu Province of contemporary Vietnam from about 2000 to 1400 B.C. (see fig. 1). By about 1200 B.C., the development of wet-rice cultivation and bronze casting in the Ma River and Red River plains led to the development of the Dong Son culture, notable for its elaborate bronze drums. The bronze weapons, tools, and drums of Dong Sonian sites show a Southeast Asian influence that indicates an indigenous origin for the bronze-casting technology. Many small, ancient copper mine sites have been found in northern Vietnam. Some of the similarities between the Dong Sonian sites and other Southeast Asian sites include the presence of boat-shaped coffins and burial jars, stilt dwellings, and evidence of the customs of betel-nut-chewing and teeth-blackening.

According to the earliest Vietnamese traditions, the founder of the Vietnamese nation was Hung Vuong, the first ruler of the semi-legendary Hung dynasty (2879–258 B.C., mythological dates) of the kingdom of Van Lang. Hung Vuong, in Vietnamese mythology, was the oldest son of Lac Long Quan (Lac Dragon Lord), who came to the Red River Delta from his home in the sea, and Au Co, a Chinese immortal. Lac Long Quan, a Vietnamese cultural hero, is credited with teaching the people how to cultivate rice. The Hung dynasty, which according to tradition ruled Van Lang for eighteen generations, is associated by Vietnamese scholars with Dong Sonian culture. An important aspect of this culture by the sixth century B.C. was the tidal irrigation of rice fields through an elaborate system of canals and dikes. The fields were called Lac fields, and Lac, mentioned in Chinese annals, is the earliest recorded name for the Vietnamese people.

The Hung kings ruled Van Lang in feudal fashion with the aid of the Lac lords, who controlled the communal settlements around each irrigated area, organized construction and maintenance of the dikes, and regulated the supply of water. Besides cultivating rice, the people of Van Lang grew other grains and beans and raised stock, mainly buffaloes, chickens, and pigs. Pottery-making and bamboo-working were highly developed crafts, as were basketry, leather-working, and the weaving of hemp, jute, and silk. Both transport and communication were provided by dugout canoes, which plied the network of rivers and canals.

The last Hung king was overthrown in the third century B.C. by An Duong Vuong, the ruler of the neighboring upland kingdom of Thuc. An Duong Vuong united Van Lang with Thuc to form Au Lac, building his capital and citadel at Co Loa, thirty-five kilometers north of present-day Hanoi. An Duong's kingdom was short-lived, however, being conquered in 208 B.C. by the army of the Chinese Qin dynasty (221–207 B.C.) military commander Trieu Da (Zhao Tuo in Chinese). Reluctant to accept the rule of the Qin dynasty's successor, the new Han dynasty (206 B.C.–A.D. 220), Trieu Da combined the territories under his control in southern China and northern Vietnam and established the kingdom of Nam Viet (Nan Yue in Chinese), meaning Southern Viet. Viet (Yue) was the term applied by the Chinese to the various peoples on the southern fringes of the Han empire, including the people of the Red River Delta. Trieu Da divided his kingdom of Nam Viet into nine military districts; the southern three (Giao Chi, Cuu Chan, and Nhat Nam) included the northern part of present-day Vietnam. The Lac lords continued to rule in the Red River Delta, but as vassals of Nam Viet (see fig. 3).

The Chinese Millennium

Vietnamese historians regard Trieu Da as a defender of their homeland against an expanding Han empire. In 111 B.C., however, the Chinese armies of Emperor Wu Di defeated the successors of Trieu Da and incorporated Nam Viet into the Han empire. The Chinese were anxious to extend their control over the fertile Red River Delta, in part to serve as a convenient supply point for Han ships engaged in the growing maritime trade with India and Indonesia. During the first century or so of Chinese rule, Vietnam was governed leniently, and the Lac lords maintained their feudal offices. In the first century A.D., however, China intensified its efforts to assimilate its new territories by raising taxes and instituting marriage reforms aimed at turning Vietnam into a patriarchal society more amenable to political authority. In response to increased Chinese domination, a revolt broke out in Giao Chi, Cuu Chan, and Nhat Nam in A.D. 39, led by Trung Trac, the wife of a Lac lord who had been put to death by the Chinese, and her sister Trung Nhi. The insurrection was put down within two years by the Han general Ma Yuan, and the Trung sisters drowned themselves to avoid capture by the Chinese. Still celebrated as heroines by the Vietnamese, the Trung sisters exemplify the relatively high status of women in Vietnamese society as well as the importance to Vietnamese of resistance to foreign rule.

Following the ill-fated revolt, Chinese rule became more direct, and the feudal Lac lords faded into history. Ma Yuan established a Chinese-style administrative system of three prefectures and fifty-six districts ruled by scholar-officials sent by the Han court. Although Chinese administrators replaced most former local officials, some members of the Vietnamese aristocracy were allowed to fill lower positions in the bureaucracy. The Vietnamese elite in particular received a thorough indoctrination in Chinese cultural, religious, and political traditions. One result of Sinicization, however, was the creation of a Confucian bureaucratic, family, and social structure that gave the Vietnamese the strength to resist Chinese political domination in later centuries, unlike most of the other Yue peoples who were sooner or later assimilated into the Chinese cultural and political world. Nor was Sinicization so total as to erase the memory of pre-Han Vietnamese culture, especially among the peasant class, which retained the Vietnamese language and many Southeast Asian customs. Chinese rule had the dual effect of making the Vietnamese aristocracy more receptive to Chinese culture and cultural leadership while at the same time instilling resistance and hostility toward Chinese political domination throughout Vietnamese society.

Chinese Cultural Impact

In order to facilitate administration of their new territories, the Chinese built roads, waterways, and harbors, largely with corvée labor (unpaid labor exacted by government authorities, particularly for public works projects). Agriculture was improved with better irrigation methods and the use of ploughs and draft animals, innovations which may have already been in use by the Vietnamese on a lesser scale. New lands were opened up for agriculture, and settlers were brought in from China. After a few generations, most of the Chinese settlers probably intermarried with the Vietnamese and identified with their new homeland.

The first and second centuries A.D. saw the rise of a Han-Viet ruling class owning large tracts of rice lands. More than 120 brick Han tombs have been excavated in northern Vietnam, indicating Han families that, rather than returning to China, had become members of their adopted society and were no longer, strictly speaking, Chinese. Although they brought Chinese vocabulary and

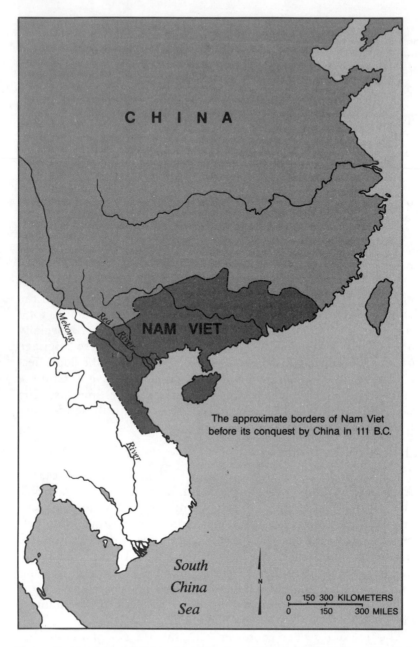

Source: Based on information from Joseph Buttinger, *Vietnam: A Political History,* New York, 1963, 23.

Figure 3. Nam Viet Before Conquest by China in 111 B.C.

technical terms into their new culture, after a generation or two, they probably spoke Vietnamese.

The second century A.D. was a time of rebellion in Giao Chi, Cuu Chan, and Nhat Nam, largely due to the declining quality of the Han administrators, who concentrated their energies on making their fortunes and returning north as soon as possible. Revolts against corrupt and repressive Chinese officials were often led by the Han-Viet families. The fall of the Han dynasty in China in 220 A.D. further strengthened the allegiance of the Han-Viet ruling elite to their new society and gave them a sense of their own independent political power. Meanwhile, among the peasant class there was also a heightened sense of identity fostered by the spread of Buddhism by sea from India to Vietnam by the early third century. The new religion was often adapted to blend with indigenous religions. Buddhist temples were sometimes dedicated to the monsoon season, for example, or identified with the guardian spirit of agricultural fertility. Although ruling-class Vietnamese tended to cling to Confucianism, various local rulers patronized the Buddhist religion, thus helping to legitimize their own rule in the eyes of the common people.

After the demise of the Han dynasty, the period of the third to the sixth century was a time of turbulence in China, with six different dynasties in succession coming to power. The periods between dynasties or the periods when dynasties were weak in China were usually the most peaceful in Vietnam. When dynasties were strong and interfered with local rule, the Vietnamese aristocracy engaged in a series of violent revolts that weakened China's control over its southern territory. A rebellion led by the noblewoman Trieu Au (Lady Trieu) in A.D. 248 was suppressed after about six months, but its leader earned a place in the hearts and history of the Vietnamese people. Despite pressure to accept Chinese patriarchal values, Vietnamese women continued to play an important role and to enjoy considerably more freedom than their northern counterparts.

Political Resistance to the Chinese

The sixth century was an important stage in the Vietnamese political evolution toward independence. During this period, the Vietnamese aristocracy became increasingly independent of Chinese authority, while retaining Chinese political and cultural forms. At the same time, indigenous leaders arose who claimed power based on Vietnamese traditions of kingship. A series of failed revolts in the late sixth and early seventh centuries increased the Vietnamese national consciousness. Ly Bi, the leader of a successful revolt in

11

543 against the Liang dynasty (502–556), was himself descended from a Chinese family that had fled to the Red River Delta during a period of dynastic turbulence in the first century A.D. Ly Bi declared himself emperor of Nam Viet in the tradition of Trieu Da and organized an imperial court at Long Bien (vicinity of Hanoi). Ly Bi was killed in 547, but his followers kept the revolt alive for another fifty years, establishing what is sometimes referred to in Vietnamese history as the Earlier Ly dynasty.

While the Ly family retreated to the mountains and attempted to rule in the style of their Chinese overlords, a rebel leader who based his rule on an indigenous form of kingship arose in the Red River Delta. Trieu Quang Phuc made his headquarters on an island in a vast swamp. From this refuge, he could strike without warning, seizing supplies from the Liang army and then slipping back into the labyrinthine channels of the swamp. Despite the initial success of such guerrilla tactics, by which he gained control over the Red River Delta, Trieu Quang Phuc was defeated by 570. According to a much later Vietnamese revolutionary, General Vo Nguyen Giap, Vietnamese concepts of protracted warfare were born in the surprise offensives, night attacks, and hit-and-run tactics employed by Trieu Quang Phuc.

The Chinese Tang dynasty (618–907) instituted a series of administrative reforms culminating in 679 in the reorganization of Vietnamese territory as the Protectorate of Annam (or Pacified South), a name later used by the French to refer to central Vietnam. The Tang dynastic period was a time of heavy Chinese influence, particularly in Giao Chau Province (in 203 the district of Giao Chi, had been elevated to provincial status and was renamed Giao Chau), which included the densely populated Red River plain. The children of ambitious, aristocratic families acquired a classical Confucian education, as increased emphasis was placed on the Chinese examination system for training local administrators. As a result, literary terms dating from the Tang dynasty constitute the largest category of Chinese loan words in modern Vietnamese. Despite the stress placed on Chinese literature and learning, Vietnamese, enriched with Chinese literary terms, remained the language of the people, while Chinese was used primarily as an administrative language by a small elite. During the Tang era, Giao Chau Province also became the center of a popular style of Buddhism based on spirit cults, which evolved as the dominant religion of Vietnam after the tenth century. Buddhism, along with an expanding sea trade, linked Vietnam more closely with South and Southeast Asia as Buddhist pilgrims traveled to India, Sumatra, and Java aboard merchant vessels laden with silk, cotton, paper, ivory, pearls, and incense.

尚書當領侍衛大臣叔青潘公像

Saigon scholar-official, late nineteenth century
Courtesy Library of Congress

13

As Tang imperial power became more corrupt and oppressive during the latter part of the dynasty, rebellion flared increasingly, particularly among the minority peoples in the mountain and border regions. Although the Viet culture of Giao Chau Province, as it developed under Tang hegemony, depended upon Chinese administration to maintain order, there was growing cultural resistance to the Tang in the border regions. A revolt among the Muong people, who are closely related to the central Vietnamese, broke out in the early eighth century. The rebels occupied the capital at Tong Binh (Hanoi), driving out the Tang governor and garrison, before being defeated by reinforcements from China. Some scholars mark this as the period of final separation of the Muong peoples from the central Vietnamese, which linguistic evidence indicates took place near the end of the Tang dynasty. In the mid-ninth century, Tai minority rebels in the border regions recruited the assistance of Nan-chao, a Tai mountain kingdom in the southern Chinese province of Yunnan, which seized control of Annam in 862. Although the Tang succeeded in defeating the Nan-chao forces and restoring Chinese administration, the dynasty was in decline and no longer able to dominate the increasingly autonomous Vietnamese. The Tang finally collapsed in 907 and by 939 Ngo Quyen, a Vietnamese general, had established himself as king of an independent Vietnam.

Nine Centuries of Independence

Having driven out the Chinese, Ngo Quyen defeated a series of local rival chiefs and, seeking to identify his rule with traditional Vietnamese kingship, established his capital at Co Loa, the third century B.C. citadel of An Duong Vuong. The dynasty established by Ngo Quyen lasted fewer than thirty years, however, and was overthrown in 968 by a local chieftain, Dinh Bo Linh, who reigned under the name Dinh Tien Hoang. He brought political unity to the country, which he renamed Dai Co Viet (Great Viet). The major accomplishments of Dinh Bo Linh's reign were the establishment of a diplomatic basis for Vietnamese independence and the institution of universal military mobilization. He organized a 100,000-man peasant militia called the Ten Circuit Army, comprising ten circuits (geographical districts). Each circuit was defended by ten armies, and each army was composed of ten brigades. Brigades in turn were made up of ten companies with ten ten-member squads apiece. After uniting the Vietnamese and establishing his kingdom, Dinh Bo Linh sent a tributary mission to the newly established Chinese Northern Song dynasty (960–1125). This diplomatic maneuver was a successful attempt to stave off China's reconquest of its former vassal. The Song emperor gave his recognition to Dinh Bo Linh, but only as "King of Giao Chi Prefecture," a state within the Chinese empire. Not until the rise of the Ly dynasty (1009–1225), however, did the Vietnamese monarchy consolidate its control over the country.

The Great Ly Dynasty and the Flowering of Buddhism

Following the death of Dinh Bo Linh in 979, the Song rulers attempted to reassert Chinese control over Vietnam. Le Hoan, the commander in chief of Dinh Bo Linh's army, seized the throne and successfully repulsed the Chinese army in 981. Ly Cong Uan, a former temple orphan who had risen to commander of the palace guard, succeeded Le Hoan in 1009, thereby founding the great Ly dynasty that lasted until 1225. Taking the reign name Ly Thai To, he moved his capital to Dai La (modern Hanoi). The early Ly kings established a prosperous state with a stable monarchy at the head of a centralized administration. The name of the country was changed to Dai Viet by Emperor Ly Thanh Tong in 1054.

The first century of Ly rule was marked by warfare with China and the two Indianized kingdoms to the south, Cambodia and Champa. After these threats were dealt with successfully, the second century of Ly rule was relatively peaceful enabling the Ly kings to establish a Buddhist ruling tradition closely related to the other Southeast Asian Buddhist kingdoms of that period. Buddhism became a kind of state religion as members of the royal family and the nobility made pilgrimages, supported the building of pagodas, sometimes even entered monastic life, and otherwise took an active part in Buddhist practices. Bonzes (see Glossary) became a privileged landed class, exempt from taxes and military duty. At the same time, Buddhism, in an increasingly Vietnamized form associated with magic, spirits, and medicine, grew in popularity with the people (see Religion, ch. 2).

During the Ly dynasty, the Vietnamese began their long march to the south (*nam tien*) at the expense of the Cham and the Khmer. Le Hoan had sacked the Cham capital of Indrapura in 982, whereupon the Cham established a new capital at Vijaya. This was captured twice by the Vietnamese, however, and in 1079 the Cham were forced to cede to the Ly rulers their three northern provinces. Soon afterwards, Vietnamese peasants began moving into the untilled former Cham lands, turning them into rice fields and moving relentlessly southward, delta by delta, along the narrow coastal plain. The Ly kings supported the improvement of Vietnam's agricultural system by constructing and repairing dikes and canals and by allowing soldiers to return to their villages to work for six months of each year. As their territory and population expanded, the Ly kings looked to China as a model for organizing a strong, centrally administered state. Minor officials were chosen by examination for the first time in 1075, and a civil service training institute and an imperial academy were set up in 1076. In 1089 a fixed hierarchy of state officials was established, with nine degrees of civil and military scholar-officials. Examinations for public office were made compulsory, and literary competitions were held to determine the grades of officials.

The Tran Dynasty and the Defeat of the Mongols

In 1225 the Tran family, which had effectively controlled the Vietnamese throne for many years, replaced the Ly dynasty by arranging a marriage between one of its members and the last Ly monarch, an eight-year-old princess. Under the Tran dynasty (1225–1400), the country prospered and flourished as the Tran rulers carried out extensive land reform, improved public administration, and encouraged the study of Chinese literature. The Tran, however, are best remembered for their defense of the country against the Mongols and the Cham. By 1225, the Mongols controlled most of northern China and Manchuria and were eyeing southern China, Vietnam, and Champa. In 1257, 1284, and 1287, the Mongol armies of Kublai Khan invaded Vietnam, sacking the capital at Thang Long (renamed Hanoi in 1831) on each occasion, only to find that the Vietnamese had anticipated their attacks and evacuated the city beforehand. Disease, shortage of supplies, the climate, and the Vietnamese strategy of harassment and scorched-earth tactics foiled the first two invasions. The third Mongol invasion, of 300,000 men and a vast fleet, was also defeated by the Vietnamese under the leadership of General Tran Hung Dao. Borrowing a tactic used by Ngo Quyen in 938 to defeat an invading Chinese fleet, the Vietnamese drove iron-tipped stakes into the bed of the Bach Dang River (located in northern Vietnam in present-day Ha Bac, Hai Hung, and Quang Ninh provinces), and then, with a small Vietnamese flotilla, lured the Mongol fleet into the river just as the tide was starting to ebb. Trapped or impaled by the iron-tipped stakes, the entire Mongol fleet of 400 craft was sunk, captured, or burned by Vietnamese fire arrows. The Mongol army retreated to China, harassed enroute by Tran Hung Dao's troops.

The fourteenth century was marked by wars with Champa, which the Tran reduced to a feudatory state by 1312 (see fig. 4). Champa freed itself again by 1326 and, under the leadership of Cham hero Che Bong Nga, staged a series of attacks on Vietnam between 1360 and 1390, sacking Thang Long in 1371. The Vietnamese again gained the upper hand following the death of Che Bong Nga and resumed their southward advance at Champa's expense. Despite their earlier success, the quality of the Tran rulers had declined markedly by the end of the fourteenth century, opening the way for exploitation of the peasantry by the feudal landlord class, which caused a number of insurrections. In 1400 General Ho Quy Ly seized the throne and proclaimed himself founder of the short-lived Ho dynasty (1400–07). He instituted a number of reforms that were unpopular with the feudal landlords, including a limit on the amount of land a family could hold and the rental of excess land by the state to landless peasants; proclamations printed in Vietnamese, rather than Chinese; and free schools in provincial capitals. Threatened by the reforms, some of the landowners appealed to China's Ming Dynasty (1368–1644) to intervene. Using reinstatement of the Tran dynasty as an excuse, the Ming reasserted Chinese control in 1407.

Renewed Chinese Influence

The Ming administered the country as if it were a province of China and ruled it harshly for the next twenty years. The forced labor of its people was used to exploit Vietnam's mines and forests solely for China's enrichment. Taxes were levied on all products including salt, a dietary staple. Under the Ming, Vietnamese cultural traditions, including the chewing of betel nut, were forbidden, and men were required to wear their hair long and women to dress in the Chinese style. Vietnamese Buddhism was replaced at court by Ming-sponsored neo-Confucianism, but Ming attempts to supplant popular Vietnamese religious traditions with an officially sponsored form of Buddhism were less successful.

The Chinese impact on Vietnamese culture was probably as great, or greater, in the centuries following independence as it was during the 1,000 years of Chinese political domination. Much of China's cultural and governmental influence on Vietnam dates from the Ming period. Other aspects of Chinese culture were introduced later by Vietnamese kings struggling to bring a Confucian order to their unruly kingdom. Chinese administrative reforms and traditions, when sponsored by Vietnamese kings and aristocracy, tended to be more palatable and hence more readily assimilated than those imposed by Chinese officials. Although the Vietnamese upper classes during the Ming period studied Chinese classical literature and subscribed to the Chinese patriarchal family system, the majority of the Vietnamese people recognized these aspects of Chinese culture mainly as ideals. Less exposed to Chinese influence, the peasantry retained the Vietnamese language and many cultural

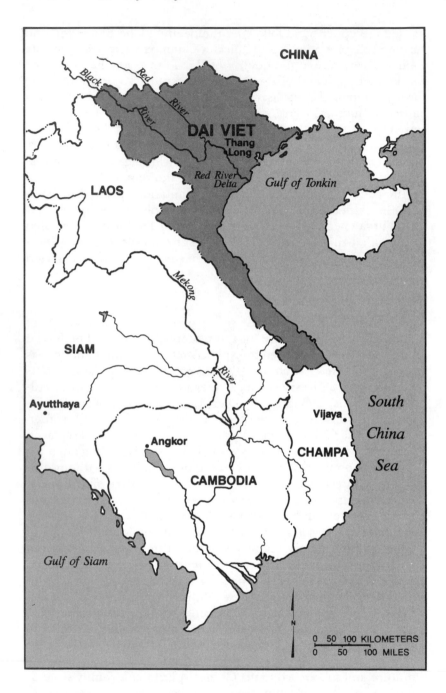

Figure 4. Vietnam (Dai Viet) and Its Neighbors, circa 1350

traditions that predated Chinese rule. Other factors also encouraged the preservation of Vietnamese culture during the periods of Chinese rule. Contact with the Indianized Cham and Khmer civilizations, for example, widened the Vietnamese perspective and served as a counterweight to Chinese influence. Vietnam's location on the South China Sea and the comings and goings of merchants and Buddhists encouraged contact with other cultures of South and Southeast Asia. China, itself, once it developed the port of Guangzhou (Canton), had less need to control Vietnam politically in order to control the South China Sea. Moreover, the Vietnamese who moved southward into lands formerly occupied by the Cham and the Khmer became less concerned about the threat from China.

The Le Dynasty and Southward Expansion

Le Loi, one of Vietnam's most celebrated heroes, is credited with rescuing the country from Ming domination in 1428. Born of a wealthy landowning family, he served as a senior scholar-official until the advent of the Ming, whom he refused to serve. After a decade of gathering a resistance movement around him, Le Loi and his forces finally defeated the Chinese army in 1428. Rather than putting to death the captured Chinese soldiers and administrators, he magnanimously provided ships and supplies to send them back to China. Le Loi then ascended the Vietnamese throne, taking the reign name Le Thai To and establishing the Le dynasty (1428–1788).

The greatest of the Le dynasty rulers was Le Thanh Tong (1460–97), who reorganized the administrative divisions of the country and upgraded the civil service system. He ordered a census of people and landholdings to be taken every six years, revised the tax system, and commissioned the writing of a national history. During his reign he accomplished the conquest of Champa in 1471, the suppression of Lao-led insurrections in the western border area, and the continuation of diplomatic relations with China through tribute missions established under Le Thai To. Le Thanh Tong also ordered the formulation of the Hong Duc legal code, which was based on Chinese law but included distinctly Vietnamese features, such as recognition of the higher position of women in Vietnamese society than in Chinese society. Under the new code, parental consent was not required for marriage, and daughters were granted equal inheritance rights with sons. Le Thanh Tong also initiated the construction and repair of granaries, dispatched his troops to rebuild irrigation works following floods, and provided for medical aid during epidemics. A noted writer and poet himself, he encouraged and emphasized employment of the Confucian examination system.

A great period of southward expansion also began under Le Thanh Tong. The *don dien* system of land settlement, borrowed from the Chinese, was used extensively to occupy and develop territory wrested from Champa. Under this system, military colonies were established in which soldiers and landless peasants cleared a new area, began rice production on the new land, established a village, and served as a militia to defend it. After three years, the village was incorporated into the Vietnamese administrative system, a communal village meeting house (*dinh*) was built, and the workers were given an opportunity to share in the communal lands given by the state to each village. The remainder of the land belonged to the state. As each area was cleared and a village established, the soldiers of the *don dien* would move on to clear more land. This method contributed greatly to the success of Vietnam's southward expansion (see fig. 5).

Although the Le rulers had ordered widespread land distribution, many peasants remained landless, while the nobility, government officials, and military leaders continued to acquire vast tracts. The final conquest of Champa in 1471 eased the situation somewhat as peasants advanced steadily southward along the coast into state-owned communal lands. However, most of the new land was set aside for government officials and, although the country grew wealthier, the social structure remained the same. Following the decline of the Le dynasty, landlessness was a major factor leading to a turbulent period during which the peasantry questioned the mandate of their rulers.

In the Confucian world view, emperors were said to have the "mandate of heaven" to rule their people, who, in turn, owed the emperor total allegiance. Although his power was absolute, an emperor was responsible for the prosperity of his people and the maintenance of justice and order. An emperor who did not fulfill his Confucian responsibilities could, in theory, lose his mandate. In practice, the Vietnamese people endured many poor emperors, weak and strong. Counterbalancing the power of the emperor was the power of the village, illustrated by the Vietnamese proverb, "The laws of the emperor yield to the customs of the village." Village institutions served both to restrain the power of the emperor and to provide a buffer between central authority and the individual villager. Each village had its council of notables, which was responsible for the obligations of the village to the state. When the central government imposed levies for taxes, for corvée labor for public projects, or for soldiers for defense, these levies were based on the council of notables' report of the resources of the villages, which was often underestimated to protect the village. Moreover, there was a division between state and local responsibilities. The central government assumed responsibility for military, judicial, and religious functions, while village authorities oversaw the construction of public works projects such as roads, dikes, and bridges, which were centrally planned. The autonomy of the villages, however, contributed to the weakness of the Vietnamese political system. If the ruling dynasty could no longer protect a village, the village would often opt for the protection of political movements in opposition to the dynasty. These movements, in turn, would have difficulty maintaining the allegiance of the villages unless they were able both to provide security and to institutionalize their political power. Although it insured the preservation of a sense of national and cultural identity, the strength of the villages was a factor contributing to the political instability of the society as it expanded southward.

Partition and the Advent of the Europeans

The degenerated Le dynasty, which endured under ten rulers between 1497 and 1527, in the end was no longer able to maintain control over the northern part of the country, much less the new territories to the south. The weakening of the monarchy created a vacuum that the various noble families of the aristocracy were eager to fill. In 1527 Mac Dang Dung, a scholar-official who had effectively controlled the Le for a decade, seized the throne, prompting other families of the aristocracy, notably the Nguyen and Trinh, to rush to the support of the Le. An attack on the Mac forces led by the Le general Nguyen Kim resulted in the partition of Vietnam in 1545, with the Nguyen family seizing control of the southern part of the country as far north as what is now Thanh Hoa Province. The Nguyen, who took the hereditary title *chua* (see Glossary), continued to profess loyalty to the Le dynasty. By the late sixteenth century the Trinh family had ousted the Mac family and had begun to rule the northern half of the country also in the name of the Le dynasty. The Trinh, who, like the Nyuyen, took the title *chua,* spent most of the seventeenth century attempting to depose the Nguyen. In order to repulse invading Trinh forces, the Nguyen in 1631 completed the building of two great walls, six meters high and eighteen kilometers long, on their northern frontier. The Trinh, with 100,000 troops, 500 elephants, and 500 large junks, were numerically far superior to their southern foe. The Nguyen, however, were better equipped, having by this time acquired Portuguese weapons and gunpowder, and, as the defending force, had the support of the local people. In addition, the Nguyen had the advantage of

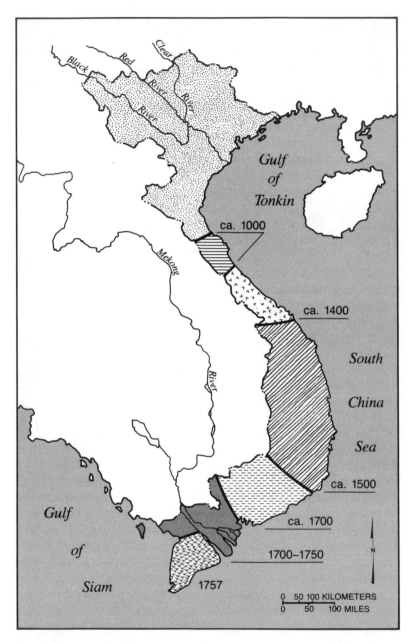

Source: Based on information from Joseph Buttinger, *Vietnam: A Political History,* New York, 1968, 50.

Figure 5. Vietnam's Southern Expansion, A.D. 1000–1757

controlling vast open lands in the Mekong Delta, wrested from the Khmer, with which to attract immigrants and refugees from the north. Among those who took up residence in the delta were an estimated 3,000 Chinese supporters of the defunct Ming dynasty, who arrived in 1679 aboard fifty junks and set about becoming farmers and traders. The Nguyen, aided by the Chinese settlers, succeeded in forcing the Khmer completely out of the Mekong Delta by 1749.

After major offensives by the Trinh in 1661 and 1672 foundered on the walls built by the Nguyen, a truce in the fighting ensued that lasted nearly 100 years. During that time, the Nguyen continued its southward expansion into lands held, or formerly held, by the Cham and the Khmer. The Trinh, meanwhile, consolidated its authority in the north, instituting administrative reforms and supporting scholarship. The nobility and scholar-officials of both north and south, however, continued to block the development of manufacturing and trade, preferring to retain a feudal, peasant society, which they could control.

The seventeenth century was also a period in which European missionaries and merchants became a serious factor in Vietnamese court life and politics. Although both had arrived by the early sixteenth century, neither foreign merchants nor missionaries had much impact on Vietnam before the seventeenth century. The Portuguese, Dutch, English, and French had all established trading posts in Pho Hien by 1680. Fighting among the Europeans and opposition by the Vietnamese made the enterprises unprofitable, however, and all of the foreign trading posts were closed by 1700.

European missionaries had occasionally visited Vietnam for short periods of time, with little impact, beginning in the early sixteenth century. The best known of the early missionaries was Alexandre de Rhodes, a French Jesuit who was sent to Hanoi in 1627, where he quickly learned the language and began preaching in Vietnamese. Initially, Rhodes was well-received by the Trinh court, and he reportedly baptized more than 6,000 converts; however, his success probably led to his expulsion in 1630. He is credited with perfecting a romanized system of writing the Vietnamese language (*quoc ngu*), which was probably developed as the joint effort of several missionaries, including Rhodes. He wrote the first catechism in Vietnamese and published a Vietnamese-Latin-Portuguese dictionary; these works were the first books printed in *quoc ngu*. Romanized Vietnamese, or *quoc ngu*, was used initially only by missionaries; classical Chinese, or *chu nom*, continued to be used by the court and the bureaucracy. The French later supported the use of *quoc ngu*, which, because of its simplicity, led to a high degree of literacy and a flourishing of Vietnamese litera-ture. After being expelled from Vietnam, Rhodes spent the next thirty years seeking support for his missionary work from the Vati-can and the French Roman Catholic hierarchy as well as making several more trips to Vietnam.

The stalemate between the Trinh and the Nguyen families that began at the end of the seventeenth century did not, however, mark the beginning of a period of peace and prosperity. Instead, the decades of continual warfare between the two families had left the peasantry in a weakened state, the victim of taxes levied to sup-port the courts and their military adventures. Having to meet their tax obligations had forced many peasants off the land and facili-tated the acquisition of large tracts by a few wealthy landowners, nobles, and scholar-officials. Because scholar-officials were exempted from having to pay a land tax, the more land they acquired, the greater was the tax burden that fell on those peasants who had been able to retain their land. In addition, the peasantry faced new taxes on staple items such as charcoal, salt, silk, and cinnamon, and on commercial activities such as fishing and mining. The desperate condition of the economy led to neglect of the extensive network of irrigation systems as well. As they fell into disrepair, disastrous flooding and famine resulted, causing great numbers of starving and landless people to wander the countryside. The widespread suffering in both north and south led to numerous peasant revolts between 1730 and 1770. Although the uprisings took place through-out the country, they were essentially local phenomena, breaking out spontaneously from similar local causes. The occasional coordi-nation between and among local movements did not result in any national organization or leadership. Moreover, most of the upris-ings were conservative, in that the leaders supported the restora-tion of the Le dynasty. They did, however, put forward demands for land reform, more equitable taxes, and rice for all. Landless peasants accounted for most of the initial support for the various rebellions, but they were often joined later by craftsmen, fisher-men, miners, and traders, who had been taxed out of their occupa-tions. Some of these movements enjoyed limited success for a short time, but it was not until 1771 that any of the peasant revolts had a lasting national impact.

The Tay Son Rebellion

The Tay Son Rebellion (1771–1802), which ended the Le and Trinh dynasties, was led by three brothers from the village of Tay Son in Binh Dinh Province. The brothers, who were of the Ho clan (to which Ho Quy Ly had belonged), adopted the name

Nguyen. The eldest brother, Nguyen Nhac, began an attack on the ruling Nguyen family by capturing Quang Nam and Binh Dinh provinces in 1772. The chief principle and main slogan of the Tay Son was "seize the property of the rich and distribute it to the poor." In each village the Tay Son controlled, oppressive landlords and scholar-officials were punished and their property redistributed. The Tay Son also abolished taxes, burned the tax and land registers, freed prisoners from local jails, and distributed the food from storehouses to the hungry. As the rebellion gathered momentum, it gained the support of army deserters, merchants, scholars, local officials, and bonzes.

In 1773 Nguyen Nhac seized Qui Nhon, which became the Tay Son capital. By 1778 the Tay Son had effective control over the southern part of the country, including Gia Dinh (later Saigon). The ruling Nguyen family were all killed by the Tay Son rebels, with the exception of Nguyen Anh, the sixteen-year-old nephew of the last Nguyen lord, who escaped to the Mekong Delta. There he was able to gather a body of supporters and retake Gia Dinh. The city changed hands several times until 1783, when the Tay Son brothers destroyed Nguyen Anh's fleet and drove him to take refuge on Phu Quoc Island. Soon thereafter, he met with French missionary bishop Pigneau de Béhaine and asked him to be his emissary in obtaining French support to defeat the Tay Son. Pigneau de Béhaine took Nguyen Anh's five-year-old son, Prince Canh, and departed for Pondichéry in French India to plead for support for the restoration of the Nguyen. Finding none there, he went to Paris in 1786 to lobby on Nguyen Anh's behalf. Louis XVI ostensibly agreed to provide four ships, 1,650 men, and supplies in exchange for Nguyen Anh's promise to cede to France the port of Tourane (Da Nang) and the island of Poulo Condore. However, the local French authorities in India, under secret orders from the king, refused to supply the promised ships and men. Determined to see French military intervention in Vietnam, Pigneau de Béhaine himself raised funds for two ships and supplies from among the French merchant community in India, hired deserters from the French navy to man them, and sailed back to Vietnam in 1789.

In the meantime, by 1786 the Tay Son had overcome the crumbling Trinh dynasty and seized all of the north, thus uniting the country for the first time in 200 years. The Tay Son made good their promise to restore the Le dynasty, at least for ceremonial purposes. The three Nguyen brothers installed themselves as kings of the north, central, and southern sections of the country, respectively, while continuing to acknowledge the Le emperor in Thang Long. In 1788, however, the reigning Le emperor fled north to seek

Chinese assistance in defeating the Tay Son. Eager to comply, a Chinese army of the Qing dynasty (1644–1911) invaded Vietnam, seized Thang Long, and invested the Le ruler as "King of Annam." That same year, the second eldest Tay Son brother, Nguyen Hue, proclaimed himself Emperor Quang Trung. Marching north with 100,000 men and 100 elephants, Quang Trung attacked Thang Long at night and routed the Chinese army of 200,000, which retreated in disarray. Immediately following his victory, the Tay Son leader sought to reestablish friendly relations with China, requesting recognition of his rule and sending the usual tributary mission.

Quang Trung stimulated Vietnam's war-ravaged economy by encouraging trade and crafts, ordering the recultivation of fallow lands, reducing or abolishing taxes on local products, and resettling landless peasants on communal lands in their own villages. Quang Trung also established a new capital at Phu Xuan (near modern Hue), a more central location from which to administer the country. He reorganized the government along military lines, giving key posts to generals, with the result that military officials for the first time outranked civilian officials. Vietnamese was substituted for Chinese as the official national language, and candidates for the bureaucracy were required to submit prose and verse compositions in *chu nom* rather than in classical Chinese.

Quang Trung died in 1792, without leaving a successor strong enough to assume leadership of the country, and the usual factionalism ensued. By this time, Nguyen Anh and his supporters had won back much of the south from Nguyen Lu, the youngest and least capable of the Tay Son brothers. When Pigneau de Béhaine returned to Vietnam in 1789, Nguyen Anh was in control of Gia Dinh. In the succeeding years, the bishop brought Nguyen Anh a steady flow of ships, arms, and European advisers, who supervised the building of forts, shipyards, cannon foundries and bomb factories, and instructed the Vietnamese in the manufacture and use of modern armaments. Nguyen's cause was also greatly aided by divisions within the Tay Son leadership, following the death of Quang Trung, and the inability of the new leaders to deal with the problems of famine and natural disasters that wracked the war-torn country. After a steady assault on the north, Nguyen Anh's forces took Phu Xuan in June 1801 and Thang Long a year later.

The Nguyen Dynasty and Expanding French Influence

In June 1802, Nguyen Anh adopted the reign name Gia Long to express the unifying of the country—Gia from Gia Dinh (Saigon) and Long from Thang Long (Hanoi). As a symbol of this unity,

A gate to the "Imperial City" of Hue, constructed by Emperor Gia Long in the early nineteenth century
Courtesy New York Times, *Paris Collection, National Archives*

Gia Long changed the name of the country from Dai Viet to Nam Viet. For the Chinese, however, this was too reminiscent of the wayward General Trieu Da. In conferring investiture on the new government, the Chinese inverted the name to Viet Nam, the first use of that name for the country. Acting as a typical counterrevolutionary government, the Gia Long regime harshly suppressed any forces opposing it or the interests of the bureaucracy and the landowners. In his drive for control and order, Gia Long adopted the Chinese bureaucratic model to a greater degree than any previous Vietnamese ruler. The new capital at Hue, two kilometers northeast of Phu Xuan, was patterned after the Chinese model in Beijing, complete with a Forbidden City, an Imperial City, and a Capital City. Vietnamese bureaucrats were required to wear Chinese-style gowns and even adopt Chinese-style houses and sedan chairs. Vietnamese women, in turn, were compelled to wear Chinese-style trousers. Gia Long instituted a law code, which followed very closely the Chinese Qing dynasty (1644–1911) model. Under the Gia Long code, severe punishment was meted out for any form of resistance to the absolute power of the government. Buddhism, Taoism, and indigenous religions were forbidden under the Confucianist administration. Traditional Vietnamese laws and customs, such as the provisions of the Hong Duc law code protecting the rights and status of women, were swept away by the new code. Taxes that had been reduced or abolished under the

27

Tay Son were levied again under the restored Nguyen dynasty. These included taxes on mining, forestry, fisheries, crafts, and on various domestic products, such as salt, honey, and incense. Another heavy burden on the peasantry was the increased use of corvéc labor to build not only roads, bridges, ports, and irrigation works but also palaces, fortresses, shipyards, and arsenals. All but the privileged classes were required to work on such projects at least sixty days a year, with no pay but a rice ration. The great Mandarin Road, used by couriers and scholar-officials as a link between Gia Dinh, Hue, and Thang Long, was started during this period in order to strengthen the control of the central government. Military service was another burden on the peasantry; in some areas one out of every three men was required to serve in the Vietnamese Imperial Army. Land reforms instituted under the Tay Son were soon lost under the restored Nguyen dynasty, and the proportion of communal lands dwindled to less than 20 percent of the total. Although *chu nom* was retained as the national script by Gia Long, his son and successor Minh Mang, who gained the throne upon his father's death in 1820, ordered a return to the use of Chinese ideographs.

Peasant rebellion flared from time to time throughout the first half of the nineteenth century, fueled by government repression and such calamities as floods, droughts, epidemics, and famines. Minority groups, including the Tay-Nung, Muong, and Cham, were also in revolt. Although they were primarily peasant rebellions, some of these movements found support from, or were led by, disaffected scholars or some of the surviving pretenders to the Le throne. Vietnam's foreign relations were also a drain on the central government during this period. Tributary missions were sent biennially to the Qing court in Beijing, bearing the requisite 600 pieces of silk, 200 pieces of cotton, 1,200 ounces of perfume, 600 ounces of aloes wood, 90 pounds of betel nuts, 4 elephant tusks, and 4 rhinoceros horns. Other missions to pay homage (also bearing presents) were sent every four years. At the same time, Vietnam endeavored to enforce tributary relations with Cambodia and Laos. In 1834, attempts to make Cambodia a Vietnamese province led to a Cambodian revolt and to Siamese intervention, with the result that a joint Vietnamese-Siamese protectorate was established over Cambodia in 1847. Other foreign adventures included Vietnamese support for a Laotian rebellion against Siamese overlordship in 1826–27.

The most serious foreign policy problem for the Nguyen rulers, however, was dealing with France through the French traders, missionaries, diplomats, and naval personnel who came in increasing

Magistrate supervising punishment, late nineteenth century
Courtesy Library of Congress

numbers to Vietnam. The influence of missionaries was perceived as the most critical issue by the court and scholar-officials. The French Société des Missions Étrangères reported 450,000 Christian converts in Vietnam in 1841. The Vietnamese Christians were for the most part organized into villages that included all strata of society, from peasants to landowners. The Christian villages, with their own separate customs, schools, and hierarchy, as well as their disdain for Confucianism, were viewed by the government as breeding grounds for rebellion—and in fact they often were. The French presence did, however, enjoy some support at high levels. Gia Long felt a special debt to Pigneau de Béhaine and to his two chief French naval advisers, Jean-Baptiste Chaigneau and Philippe Vannier, both of whom remained in the country until 1824. There were also members of the Vietnamese court who urged the monarchy to undertake a certain degree of westernization and reform in order to strengthen itself in the areas of administration, education, and defense. In the southern part of the country, Christians enjoyed the protection of Viceroy Le Van Duyet until his death in 1832. Soon thereafter the Nguyen government began a serious attempt to rid itself of French missionaries and their influence. A series of edicts forbade the practice of Christianity, forcing the Christian communities underground. An estimated ninety-five priests and members of the laity were executed by the Vietnamese during the following quarter of a century.

In response, the missionaries stepped up their pressure on the French government to intervene militarily and to establish a French protectorate over Vietnam. During this period, French traders became interested in Vietnam once more, and French diplomats in China began to express the view that France was falling behind the rest of Europe in gaining a foothold in Asia. Commanders of a French naval squadron, permanently deployed in the South China Sea after 1841, also began to agitate for a stronger role in protecting the lives and interests of the missionaries. Given tacit approval by Paris, naval intervention grew steadily. In 1847 two French warships bombarded Tourane (Da Nang), destroying five Vietnamese ships and killing an estimated 10,000 Vietnamese. The purpose of the attack was to gain the release of a missionary, who had, in fact, already been released. In the following decade, persecution of missionaries continued under Emperor Tu Duc, who came to the throne in 1848. While the missionaries stepped up pressure on the government of Louis Napoleon (later Napoleon III), which was sympathetic to their cause, a Commission on Cochinchina made the convincing argument that France risked becoming a second-class power by not intervening.

Under French Rule

By 1857 Louis-Napoleon had been persuaded that invasion was the best course of action, and French warships were instructed to take Tourane without any further efforts to negotiate with the Vietnamese. Tourane was captured in late 1858 and Gia Dinh (Saigon and later Ho Chi Minh City) in early 1859. In both cases Vietnamese Christian support for the French, predicted by the missionaries, failed to materialize. Vietnamese resistance and outbreaks of cholera and typhoid forced the French to abandon Tourane in early 1860. Meanwhile, fear was growing in Paris that if France withdrew the British would move in. Also current in Paris at that time was the rationalization that France had a civilizing mission—a duty to bring the benefits of its superior culture to the less fortunate lands of Asia and Africa. (This was a common justification for the colonial policies of most of the Western countries.) Meanwhile, French business and military interests increased their pressure on the government for decisive action. Thus in early 1861, a French fleet of 70 ships and 3,500 men reinforced Gia Dinh and, in a series of bloody battles, gained control of the surrounding provinces. In June 1862, Emperor Tu Duc, signed the Treaty of Saigon agreeing to French demands for the cession of three provinces around Gia Dinh (which the French had renamed Saigon) and Poulo Condore, as well as for the opening of three ports to trade, free passage of French warships up the Mekong to Cambodia, freedom of action for the missionaries, and payment of a large indemnity to France for its losses in attacking Vietnam.

Even the French were surprised by the ease with which the Vietnamese agreed to the humiliating treaty. Why, after successfully resisting invasions by the Chinese for the previous 900 years, did the monarchy give in so readily to French demands? Aside from the seriousness of the loss of Saigon and the possible overestimation of French strength, it appears that the isolation of the monarchy from the people created by decades of repression prevented Tu Duc and his court from attempting to rally the necessary popular support to drive out the French. In fact, by placating the French in the south, Tu Duc hoped to free his forces to put down a widespread Christian-supported rebellion in Bac Bo, which he indeed crushed by 1865. French missionaries, who had urged their government to support this rebellion, were disillusioned when it did not, especially after thousands of Christians were slaughtered by Tu Duc's forces following the rebellion. The missionaries, however, had served only as an initial excuse for French intervention in Vietnam; military and economic interests soon became the primary reasons for remaining there.

The French navy was in the forefront of the conquest of Indochina. In 1863 Admiral de la Grandière, the governor of Cochinchina (as the French renamed Nam Bo), forced the Cambodian king to accept a French protectorate over that country, claiming that the Treaty of Saigon had made France heir to Vietnamese claims in Cambodia. In June 1867, the admiral completed the annexation of Cochinchina by seizing the remaining three western provinces. The following month, the Siamese government agreed to recognize a French protectorate over Cambodia in return for the cession of two Cambodian provinces, Angkor and Battambang, to Siam. With Cochinchina secured, French naval and mercantile interests turned to Tonkin (as the French referred to Bac Bo). The 1873 storming of the citadel of Hanoi, led by French naval officer Francis Garnier, had the desired effect of forcing Tu Duc to sign a treaty with France in March 1874 that recognized France's "full and entire sovereignty" over Cochinchina, and opened the Red River to commerce. In an attempt to secure Tonkin, Garnier was killed and his forces defeated in a battle with Vietnamese regulars and Black Flag forces (see Glossary). The latter were Chinese soldiers, who had fled south following the Taiping Rebellion in that country and had been hired by the Hue court to keep order in Tonkin.

In April 1882, a French force again stormed the citadel of Hanoi, under the leadership of naval officer Henri Rivière. Rivière and part of his forces were wiped out in a battle with a Vietnamese-Black Flag army, a reminder of Garnier's fate a decade earlier. While Garnier's defeat had led to a partial French withdrawal from Tonkin, Rivière's loss strengthened the resolve of the French government to establish a protectorate by military force. Accordingly, additional funds were appropriated by the French Parliament to support further military operations, and Hue fell to the French in August 1883, following the death of Tu Duc the previous month. A Treaty of Protectorate, signed at the August 1883 Harmand Convention, established a French protectorate over North and Central Vietnam and formally ended Vietnam's independence. In June 1884, Vietnamese scholar-officials were forced to sign the Treaty of Hue, which confirmed the Harmand Convention agreement. By the end of 1884, there were 16,500 French troops in Vietnam. Resistance to French control, however, continued. A rebellion known as the Can Vuong (Loyalty to the King) movement formed in 1885 around the deposed Emperor Ham Nghi and attracted support from both scholars and peasants. The rebellion was essentially subdued with the capture and exile of Ham Nghi in 1888. Scholar and patriot Phan Dinh Phung continued to lead the resistance until his death in 1895. Although unsuccessful in driving out the French, the Can Vuong movement, with its heroes and patriots, laid important groundwork for future Vietnamese independence movements (see fig. 6).

Colonial Administration

Not all Vietnamese resisted the French conquest, and some even welcomed it. The monarchy, through decades of repression, had lost the support of the people; and Tu Duc, in the eyes of large segments of the peasantry, had lost his mandate to rule. He had been able to protect his people neither from foreign aggression nor from an unusually high incidence of natural disasters such as floods, famines, locusts, droughts, and a cholera epidemic in 1865 that killed more than 1 million people. Tu Duc's repression of Catholics also created a large opposition group ready to cooperate with the French, and those who did were often rewarded with lands vacated during the French invasion. Much of this land, however, was given to French *colons* (colonial settlers), often in sizable holdings of 4,000 hectares or more. Gradually a French-Vietnamese landholding class developed in Cochinchina. Vietnamese, however, were appointed only to the lower levels of the bureaucracy established to administer the new colony. Seeking to finance the growing bureaucracy, the early admiral-governors of Vietnam viewed the colony as the source of the necessary revenue. Rice exports, forbidden under the monarchy, reached 229,000 tons annually in 1870. Taxes extracted from Cochinchina increased tenfold in the first decade of French control. State monopolies and excise taxes on opium, salt, and alcohol eventually came to provide 70 percent of the government's operating revenue.

In 1887 France formally established the Indochinese Union, comprising the colony of Cochinchina and the protectorates of Annam, Tonkin, and Cambodia, with Laos being added as a protectorate in 1893. There was a rapid turnover among governors-general of the Indochinese Union, and few served a full five-year term. One who did, Paul Doumer (1897–1902), is considered to have been the architect of a colonial system under which Vietnam was politically dominated and economically exploited. Following the partitioning of Vietnam into three parts, the emperor was stripped of the last vestiges of his authority. In 1897 the powers of the *kinh luoc* (emperor's viceroy) were transferred to the Resident Superieur at Hanoi, who governed in the name of the emperor. That same year, the Privy Council or Co Mat Vien (see Glossary) in Annam was replaced with a French-controlled Council of Ministers. The following year in Annam, the French took over tax collection and payment of officials. Most of the Vietnamese scholar-officials had refused to cooperate with the French, but those who did were restricted to minor or ceremonial positions. Consequently, Frenchmen were recruited to staff a new, continually expanding bureaucracy. By 1925 there were 5,000 European administrators ruling an Indochinese population of 30 million, roughly the same number used to administer British India, which had a population more than ten times as large. Under the French laws applicable to individuals, Vietnamese were prohibited from traveling outside their districts without identity papers; and they were not allowed to publish, meet, or organize. They were subject to corvée, and they could be imprisoned at the whim of any French magistrate. The colonial police enforced the law through a network of French and Vietnamese agents.

Land alienation was the cornerstone of economic exploitation under the colonial government. By 1930 more than 80 percent of the riceland in Cochinchina was owned by 25 percent of the landowners, and 57 percent of the rural population were landless peasants working on large estates. Although the situation was somewhat better in the north, landless peasants in Annam totaled 800,000 and in Tonkin nearly 1 million. Heavy taxes and usurious interest rates on loans were added burdens on the peasants. More than 90 percent of rubber plantations were French owned. Two-thirds of

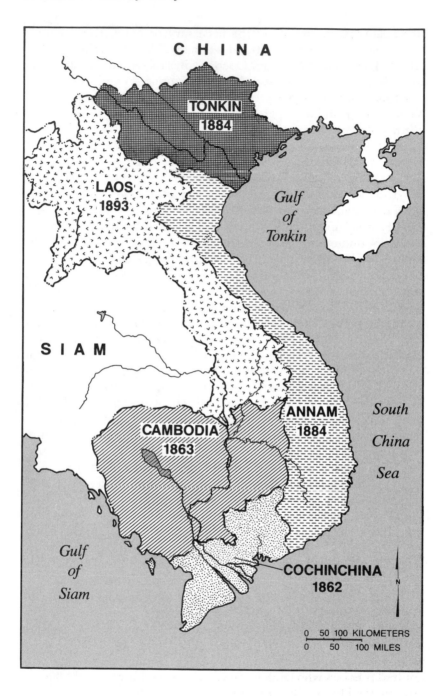

Figure 6. French Acquisitions in Indochina in the Nineteenth Century

the coal mined in Vietnam (nearly two million tons in 1927) was exported. Manufacturing was limited to cement and textiles, partly to placate French industrialists who saw Indochina as a market for their own goods. Naval shipyards and armament factories built under the Nguyen dynasty were dismantled under the French. Much of the craft industry survived, however, because it produced affordable consumer goods in contrast to imported French goods, which only the French colons or wealthy Vietnamese could afford.

French efforts at education in the early decades of colonial rule were negligible. A few government *quoc ngu* schools were established along with an Ecole Normale to train Vietnamese clerks and interpreters. A few Vietnamese from wealthy families, their numbers rising to about ninety by 1870, were sent to France to study. Three lycées (secondary schools), located in Hanoi, Hue, and Saigon, were opened in the early 1900s, using French as the language of instruction. The number of *quoc ngu* elementary schools was gradually increased, but even by 1925 it was estimated that no more than one school-age child in ten was receiving schooling. As a result, Vietnam's high degree of literacy declined precipitously during the colonial period. The University of Hanoi, founded in 1907 to provide an alternative for Vietnamese students beginning to flock to Japan, was closed for a decade the following year because of fear of student involvement in a 1908 uprising in Hanoi. In Tonkin and Annam, traditional education based on Chinese classical literature continued to flourish well into the twentieth century despite French efforts to discourage it, but the triennial examinations were abolished in 1915 in Tonkin and in 1918 in Annam. China, which had always served as a source of teaching materials and texts, by the turn of the century was beginning to be a source of reformist literature and revolutionary ideas. Materials filtering in from China included both Chinese texts and translations of Western classics, which were copied and spread from province to province.

Phan Boi Chau and the Rise of Nationalism

By the turn of the century, a whole generation of Vietnamese had grown up under French control. The people continued, as in precolonial times, to look to the scholar-gentry class for guidance in dealing with French imperialism and the loss of their country's independence. A few scholar-officials collaborated with the French, but most did not. Among those who refused was a group of several hundred scholars who became actively involved in the anticolonial movement. The best known among them was Phan Boi Chau, a scholar from Nghe An Province, trained in the Confucian tradition under his father and other local teachers. In 1885 Phan Boi

Chau observed at close range the actions of French troops in crushing scholar-gentry resistance to the colonial overlords. For the next decade he devoted himself to his studies and finally passed the regional examination with highest honors in 1905. During the following five years, he traveled about the country making contacts with other anticolonial scholars and seeking out in particular the survivors of the Can Vuong movement, with whom he hoped to launch a rebellion against the French. He also sought to identify a member of the Nguyen ruling family sympathetic to the cause, who would serve as titular head of the independence movement and as a rallying point for both moral and financial support. Chosen to fill this role was Cuong De, a direct descendant of Gia Long.

In 1904 Phan Boi Chau and about twenty others met in Quang Nam to form the Duy Tan Hoi (Reformation Society), the first of a number of revolutionary societies he organized. The following year, he went to Japan to meet with Japanese and Chinese revolutionaries and seek financial support for the Vietnamese cause. The Japanese defeat of the Russian fleet at Tsushima the month before his arrival had caused great excitement among the various Asian anticolonialist movements. Phan Boi Chau brought Cuong De, along with several Vietnamese students, to Japan in 1906. That same year he convinced the other great Vietnamese nationalist leader of the period, Phan Chu Trinh, to visit him in Tokyo. After two weeks of discussions, however, they were unable to resolve their basic tactical differences. Whereas Phan Boi Chau favored retaining the monarchy as a popular ideological symbol and a means of attracting financial support, Phan Chu Trinh wanted primarily to abolish the monarchy in order to create a base on which to build national sovereignty. Furthermore, he was greatly influenced by the writings of French political philosophers Rousseau and Montesquieu, and he believed that the French colonial administration could serve as a progressive force to establish a Western democratic political structure through peaceful reform. Phan Boi Chau, conversely, wanted to drive out the French immediately through armed resistance and restore Vietnamese independence.

In 1907 Phan Boi Chau organized the Viet Nam Cong Hien Hoi (Vietnam Public Offering Society) to unite the 100 or so Vietnamese then studying in Japan. The organization was important because of the opportunity it provided for the students to think and work together as Vietnamese, rather than as Cochinchinese, Annamese, or Tonkinese, as the French called them. The following year, however, the Japanese, under pressure from the French, expelled the students, forcing most of them to return home. In March 1909, Phan Boi Chau was also deported by the Japanese. He went first to Hong Kong, later to Bangkok and Guangzhou. Even during his years abroad, his writings served to influence nationalist activities in Vietnam. In 1907 the Dong Kinh Nghia Thuc (Free School of the Eastern Capital [Hanoi]) was founded to educate nationalist political activists. Phan Boi Chau's writings were studied and Phan Chu Trinh gave lectures at the school. Suspecting that Phan Boi Chau was associated with the school, however, the French closed it in less than a year. The French also blamed Phan Boi Chau for instigating antitax demonstrations in Quang Nam and Quang Ngai provinces and in Hue in early 1908. As a symbol of the movement, the demonstrators forcibly cut off men's traditional long hair. An abortive Hanoi uprising and poison plot in June 1908 was also blamed on Phan Boi Chau. In response to the uprising, the French executed thirteen of the participants and initiated a crackdown on Vietnamese political activists, sending hundreds of scholar-officials, including Phan Chu Trinh, to prison on Poulo Condore (now Con Dao). A major expedition was also launched in 1909 against De Tham, a resistance leader who was involved in the Hanoi uprising. De Tham, who had led a thirty-year campaign against the French in the mountains around Yen The in the northeastern part of Tonkin, managed to hold out until he was assassinated in 1913 .

Stimulated by the Chinese Revolution led by Sun Yat-sen in 1911, Phan Boi Chau and the other Vietnamese nationalists in exile in Guangzhou formed a new organization in 1912 to replace the moribund Duy Tan Hoi. The main goals of the newly organized Viet Nam Quang Phuc Hoi (Vietnam Restoration Society) included expulsion of the French, recovery of Vietnamese independence, and establishment of a "Vietnamese democratic republic." Phan Boi Chau had by this time given up his monarchist position, although Cuong De was accorded presidential status within the organization's provisional government. In order to gain support and financial backing for the new organization, Phan Boi Chau organized a number of terrorist bombings and assassinations in 1913, to which the French responded harshly. By 1914 the counterrevolutionary government of Yuan Shi-kai was in charge in China, and, by French request, Phan Boi Chau and other Vietnamese exiles in that country were imprisoned.

World War I began shortly thereafter, and some 50,000 Vietnamese troops and 50,000 Vietnamese workers were sent to Europe. The Vietnamese also endured additional heavy taxes to help pay for France's war efforts. Numerous anticolonial revolts occurred in Vietnam during the war, all easily suppressed by the French. In May 1916, the sixteen-year-old king, Duy Tan, escaped from his palace in order to take part in an uprising of Vietnamese troops.

The French were informed of the plan and the leaders arrested and executed. Duy Tan was deposed and exiled to Réunion in the Indian Ocean. One of the most effective uprisings during this period was in the northern Vietnamese province of Thai Nguyen. Some 300 Vietnamese soldiers revolted and released 200 political prisoners, whom, in addition to several hundred local people, they armed. The rebels held the town of Thai Nguyen for several days, hoping for help from Chinese nationalists. None arrived, however, and the French retook the town and hunted down most of the rebels.

In 1917, Phan Boi Chau was released from prison. He spent the next eight years in exile in China, studying and writing but exerting little direct influence on the Vietnamese nationalist movement. In 1925 he was kidnaped by the French in Shanghai and returned to Hanoi, where he was tried and sentenced to hard labor for life. The sentence was later changed to house arrest until his death in 1940. Vietnamese historians view Phan Boi Chau's contribution to the country's independence as immeasurable. He advocated forcibly expelling the French, although he was not able to solve the problems involved in actually doing it. He suggested learning from other Asian independence movements and leaders, while realizing that in the end only the Vietnamese could win their own independence. His greatest weakness, according to many historians, was his failure to involve the Vietnamese peasantry, who composed 80 percent of the population, in his drive for independence. Rather than recruiting support at the village level, Phan Boi Chau and his followers concentrated on recruiting the elite, in the belief that the peasant masses would automatically rally around the scholar-gentry. Future Vietnamese independence leaders took inspiration from the efforts of the early nationalists and learned from their mistakes the importance of winning support at the local level.

An important development in the early part of the twentieth century was the increased use of *quoc ngu* in the northern part of the country through a proliferation of new journals printed in that script. There had been *quoc ngu* publications in Cochinchina since 1865, but in 1898 a decree of the colonial government prohibited publication without permission, in the protectorate areas, of periodicals in *quoc ngu* or Chinese that were not published by a French citizen. In 1913 Nguyen Van Vinh succeeded in publishing *Dong Duong Tap Chi* (Indochinese Review), a strongly antitraditional but pro-French journal. He also founded a publishing house that translated such Vietnamese classics as the early nineteenth century poem *Kim Van Kieu* as well as Chinese classics into *quoc ngu*. Nguyen Van Vinh's publications, while largely pro-Western, were the major impetus for the increasing popularity of *quoc ngu* in Annam and Tonkin. In 1917 the moderate reformist journalist Pham Quynh began publishing in Hanoi the *quoc ngu* journal *Nam Phong,* which addressed the problem of adopting modern Western values without destroying the cultural essence of the Vietnamese nation. By World War I, *quoc ngu* had become the vehicle for the dissemination of not only Vietnamese, Chinese, and French literary and philosophical classics but also a new body of Vietnamese nationalist literature emphasizing social comment and criticism.

In the years immediately following World War I, the scholar-led Vietnamese independence movement in Cochinchina began a temporary decline as a result, in part, of tighter French control and increased activity by the French-educated Vietnamese elite. The decrease of both French investments in and imports to Vietnam during the war had opened opportunities to entrepreneurial Vietnamese, who began to be active in light industries such as rice milling, printing, and textile weaving. The sale of large tracts of land in the Mekong Delta by the colonial government to speculators at cheap prices resulted in the expansion of the Vietnamese landed aristocracy. These factors in combination led to the rise of a wealthy Vietnamese elite in Cochinchina that was pro-French but was frustrated by its own lack of political power and status.

Prominent among this group was Bui Quang Chieu, a French-trained agricultural engineer, who helped organize the Constitutionalist Party in 1917. Founded with the hope that it would be able to exert pressure on the Colonial Council of Cochinchina, the governing body of the colony, the party drew its support from Vietnamese who were large landowners, wealthy merchants, industrialists, and senior civil servants. The Colonial Council, established in 1880, was controlled by French interests, having only ten Vietnamese members out of twenty-four by 1922. The demands of the party included increased Vietnamese representation on the Colonial Council, higher salaries for Vietnamese officials, replacement of the scholar-official administration system with a modern bureaucracy, and reform of the naturalization law to make it easier for Vietnamese to become French citizens.

When the party failed to gain acceptance of any of these demands, it turned to its most pressing economic grievance, the ethnic Chinese domination of the Cochinchinese economy. Although French investors exercised almost exclusive control over industry and shared control of agriculture with the Vietnamese, the ethnic Chinese were sought out by the French to act as middlemen and came to dominate rice trade and retail business in both urban and rural areas. A boycott of Chinese goods organized by the party, however, was largely

unsuccessful because it primarily served the interests of the entrepreneurial elite. By the mid-1920s, Constitutionalist Party goals
were too elitist and too moderate to attract a popular following.
Although the party grew increasingly critical of the French, it failed
to advocate anything more than continued Franco-Vietnamese col-
laboration. Its place in the Vietnamese nationalist movement was
effectively usurped by more progressive political groups seeking
Vietnam's independence.

The mid-1920s also brought a period of increased activity among
the growing Vietnamese worker class; and pedicab drivers, dye
workers, and textile workers launched strikes with some success.
In August 1925, workers belonging to an underground union struck
at the Ba Son naval arsenal in Saigon-Cholon, ostensibly for higher
pay but in actuality to block two French naval ships from being
sent to Shanghai to pressure striking Chinese workers. The strik-
ers were successful in their demands and, in November, held massive demonstrations in Saigon to protest the arrest of Phan Boi Chau
in Shanghai.

Ho Chi Minh and the Communist Movement

The year 1925 also marked the founding of the Viet Nam Thanh
Nien Cach Menh Dong Chi Hoi (Revolutionary Youth League)
in Guangzhou by Ho Chi Minh. Born Nguyen Sinh Cung in Kim
Lien village, Nghe An Province in May 1890, Ho was the son of
Nguyen Sinh Sac (or Huy), a scholar from a poor peasant family.
Following a common custom, Ho's father renamed him Nguyen
Tat Thanh at about age ten. Ho was trained in the classical Confucian tradition and was sent to secondary school in Hue. After
working for a short time as a teacher, he went to Saigon where
he took a course in navigation and in 1911 joined the crew of a
French ship. Working as a kitchen hand, Ho traveled to North
America, Africa, and Europe. While in Paris from 1919–23, he
took the name Nguyen Ai Quoc (Nguyen the Patriot). In 1919 he
attempted to meet with United States President Woodrow Wilson
at the Versailles Peace Conference in order to present a proposal
for Vietnam's independence, but he was turned away and the
proposal was never officially acknowledged. During his stay in Paris,
Ho was greatly influenced by Marxist-Leninist literature, particularly Lenin's *Theses on the National and Colonial Questions* (1920), and
in 1920 he became a founding member of the French Communist
Party. He read, wrote, and spoke widely on Indochina's problems
before moving to Moscow in 1923 and attending the Fifth Congress of the Communist International (see Glossary), also called
the Comintern, in 1924. In late 1924, Ho arrived in Guangzhou,

where he spent the next two years training more than 200 Vietnamese cadres in revolutionary techniques. His course of instruction included study of Marxism-Leninism, Vietnamese and Asian revolutionary history, Asian leaders such as Gandhi and Sun Yat-sen, and the problem of organizing the masses. As a training manual, Ho used his own publication *Duong Cach Menh* (The Revolutionary Path), written in 1926 and considered his primer on revolution. Going by the name Ly Thuy, he formed an inner communist group, Thanh Nien Cong San Doan (Communist Youth League), within the larger Thanh Nien (Youth) organization. The major activity of Thanh Nien was the production of a journal, *Thanh Nien,* distributed clandestinely in Vietnam, Siam, and Laos, which introduced communist theory into the Vietnamese independence movement. Following Chiang Kai-shek's April 1927 coup and the subsequent suppression of the communists in southern China, Ho fled to Moscow.

In December of that year, a teacher from a Vietnamese peasant family, Nguyen Thai Hoc, founded Viet Nam Quoc Dan Dang (VNQDD, Vietnamese Nationalist Party), in Hanoi. With a membership largely of students, low-ranking government employees, soldiers, and a few landlords and rich peasants, VNQDD was patterned after the Chinese Nationalist Party (Kuomintang), from which it received financial support in the 1930s. Another source of funds for the VNQDD was the Vietnam Hotel in Hanoi, which it opened in 1928 as both a commercial enterprise and the party headquarters. The hotel restaurant, however, provided French agents with an easy means of penetrating the party and monitoring its activities. At various times, the VNQDD attempted, without success, to form a united front with Thanh Nien and other independence organizations. Thanh Nien, being two years older, however, had had a head start over VNQDD in organizing in schools, factories, and local government, which it had done with patience and planning. The VNQDD therefore concentrated instead on recruitment of Vietnamese soldiers and the overthrow of French rule through putschist-style activities.

In February 1929, the French official in charge of recruiting coolie labor was killed by an assassin connected with the VNQDD. The French immediately arrested several hundred VNQDD leaders and imprisoned seventy-eight. VNQDD leaders Nguyen Thai Hoc and Nguyen Khac Nhu escaped, but most members of the Central Committee were captured. The remaining leadership under Nguyen Thai Hoc decided to stage a general uprising as soon as possible. All dissent to the plan was overridden, and the party began manufacturing and stockpiling weapons. On February 9, 1930, a revolt instigated by the VNQDD broke out at Yen Bai among the Vietnamese garrison, but it was quickly suppressed. Simultaneous attacks on other key targets, including Son Tay and Lam Thu, were also unsuccessful because of poor preparation and communication. The Yen Bai uprising was disastrous for the VNQDD. Most of the organization's top leaders were executed, and villages that had given refuge to the party were shelled and bombed by the French. After Yen Bai, the VNQDD ceased to be of importance in the anticolonial struggle. Although more modernist and less bound by tradition than the scholar-patriots of the Phan Boi Chau era, the VNQDD had remained a movement of urban intellectuals who were unable to involve the masses in their struggle and too often favored reckless exploits over slow and careful planning.

On June 17, 1929, the founding conference of the first Indochinese Communist Party (ICP, Dang Cong San Dong Duong) was held in Hanoi under the leadership of a breakaway faction of Thanh Nien radicals. The party immediately began to publish several journals and to send out representatives to all parts of the country for the purpose of setting up branches. A series of strikes supported by the party broke out at this time, and their success led to the convening of the first National Congress of Red Trade Unions the following month in Hanoi. Other communist parties were founded at this time by both supporting members of Thanh Nien and radical members of yet another revolutionary party with Marxist leanings but no direct tie with the Comintern, called the New Revolutionary Party or Tan Viet Party. At the beginning of 1930, there were actually three communist parties in French Indochina competing for members. The establishment of the ICP prompted remaining Thanh Nien members to transform the Communist Youth League into a communist party, the Annam Communist Party (ACP, Annam Cong San Dang), and Tan Viet Party members followed suit by renaming their organization the Indochinese Communist League (Dong Duong Cong San Lien Doan). As a result, the Comintern issued a highly critical indictment of the factionalism in the Vietnamese revolutionary movement and urged the Vietnamese to form a united communist party. Consequently, the Comintern leadership sent a message to Ho Chi Minh, then living in Siam, asking him to come to Hong Kong to unify the groups. On February 3, 1930, in Hong Kong, Ho presided over a conference of representatives of the two factions derived from Thanh Nien (members of the Indochinese Communist League were not represented but were to be permitted membership in the newly formed party as individuals) at which a unified Vietnamese Communist Party (VCP) was founded, the Viet Nam Cong San Dang.

At the Comintern's request, the name was changed later that year at the first Party Plenum to the Indochinese Communist Party, thus reclaiming the original name of the party founded in 1929. At the founding meeting, it was agreed that a provisional Central Committee of nine members (three from Bac Bo, two from Trung Bo, two from Nam Bo, and two from Vietnam's overseas Chinese community) should be formed and that recognition should be sought from the Comintern. Various mass organizations including unions, a peasants' association, a women's association, a relief society, and a youth league were to be organized under the new party. Ho drew up a program of party objectives, which were approved by the conference. The main points included overthrow of the French; establishment of Vietnamese independence; establishment of a workers', peasants', and soldiers' government; organization of a workers' militia; cancellation of public debts; confiscation of means of production and their transfer to the proletarian government; distribution of French-owned lands to the peasants; suppression of taxes; establishment of an eight-hour work day; development of crafts and agriculture; institution of freedom of organization; and establishment of education for all.

The formation of the ICP came at a time of general unrest in the country, caused in part by a global worsening of economic conditions. Although the size of the Vietnamese urban proletariat had increased four times, to about 200,000, since the beginning of the century, working conditions and salaries had improved little. The number of strikes rose from seven in 1927 to ninety-eight in 1930. As the effects of the worldwide depression began to be felt, French investors withdrew their money from Vietnam. Salaries dropped 30 to 50 percent, and employment dropped approximately 33 percent. Between 1928 and 1932, the price of rice on the world market decreased by more than half. Rice exports totaling nearly 2 million tons in 1928 fell to less than 1 million tons in 1931. Although both French colons and wealthy Vietnamese landowners were hit by the crisis, it was the peasant who bore most of the burden because he was forced to sell at least twice as much rice to pay the same amount in taxes or other debts. Floods, famine, and food riots plagued the countryside. By 1930 rubber prices had plummeted to less than one-fourth their 1928 value. Coal production was cut, creating more layoffs. Even the colonial government cut its staff by one-seventh and salaries by one-quarter.

The Nghe-Tinh Revolt

Strikes grew more frequent in Nam Bo in early 1930 and led to peasant demonstrations in May and June of that year. The focus of reaction to the worsening economic conditions, however, was Nghe An Province, which had a long history of support for peasant revolts. Plagued by floods, drought, scarcity of land, and colonial exploitation, the people of Nghe An had been supporters of the Can Vuong movement and the activities of Phan Boi Chau. By late 1929, the ICP had begun organizing party cells, trade unions, and peasant associations in the province. By early 1930, it had established a provincial committee in the provincial capital of Vinh and had begun to found mass organizations throughout Nghe An. French sources reported that by mid-summer 1930 there were about 300 communist activists in Nghe An and the neighboring province of Ha Tinh. This figure rose to 1,800 a few months later. The communists helped to mobilize the workers and peasants of Nghe-Tinh, as the two-province area was known, to protest the worsening conditions. Peasant demonstrators demanded a moratorium on the payment of the personal tax and a return of village communal lands that were in the hands of wealthy landowners. When the demands were ignored, demonstrations turned to riots; government buildings, manor houses, and markets were looted and burned, and tax rolls were destroyed. Some village notables joined in the uprisings or refused to suppress them. Local officials fled, and government authority rapidly disintegrated. In some of the districts, the communists helped organize the people into local village associations called soviets (using the Bolshevik term). The soviets, formed by calling a meeting of village residents at the local *dinh,* elected a ruling committee to annul taxes, lower rents, distribute excess rice to the needy, and organize the seizure of communal land confiscated by the wealthy. Village militias were formed, usually armed only with sticks, spears, and knives.

By September the French had realized the seriousness of the situation and brought in Foreign Legion troops to suppress the rebellion. On September 9, French planes bombed a column of thousands of peasants headed toward the provincial capital. Security forces rounded up all those suspected of being communists or of being involved in the rebellion, staged executions, and conducted punitive raids on rebellious villages. By early 1931, all of the soviets had been forced to surrender. Of the more than 1,000 arrested, 400 were given long prison sentences, and 80, including some of the party leaders, were executed. With the aid of other Asian colonial authorities, Vietnamese communists in Singapore, China, and Hong Kong were also arrested.

The early 1930s was a period of recovery and rebuilding for the ICP in Vietnam. Reorganization and recruitment were carried on even among political prisoners, of whom there were more than

10,000 by 1932. In the prison of Poulo Condore, Marxist literature circulated secretly, an underground journal was published,
and party members (among them future party leaders Pham Van
Dong and Le Duan) organized a university, teaching courses in
sciences, literature, languages, geography, and Marxism-Leninism
(see Development of the Vietnamese Communist Party, ch. 4;
Appendix B). The party also began to recruit increasingly from
among Vietnamese minorities, particularly the Tay-Nung ethnic
groups living in Viet Bac. Located along Vietnam's northern border
with China, this remote mountainous region includes the modern
provinces of Lang Son, Cao Bang, Bac Thai, and Ha Tuyen (see
fig. 7).

This period also marked the rise of a Trotskyite faction within
the communist movement, which in 1933 began publishing a widely
read journal called *La Lutte* (Struggle). The Comintern's hostility
toward Trotskyites prevented their formal alliance with the ICP,
although informal cooperation did exist. In 1935 a combined slate
of ICP members and Trotskyites managed to elect four candidates
to the Saigon municipal council. Cooperation between the two
groups began to break down, however, when a Popular Front
government led by the French Socialist Party under Léon Blum
was elected in Paris. The Trotskyites complained that, despite the
change of leadership in France, nothing had changed in Indochina.
From the communist viewpoint, the major contribution to Vietnamese independence made by the Popular Front government was
an amnesty declared in 1936 under which 1,532 Vietnamese political
prisoners were freed.

World War II and Japanese Occupation

The signing of the Nazi-Soviet Non-Agression pact in August
1939, caused France immediately to ban the French Communist
Party and, soon afterwards, to declare illegal all Vietnamese political parties including the ICP. The colonial authorities began a crackdown on communists, arresting an estimated 2,000 and closing
down all communist and radical journals. The party consequently
was forced to shift its activities to the countryside, where French
control was weaker—a move that was to benefit the communists
in the long run. In November the ICP Central Committee held
its Sixth Plenum with the goal of mapping out a new united front
strategy, the chief task of which was national liberation. According to the new strategy, support would now be welcomed from the
middle class and even the landlord class, although the foundation
of the party continued to be the proletarian-peasant alliance.

After the fall of France to the Nazis in June 1940, Japan demanded

Source: Based on information from Thomas Hodgkin, *Vietnam: The Revolutionary Path,* New York, 1981, Map No. 5.

Figure 7. Viet Bac, Viet Minh Base Area, 1941-45

that the French colonial government close the Hanoi-Kunming railway to shipments of war-related goods to China. In an agreement with the Vichy government in France in August, Japan formally recognized French sovereignty in Indochina in return for access to military facilities, transit rights, and the right to station occupation troops in Tonkin. On September 22, however, Japanese troops invaded from China, seizing the Vietnamese border towns of Dong Dang and Lang Son. As the French retreated southward, the Japanese encouraged Vietnamese troops to support the invasion. The communists in the Bac Son district border area moved to take advantage of the situation, organizing self-defense units and establishing a revolutionary administration. The French protested to the Japanese, however, and a cease-fire was arranged whereby the French forces returned to their posts and promptly put down all insurrection. Most of the communist forces in Tonkin were able to retreat to the mountains. In similar short-lived uprisings that took place in the Plain of Reeds area of Cochinchina, however, the communist rebel forces had nowhere to retreat and most were destroyed by the French.

Establishment of the Viet Minh

In early 1940, Ho Chi Minh returned to southern China, after having spent most of the previous seven years studying and teaching at the Lenin Institute in Moscow. In Kunming he reestablished contact with the ICP Central Committee and set up a temporary headquarters, which became the focal point for communist policy-making and planning. After thirty years absence, Ho returned to Vietnam in February 1941 and set up headquarters in a cave at Pac Bo, near the Sino-Vietnamese border, where in May the Eighth Plenum of the ICP was held. The major outcome of the meeting was the reiteration that the struggle for national independence took primacy over class war or other concerns of socialist ideology. To support this strategy, the League for the Independence of Vietnam (Viet Nam Doc Lap Dong Minh Hoi, Viet Minh for short—see Glossary) was established. In this new front group, which would be dominated by the party, all patriotic elements were welcomed as potential allies. The party would be forced in the short term to modify some of its goals and soften its rhetoric, supporting, for example, the reduction of land rents rather than demanding land seizures. Social revolution would have to await the defeat of the French and the Japanese. The Eighth Plenum also recognized guerrilla warfare as an integral part of the revolutionary strategy and established local self-defense militias in all villages under Viet Minh control. The cornerstone of the party's strategy, of which Ho appears to have been the chief architect, was the melding of the forces of urban nationalism and peasant rebellion into a single independence effort.

In order to implement the new strategy, two tasks were given priority: the establishment of a Viet Minh apparatus throughout the country and the creation of a secure revolutionary base in the Viet Bac border region from which southward expansion could begin. This area had the advantages of being remote from colonial control but accessible to China, which could serve both as a refuge and training ground. Moreover, the Viet Bac population was largely sympathetic to the communists. Viet Minh influence began to permeate the area, and French forces attempted, but failed, to regain control of the region in 1941. The liberation zone soon spread to include the entire northern frontier area until it reached south of Cao Bang, where an ICP Interprovincial Committee established its headquarters. A temporary setback for the communists occurred in August 1942, when Ho Chi Minh, while on a trip to southern China to meet with Chinese Communist Party officials, was arrested and imprisoned for two years by the Kuomintang. By August 1944, however, he had convinced the regional Chinese commander to support his return to Vietnam at the head of a guerrilla force. Accordingly, Ho returned to Vietnam in September with eighteen men trained and armed by the Chinese. Upon his arrival, he vetoed, as too precipitate, a plan laid by the ICP in his absence to launch a general uprising in Viet Bac within two months. Ho did, however, approve the establishment of armed propaganda detachments with both military and political functions.

As World War II drew to a close, the ICP sought to have the Vietnamese independence movement recognized as one of the victorious Allied forces under the leadership of the United States. With this in mind, Ho returned again to southern China in January 1945 to meet with American and Free French units there. From the Americans he solicited financial support, while from the French he sought, unsuccessfully, guarantees of Vietnamese independence. On March 9, 1945, the Japanese gave the French an ultimatum demanding that all French and Indochinese forces be placed under Japanese control. Without waiting for the French reply, the Japanese proceeded to seize administrative buildings, radio stations, banks, and industries and to disarm the French forces. Bao Dai, the Nguyen ruler under the French, was retained as emperor, and a puppet government was established with Tran Trong Kim, a teacher and historian, as prime minister. Japan revoked the Franco-Vietnamese Treaty of Protectorate of 1883, which had established Indochina as a French protectorate, and declared the independence of Vietnam under Japanese tutelage.

The communists concluded that the approaching end of the war and the defeat of the Japanese meant that a propitious time for a general uprising of the Vietnamese people was close at hand. Accordingly, the ICP began planning to take advantage of the political vacuum produced by the French loss of control and the confinement of Japanese power largely to urban and strategic areas. Moreover, famine conditions prevailed in the countryside, and unemployment was rampant in the cities. In the Red River Delta alone, more than 500,000 people died of starvation between March and May 1945. Because Japan was considered the main enemy, the communists decided that a United Front should be formed that included patriotic French resistance groups and moderate urban Vietnamese bourgeoisie. The overall ICP strategy called for a two-stage revolt, beginning in rural areas and then moving to the cities. Accordingly, communist military forces responded to the plan. Armed Propaganda units under ICP military strategist Vo Nguyen Giap began moving south from Cao Bang into Thai Nguyen Province (see the Armed Forces, ch. 5). To the east, the 3,000-man National Salvation Army commanded by Chu Van Tan began liberating the provinces of Tuyen Quang and Lang Son and establishing revolutionary district administrations. At the first major military conference of the ICP, held in April in Bac Giang Province, the leaders determined that a liberated zone would be established in Viet Bac and that existing ICP military units would be united to form the new Vietnam Liberation Army (VLA), later called the People's Army of Vietnam (PAVN—see Glossary) (see The Armed Forces, ch. 5). Giap was named Commander in Chief of the VLA and chairman of the Revolution Military Committee, later called the Central Military Party Committee (CMPC). Meanwhile, the ICP was expanding its influence farther south by forming mass organizations known as national salvation associations (*cuu quoc hoi*) for various groups, including workers, peasants, women, youth, students, and soldiers. As a result of labor unrest in Hanoi, 2,000 workers were recruited into salvation associations in early 1945, and 100,000 peasants had been enlisted into salvation associations in Quang Ngai Province by mid-summer. In Saigon, a youth organization, Thanh Nien Tien Phong (Vanguard Youth), established by the communists in 1942, had recruited 200,000 by early summer. Thanh Nien Tien Phong became the focal point for the communist effort in the south and soon expanded to more than one million members throughout Cochinchina. By June 1945, in the provinces of Viet Bac, the Viet Minh had set up people's revolutionary committees at all levels, distributed communal and French-owned lands to the poor, abolished the corvée, established *quoc ngu* classes, set up local self-defense militias in the villages, and declared universal suffrage and democratic freedoms. The Viet Minh then established a provisional directorate, headed by Ho Chi Minh, as the governing body for the liberated zone, comprising an estimated one million people.

Despite its success in the north, the ICP faced a range of serious obstacles in Cochinchina, where the Japanese maintained 100,000 well-armed troops. In addition, the Japanese also supported the neo-Buddhist Cao Dai sect (see Glossary) of more than one million members, including a military force of several battalions. Another sect, the Hoa Hao (see Glossary), founded and led by the fanatical Huynh Phu So, eschewed temples and hierarchy and appealed to the poor and oppressed. Although lacking the military force of the Cao Dai, the Hoa Hao was also closely connected with the Japanese. Meanwhile, the Japanese had also gained control of the Viet Nam Phuc Quoc Dong Minh Hoi (League for the Restoration of Vietnam), established in 1939 as an outgrowth of Viet Nam Quang Phuc Hoi. Mobilized by the communists to face this array of forces in Cochinchina were the Vanguard Youth and the Vietnam Trade Union Federation, with 100,000 members in 300 unions.

The General Uprising and Independence

On August 13, 1945, the ICP Central Committee held its Ninth Plenum at Tan Trao to prepare an agenda for a National Congress of the Viet Minh a few days later. At the plenum, convened just after the dropping of the atomic bombs on Hiroshima and Nagasaki, an order for a general uprising was issued, and a national insurrection committee was established headed by ICP general secretary Truong Chinh (see Development of the Vietnamese Communist Party, ch. 4; Appendix B). On August 16, the Viet Minh National Congress convened at Tan Trao and ratified the Central Committee decision to launch a general uprising. The Congress also elected a National Liberation Committee, headed by Ho Chi Minh (who was gravely ill at the time), to serve as a provisional government. The following day, the Congress, at a ceremony in front of the village *dinh,* officially adopted the national red flag with a gold star, and Ho read an appeal to the Vietnamese people to rise in revolution.

By the end of the first week following the Tan Trao conference, most of the provincial and district capitals north of Hanoi had fallen to the revolutionary forces. When the news of the Japanese surrender reached Hanoi on August 16, the local Japanese military command turned over its powers to the local Vietnamese authorities. By August 17, Viet Minh units in the Hanoi suburbs had deposed the local administrations and seized the government seals symbolizing political authority. Self-defense units were set up and armed with guns, knives, and sticks. Meanwhile, Viet Minh-led demonstrations broke out inside Hanoi. The following morning, a member of the Viet Minh Municipal Committee announced to a crowd of 200,000 gathered in Ba Dinh Square that the general uprising had begun. The crowd broke up immediately after that and headed for various key buildings around the city, including the palace, city hall, and police headquarters, where they accepted the surrender of the Japanese and local Vietnamese government forces, mostly without resistance. The Viet Minh sent telegrams throughout Tonkin announcing its victory, and local Viet Minh units were able to take over most of the provincial and district capitals without a struggle. In Annam and Cochinchina, however, the communist victory was less assured because the ICP in those regions had neither the advantage of long, careful preparation nor an established liberated base area and army. Hue fell in a manner similar to Hanoi, with the takeover first of the surrounding area. Saigon fell on August 25 to the Viet Minh, who organized a nine-member, multiparty Committee of the South, including six members of the Viet Minh, to govern the city. The provinces south and west of Saigon, however, remained in the hands of the Hoa Hao. Although the Hoa Hao and Cao Dai were anti-French, both were more interested in regional autonomy than in communist-led national independence. As a result, clashes between the Hoa Hao and the Viet Minh broke out in the Mekong Delta in September.

Ho Chi Minh moved his headquarters to Hanoi shortly after the Viet Minh takeover of the city. On August 28, the Viet Minh announced the formation of the provisional government of the Democratic Republic of Vietnam (DRV) with Ho as president and minister of foreign affairs. Vo Nguyen Giap was named minister of interior and Pham Van Dong minister of finance. In order to broaden support for the new government, several noncommunists were also included. Emperor Bao Dai, whom the communists had forced to abdicate on August 25, was given the position of high counselor to the new government. On September 2, half a million people gathered in Ba Dinh Square to hear Ho read the Vietnamese Declaration of Independence, based on the American Declaration of Independence and the French Declaration of the Rights of Man and the Citizen. After indicting the French colonial record in Vietnam, he closed with an appeal to the victorious Allies to recognize the independence of Vietnam.

Despite the heady days of August, major problems lay ahead for the ICP. Noncommunist political parties, which had been too weak and disorganized to take advantage of the political vacuum left by the fall of the Japanese, began to express opposition to communist control of the new provisional government. Among these parties, the nationalist VNQDD and Viet Nam Phuc Quoc Dong Minh Hoi parties had the benefit of friendship with the Chinese expeditionary forces of Chiang Kai-shek, which began arriving in northern Vietnam in early September. At the Potsdam Conference in July 1945, the Allies had agreed that the Chinese would accept the surrender of the Japanese in Indochina north of the 16°N parallel and the British, south of that line. The Vietnamese nationalists, with the help of Chinese troops, seized some areas north of Hanoi, and the VNQDD subsequently set up an opposition newspaper in Hanoi to denounce "red terror." The communists gave high priority to avoiding clashes with Chinese troops, which soon numbered 180,000. To prevent such encounters, Ho ordered VLA troops to avoid provoking any incidents with the Chinese and agreed to the Chinese demand that the communists negotiate with the Vietnamese nationalist parties. Accordingly, in November 1945, the provisional government began negotiations with the VNQDD and the Viet Nam Phuc Quoc Dong Minh Hoi, both of which initially took a hard line in their demands. The communists resisted, however, and the final agreement called for a provisional coalition government with Ho as president and nationalist leader Nguyen Hai Than as vice president. In the general elections scheduled for early January, 50 of the 350 National Assembly seats were to be reserved for the VNQDD and 20 for Viet Nam Phuc Quoc Dong Minh Hoi regardless of the results of the balloting.

At the same time, the communists were in a far weaker political position in Cochinchina because they faced competition from the well-organized, economically influential, moderate parties based in Saigon and from the Hoa Hao and Cao Dai in the countryside. Moreover, the commander of the British expeditionary forces, which arrived in early September, was unsympathetic to Vietnamese desires for independence. French troops, released from Japanese prisons and rearmed by the British, provoked incidents and seized control of the city. A general strike called by the Vietnamese led to clashes with the French troops and mob violence in the French sections of the city. Negotiations between the French and the Committee of the South broke down in early October, as French troops began to occupy towns in the Mekong Delta. Plagued by clashes with the religious sects, lack of weapons, and a high desertion rate, the troops of the Viet Minh were driven deep into the delta, forests, and other inaccessible areas of the region.

Meanwhile, in Hanoi candidates supported by the Viet Minh won 300 seats in the National Assembly in the January 1946 elections. In early March, however, the threat of the imminent arrival of French troops in the north forced Ho to negotiate a compromise with France. Under the terms of the agreement, the French government recognized the DRV as a free state with its own army, legislative body, and financial powers, in return for Hanoi's acceptance of a small French military presence in northern Vietnam and membership in the French Union. Both sides agreed to a plebiscite in Cochinchina. The terms of the accord were generally unpopular with the Vietnamese and were widely viewed as a sell-out of the

Ho Chi Minh, accompanied by
Pham Van Dong, arriving in Paris, 1946
Courtesy New York Times, *Paris Collection, National Archives*

revolution. Ho, however, foresaw grave danger in refusing to compromise while the country was still in a weakened position. Soon after the agreement was signed, some 15,000 French troops arrived in Tonkin, and both the Vietnamese and the French began to question the terms of the accord. Negotiations to implement the agreement began in late spring at Fontainbleau, near Paris, and dragged on throughout the summer. Ho signed a modus vivendi (temporary agreement), which gave the Vietnamese little more than the promise of negotiation of a final treaty the following January, and returned to Vietnam.

First Indochina War

Ho's efforts during this period were directed primarily at conciliating both the French themselves and the militantly anti-French members of the ICP leadership. The growing frequency of clashes between French and Vietnamese forces in Haiphong led to a French naval bombardment of that port city in November 1946. Estimates of Vietnamese casualties from the action range from 6,000 to 20,000. This incident and the arrival of 1,000 troops of the French Foreign Legion in central and northern Vietnam in early December convinced the communists, including Ho, that they should prepare for war. On December 19, the French demanded that the Vietnamese forces in the Hanoi area disarm and transfer responsibility for law and order to French authority. That evening, the Viet Minh responded by attacking the city's electric plant and other French installations around the area. Forewarned, the French seized Gia Lam airfield and took control of the central part of Hanoi, as full-scale war broke out. By late January, the French had retaken most of the provincial capitals in northern and central Vietnam. Hue fell in early February, after a six-week siege. The Viet Minh, which avoided using its main force units against the French at that time, continued to control most of the countryside, where it concentrated on building up its military strength and setting up guerrilla training programs in liberated areas. Seizing the initiative, however, the French marched north to the Chinese border in the autumn of 1947, inflicting heavy casualties on the Viet Minh and retaking much of the Viet Bac region.

Meanwhile, in April 1947 the Viet Minh in Cochinchina had destroyed all chance for alliance with the religious sects by executing Huynh Phu So, leader of the Hoa Hao. Both the Hoa Hao and the Cao Dai formed alliances soon afterward with the French. The Committee for the South, which had seriously damaged the communist image in Cochinchina by its hard-line approach, was replaced in 1951 by the Central Office for South Vietnam (COSVN,

Trung Uong Cuc Mien Nam), headed by Le Duan. In the north, however, the political and military situation had begun to improve for the communists by late 1948. The Viet Minh had increased the number of its troops to more than 250,000 and, through guerrilla activities, the communists had managed to retake part of Viet Bac as well as a number of small liberated base areas in the south. ICP political power was also growing, although lack of a land reform program and the continued moderate policy toward the patriotic landed gentry discouraged peasant support for the communists. In 1948, the French responded to the growing strength of the Viet Minh by granting nominal independence to all of Vietnam in the guise of "associated statehood" within the French Union. The terms of the agreement made it clear, however, that Vietnam's independence was, in reality, devoid of any practical significance. The new government, established with Bao Dai as chief of state, was viewed critically by nationalists as well as communists. Most prominent nationalists, including Ngo Dinh Diem (president, Republic of Vietnam, South Vietnam, 1955–63), refused positions in the government, and many left the country.

The United States recognized the Associated State of Vietnam in early 1950, but this action was counterbalanced a few days later with the recognition of the DRV by the new People's Republic of China. In March, Ho Chi Minh signed an agreement with Beijing that called for limited assistance to Hanoi. Shortly thereafter, Moscow also formally recognized the DRV, and the Viet Minh became more openly affiliated with the communist camp. Mao Zedong's model of revolution was openly praised in the Vietnamese press; and the ICP, which, on paper, had been temporarily dissolved in 1945 to obscure the Viet Minh's communist roots, surfaced under a new name in 1951 that removed all doubt of its communist nature. More than 200 delegates, representing some 500,000 party members, gathered at the Second National Party Congress of the ICP, held in February 1951 in Tuyen Quang Province. Renaming the ICP the Vietnam Workers' Party (VWP, Dang Lao Dong Viet Nam), the delegates elected Ho as party chairman and Truong Chinh as general secretary.

Dien Bien Phu

With Beijing's promise of limited assistance to Hanoi, the communist military strategy concentrated on the liberation of Tonkin and consigned Cochinchina to a lower priority. The top military priority, as set by Giap, was to free the northern border areas in order to protect the movement of supplies and personnel from China. By autumn of 1950, the Viet Minh had again liberated

Viet Bac in decisive battles that forced the French to evacuate the entire border region, leaving behind a large quantity of ammunition. From their liberated zone in the northern border area, the Viet Minh were free to make raids into the Red River Delta. The French military in Vietnam found it increasingly difficult to convince Paris and the French electorate to give them the manpower and matériel needed to defeat the Viet Minh. For the next two years, the Viet Minh, well aware of the growing disillusionment of the French people with Indochina, concentrated its efforts on wearing down the French military by attacking its weakest outposts and by maximizing the physical distance between engagements to disperse French forces. Being able to choose the time and place for such engagements gave the guerrillas a decided advantage. Meanwhile, political activity was increased until, by late 1952, more than half the villages of the Red River Delta were under Viet Minh control.

The newly appointed commander of French forces in Vietnam, General Henri Navarre, decided soon after his arrival in Vietnam that it was essential to halt a Viet Minh offensive underway in neighboring Laos. To do so, Navarre believed it was necessary for the French to capture and hold the town of Dien Bien Phu, sixteen kilometers from the Laotian border. For the Viet Minh, control of Dien Bien Phu was an important link in the supply route from China. In November 1953, the French occupied the town with paratroop battalions and began reinforcing it with units from the French military post at nearby Lai Chau.

During that same month, Ho indicated that the DRV was willing to examine French proposals for a diplomatic settlement announced the month before. In February 1954, a peace conference to settle the Korean and Indochinese conflicts was set for April in Geneva, and negotiations in Indochina were scheduled to begin on May 8. Viet Minh strategists, led by Giap, concluded that a successful attack on a French fortified camp, timed to coincide with the peace talks, would give Hanoi the necessary leverage for a successful conclusion of the negotiations.

Accordingly, the siege of Dien Bien Phu began on March 13, by which time the Viet Minh had concentrated nearly 50,000 regular troops, 55,000 support troops, and almost 100,000 transport workers in the area. Chinese aid, consisting mainly of ammunition, petroleum, and some large artillery pieces carried a distance of 350 kilometers from the Chinese border, reached 1,500 tons per month by early 1954. The French garrison of 15,000, which depended on supply by air, was cut off by March 27, when the Viet Minh artillery succeeded in making the airfield unusable. An

56

United States Vice President
Richard M. Nixon
visiting Vietnam in 1953
Courtesy Indochina Archives

Treating wounded
French soldiers at
Dien Bien Phu, April 1954
Courtesy New York Times,
Paris Collection,
National Archives

elaborate system of tunnels dug in the mountainsides enabled the Viet Minh to protect its artillery pieces by continually moving them to prevent discovery. Several hundred kilometers of trenches permitted the attackers to move progressively closer to the French encampment. In the final battle, human wave assaults were used to take the perimeter defenses, which yielded defensive guns that were then turned on the main encampment. The French garrison surrendered on May 7, ending the siege that had cost the lives of about 25,000 Vietnamese and more than 1,500 French troops.

The following day, peace talks on Indochina began in Geneva, attended by the DRV, the Associated State of Vietnam, Cambodia, Laos, France, Britain, China, the Soviet Union, and the United States. In July a compromise agreement was reached consisting of two documents: a cease-fire and a final declaration. The cease-fire agreement, which was signed only by France and the DRV, established a provisional military demarcation line at about the 17°N parallel and required the regrouping of all French military forces south of that line and of all Viet Minh military forces north of the line. A demilitarized zone (DMZ), no more than five kilometers wide, was established on either side of the demarcation line. The cease-fire agreement also provided for a 300-day period, during which all civilians were free to move from one zone to the other, and an International Control Commission, consisting of Canada, India, and Poland, to supervise the cease-fire. The final declaration was endorsed through recorded oral assent by the DRV, France, Britain, China, and the Soviet Union. It provided for the holding of national elections in July 1956, under the supervision of the International Control Commission, and stated that the military demarcation line was provisional and "should not in any way be interpreted as constituting a political territorial boundary." Both the United States and the Associated State of Vietnam, which France had recognized on June 4 as a "fully independent and sovereign state," refused to approve the final declaration and submitted separate declarations stating their reservations.

The Aftermath of Geneva

The Geneva Agreements were viewed with doubt and dissatisfaction on all sides. Concern over possible United States intervention, should the Geneva talks fail, was probably a major factor in Hanoi's decision to accept the compromise agreement. The United States had dissociated itself from the final declaration, although it had stated that it would refrain from the threat or use of force to disturb the agreements. President Dwight D. Eisenhower wrote to the new Prime Minister of the Bao Dai government, Ngo Dinh

*Charles DeGaulle and
Ho Chi Minh are hanged in
effigy during the National
Shame Day celebration in
Saigon, July 1964, observing
the tenth anniversary
of the July 1954
Geneva Agreements.
Courtesy United States Army*

*Northern Roman Catholic
peasant refugee, 1954
Courtesy Indochina Archives*

Diem, in September 1954 promising United States support for a noncommunist Vietnam. Direct United States aid to South Vietnam began in January 1955, and American advisors began arriving the following month to train South Vietnamese army troops. By early 1955, Diem had consolidated his control by moving against lawless elements in the Saigon area and by suppressing the religious sects in the Mekong Delta. He also launched a "denounce the communists" campaign, in which, according to communist accounts, 25,000 communist sympathizers were arrested and more than 1,000 killed. In August 1955, Diem issued a statement formally refusing to participate in consultations with the DRV, which had been called for by the Geneva Agreement to prepare for national elections. In October, he easily defeated Bao Dai in a seriously tainted referendum and became president of the new Republic of Vietnam.

Despite the growing likelihood that national elections would not be held, the communist leadership in Hanoi decided for the time being to continue to concentrate its efforts on the political struggle. Several factors led to this decision, including the weakness of the party apparatus in the South, the need to concentrate on strengthening the war-weakened North, and pressure from the communist leadership of the Soviet Union, which, under General Secretary Nikita Khrushchev, had inaugurated its policy of peaceful coexistence with the West. By 1957, however, a shift to a more militant approach to the reunification of the country was apparent. Partly in response to Diem's anticommunist campaign, the Party stepped up terrorist activities in the South, assassinating several hundred officials of the Diem government. This led to the arrest of another 65,000 suspected communists and the killing of more than 2,000 by the Saigon government in 1957. Repression by the Diem regime led to the rise of armed rebel self-defense units in various parts of the South, with the units often operating on their own without any party direction. Observing that a potential revolutionary situation had been created by popular resentment of the Diem government and fearing that the government's anticommunist policy would destroy or weaken party organization in the South, the VWP leadership determined that the time had come to resort to violent struggle.

Second Indochina War

By 1959 some of the 90,000 Viet Minh troops that had returned to the North following the Geneva Agreements had begun filtering back into the South to take up leadership positions in the insurgency apparatus. Mass demonstrations, punctuated by an occasional raid on an isolated post, were the major activities in the initial stage of this insurgency. Communist-led uprisings launched in 1959 in the lower Mekong Delta and Central Highlands resulted in the establishment of liberated zones, including an area of nearly fifty villages in Quang Ngai Province. In areas under communist control in 1959, the guerrillas established their own government, levied taxes, trained troops, built defense works, and provided education and medical care. In order to direct and coordinate the new policies in the South, it was necessary to revamp the party leadership apparatus and form a new united front group. Accordingly, COSVN, which had been abolished in 1954, was reestablished with General Nguyen Chi Thanh, a northerner, as chairman and Pham Hung, a southerner, as deputy chairman. On December 20, 1960, the National Front for the Liberation of South Vietnam, informally called the National Liberation Front (NLF, Mat Tran Dan Toc Giai Phong Mien Nam), was founded, with representatives on its Central Committee from all social classes, political parties, women's organizations, and religious groups, including Hoa Hao, Cao Dai, the Buddhists, and the Catholics. In order to keep the NLF from being obviously linked with the VWP and the DRV, its executive leadership consisted of individuals not publicly identified with the communists, and the number of party members in leadership positions at all levels was strictly limited. Furthermore, in order not to alienate patriotic noncommunist elements, the new front was oriented more toward the defeat of the United States-backed Saigon government than toward social revolution.

The Fall of Ngo Dinh Diem

In 1961 the rapid increase of insurgency in the South Vietnamese countryside led President John F. Kennedy's administration to decide to increase United States support for the Diem regime. Some $US65 million in military equipment and $US136 million in economic aid were delivered that year, and by December 3,200 United States military personnel were in Vietnam. The United States Military Assistance Command, Vietnam (MACV) was formed under the command of General Paul D. Harkins in February 1962. The cornerstone of the counterinsurgency effort was the strategic hamlet program, which called for the consolidation of 14,000 villages of South Vietnam into 11,000 secure hamlets, each with its own houses, schools, wells, and watchtowers. The hamlets were intended to isolate guerrillas from the villages, their source of supplies and information, or, in Maoist terminology, to separate the fish from the sea in which they swim. The program had its problems, however, aside from the frequent attacks on the hamlets by guerrilla units. The self-defense units for the hamlets were often poorly trained, and support from the Army of the Republic of Vietnam (ARVN—see Glossary) was inadequate. Corruption, favoritism, and the resentment of a growing number of peasants who were forcibly resettled plagued the program. It was estimated that of the 8,000 hamlets established, only 1,500 were viable.

In response to increased United States involvement, all communist armed units in the South were unified into a single People's Liberation Armed Force (PLAF) in 1961. These troops expanded in number from fewer than 3,000 in 1959 to more than 15,000 by 1961, most of whom were assigned to guerrilla units. Southerners trained in the North who infiltrated back into the South composed an important element of this force. Although they accounted numerically for only about 20 percent of the PLAF, they provided a well-trained nucleus for the movement and often served as officers or political cadres. By late 1962, the PLAF had achieved the capability to attack fixed positions with battalion-sized forces. The NLF was also expanded to include 300,000 members and perhaps 1 million sympathizers by 1962. Land reform programs were begun in liberated areas, and by 1964 approximately 1.52 million hectares had been distributed to needy peasants, according to communist records. In the early stages, only communal lands, uncultivated lands, or lands of absentee landlords were distributed. Despite local pressure for more aggressive land reform, the peasantry generally approved of the program, and it was an important factor in gaining support for the liberation movement in the countryside. In the cities, the Workers' Liberation Association of Vietnam (Hoi Lao Dong Giai Phong Mien Nam), a labor organization affiliated with the NLF, was established in 1961.

Diem grew steadily more unpopular as his regime became more repressive. His brother and chief adviser, Ngo Dinh Nhu, was identified by regime opponents as the source of many of the government's repressive measures. Harassment of Buddhist groups by ARVN forces in early 1963 led to a crisis situation in Saigon. On May 8, 1963, ARVN troops fired into a crowd of demonstrators protesting the Diem government's discriminatory policies toward Buddhists, killing nine persons. Hundreds of Buddhist bonzes responded by staging peaceful protest demonstrations and by fasting. In June a bonze set himself on fire in Saigon as a protest, and, by the end of the year, six more bonzes had committed self-immolation. On August 21, special forces under the command of Ngo Dinh Nhu raided the pagodas of the major cities, killing many bonzes and arresting thousands of others. Following demonstrations at Saigon University on August 24, an estimated 4,000

Peasants suspected of being communists, 1966
Courtesy United States Army

students were rounded up and jailed, and the universities of Saigon and Hue were closed. Outraged by the Diem regime's repressive policies, the Kennedy administration indicated to South Vietnamese military leaders that Washington would be willing to support a new military government. Diem and Nhu were assassinated in a military coup in early November, and General Duong Van Minh took over the government.

Escalation of the War

Hanoi's response to the fall of the Diem regime was a subject of intense debate at the Ninth Plenum of the VWP Central Committee held in December 1963. It appeared that the new administration of President Lyndon B. Johnson (who assumed office following the assassination of President Kennedy on November 22) was not planning to withdraw from Vietnam but, rather, to increase its support for the new Saigon government. The VWP leadership concluded that only armed struggle would lead to success and called for an escalation of the war. The critical issues then became the reactions of the United States and the Soviet Union. Hanoi clearly hoped that the United States would opt for a compromise solution, as it had in Korea and Laos, and the party leaders believed that a quick and forceful escalation of the war would induce it to do so. Hanoi's decision to escalate the struggle was made in spite of the risk of damage to its relations with Moscow, which opposed the decision. The new policy also became an issue in the developing rift between Beijing and Moscow because China expressed its full support for the Vietnamese war of national liberation. As a result, Moscow's aid began to decrease as Beijing's grew.

Escalation of the war resulted in some immediate success for the struggle in the South. By 1964 a liberated zone had been established from the Central Highlands to the edge of the Mekong Delta, giving the communists control over more than half the total land area and about half the population of the South. PLAF forces totaled between 30 and 40 battalions, including 35,000 guerrillas and 80,000 irregulars. Moreover, with the completion of the so-called Ho Chi Minh Trail (see Glossary) through Laos, the number of PAVN troops infiltrated into the South began to increase. ARVN control was limited mainly to the cities and surrounding areas, and in 1964 and 1965 Saigon governments fell repeatedly in a series of military and civilian coups.

The Johnson administration remained hesitant to raise the American commitment to Vietnam. However, in August 1964, following the reputed shelling of United States warships in the Gulf of Tonkin off the North Vietnamese coast, Johnson approved air

THE PEOPLE OF TAY-NINH ARE DEEPLY GRATEFUL TO THE
COMRADES OF THE U.S 25 TH INFANTRY DIVISION

*Citizens of Tay Ninh welcome the United States Army's
25th Infantry Division, August 1966.
Courtesy United States Army*

strikes against North Vietnamese naval bases. At President Johnson's urgent request, the United States Congress passed the Gulf
of Tonkin Resolution, which gave the president the power "to take
all necessary measures to repel any armed attack against the forces
of the United States and to prevent further aggression." This
tougher United States stance was matched in Moscow in October
when Leonid Brezhnev and Aleksey Kosygin took over control of
the government following the fall from power of Nikita Khrushchev.
The new Soviet government pledged increased military support
for Hanoi, and the NLF set up a permanent mission in Moscow.

United States support for South Vietnam, which had begun as
an effort to defend Southeast Asia from the communist threat,
developed into a matter of preserving United States prestige. The
Johnson administration, nevertheless, was reluctant to commit combat troops to Vietnam, although the number of United States military advisers including their support and defense units had reached
16,000 by July 1964. Instead, in February 1965 the United States
began a program of air strikes known as Operation Rolling Thun-
der against military targets in North Vietnam. Despite the bombing of the North, ARVN losses grew steadily, and the political
situation in Saigon became precarious as one unstable government
succeeded another. General William C. Westmoreland, commander

of MACV from June 1964 to March 1968, urged the use of United States combat troops to stop the communist advance, which he predicted could take over the country within a year. The first two battalions of United States Marines (3,500 men) arrived in Vietnam in March 1965 to protect the United States airbase at Da Nang. The following month, Westmoreland convinced the administration to commit sufficient combat troops to secure base areas and mount a series of search and destroy missions (see Glossary). By late 1965, the United States expeditionary force in South Vietnam numbered 180,000, and the military situation had stabilized somewhat. Infiltration from the north, however, had also increased, although still chiefly by southerners who had gone north in 1954 and received military training. PLAF strength was estimated to be about 220,000, divided almost equally between guerrillas and main force troops, the latter including units of PAVN regulars totalling about 13,000 troops.

The United States decision to escalate the war was a surprise and a blow to party strategists in Hanoi. At the Twelfth Plenum of the Central Committee in December 1965, the decision was made to continue the struggle for liberation of the South despite the escalated American commitment. The party leadership concluded that a period of protracted struggle lay ahead in which it would be necessary to exert constant military pressure on the Saigon government and its ally in order to make the war sufficiently unpopular in Washington. Efforts were to be concentrated on the ARVN troops, which had suffered 113,000 desertions in 1965 and were thought to be on the verge of disintegration. In early 1965, Hanoi had been encouraged by Moscow's decision to increase its economic and military assistance substantially. The resulting several hundred million dollars in Soviet aid, including surface-to-air missiles, had probably been tied to a promise by Hanoi to attend an international conference on Indochina that had been proposed by Soviet premier Kosygin in February. As preconditions for these negotiations, Hanoi and Washington, however, had each presented demands that were unacceptable to the other side. The DRV had called for an immediate and unconditional halt to the bombing of the north, and the United States had demanded the removal of PAVN troops from the South. Although both Hanoi and Washington had been interested in a negotiated settlement, each had preferred to postpone negotiations until it had achieved a position of strength on the battlefield.

By mid-1966 United States forces, now numbering 350,000, had gained the initiative in several key areas, pushing the communists out of the heavily populated zones of the south into the more remote mountainous regions and into areas along the Cambodian border. Revolutionary forces in the South, under the command of General Nguyen Chi Thanh, responded by launching an aggressive campaign of harassment operations and full-scale attacks by regiment-sized units. This approach proved costly, however, in terms of manpower and resources, and by late 1966 about 5,000 troops, including main force PAVN units, were being infiltrated from the North each month to help implement this strategy. At the same time, North Vietnam placed its economy on a war footing, temporarily shelving non-war-related construction efforts. As a consequence of the heavy United States bombing of the North, industries were dismantled and moved to remote areas. Young men were conscripted into the army and their places in fields and factories were filled by women, who also served in home defense and antiaircraft units. Such measures were very effective in countering the impact of the bombing on the North's war effort. The Johnson administration, however, showed no sign of willingness to change its bombing strategy or to lessen its war effort (see fig. 8; fig. 9).

During this difficult period, the communists returned to protracted guerrilla warfare and political struggle. The party leadership called for increased efforts to infiltrate moderate political parties and religious organizations. The underground communist leadership in Saigon was instructed to prepare for a general uprising by recruiting youths into guerrilla units and training women to agitate against the city's poor living conditions and the injustices of the Saigon government. Total victory, according to the party leadership, would probably occur when military victories in rural areas were combined with general uprisings in the cities.

In mid-1967, with United States troop levels close to the half million mark, Westmoreland requested 80,000 additional troops for immediate needs and indicated that further requests were being contemplated. United States forces in Tay Ninh, Binh Dinh, Quang Ngai, and Dinh Tuong provinces had initiated major offensives in late 1966 and in early 1967, and more troops were needed to support these and other planned operations. As a result of these deployments, United States forces were scattered from the DMZ to the Mekong Delta by mid-1967. Opposition to the war, meanwhile, was mounting in the United States; and among the Vietnamese facing one another in the South, the rising cost of men and resources was beginning to take its toll on both sides. The level of PLAF volunteers declined to less than 50 percent in 1967 and desertions rose, resulting in an even greater increase in northern troop participation. Morale declined among communist sympathizers and Saigon

67

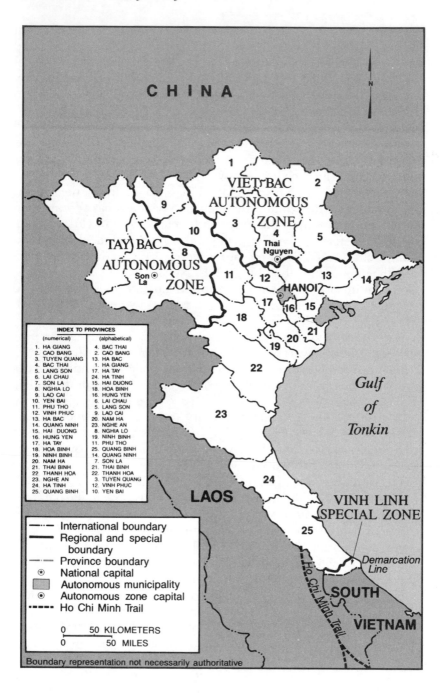

Figure 8. North Vietnam's Administrative Divisions, 1966

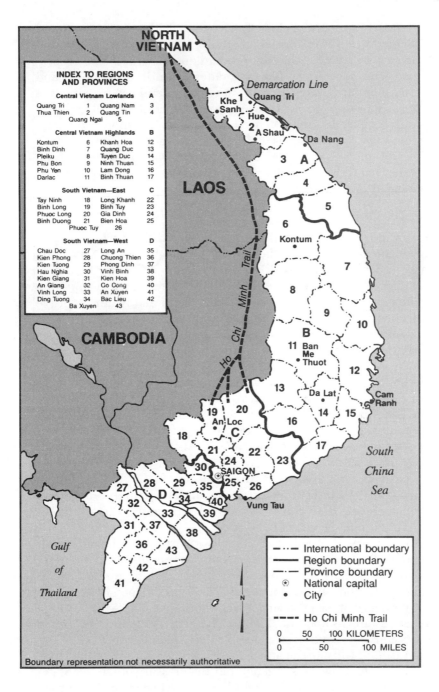

**INDEX TO REGIONS
AND PROVINCES**

Central Vietnam Lowlands			A
Quang Tri	1	Quang Nam	3
Thua Thien	2	Quang Tin	4
		Quang Ngai	5

Central Vietnam Highlands			B
Kontum	6	Khanh Hoa	12
Binh Dinh	7	Quang Duc	13
Pleiku	8	Tuyen Duc	14
Phu Bon	9	Ninh Thuan	15
Phu Yen	10	Lam Dong	16
Darlac	11	Binh Thuan	17

South Vietnam—East			C
Tay Ninh	18	Long Khanh	22
Binh Long	19	Binh Tuy	23
Phuoc Long	20	Gia Dinh	24
Binh Duong	21	Bien Hoa	25
		Phuoc Tuy	26

South Vietnam—West			D
Chau Doc	27	Long An	35
Kien Phong	28	Chuong Thien	36
Kien Tuong	29	Phong Dinh	37
Hau Nghia	30	Vinh Binh	38
Kien Giang	31	Kien Hoa	39
An Giang	32	Go Cong	40
Vinh Long	33	An Xuyen	41
Ding Tuong	34	Bac Lieu	42
		Ba Xuyen	43

International boundary
Region boundary
Province boundary
National capital
City

Ho Chi Minh Trail

0   50   100 KILOMETERS
0   50   100 MILES

Boundary representation not necessarily authoritative

Figure 9. South Vietnam's Administrative Divisions, 1966

government supporters alike. In elections held in South Vietnam in September 1967, former generals Nguyen Van Thieu and Nguyen Cao Ky were elected president and vice president, respectively. A number of popular candidates, including Buddhists and peace candidates, were barred from running, and newspapers were largely suppressed during the campaign. Even so, the military candidates received less than 35 percent of the vote, although the election took place only in areas under the Saigon government's control. When proof of widespread election fraud was produced by the defeated candidates, students and Buddhists demonstrated and demanded that the elections be annulled.

The Tet Offensive

In mid-1967 the costs of the war mounted daily with no military victory in sight for either side. Against this background, the party leadership in Hanoi decided that the time was ripe for a general offensive in the rural areas combined with a popular uprising in the cities. The primary goals of this combined major offensive and uprising were to destabilize the Saigon regime and to force the United States to opt for a negotiated settlement. In October 1967, the first stage of the offensive began with a series of small attacks in remote and border areas designed to draw the ARVN and United States forces away from the cities. The rate of infiltration of troops from the North rose to 20,000 per month by late 1967, and the United States command in Saigon predicted a major communist offensive early the following year. The DMZ area was expected to bear the brunt of the attack. Accordingly, United States troops were sent to strengthen northern border posts, and the security of the Saigon area was transferred to ARVN forces. Despite warnings of the impending offensive, in late January more than one-half of the ARVN forces were on leave because of the approaching Tet (Lunar New Year) holiday.

On January 31, 1968, the full-scale offensive began, with simultaneous attacks by the communists on five major cities, thirty-six provincial capitals, sixty-four district capitals, and numerous villages. In Saigon, suicide squads attacked the Independence Palace (the residence of the president), the radio station, the ARVN's joint General Staff Compound, Tan Son Nhut airfield, and the United States embassy, causing considerable damage and throwing the city into turmoil. Most of the attack forces throughout the country collapsed within a few days, often under the pressure of United States bombing and artillery attacks, which extensively damaged the urban areas. Hue, which had been seized by an estimated 12,000 communist troops who had previously infiltrated the city, remained

*Newly arrived United States troops board
buses at the Bien Hoa Air Terminal, February 1970.
Courtesy United States Army*

in communist hands until late February. A reported 2,000 to 3,000 officials, police, and others were executed in Hue during that time as counterrevolutionaries.

The Tet offensive is widely viewed as a turning point in the war despite the high cost to the communists (approximately 32,000 killed and about 5,800 captured) for what appeared at the time to be small gains. Although they managed to retain control of some of the rural areas, the communists were forced out of all of the towns and cities, except Hue, within a few weeks. Nevertheless, the offensive emphasized to the Johnson administration that victory in Vietnam would require a greater commitment of men and resources than the American people were willing to invest. On March 31, 1968, Johnson announced that he would not seek his party's nomination for another term of office, declared a halt to the bombing of North Vietnam (except for a narrow strip above the DMZ), and urged Hanoi to agree to peace talks. In the meantime, with United States troop strength at 525,000, a request by Westmoreland for an additional 200,000 troops was refused by a presidential commission headed by the new United States secretary of defense, Clark Clifford.

Following the Tet Offensive, the communists attempted to maintain their momentum through a series of attacks directed mainly at cities in the delta. Near the DMZ, some 15,000 PAVN and PLAF troops were also thrown into a three-month attack on the United States base at Khe Sanh. A second assault on Saigon, complete with rocket attacks, was launched in May. Through these and other attacks in the spring and summer of 1968, the communists kept up pressure on the battlefield in order to strengthen their position in a projected series of four-party peace talks scheduled to begin in January 1969 that called for representatives of the United States, South Vietnam, North Vietnam, and the National Liberation Front to meet in Paris. In June 1969, the NLF and its allied organizations formed the Provisional Revolutionary Government of the Republic of South Vietnam (PRG), recognized by Hanoi as the legal government of South Vietnam. At that time, communist losses dating from the Tet Offensive numbered 75,000, and morale was faltering, even among the party leadership.

Peace Negotiations

With negotiations making little progress, the United States military commander in Saigon, General Creighton W. Abrams, who had held that post since mid-1968, requested and was given permission by President Richard M. Nixon to launch secret bombing attacks, beginning March 18, 1970, on what were described as Vietnamese communist sanctuaries and supply routes inside Cambodia. In late March, Prince Norodom Sihanouk of Cambodia was ousted as chief of state in a military coup led by Premier and Defense Minister, General Lon Nol. Shortly thereafter, the Lon Nol government cancelled an agreement that had allowed North Vietnam to use the port at Sihanoukville. Hanoi reacted by increasing support to the Khmer (Kampuchean) Communist Party, by then under the leadership of the radical Pol Pot. In April, Nixon authorized the invasion of Cambodia by a joint United States-ARVN force of 30,000 troops for the purpose of destroying communist bases across the border. Little more than short-term gains were accomplished by the invasion, which resulted in massive protests in the United States, leading to the passage of legislation by Congress requiring the removal of United States troops from Cambodia by the end of June.

In 1971 and 1972, the communists faced some serious problems unrelated to United States offensive operations. The Saigon government began to gain some support in the Mekong Delta because of the implementation of a ''land-to-the-tiller'' reform program pressed on the Thieu government by Washington in 1970. Almost 400,000 farmers received a total of 600,000 hectares, and by 1972 tenancy reportedly had declined from about 60 percent to 34 percent in some rural areas. In addition, a People's Self-Defense Force Program begun about this time had some success in freeing ARVN troops for combat duty, as United States forces were gradually withdrawn. Although it wasn't clear at the time whether the withdrawal of United States troops would cause the ARVN to crumble instantly, as predicted by the communists, the decisive defeat of an ARVN operation mounted against the Ho Chi Minh Trail in Laos in March 1971 was an early indication. At the time of the ARVN defeat, however, the communists were coping with deteriorating morale and with dwindling numbers of troops; a rising desertion rate and falling recruitment levels had reduced PLAF strength from 250,000 in 1968 to less than 200,000 in 1971.

Both on the battlefield and at the conference table, a stalemate of sorts was reached by mid-1971. In negotiations there was some flexibility, as Washington offered a unilateral withdrawal of United States forces provided Hanoi stopped its infiltration of the South; and Hanoi countered by agreeing to a coalition government in Saigon along with a United States troop withdrawal and to a cease-fire following the formation of a new government. The main point of debate was the retention of President Thieu as head of the South Vietnamese government, which Washington demanded and Hanoi rejected. To break the deadlock, the party leadership in Hanoi turned again to the strategy of a general offensive and uprising. Accordingly, the so-called Easter offensive was launched beginning on March 30, 1972, with a three-pronged attack across the DMZ through the A Shau Valley. The following day the communists attacked the city of Kontum and the provinces of Binh Dinh and Phuoc Tuy, threatening to cut South Vietnam in two. A few days later, three PAVN divisions attacked Binh Long Province along the Cambodian border, placing the capital, An Loc, under siege. In May the communists captured Quang Tri Province, including the capital, which was not recaptured by the ARVN until September. By that time, Quang Tri city had been virtually leveled by United States air strikes. Although the Easter offensive did not result in the fall of the Saigon government, as the communists had hoped, it did further destabilize the government and reveal the ARVN's weaknesses. The costs were great on both sides, however, and by October both Hanoi and Washington were more inclined to negotiate. By then Hanoi had agreed to accept Thieu as president of a future Saigon government in exchange for the removal of United States forces without a corresponding removal of PAVN troops. Thieu's objections to the failure to require the removal of North Vietnamese forces was in the end ignored, and the Agreement on

Interment for 300 unidentified victims
of communist occupation of Hue in 1968
Courtesy United States Army

Ending the War and Restoring Peace in Vietnam was signed in Paris on January 27, 1973.

The Final Campaign

Although the terms of the peace agreement were less than the communists had hoped for, the accords did permit them to participate in the new government legally and recognized their right to control certain areas. Most important, the removal of United States forces gave the communists a welcome breathing space, allowing them to concentrate on political efforts. In the initial period after the signing of the agreement, the party leadership viewed armed struggle as a last resort only because it was feared that the United States might reintroduce its forces. PLAF troops were instructed to limit their use of force to self-defense. Meanwhile, the Thieu government embarked on pacification efforts along the central coast and in the Mekong Delta, which resulted in a reduction of the area under official communist control to about 20 percent of the South. The Saigon government, however, faced serious difficulties, including the negative effect on the economy of the withdrawal of United States forces and a critical refugee problem. During the course of the war, several million Vietnamese had been evacuated or had fled from their villages to find safety and jobs in urban areas. Most of these remained unemployed and, together with militant Buddhist groups, the Cao Dai, and the Hoa Hao, represented a sizable wellspring of discontent with the Thieu government.

In early 1974, the communists launched a campaign to regain the territory they had lost since the cease-fire. Raids were conducted on roads, airfields, and economic installations; the flow of supplies and equipment from the North was stepped up; and a 19,000-kilometer network of roads leading from the DMZ in Quang Tri Province to Loc Ninh, northwest of Saigon, was completed. By summer the communists were moving cautiously forward, seizing vulnerable areas in the Central Highlands and in the provinces around Saigon. There was no direct response from the United States, and the resignation of Nixon in August convinced the party leadership that further United States intervention was unlikely. ARVN forces continued to deteriorate, suffering high casualties and facing a lack of ammunition and spare parts. The party leadership met in October to plan a 1975 military offensive concentrating on the Cambodian border area and the Central Highlands. The taking of the Phuoc Long province capital, Phuoc Binh (now Ba Ra in Song Be Province), in early January was followed by a surprise attack in March on Ban Me Thuot, the largest city in the Central Highlands. President Thieu ordered ARVN units at Pleiku

Kham Thien Street Memorial in Hanoi depicting a mother and child standing on a United States Air Force bomb fragment
Courtesy Bill Herod

Bicycles used to transport rice on the Ho Chi Minh Trail, captured during United States operations in Cambodia, spring 1970
Courtesy United States Army

and Kontum to leave the highlands and withdraw to the coast to regroup for a counterattack on Ban Me Thuot. The ARVN strategic withdrawal became a rout, however, because PAVN units had already cut the main roads to the coast and fleeing civilians clogged the secondary roads as panic ensued. By the end of March, eight northern provinces had fallen to the communist forces, including the cities of Hue and Da Nang. Buoyed by this stunning victory, the party leadership directed the commander of revolutionary forces in the South, General Van Tien Dung to prepare for an offensive against Saigon. In early April, PAVN and PLAF troops moved south and began an encirclement of the capital. On April 20, after ten days of stiff resistance, the ARVN Eighteenth Division, stationed thirty kilometers north of Saigon, finally crumbled under the attack of three PAVN divisions. With Saigon in a state of panic, President Thieu resigned the following day and was replaced by Vice President Tran Van Huong. Duong Van Minh, thought to be more acceptable to the communists, took over the presidency on April 28. The communists refused to negotiate, however, and fifteen PAVN battalions began to move toward Saigon. On April 30, communist forces entered the capital, and Duong Van Minh ordered ARVN troops to lay down their arms.

Nearly thirty years had passed since Ho Chi Minh first declared Vietnam's independence as a unified nation in September 1945. In the interim, an entire generation of Vietnamese had endured a divided Vietnam, knowing only continuous warfare. The events of April 1975 not only abruptly concluded the war but also prepared the way for the official reunification of the country the following year, when the Vietnamese people were brought together under one independent government for the first time in more than a century.

*　　*　　*

The body of literature in English on the history of Vietnam has increased dramatically since the mid-1960s. Most of the writing, however, has focused on the three decades of war in that country following World War II. The increased interest in Vietnam, nevertheless, has prompted a number of historians to take the longer view—the Vietnamese view—of history and to examine earlier time periods.

Based on Vietnamese and Chinese sources, and particularly useful for Vietnamese history from the earliest traditions up to the end of the Chinese millennium, is Keith Weller Taylor's *Birth of Vietnam*. Also treating this period, as well as the period up through

World War II, is Thomas Hodgkin's, *Vietnam. The Revolutionary Path.* Hodgkin gives detailed coverage of the 900-year period of Vietnamese independence, while D.G.E. Hall's classic *History of South-East Asia* provides a description and analysis of that period within the larger Southeast Asian context. Another useful single-volume history of Vietnam up to 1968 is Joseph Buttinger's *Vietnam: A Political History.* Finally, Alexander Woodside in *Vietnam and the Chinese Model* presents an interesting analysis, based on Vietnamese and Chinese sources, of Chinese influence on Vietnamese education, administration, literature, and law during the nineteenth century.

J. F. Cady treats in detail the French conquest and early colonial period in *The Roots of French Imperialism in Eastern Asia.* David Marr uses Vietnamese source materials to examine the roots of Vietnamese nationalism in *Vietnamese Anticolonialism, 1885–1925,* and William Duiker in *The Rise of Nationalism in Vietnam, 1900–1941* carries the examination of the nationalist movement up to the early period of Japanese occupation. Duiker also traces the communist movement from its origins to the reunification of the country in *The Communist Road to Power in Vietnam.*

Although their focus is somewhat peripheral to an overview history of Vietnam, there are a number of accounts of the United States involvement in Vietnam that bear mentioning, including: William Turley's *The Second Indochina War;* Ronald Spector's *Advice and Support: The Early Years, 1941–1960;* R.B. Smith's *An International History of the Vietnam War;* Stanley Karnow's *Vietnam. A History;* and George McT. Kahin's, *Intervention. How America Became Involved in Vietnam.* (For further information and complete citations, see Bibliography.)

Chapter 2. The Society and Its Environment

Village official, late French colonial period

SEVERAL MONTHS BEFORE his death in 1969, Ho Chi Minh declared that Vietnam would ''certainly be reunified under the same roof''no matter what difficulties and hardships might lie ahead. In 1976 the country was territorially reunited—under Hanoi's roof—after more than twenty years of separation. This historic event proved, however, to be only the first step toward the ultimate test of reunification—the development of sociocultural, economic, and political processes that could best serve the aspirations and needs of the Vietnamese people. In 1987 Vietnam was, in some respects, still a divided nation and still at war—not for liberation from the bondage of neo-colonialism but for the triumph of socialism in what was officially called the struggle between the socialist and the capitalist paths.

The struggle between socialism and capitalism unfolded in an environment of social and religious patterns molded by centuries of cultural influences from Confucianism, Buddhism, Taoism, indigenous animism, and, more recently, Roman Catholicism. The communist government disparaged some of these influences as feudal, backward, superstitious, reactionary, or bourgeois and targeted them for reform. Others, including Buddhism, Catholicism, and minor faiths, were tolerated.

The Vietnamese people were continually urged to discard vestiges of the old society and to adopt instead new values associated with love of labor, collective ownership, patriotism, socialism, and the proletarian dictatorship under the Vietnamese Communist Party (VCP, Viet Nam Cong San Dang). In 1987 these values were at best an abstraction to most Vietnamese, except perhaps for a fraction of the party's fewer than 2 million members. Despite the increasing dependence of families, simply for subsistence, on organizations sponsored by collectives and the state, the strongest bond in the society by far was that of family loyalty. Such loyalty was particularly evident after the mid-1970s, when living conditions deteriorated amid indications of growing government corruption.

Much of Vietnam's contemporary history has been a grim struggle, not on behalf of patriotism or socialism but for survival. With a per capita income estimated at less than US$200 per year, the Vietnamese people in the 1980s remained among the poorest in the world. In 1987 the society was predominantly rural; more than 80 percent of the population resided in villages and engaged primarily in farming. Among the urban population, party and government officials supplanted the former elite, whose privileged status had been derived mainly from wealth and higher education. In theory, Vietnam had eliminated all exploiting classes by developing a class structure composed of workers, peasants, and socialist intellectuals. In practice, a small-scale bourgeoisie continued to operate in the South's industrial sector with the permission of the state, and, according to an official source, some cadres in the south were exploiting peasants in the tradition of former landowners.

Theoretically the society is multiracial, but actually it is dominated by an ethnic Vietnamese elite. Vietnamese, who outnumber other ethnic groups, are overwhelmingly lowlanders; minority peoples, who are divided into nearly sixty groups of various sizes and backgrounds, are mostly highlanders. With the exception of the Chinese, or Hoa (see Glossary), who are mostly lowlanders, the minority peoples traditionally lived apart from one another and from the Vietnamese. In the 1980s, however, the distance between the highland and lowland communities gradually narrowed as a result of the government policy of population redistribution and political integration.

Under this policy, lowlanders were sent to remote, uninhabited areas of the highlands both to relieve overcrowding in the cities and in the congested Red River Delta and to increase food production. Both aims were part of the government's effort to raise the standard of living, which in turn was linked to another urgent national priority—family planning. In 1987 the rate of population growth continued to outstrip food production. Given the people's traditional belief in large families, the government faced a major challenge in its attempt to reduce the annual rate of population growth to 1.7 percent or less by 1990.

Geography

Vietnam is located in the southeastern extremity of the Indo-chinese peninsula and occupies about 331,688 square kilometers, of which about 25 percent was under cultivation in 1987. The S-shaped country has a north-to-south distance of 1,650 kilometers and is about 50 kilometers wide at the narrowest point. With a coastline of 3,260 kilometers, excluding islands, Vietnam claims 12 nautical miles as the limit of its territorial waters, an additional 12 nautical miles as a contiguous customs and security zone, and 200 nautical miles as an exclusive economic zone.

The boundary with Laos, settled, on an ethnic basis, between the rulers of Vietnam and Laos in the mid-seventeenth century, was formally defined by a delimitation treaty signed in 1977 and ratified in 1986. The frontier with Cambodia, defined at the time of French annexation of the western part of the Mekong River Delta in 1867, remained essentially unchanged, according to Hanoi, until some unresolved border issues were finally settled in the 1982–85 period. The land and sea boundary with China, delineated under the France-China treaties of 1887 and 1895, is "the frontier line" accepted by Hanoi that China agreed in 1957–58 to respect. However, in February 1979, following China's limited invasion of Vietnam, Hanoi complained that from 1957 onward China had provoked numerous border incidents as part of its anti-Vietnam policy and expansionist designs in Southeast Asia. Among the territorial infringements cited was the Chinese occupation in January 1974 of the Paracel Islands, claimed by both countries in a dispute left unresolved in the 1980s (see Foreign Relations, ch. 4).

Vietnam is a country of tropical lowlands, hills, and densely forested highlands, with level land covering no more than 20 percent of the area. The country is divided into the highlands and the Red River Delta in the north; and the Giai Truong Son (Central mountains, or the Chaîne Annamitique, sometimes referred to simply as the Chaîne), the coastal lowlands, and the Mekong River Delta in the south.

The Red River Delta, a flat, triangular region of 3,000 square kilometers, is smaller but more intensely developed and more densely populated than the Mekong River Delta. Once an inlet of the Gulf of Tonkin, it has been filled in by the enormous alluvial deposits of the rivers, over a period of millennia, and it advances one hundred meters into the gulf annually. The ancestral home of the ethnic Vietnamese, the delta accounted for almost 70 percent of the agriculture and 80 percent of the industry of North Vietnam before 1975.

The Red River (Song Hong in Vietnamese), rising in China's Yunnan Province, is about 1,200 kilometers long. Its two main tributaries, the Song Lo (also called the Lo River, the Rivière Claire, or the Clear River) and the Song Da (also called the Black River or Rivière Noire), contribute to its high water volume, which averages 500 million cubic meters per second, but may increase by more than 60 times at the peak of the rainy season. The entire delta region, backed by the steep rises of the forested highlands, is no more than three meters above sea level, and much of it is one meter or less. The area is subject to frequent flooding; at some places the high-water mark of floods is fourteen meters above the surrounding countryside. For centuries flood control has been an integral part of the delta's culture and economy. An extensive system of dikes and canals has been built to contain the Red River and to irrigate the rich rice-growing delta. Modeled on that of

China, this ancient system has sustained a highly concentrated population and has made double-cropping wet-rice cultivation possible throughout about half the region (see Agriculture, ch. 3; fig. 10).

The highlands and mountain plateaus in the north and northwest are inhabited mainly by tribal minority groups. The Giai Truong Son originates in the Xizang (Tibet) and Yunnan regions of southwest China and forms Vietnam's border with Laos and Cambodia. It terminates in the Mekong River Delta north of Ho Chi Minh City (formerly Saigon).

These central mountains, which have several high plateaus, are irregular in elevation and form. The northern section is narrow and very rugged; the country's highest peak, Fan Si Pan, rises to 3,142 meters in the extreme northwest. The southern portion has numerous spurs that divide the narrow coastal strip into a series of compartments. For centuries these topographical features not only rendered north-south communication difficult but also formed an effective natural barrier for the containment of the people living in the Mekong basin.

Within the southern portion of Vietnam is a plateau known as the Central Highlands (Tay Nguyen), approximately 51,800 square kilometers of rugged mountain peaks, extensive forests, and rich soil. Comprising 5 relatively flat plateaus of basalt soil spread over the provinces of Dac Lac and Gia Lai-Kon Tum, the highlands account for 16 percent of the country's arable land and 22 percent of its total forested land (see fig. 1). Before 1975 North Vietnam had maintained that the Central Highlands and the Giai Truong Son were strategic areas of paramount importance, essential to the domination not only of South Vietnam but also of the southern part of Indochina. Since 1975 the highlands have provided an area in which to relocate people from the densely populated lowlands. The narrow, flat coastal lowlands extend from south of the Red River Delta to the Mekong River basin. On the landward side, the Giai Truong Son rises precipitously above the coast, its spurs jutting into the sea at several places. Generally the coastal strip is fertile and rice is cultivated intensively.

The Mekong, which is 4,220 kilometers long, is one of the 12 great rivers of the world. From its source in the Xizang plateau, it flows through the Xizang and Yunnan regions of China, forms the boundary between Laos and Burma as well as between Laos and Thailand, divides into two branches—the Song Han Giang and Song Tien Giang—below Phnom Penh, and continues through Cambodia and the Mekong basin before draining into the South China Sea through nine mouths or *cuu long* (nine dragons). The

river is heavily silted and is navigable by seagoing craft of shallow draft as far as Kompong Cham in Cambodia. A tributary entering the river at Phnom Penh drains the Tonle Sap, a shallow freshwater lake that acts as a natural reservoir to stabilize the flow of water through the lower Mekong. When the river is in flood stage, its silted delta outlets are unable to carry off the high volume of water. Floodwaters back up into the Tonle Sap, causing the lake to inundate as much as 10,000 square kilometers. As the flood subsides, the flow of water reverses and proceeds from the lake to the sea. The effect is to reduce significantly the danger of devastating floods in the Mekong delta, where the river floods the surrounding fields each year to a level of one to two meters.

The Mekong delta, covering about 40,000 square kilometers, is a low-level plain not more than three meters above sea level at any point and criss-crossed by a maze of canals and rivers. So much sediment is carried by the Mekong's various branches and tributaries that the delta advances sixty to eighty meters into the sea every year. An official Vietnamese source estimates the amount of sediment deposited annually to be about 1 billion cubic meters, or nearly 13 times the amount deposited by the Red River. About 10,000 square kilometers of the delta are under rice cultivation, making the area one of the major rice-growing regions of the world. The southern tip, known as the Ca Mau Peninsula, is covered by dense jungle and mangrove swamps.

Vietnam has a tropical monsoon climate, with humidity averaging 84 percent throughout the year. However, because of differences in latitude and the marked variety of topographical relief, the climate tends to vary considerably from place to place. During the winter or dry season, extending roughly from November to April, the monsoon winds usually blow from the northeast along the China coast and across the Gulf of Tonkin, picking up considerable moisture; consequently the winter season in most parts of the country is dry only by comparison with the rainy or summer season. During the southwesterly summer monsoon, occurring from May to October, the heated air of the Gobi Desert rises, far to the north, inducing moist air to flow inland from the sea and deposit heavy rainfall.

Annual rainfall is substantial in all regions and torrential in some, ranging from 120 centimeters to 300 centimeters. Nearly 90 percent of the precipitation occurs during the summer. The average annual temperature is generally higher in the plains than in the mountains and plateaus. Temperatures range from a low of 5°C in December and January, the coolest months, to more than 37°C in April, the hottest month. Seasonal divisions are more clearly marked in the northern half than in the southern half of the country, where, except in some of the highlands, seasonal temperatures vary only a few degrees, usually in the 21°C–28°C range.

Population

According to Hanoi, the population of Vietnam was almost 60 million at the end of 1985 (Western sources estimated about a half million more than that in mid-1985). Vietnamese officials estimated that the population would be at least 66 million by 1990 and 80 million by the year 2000, unless the growth rate of 2 percent per year used for these estimates was lowered to 1.7 percent by 1990. With declining mortality rates achieved through improved health conditions, the population increased by 1.2 million or more per year between 1981 and 1986 (1.5 million in 1985 alone), worsening the country's chronic food shortage. In the 1980s, Vietnam needed to produce an additional 400,000 tons of food each year just to keep pace with its rapidly increasing population.

Census results of October 1979 showed the total population of reunified Vietnam to be 52.7 million of which 52 percent lived in the North and 48 percent in the South. About 19 percent of the population was classified as urban and 81 percent as rural. Females outnumbered males by 3 percent, and the average life expectancy at birth was 66 for females and 63 for males. With 52 percent of the total under 20 years of age, the population was young. Ethnically, 87 percent were Vietnamese-speaking lowlanders known as Viet or Kinh, and the remainder were Hoa or members of highland minority groups (see Ethnic Groups and Languages, this ch.). In December 1986, Hanoi estimated that more than 1 million Vietnamese lived overseas, 50 percent of them in the United States. A Vietnamese source in Paris claimed that about half of Ho Chi Minh City's population lived completely or partially on family aid packages sent by Vietnamese émigrés abroad.

Beginning in the early 1960s, the socioeconomic implications of rapid population growth became an increasing concern of the government in Hanoi. A family planning drive, instituted in 1963, was claimed by the government to have accounted for a decline in the annual growth rate in the North from 3.4 percent in 1960 to 2.7 percent in 1975. In the South, however, family planning was actively encouraged only after 1976, and the results were mixed, consistently falling short of announced goals. In 1981 Hanoi set a national goal of 1.7 percent growth rate to be achieved by the end of 1985: a growth rate of 1.3 to 1.5 percent was established for the North, 1.5 to 1.7 percent for the South, and 1.7 to 2.0 percent for the sparsely settled highland provinces. In 1987, the growth rate, according to Vietnamese sources, was about 2.0 percent (see table 2, Appendix A).

Family planning was described as voluntary and dependent upon persuasion. The program's guidelines called for two children per couple, births spaced five years apart, and a minimum age of twenty-two for first-time mothers—a major challenge in a society where the customary age for women to marry, especially in the rural areas, was sixteen to twenty. Campaign workers were instructed to refrain tactfully from mentioning abortion and to focus instead on pregnancy prevention when dealing with people of strong religious conviction. Enlisting the support of Catholic priests for the campaign was strongly encouraged. In 1987 it was evident that the government was serious about family planning; a new law on marriage and the family adopted in December 1986 made family planning obligatory, and punitive measures, such as pay cuts and denial of bonuses and promotions, were introduced for non-compliance (see The Family since 1954, this ch.).

A substantial portion of the population had mixed feelings about birth control and sex education, and the number of women marrying before age twenty remained high. Typically, a woman of child-bearing age had four or more children. The 1986 family law that raised the legal marriage age for women to twenty-two met with strenuous opposition. Critics argued that raising the legal age offered no solution to the widespread practice among Vietnamese youth of "falling in love early, having sexual relations early, and getting married early." Some critics even advanced the view that the population should be increased to further economic development; others insisted that those who could grow enough food for themselves need not practice birth control. A significant proportion of the population retained traditional attitudes which favored large families with many sons as a means of insuring the survival of a family's lineage and providing for its security. Although problems associated with urban living, such as inadequate housing and unemployment, created a need for change in traditional family-size standards, old ways nevertheless persisted. They were perpetuated in proverbs like "If Heaven procreates elephants, it will provide enough grass to feed them" or "To have one son is to have; to have ten daughters is not to have."

Government authorities were concerned over the lack of coordination among agencies involved in family planning and the lack of necessary clinics and funding to provide convenient, safe, and efficient family planning services in rural areas. Even more disturbing was the knowledge that many local party committees and government agencies were only going through the motions of supporting the family planning drive. To remedy the situation, the government in 1984 created the National Committee on Family Planning (also known as the National Commission on Demography and Family Planning, or the National Population and Parenthood Commission). The commission was directed to increase the rate of contraceptive use among married couples from about 23 percent in 1983 to 70 percent by 1990 and to limit the population to between 75 and 80 million by the year 2000. The latter goal was to be based on an annual growth rate of 1.7 percent or less, a figure that in 1987 seemed unrealistically low. According to a National Committee on Family Planning report released in February 1987, the population grew by 2.2 percent in 1986 (Western analysts estimate the increase to have been between 2.5 and 2.8 percent). In light of the 1986 growth rate, the committee's target for 1987 was revised at the beginning of the year to 1.9 percent. Even if such a goal were met, Vietnam's population at the end of 1987 would stand in excess of 63 million inhabitants.

The average population density in 1985 was 179 persons per square kilometer. Population density varied widely, however, and was generally lower in the southern provinces than in the northern ones; in both North and South it was also lower in the highlands and mountainous regions than in the lowlands. The most densely settled region was the Red River Delta, accounting for roughly 75 percent of the population of the North. Also heavily settled was the Mekong River Delta, with nearly half of the southern population.

After 1976, population redistribution became a pressing issue because of food shortages and unemployment in the urban areas. A plan unveiled at the Fourth National Party Congress in December 1976 called for the relocation of 44 million people by 1980 and an additional 10 million by the mid-1990s. The plan also called for opening up 1 million hectares of virgin land to cultivation and introduced a measure designed to divert some armed forces personnel to the building of new economic zones (see Glossary). The relocation was to involve an interregional transfer of northerners to the South as well as an intraregional movement of lowlanders to upland areas in both the North and the South. Between 1976 and 1980, most of the 4 million people who were relocated to rural areas and the new economic zones were from Ho Chi Minh City and other southern cities. In the 1981–85 period, a total of about 0.6 million workers and 1.3 million dependents were relocated, causing the country's urban population to decline from 19.3 percent of the total in 1979 to 18 percent in 1985. The country's long-range goal, established in 1976, called for the population to be distributed more or less evenly throughout Vietnam's 443 districts with an average for each district of 200,000 persons living on 20,000 hectares (see fig. 11).

Ethnic Groups and Languages

The ethnic Vietnamese are concentrated largely in the alluvial deltas and in the coastal plains, having little in common with the minority peoples of the highlands, whom they historically have regarded as hostile and barbaric. A homogenous social group, the Vietnamese exert influence on national life through their control of political and economic affairs and their role as purveyors of the dominant culture. By contrast, the ethnic minorities, except for the Hoa, are found mostly in the highlands that cover two-thirds of the national territory. The Hoa, the largest minority, are mainly lowlanders. Officially, the ethnic minorities are referred to as national minorities.

Vietnamese

The origins of the Vietnamese are generally traced to the inhabitants of the Red River Delta between 500 and 200 B.C., people who were a mixture of Australoid, Austronesian, and Mongoloid stock. Like their contemporary descendants, they were largely villagers, skilled in rice cultivation and fishing (see Early History, ch. 1).

Contemporary ethnic Vietnamese live in urban as well as rural areas, are engaged in a variety of occupations, and are represented at all levels on the socioeconomic scale. The power elite (senior officials in the party, government, and military establishments), in particular, is dominated by ethnic Vietnamese. Although predominantly Buddhist, the Vietnamese people's religious beliefs and practices nevertheless include remnants of an earlier animistic faith. A sizable minority is Roman Catholic. Despite some regional and local differences in customs and speech, the people retain a strong sense of ethnic identity that rests on a common language and a shared cultural heritage.

Vietnamese, the official language, is the mother tongue of the vast majority of the people and is understood by many national minority members. According to a widely accepted theory, Vietnamese is believed to be related to the Austroasiatic family of languages, which includes various languages, dialects, and subdialects spoken in mainland Southeast Asia from Burma to Vietnam. Scholarship nonetheless is tentative on whether Vietnamese, which was spoken in the Red River Delta long before the Christian era, was influenced by Mon-Khmer or Tai, both Austroasiatic subsets.

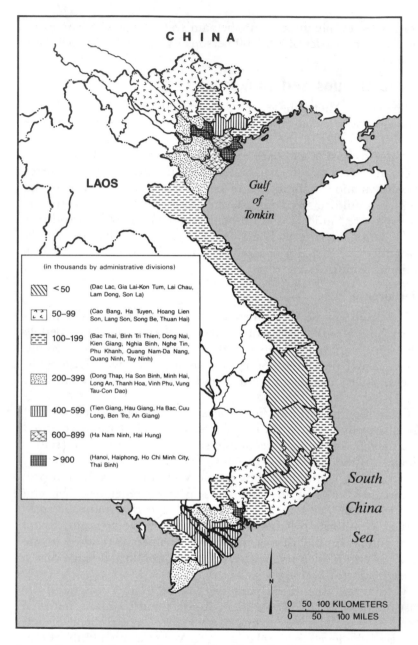

(in thousands by administrative divisions)

⧄	< 50	(Dac Lac, Gia Lai-Kon Tum, Lai Chau, Lam Dong, Son La)
	50–99	(Cao Bang, Ha Tuyen, Hoang Lien Son, Lang Son, Song Be, Thuan Hai)
	100–199	(Bac Thai, Binh Tri Thien, Dong Nai, Kien Giang, Nghia Binh, Nghe Tin, Phu Khanh, Quang Nam-Da Nang, Quang Ninh, Tay Ninh)
	200–399	(Dong Thap, Ha Son Binh, Minh Hai, Long An, Thanh Hoa, Vinh Phu, Vung Tau-Con Dao)
	400–599	(Tien Giang, Hau Giang, Ha Bac, Cuu Long, Ben Tre, An Giang)
	600–899	(Ha Nam Ninh, Hai Hung)
	> 900	(Hanoi, Haiphong, Ho Chi Minh City, Thai Binh)

Source: Based on information from Tong Cuc Thong Ke, *So Lieu Thong Ke, 1930–1984,* Hanoi, 1985, 7–8.

Figure 11. Population Distribution, 1984

Actually, the Vietnamese language was influenced more by classical Chinese than by any other language. During more than 1,000 years of Chinese rule and for centuries afterwards, Chinese was the language of officialdom, scholarship, and literature. The Chinese language had special status because of its identification with the ruling class of scholar-officials. Nevertheless, Vietnamese continued to be the popular language, even though knowledge of Chinese was a prerequisite to government employment and social advancement.

Beginning in the eighth or ninth century, the Vietnamese devised a popular script based on Chinese characters to express written ideas and to standardize the phonetics of their own language. Well developed by the thirteenth century, this system, which combined ideographs and phonetics, became the medium for a growing popular literature. The system is known as *chu nom,* literally "southern character" or "southern writing," or simply *nom.* Although disdained by orthodox Confucian scholars, *chu nom* had a distinct place in the evolution of Vietnam's vernacular literature through the end of the nineteenth century.

In the seventeenth century, the Vietnamese language evolved further when Portuguese and French missionaries developed a new transcription that used roman letters instead of Chinese characters. The new system, called *quoc ngu,* was devised as a tool for their missionary activities, including the translation of prayer books and catechisms. By the end of the nineteenth century, it had become the common method of writing, gradually replacing classical Chinese and *chu nom. Quoc ngu* uses diacritical marks above or below letters to indicate variations in the pronunciation of vowels and of consonants, and differentiations in tones. Since most single syllables function as meaningful words identified only by tone, and each of these phonetic syllables can have numerous meanings, the diacritical marks are an essential part of the new writing system (see Nine Centuries of Independence, ch. 1).

Under French rule, the French language was widely used in the cities, and it was read and spoken by all secondary-school graduates. Many less educated people, including merchants, low-ranking civil servants, army veterans, and domestics working for French households, also had some familiarity with the language, although their knowledge might be limited to a form of pidgin French. In the rural areas the language generally was less well-known, but a number of minority peoples learned its rudiments in school or during service with the French army. Use of the French language resulted in minor changes in the grammatical structure of Vietnamese and in the addition of some new technical, scientific, and popular terms.

Vietnam: A Country Study

Minorities

Living somewhat separately from the dominant ethnic Vietnamese are the numerous minorities. The 1979 census listed fifty-
three minorities accounting for 12.5 percent (6.6 million persons)
of the national population. This figure included the Hoa (Han
Chinese), the single largest bloc—representing approximately 1.8
percent of the total population, or about 935,000 people—in the
lowland urban centers of both the North and the South. Of the
other minority groups, thirty, comprising 68 percent of the minority
population (4.5 million persons), resided in the North, while the
remaining twenty-two groups, comprising 32 percent of the minority population (2.1 million persons) lived in the South. The size
of each community ranged from fewer than 1,000 to as many as
0.9 million persons, and 10 major groups comprised about 85 percent of the minority population (see table 3, Appendix A).

Minorities that live in the mountainous regions are known by
their generic name, Montagnards. The Vietnamese also disparagingly call them "moi," meaning savage. The government attrib-
utes the backwardness of the Montagnards to the overwhelming
influence of their history as exploited and oppressed peoples. They
are darker skinned than their lowland neighbors.

The origins of the non-Vietnamese minorities are far from clear,
but scholars generally believe that some, like the Hmong (Meo),
Zao, Nung, San Chay, Cao Lan, Giay, and Lolo, are descendants
of the ancient migrants from southern China who settled in the
northern border regions. Others, like the Tay, Muong, and Thai,
are believed to be related to the lowland natives of Malay stock
who were forced into the highlands by successive invasions of
Mongoloid peoples from China. Among these indigenous minorities are the Cham of central Vietnam, remnants of a kingdom that
ruled the central coast of the country until overrun by the Vietnamese in the fifteenth century, and the Khmer, whose Cambodian
forebears controlled the Mekong delta region until displaced in the
late eighteenth century by the Vietnamese (see Nine Centuries of
Independence, ch. 1). The Khmer and the Cham are lowlanders
of the south and are considered, along with the Tay, Muong, and
Thai of the north, to be culturally more developed than other
minority ethnic groups but less so than the Vietnamese.

The non-Chinese minority peoples, however, are for the most
part highlanders who live in relative independence and follow their
own traditional customs and culture. They are classified as either
sedentary or nomadic. The sedentary groups, the more numerous
of the two kinds, are engaged mainly in the cultivation of wet rice

96

Tonkinese woman, late nineteenth century
Courtesy New York Times, *Paris Collection, National Archives*

and industrial crops; the nomadic groups, in slash-and-burn farming where forested land is cleared for a brief period of cultivation and then abandoned. Both groups inhabit the same four major areas: the northern border region and the uplands adjacent to the Red River Delta, the northwestern border region adjoining Laos and China, the Central Highlands and the area along the Giai Truong Son, and parts of the Mekong River Delta and the central coastal strip. These groups are notable for their diverse cultural characteristics. They are distinguished from one another not only by language but also by such other cultural features as architectural styles, colors and shapes of dress and personal ornaments, shapes of agricultural implements, religious practices, and systems of social organization.

The number and variety of languages used by Vietnam's minorities reflect the country's ethnic complexity. Minority groups are distinguished by more than a dozen distinct languages and numerous dialects; the origins and distribution of many of these languages have not yet been conclusively established. They can, however, be classified loosely into three major language families, which in turn can be divided into several subgroups. Eleven of the minority groups—Tay, Thai, Nung, Hmong, Muong, Cham, Khmer, Kohor, Ede, Bahnar, and Jarai—have their own writing systems.

Religious practices among highland minorities tend to be rooted in animistic beliefs. Most worship a pantheon of spirits, but a large number are Catholics or Protestants. In contrast to the Mahayana Buddhist beliefs of the majority of Vietnamese, the Khmer practice Theravada (or Hinayana) Buddhism, and the Cham subscribe to both Islam and Hindu beliefs (see Religion, this ch.).

Before the arrival of the French in the nineteenth century, the highland minorities lived in isolation from the lowland population. Upon the consolidation of French rule, however, contacts between the two groups increased. The French, interested in the uplands for plantation agriculture, permitted the highlanders their linguistic and cultural autonomy, and administered their areas separately from the rest of Vietnam. Conferring this special status gave the French a free hand in cultivating the largely unexploited highlands, where their administrators and Christian missionaries also set up schools, hospitals, and leprosariums.

Often, however, conflicts arose between the upland communities and the French, who were distrusted as exploitative, unwelcome interlopers. The French, however, eventually overcame the unrest and successfully developed some of the highland areas, especially those of the Ede and Jarai, where they established large rubber, coffee, and tea plantations.

*Montagnard tribesman
Courtesy
United States Army*

After the mid-1950s, North and South Vietnam dealt with the minorities differently. The Hanoi regime in the North, recognizing the traditional separatist attitudes of the tribal minorities, initiated a policy of accommodation by setting up two autonomous zones for the highlanders in return for their acceptance of Hanoi's political control. By offering limited self-government, Hanoi's leaders hoped that integration of the minorities into Vietnamese society could eventually be achieved. By contrast, the noncommunist Saigon administration in the South, under Ngo Dinh Diem, opted for direct, centralized control of the tribal minorities and incurred their enduring wrath by seizing ancestral tribal lands for the resettlement of displaced Catholic refugees from the North.

After Diem's death in 1963, successive Saigon administrations granted a modicum of autonomy, but the strategic hamlet program, introduced in the South in the 1960s, caused further disruption by forcing highlanders to relocate to fortified enclaves. The program was proposed to improve the physical security of Montagnards as well as to deny food and services to Viet Cong (see Glossary) guerrillas, but it largely embittered its minority participants, who wanted to be left alone to continue living on their ancestral lands in the traditional manner. In an act of resistance, some tribal leaders gathered in 1964 to announce the formation of the Unified Front for the Struggle of Oppressed Races (Front Unifié pour la Lutte des Races Opprimées—FULRO), representing the Bahnar,

Cham, Ede, Hre, Jarai, Mnong, Raglai, Sadang, Stieng, and other groups.

After 1975 a number of northern minority cadres were sent to the Central Highlands to lay the groundwork for socio-economic development. In 1977 a university was set up at Buon Me Thuot, capital of Dac Lac Province, to train a corps of minority cadres. These tactics were designed to narrow the socioeconomic gap not only between the highlanders and the lowlanders but also among the minorities themselves.

In the mid-1980s, the party and media expressed satisfaction with the cadres' training and commended certain highland provinces for progress in agricultural cooperativization, noting that a growing number of slash-and-burn farmers had turned to sedentary farming and that further improvements in cultural and health facilities were planned. By 1986 about 43 percent of the estimated 2.2 million nomadic minority members were reported to have adopted a more sedentary life. There were also glowing claims that minorities were now full-fledged participants in national affairs, as was evidenced by their representation in the National Assembly (see Glossary) and in other government and party organizations.

A cursory examination reveals, however, that progress was spotty. The living conditions of highlanders continued to lag behind those of lowlanders. In remote areas, "backward customs and practices" remained unchanged, minority groups were insufficiently represented among cadres, and sorely needed resources for material improvements were lacking. Official claims that closer unity and greater harmony were being achieved in a multinational Vietnam were belied by the government's frequent admonishments against "narrow nationalism" (the parochialism of the minority groups) and against "big nationality prejudices" (the ingrained Vietnamese biases against minorities). To be sure, the number of minority cadres with either general or college-level education was growing, but in 1987 these cadres represented only a small portion of the functionaries serving in the highland provinces, districts, towns, and villages. In Dac Lac Province, 91 percent of the district-level cadres and 63 percent of the key village and lower level cadres had been transferred from other places, presumably from the North or the lowlands of the South.

Under the government program of population redistribution, lowlanders continued to emigrate to the Central Highlands. In 1980 about 52 percent of the Central Highlands population consisted of ethnic Vietnamese. In 1985, as pressure mounted on the Vietnamese government to produce grain and industrial crops, a greater influx of ethnic Vietnamese was anticipated. By 1987 it seemed clear that minority groups were likely to remain unequal partners in the management of their local affairs, despite official protestations to the contrary, as increasing numbers of Vietnamese settled in the Central Highlands.

The minority question remained an issue because of its implications not only for integration but also for internal security. In the mid-1980s, there were occasional official allusions to counter-revolutionary activities attributed to FULRO. Hanoi was quick to assert, however, that these rebel activities were blown out of proportion by the Western media (see Internal Security, ch. 5). Nonetheless, the authorities were concerned about the northern border areas, where renegades of such groups as the Hmong, Zao, and Giay were said to have participated in China's anti-Vietnamese activities after 1979 as "special gangs of bandits." Official literature supported the construction of "a border cultural defense line to counter the multifaceted war of sabotage waged by the Chinese expansionists."

Hoa

The Hoa, or ethnic Chinese, are predominantly urban dwellers. A few Hoa live in small settlements in the northern highlands near the Chinese frontier, where they are also known as *Ngai*. Traditionally, as elsewhere in Southeast Asia, the Chinese have retained a distinctive cultural identity, but in 1955 North Vietnam and China agreed that the Hoa should be integrated gradually into Vietnamese society and should have Vietnamese citizenship conferred on them (see Foreign Relations, ch. 4).

Before 1975 the northern Hoa were mainly rice farmers, fishermen, and coal miners, except for those residing in cities and provincial towns. In the South they were dominant in commerce and manufacturing. According to an official source, at the end of 1974 the Hoa controlled more than 80 percent of the food, textile, chemical, metallurgy, engineering, and electrical industries, 100 percent of wholesale trade, more than 50 percent of retail trade, and 90 percent of export-import trade. Dominance over the economy enabled the Hoa to "manipulate prices" of rice and other scarce goods. This particular source further observed that the Hoa community constituted "a state within a state," inasmuch as they had built "a closed world based on blood relations, strict internal discipline, and a network of sects, each with its own chief, to avoid the indigenous administration's direct interference." It was noted by Hanoi in 1983 that as many as 60 percent of "the former bourgeoisie" of the south were of Chinese origin.

In mid-1975 the combined Hoa communities of the North and South numbered approximately 1.3 million, and all but 200,000 resided in the South, most of them in the Saigon metropolitan area. Beginning in 1975, the Hoa bore the brunt of socialist transformation in the South, especially after the communist government decided in early 1978 to abolish private trade (see Economic Roles of the Party and the Government, ch. 3). This, combined with external tensions stemming from Vietnam's dispute with Cambodia and China in 1978 and 1979 caused an exodus of about 250,000 Hoa, of whom 170,000 fled overland into China from the North and the remainder fled by boat from the South (see Foreign Relations, ch. 4; The Armed Forces, ch. 5).

The Social System

Traditional Patterns

For centuries Vietnamese society was knit together by Confucian norms based on five relationships: the subordination of subject to ruler, son to father, wife to husband, and younger brother to elder brother, and the mutual respect between friends. These norms influenced the evolution of Vietnam as a hierarchic, authoritarian society in which Confucian scholarship, monarchical absolutism, filial piety, the subordinate role of women, and the family system were regarded as integral to the natural order of the universe.

The traditional society was stratified on the basis of education and occupation into four groups: scholar-officials or mandarins, farmers, artisans, and merchants. At the pinnacle was the emperor, who ruled with the "mandate of heaven." Next were the scholar-officials, recruited through rigorous civil service examinations in Chinese classical literature and philosophy. Once a person passed the triennial examinations, he became an accredited scholar or degree holder and was eligible for appointment to the imperial civil service, the most prestigious route to power, status, and wealth. Together, the emperor, his family, and the scholar-officials constituted the ruling class.

In theory, the mandarinate was not a closed social group. Commoners were permitted to apply for the examinations, and the status of scholar-official could not be inherited. In practice, however, these officials became a self-perpetuating class of generalist-administrators, partly because their sons could afford years of academic preparation for the examinations whereas most commoners could not. Education, the key to upward mobility, was neither free nor compulsory and tended to be the preserve of the mandarins.

Although social eminence and political power were thus concentrated in the hands of the mandarins, economic power was based on landholdings and was more widely diffused as a result of progressive dismantling of the hereditary feudal nobility after the fifteenth century. This process was accomplished by breaking up the nobility's vast holdings and redistributing smaller parcels to others, such as families of royal blood, prominent scholar-officials, and influential local notables. The wealthier of these notables formed a kind of landed gentry that wielded influence in the rural towns and villages.

The society was further transformed in the nineteenth century by the imposition of French rule, the introduction of Western education, the beginnings of industrialization and urbanization, and the growth of commercial agriculture. The establishment of a new, French-dominated governing class led to a rapid decline in the power and prestige of the emperor and the mandarins, whose functions were substantially reduced. When the triennial examinations were held in 1876 and 1879, an average of 6,000 candidates took them; in 1913, only 1,330 did.

In place of the old imperial bureaucracy, in the late nineteenth and early twentieth centuries a new intellectual elite emerged that emphasized achievement in science, geography, and other modern subjects instead of the Confucian classics. The new Vietnamese intelligentsia was impressed by the power of the French and by the 1905 naval victory at Tsushima of a modernized Japan over tsarist Russia. Having viewed some of the achievements of Western culture in Europe during World War I, when nearly 150,000 Vietnamese were recruited for work in French factories, the new elite proclaimed their country's need for a modern, Western educational focus. By 1920, even in the conservative city of Hue, the last Confucian outpost, wealthy families refused to marry their daughters to the sons of distinguished scholar-official families unless the young men had acquired a modern, Western-style education. The traditional civil service examinations were held for the last time in 1919.

Traditional Confucian village schools, accustomed to teaching in Chinese, introduced instruction in Vietnamese and French into the existing curriculum. Vietnamese who had successfully acquired a higher education at home or abroad entered government service as administrators or were absorbed as doctors, engineers, and teachers as the government expanded its role in the fields of health, public works, and education. Others took up professions outside government, such as law, medicine, pharmacology, and journalism. The new elite was composed mainly of Vietnamese from Tonkin and Annam rather than from Cochinchina, a regional bias perhaps attributable to the location in Hanoi of the country's only institution of Western higher education (see fig. 6).

The French period also produced a new group of Vietnamese absentee landowners who possessed riches far in excess of the wealth anyone in the older society had enjoyed. This new group came into existence as a result of the French development of vast new tracts of land in Cochinchina. A few of these large holdings were retained by French companies or citizens, but most were held by enterprising, Western-oriented, urban Vietnamese from Annam and Tonkin who lived mainly in Hanoi and Hue. By investing in light industry and medium-sized trading concerns, they became Vietnam's first modern industrialists and entrepreneurs.

In urban centers the demand of both the expanding French government bureaucracy and the private sector for secretaries, clerks, cashiers, interpreters, minor officials, and labor foremen created a new Vietnamese white-collar group. The development of mining and industry between 1890 and 1919 also introduced a new class of workers. Because most of the natural resources as well as a large labor pool were located in the North, industrial development was concentrated there, and Hanoi and Haiphong became the country's leading industrial centers. At the same time, conditions of overcrowding and intensive farming in the North provided little room for agriculture on a commercial scale. In order to expand agriculture, the French turned their attention to the underdeveloped, warmer South, where French cultivation of such crops as rubber, coffee, tea, and, in Cochinchina, rice gave rise to a group of agricultural and plantation wage earners.

The colonial period also led to a substantial increase in the Hoa population. The country's limited foreign and domestic trade were already in the hands of Chinese when the French arrived. The French chose to promote the Chinese role in commerce and to import Chinese labor to develop road and railroad systems, mining, and industry. French colonial policy that lifted the traditional ban on rice exports at the end of the nineteenth century also attracted new waves of Chinese merchants and shopkeepers seeking to take advantage of the new export market. Vietnam's growing economy attracted even more Chinese thereafter, especially to the South. Already deeply involved in the rice trade, the Chinese expanded their interests to include rice-milling and established a virtual monopoly.

They also were a significant presence in sugar refining, coconut and peanut oil production, lumber, and shipbuilding. Many who began their careers as laborers on the French rubber plantations of Cochinchina eventually started their own tea, pepper, or rice plantations to supply local market needs. Chinese gardeners in the suburbs of Saigon monopolized the supply of fresh vegetables consumed in that city, and Chinese restaurants and hotels proliferated in virtually every urban center.

Society in the 1954–75 Period

North Vietnam

At the time of the 1954 partition, Vietnam was overwhelmingly a rural society; peasants accounted for nearly 90 percent of the total population. During the ensuing 20 years of political separation, however, the North and the South developed into two very different societies. In the North the communists had embarked on a program intended to revolutionize the socioeconomic structure. The focus of change was ostensibly economic, but its underlying motivation was both political and social as well. Based on the Marxist principle of class struggle, it involved no less than the creation of a totally new social structure. Propertied classes were eliminated, and a proletarian dictatorship was established in which workers and peasants emerged as the nominal new masters of a socialist and ultimately classless state.

As a prelude to the socialist revolution, a land reform campaign and a harsh, systematic campaign to liquidate "feudal landlords" from rural society were launched concurrently in 1955. Reminiscent of the campaign undertaken by communists in China in earlier years, the liquidation of landlords cost the lives of an estimated 50,000 people and prompted the party to acknowledge and redress "a number of serious errors" committed by its zealous cadres.

In urban sectors the party's intervention was less direct, initially at least, because large numbers of the bourgeoisie had fled the North in anticipation of the communists' coming to power. Many had fled to the South before the party gained full control. Those who remained were verbally assailed as exploiters of the people, but because the regime needed their administrative and technical skills and experience, they were otherwise treated tolerantly and allowed to retain private property.

In 1958 the regime stepped up the pace of "socialist transformation," mindful that even though the foundations of a socialist society were basically in place, the economy remained for the most part still in the hands of the private, capitalist sector. By 1960 all but a small number of peasants, artisans, handicraft workers, industrialists, traders, and merchants had been forced to join cooperatives of various kinds.

Intellectuals, many of whom had earlier been supporters of the Viet Minh (see Glossary), were first conciliated by the government, then stifled. Opposition to the government, expressed openly during and after the peasant uprisings of 1956, prompted the imposition of controls that graduated to complete suppression by 1958. Writers and artists who had established their reputations in the pre-communist era were excluded from taking any effective role in national affairs. Many were sent to the countryside to perform manual labor and to help educate a new corps of socialist intellectuals among the peasants.

The dominant group in the new social order were the high-level party officials, who constituted a new ruling class. They owed their standing more to demonstrations of political acumen and devotion to nationalism or Marxism-Leninism than to educational or professional achievements. Years of resistance against the French in the rural areas had inured them to hardship and at the same time given them valuable experience in organization and guerrilla warfare. Resistance work had also brought them into close touch with many different segments of the population.

At the apex of the new ruling class were select members of the Political Bureau of the communist Vietnam Workers Party (VWP, Dang Lao Dong Viet Nam), and a somewhat larger body of Central Committee members holding key posts in the party, the government, the military, and various party-supported organizations. Below the top echelon were the rank and file party members (500,000 by 1960), including a number of women and members of ethnic minorities. Party cadres who possessed special knowledge and experience in technical, financial, administrative, or managerial matters were posted in all social institutions to supervise the implementation of party decisions.

Occupying an intermediate position between the party and the citizenry were those persons who did not belong to the party but who, nevertheless, had professional skills or other talents needed by the regime. Noncommunists were found in various technical posts, in the school system, and in the mass organizations to which most citizens were required to belong. A few even occupied high, though politically marginal, posts in the government. The bulk of the population remained farmers, workers, soldiers, miners, porters, stevedores, clerks, tradespeople, teachers, and artisans.

Social reorganization did little to evoke mass enthusiasm for socialism, and socialist transformation of the private sector into cooperative- and state-run operations did not result in the kind of economic improvement the government needed to win over the peasants and merchants. The regime managed to provide better educational and health care services than had existed in the pre-1954 years, but poverty was still endemic. The party attributed the "numerous difficulties" it faced to "natural calamities, enemy actions, and the utterly poor and backward state of the economy," but also acknowledged its own failings. These included cadre incompetence in ideological and organizational matters as well as in financial, technical, and managerial affairs.

South Vietnam

South of the demarcation line after partition in 1954, the social system remained unchanged except that power reverted to a Vietnamese elite. The South's urban-rural network of roles, heavily dependent on the peasant economy, remained intact despite the influx of nearly a million refugees from the North; and land reform, initiated unenthusiastically in 1956, had little socioeconomic impact in the face of obstruction by the landowning class. In contrast to the North, there was no doctrinaire, organized attempt to reorganize the society fundamentally or to implant new cultural values and social sanctions. The regime of Ngo Dinh Diem was more concerned with its own immediate survival than with revolutionary social change, and if it had a vision of sociopolitical reform at all, that vision was diffusive. Furthermore, it lacked a political organization comparable in zeal to the party apparatus of Hanoi in order to achieve its goals.

In the 1960s, prolonged political instability placed social structures in the South under increasing stress. The communist insurgency, which prevented the government from extending its authority to some areas of the countryside, was partially responsible, but even more disruptive were the policies of the government itself. Isolated in Saigon, the Diem regime alienated large parts of the population by acting to suppress Buddhists and other minorities, by forcing the relocation of peasants to areas nominally controlled by the government, and by systematically crushing political opposition. Such policies fueled a growing dissatisfaction with the regime that led to Diem's assassination in November 1963 and his replacement by a series of military strongmen.

As the war in the South intensified, it created unprecedented social disruption in both urban and rural life. Countless civilians were forced to abandon their ancestral lands and sever their network of family and communal ties to flee areas controlled by the Viet Cong or exposed to government operations against the communists. By the early 1970s, as many as 12 million persons, or 63 percent of the entire southern population, were estimated to have been displaced; some were relocated to government-protected rural hamlets while others crowded into already congested urban centers. Few villages, however remote, were left untouched by the war. The urban-rural boundary, once sharply defined, seemed to disappear as throngs of uprooted refugees moved to the cities. Traditional social structures broke down, leaving the society listless and bereft of a cohesive force other than the common instinct for survival.

The disruption imposed by the war, however, did not alter conventional socioeconomic class identifiers. In the urban areas, the small upper class elite continued to be limited to high-ranking military officers, government officials, people in the professions, absentee landlords, intellectuals, and Catholic and Buddhist religious leaders. The elite retained a strong personal interest in France and French culture; many had been educated in France and many had sons or daughters residing there. In addition to wealth, Western education—particularly French education—was valued highly, and French and English were widely spoken.

The urban middle class included civil servants, lower and middle-ranking officers in the armed forces, commercial employees, school teachers, shop owners and managers, small merchants, and farm and factory managers. A few were college graduates, although the majority had only a secondary-school education. Very few had been able to study abroad.

At the bottom of the urban society were unskilled, largely uneducated wageworkers and petty tradespeople. While semiliterate themselves, they nevertheless were able to send their children to primary school. Secondary education was less common, however, particularly for girls. These children tended not to proceed far enough in school to acquire an elementary knowledge of French or English, and most adults of the lower class knew only Vietnamese unless they had worked as domestics for foreigners.

Village society, which embraced 80 percent of the population, was composed mostly of farmers, who were ranked in three socioeconomic groups. The elite were the wealthiest landowners. If they farmed, the work was done by hired laborers who planted, irrigated, and harvested under the owner's supervision. In the off-season, landowners engaged in moneylending, rice trading, or rice milling. Usually the well-to-do owners were active in village affairs as members of the village councils. After the mid-1960s, however, interest in seeking such positions waned as village leaders increasingly were targeted by Viet Cong insurgents.

The less prosperous, middle-level villagers owned or rented enough land to live at a level well above subsistence, but they tended not to acquire a surplus large enough to invest in other ventures. They worked their own fields and hired farm hands only when needed during planting or harvesting. A few supplemented their income as artisans, but never as laborers. Because of their more modest economic circumstances, members of this group tended not to assume as many communal responsibilities as did the wealthier villagers.

At the bottom of village life were owners of small farming plots and tenant farmers. Forced to spend nearly all of their time eking out a living, they could not afford to engage in village affairs. Because they could not cultivate enough land to support their families, most of them worked also as part-time laborers, and their wives and children assisted with the field work. Their children frequently went to school only long enough to learn the rudiments of reading and writing. This group also included workers in a wide range of other service occupations, such as artisans, practitioners of oriental medicine, and small tradespeople.

Vietnam after 1975

The sudden collapse of Saigon in April 1975 set the stage for a new and uncertain chapter in the evolution of Vietnamese society. The Hanoi government had to confront directly what communists have long called the struggle between the two paths of socialism and capitalism. At issue was Hanoi's ability to translate its wartime success and socialist revolutionary experience into postwar rehabilitation and reconstruction now that it controlled the South territorially.

Foremost among the regime's imperatives was that of restoring order and stability to the war-torn South. The critical question, however, was whether or not the northern conquerors could inspire the southern population to embrace communism. Initially, Hanoi appeared sanguine; the two zones had more similarities than dissimilarities, and the dissimilarities were expected to be eliminated as the South caught up with the North in socialist organization.

The December 1975 *Vietnam Courier,* an official government publication, portrayed Vietnam as two distinct, incongruent societies. The South was reported to continue to suffer from what communists consider the neo-colonialist influences and feudal ideology of the United States, while the North was considered to serve as a progressive environment for growing numbers of a new kind of socialist human being, imbued with patriotism, proletarian internationalism, and socialist virtues. The class of social exploiter had been eliminated in the North, leaving the classes of worker, collectivized peasant, and socialist intellectual, the last consisting of various groups. In contrast, the South was divided into a working class, peasantry, petit bourgeois, capitalist—or comprador (see Glossary)—class, and the remnant of a feudal landlord class.

In September 1976, Premier Pham Van Dong declared that his compatriots, North and South, were "translating the revolutionary heroism they [had] displayed in fighting into creative labor in the acquisition of wealth and strength." In the South particularly, the old society was undergoing active changes as the result of "stirring revolutionary movements" by the workers, peasants, youth, women, intellectuals, and other groups. In agriculture alone, "millions of people" participated in bringing hundreds of thousands more hectares under cultivation and in building or dredging thousands of kilometers of canals and ditches.

From all indications, however, these changes occurred more through coercion than volition. In Dong's own words, the party had initiated "various policies aimed at eliminating the comprador capitalists as a class and doing away with all vestiges of feudal exploitation." These policies radically realigned the power elite so that the ruling machine was controlled collectively by the putative vanguard of the working class—the party—and by the senior cadres of the party who were mostly from the North.

In its quest for a new socialist order in the South, Hanoi relied on other techniques apart from socialist economic transformation and socialist education. These included thought reform, population resettlement, and internal exile, as well as surveillance and mass mobilization. Party-sponsored "study sessions" were obligatory for all adults. For the former elite of the Saigon regime, a more rigorous form of indoctrination was used; hundreds of thousands of former military officers, bureaucrats, politicians, religious and labor leaders, scholars, intellectuals, and lawyers, as well as critics of the new regime were ordered to "reeducation camps" for varying periods. In mid-1985, the Hanoi government conceded that it still held about 10,000 inmates in the reeducation camps, but the actual number was believed to be at least 40,000. In 1982 there were about 120,000 Vietnamese in these camps. According to a knowledgeable American observer, the inmates faced hard labor, but only rarely torture or execution.

Population resettlement or redistribution, although heralded on economic grounds, turned out to be another instrument of social control in disguise. It was a means of defusing tensions in congested cities, which were burdened with unemployed and socially dislocated people even after most of the rural refugees had been repatriated to their native villages. These refugees had swelled the urban population to 45 percent of the southern total in 1975 (up from 33 percent in 1970). The authorities sought to address the problem of urban congestion by relocating many of the metropolitan jobless in the new economic zones hastily set up in virgin lands, often malaria-infested jungles, as part of a broader effort to boost agricultural output. In 1975 and 1976 alone, more than 600,000 people were moved from Ho Chi Minh City to these zones, in most instances, reportedly, against their will. Because of the barely tolerable living conditions in the new settlements, a considerable number of people escaped or bribed their way back to the city. The new economic zones came to be widely perceived as places of internal exile. In fact, the authorities were said to have used the threat of exile to such places against those who refused to obey party instructions or to participate in the activities of the mass organizations.

Surveillance was a familiar tool of the regime, which was bent on purging all class enemies. Counterrevolutionaries, real and suspected, were summarily interned in reform camps or forced labor camps that were set up separately from the new economic zones in several border areas and other undeveloped regions.

The Hanoi government has claimed that not a single political execution took place in the South after 1975, even in cases of grave war crimes. Generally, the foreign press corroborated this claim by reporting in 1975 that there seemed to be no overt indication of the blood bath that many Western observers had predicted would occur in the wake of the communist takeover. Some Western observers, however, have estimated that as many as 65,000 South Vietnamese may have been executed.

In March 1982, the Vietnamese Communist Party (VCP) convened its Fifth National Party Congress to assess its achievements since 1976 and to outline its major tasks for the 1980s. The congress was revealing if only because of its somber admission that revolutionary optimism was no substitute for common sense. Despite rigid social controls and mass mobilization, the party fell far short of its original expectations for socialist transition. According to the party's assessment, from 1976 through 1980 shortcomings and errors occurred in establishing transition goals and in implementing the party line.

The congress, however, reaffirmed the correctness of the party line concerning socialist transition, and directed that it be implemented with due allowances for different regional circumstances. The task was admittedly formidable. In a realistic appraisal of the regime's difficulties, *Nhan Dan,* the party's daily organ, warned in June 1982 that the crux of the problem lay in the regime itself, the shortcomings of which included lack of party discipline and corruption of party and state functionaries.

In 1987 the goal of establishing a new society remained elusive, and Vietnam languished in the first stage of the party's planned period of transition to socialism. Mai Chi Tho, mayor of Ho Chi Minh City and deputy head of its party branch, had told visiting Western reporters as early as April 1985 that socialist transition, as officially envisioned, would probably continue until the year 2000.

In the estimation of the party, Vietnamese society had succumbed to a new form of sociopolitical elitism that was just as undesirable as the much-condemned elitism of the old society. Landlords and comprador capitalists may have disappeared but in their places were party cadres and state functionaries who were no less status-conscious and self-seeking. The Sixth National Party Congress in December 1986 found it necessary to issue a stern warning against opportunism, individualism, personal gain, corruption, and a desire for special prerogatives and privileges. A report to the congress urged the party to intensify class struggle in order to combat the corrupt practices engaged in by those who had "lost their class consciousness." Official efforts to purify the ranks of the working class, peasantry, and socialist intellectuals, however, failed to strike a responsive chord. In fact, the proceedings of the Sixth Congress left the inescapable impression that the regime was barely surviving the struggle between socialism and capitalism and that an early emergence of a communist class structure was unlikely.

As ideally envisioned, the socialist sector was expected to provide 70 percent of household income, and the "household economy," or the privately controlled resources of the home, was to make up the balance. In September 1986, cadres and workers were earning their living mainly through moonlighting and, according to a Vietnamese source, remained on "the state rolls only to preserve their political prestige and to receive some ration stamps and coupons." The source further disclosed that the society's lack of class consciousness was reflected in the party's membership, among whom only about 10 percent were identified as from the working class.

The Family
Background

Using the patriarchal family as the basic social institution, the Confucianists framed their societal norm in terms of the duties and obligations of a family to a father, a child to a parent, a wife to a husband, and a younger brother to an older brother; they held that the welfare and continuity of the family group were more important than the interests of any individual member. Indeed, the individual was less an independent being than a member of a family group that included not only living members but also a long line of ancestors and of those yet to be born. A family member's life was caught up in the activities of a multitude of relatives. Members of the same household lived together, worked together, and gathered together for marriages, funerals, Tet (lunar New Year) celebrations, and rituals marking the anniversary of an ancestor's death. Family members looked first to other family members for help and counsel in times of personal crisis and guarded the interests of the family in making personal or household decisions.

Special reverence was accorded a family's ancestors. This practice, known as the family cult or cult of the ancestors, derived from the belief that after death the spirits of the departed continued to influence the world of the living. The soul was believed to become restless and likely to exert an unfavorable influence on the living, unless it was venerated in the expected manner.

Veneration of ancestors was also regarded as a means through which an individual could assure his or her own immortality. Children were valued because they could provide for the spirits of their parents after death. Family members who remained together and venerated their forebears with strict adherence to prescribed ritual found comfort in the belief that the souls of their ancestors were receiving proper spiritual nourishment and that they were insuring their own soul's nourishment after death.

The cult required an ancestral home or patrimony, a piece of land legally designated as a place devoted to the support of venerated ancestors. Ownership of land that could be dedicated to the support of the cult was, however, only a dream for most landless farmers. The cult also required a senior male of direct descent to oversee preparations for obligatory celebrations and offerings.

On the anniversary of an ancestor's death, rites were performed before the family altar to the god of the house, and sacrificial offerings were made to both the god and the ancestor. The lavishness of the offering depended on the income of the family and on the rank of the deceased within the family. A representative of each family in the lineage was expected to be present, even if this meant traveling great distances. Whenever there was an occasion of family joy or sorrow, such as a wedding, an anniversary, success in an examination, a promotion, or a funeral, the ancestors were consulted or informed of the event through sacrificial offerings.

In the traditional kinship system, the paternal line of descent was emphasized. Individuals were identified primarily by their connections through the father's male bloodline, and kin groups larger than the family—clans and lineages—were formed by kinspeople who traced their relationship to each other in this manner. It was

113

through these patrilineal descent groups that both men and women inherited property and that men assumed their primary obligation for maintaining the ancestor observances.

The patrilineal group maintained an extremely strong kin relationship. Members' ties to one another were reinforced by their shared heritage, derived from residence in the same village over many generations. Family land and tombs, located in or near the village, acted as a focus for feelings of kin loyalty, solidarity, and continuity.

The extended family rather than the nuclear one was the dominant family structure, often including three or even four generations, and typically consisting of grandparents, father and mother, children, and grandchildren, all living under the same roof. Sometimes parents had more than one married son living with them, but this often led to such tension that it was generally held preferable for a second son to live separately. All members of the household lived under the authority of the oldest male, and all contributed to the income of the family.

Despite the cultural emphasis on their obedience, women were not regarded as the weaker sex but as resilient and strong-willed. In the village, women assumed a great deal of responsibility for cultivation of paddy fields, often working harder than men, and sometimes engaged in retail trade of all kinds. A few women owned agricultural estates, factories, and other businesses, and both urban and rural women typically managed the family income. A woman's influence in family affairs could be increased by giving birth to a first male child. In general, though, a woman was expected to be dutiful and respectful toward her husband and his parents, to care for him and his children, and to perform household duties. There were few women in public life.

Besides the so-called wife of the first rank, a household sometimes included a second and third wife and their children. The consent of the first wife was required before this arrangement could be made, but, more often than not, additional wives either were established by the husband in separate households or were permitted to continue living as they had before marriage, in their own homes or with parents. Polygyny was widespread in both northern and central Vietnam, as was the taking of concubines.

Marriage was regarded primarily as a social contract and was arranged by the parents through intermediaries. The parents' choice was influenced more by considerations affecting the welfare of the lineage than by the preferences of the participants.

Interest in having children was strongly reinforced by Confucian culture, which made it imperative to produce a male heir to

Tonkinese family of Son Tay, early twentieth century
Courtesy New York Times, *Paris Collection, National Archives*

continue the family line. A couple with numerous offspring was
cnvied. If there were sons, it was assured that the lineage would
be perpetuated and the cult of the ancestors maintained; if there
was no male heir, a couple was regarded as unfortunate, and a
barren wife could be divorced or supplanted by another wife.

Fostering filial piety was of overriding importance in child-
rearing. Children were expected to be polite to their parents and
older persons, to be solicitous of their welfare, to show them respect
through proper manner and forms of address, and to carry out
prescribed tradition with respect to funeral practices and the observance of mourning. After the deaths of their parents, it was incumbent upon surviving children (and their children in turn) to
honor their parents' memory through maintenance of the ancestors' cult.

All important family occasions such as births, betrothals, marriages, funerals, and anniversaries of the deaths of ancestors were
observed by appropriate ceremonies in which members of the kin
group participated. The ceremonies had both religious and social
meaning, and many were very elaborate, in keeping with the wealth
and social status of the family. Whenever such a celebration took
place, the family was always careful to make an offering to the god
of the hearth. Prayers and sacrifices were also made when misfortune fell upon the household.

The Family since 1954

In the first decade after World War II, the vast majority of North and South Vietnamese clung tenaciously to traditional customs and practices. After the 1950s, however, some traditions were questioned, especially in the North. The timeless notion that the family was the primary focus of individual loyalty was disparaged as feudal by the communists, who also criticized the traditional concept of the family as a self-contained socioeconomic unit. Major family reform was initiated under a new law enacted in 1959 and put into effect in 1960. The law's intent was to protect the rights of women and children by prohibiting polygyny, forced marriage, concubinage, and abuse. It was designed to equalize the rights and obligations of women and men within the family and to enable women to enjoy equal status with men in social and work-related activities. Young women were encouraged to join the party as well as the Ho Chi Minh Communist Youth League and the Vietnam Women's Union, and they were trained as cadres and assigned as leaders to production teams.

In conjunction with the law, a mass campaign was launched to discourage as wasteful the dowries and lavish wedding feasts of an earlier era. Large families were also discouraged. Parents who felt themselves blessed by heaven and secure in their old age because they had many children were labeled bourgeois and reactionary. Young people were advised not to marry before the age of twenty for males and eighteen for females and to have no more than two children per household. Lectures on birth control were commonplace in the public meeting rooms of cooperatives and factories.

According to Ha Thi Que, president of the Vietnam Women's Union in the early 1980s, popularizing family reform was extremely difficult, even in 1980, because women lacked a feminist consciousness and men resisted passively. To promote equality of the sexes, members of the women's union took an active part in a consciousness-raising campaign under the slogan, "As good in running society as running the home, women must be the equals of men." Such campaigns resulted in a fairer division of labor between husbands and wives and in the decline of customs and practices based on belief in women's inferiority.

In 1980 some old habits remained. Change reportedly was slower in the mountain areas and in the countryside than in the towns. According to Ha Thi Que, in areas where state control and supervision were lax, old-fashioned habits reemerged not only among the working people but also among state employees. She also pointed out that many young people misinterpreted the notion of free

Female lathe operator
Courtesy Bill Herod

marriage, or the right of individuals to select their own marriage partners, and were engaging in love affairs without seriously intending to marry. Marriages were also being concluded for money or for status, and in the cities the divorce rate was rising.

In the North, family life was affected by the demands of the war for the liberation of the South, or the Second Indochina War (see Glossary), on the society and by the policies of a regime doctrinally committed to a major overhaul of its socioeconomic organization. Sources of stress on the family in the North in the 1960s and the 1970s included the trend toward nuclear families, rural collectivization, population redistribution from the Red River Delta region to the highlands, prolonged mobilization of a large part of the male work force for the war effort, and the consequent movement of women into the economic sector. By 1975 women accounted for more than 60 percent of the total labor force.

In the South, despite the hardships brought on by the First Indochina War (see Glossary) and Second Indochina War, the traditional family system endured. Family lineage remained the source of an individual's identity, and nearly all southerners believed that the family had first claim on their loyalties, before that of extra-familial individuals or institutions, including the state.

The first attempt to reform the family system in the South occurred in 1959, when the Catholic Diem regime passed a family

117

code to outlaw polygyny and concubinage. The code also made legal separation extremely difficult and divorce almost impossible. Under provisions equalizing the rights and obligations of spouses, a system of community property was established so that all property and incomes of husband and wife would be jointly owned and administered. The code reinforced the role of parents, grandparents, and the head of the lineage as the formal validators of marriage, divorce, or adoption, and supported the tradition of ancestor cults. The consent of parents or grandparents was required in the marriage or the adoption of a minor, and they or the head of the lineage had the right to oppose the marriage of a descendant.

In 1964 after the Diem regime had been toppled in a coup, a revised family law was promulgated. It was similar to the previous one except that separation and divorce were permitted after two years of marriage on grounds of adultery, cruelty, abandonment, or a criminal act on the part of a spouse. Concubinage, which had been expressly forbidden previously, was not mentioned, and adultery was no longer punishable by fines or imprisonment.

During the war years, family life was seriously disrupted as family members were separated and often resettled in different areas. If the distance from one another was too great, they could not assemble for the rites and celebrations that traditionally reinforced kinship solidarity. Family ties were further torn by deaths and separations caused by the war and by political loyalties, which in some instances set one kinsperson against another.

In those areas where hostilities occurred, the war was a family affair, extending to the children. Few Vietnamese children had the opportunity simply to be children. From birth they were participants in the war as well as its victims. They matured in an environment where death and suffering inflicted by war were commonplace and seemingly unavoidable.

The years of military conflicts and refugee movements tended in many parts of the South to break up the extended family units and to reinforce the bonds uniting the nuclear family. The major preoccupation of the ordinary villager and urbanite alike was to earn a livelihood and to protect his immediate family, holding his household together at any cost.

After the mid-1970s, the North and South faced the task of social reconstruction. For the South, the communist conquest and ensuing relocation and collectivization policies created an uncertain social milieu. While the return of peace reunited families, communist policies forced fathers or sons into reeducation camps or entire families into new economic zones for resettlement. For those who saw no future in a socialist Vietnam, the only alternatives were to escape by boat or escape by land.

As the pace of rural collectivization accelerated in 1987, and as the people became more receptive to family planning, it seemed likely that families in the South would gradually take on the characteristics of those in the North. This conjecture was reinforced by Hanoi's decision in 1977 to apply its own 1959 family law to the South.

According to an official 1979 survey of rural families in the Red River Delta commune of An Binh near Hanoi, a typical family was nuclear, averaging four persons (parents and two children). The An Binh study, confirmed by other studies, also showed the family to be heavily dependent on outsiders for the satisfaction of its essential needs and confirmed that the family planning drive had had some success in changing traditional desires for a large family. Seventy-five percent of those interviewed nonetheless continued to believe three or four children per family to be the most desirable number and to prefer a son to a daughter.

The An Binh study revealed in addition that almost all the parents interviewed preferred their children not to be farmers, a preference that reflected the popular conviction that farming was not the promising route to high-status occupations. Such thinking, however, was alarming to officials who considered the promotion of agriculture as essential to the regime's scheme for successful transition to a socialist economy (see Agriculture, ch. 3).

In December 1986, the government enacted a new family law that incorporated the 1959 law and added some new provisions. The goal of the new legislation was ''to develop and consolidate the socialist marriage and family system, shape a new type of man, and promote a new socialist way of life eliminating the vestiges of feudalism, backward customs, and bad or bourgeois thoughts about marriage and family.'' The law explicitly defined the ''socialist family'' as one in which ''the wife and husband are equals who love each other, who help each other to make progress, who actively participate in building socialism and defending the fatherland and work together to raise their children to be productive citizens for society.''

Reflecting the government's sense of urgency about population control, the 1986 law stipulated a new parental ''obligation'' to practice family planning, a provision that was absent from the 1959 text. The new law was notable also for its stronger wording regarding the recommended marriage age: it specified that ''only males twenty years of age or older and females eighteen years of age or older may marry.'' The 1959 text had stated only that such persons were ''eligible for marriage.''

Other noteworthy provisions concerned adoption, guardianship, and marriage between Vietnamese and foreigners. Foreigners married to Vietnamese were to comply with the provisions of the 1986 law except in matters relating to separation, divorce, adoption, and guardianship, which were to be regulated separately. The new code also called on various mass organizations to play an active role in ''teaching and campaigning among the people for the strict implementation'' of the law.

Religion

The Constitution of the Socialist Republic of Vietnam, adopted in 1980, proclaims that ''citizens enjoy freedom of worship, and may practice or not practice a religion'' but that ''no one may misuse religions to violate state laws or policies.'' Despite the Constitution's ostensible protection of the practice of religion, the status of such was precarious in Vietnam in late 1987.

Buddhism

Historically, most Vietnamese have identified themselves with Buddhism, which originated in what is now southern Nepal around 530 B.C. as an offshoot of Hinduism. Its founder was Gautama, a prince who bridled at the formalism of Hinduism as it was being interpreted by the priestly caste of Brahmans. Gautama spent years meditating and wandering as an ascetic until he discovered the path of enlightenment to nirvana, the world of endless serenity in which one is freed from the cycle of birth, death, and rebirth. According to Buddhist thought, human salvation lies in discovering the ''four noble truths''—that man is born to suffer in successive lives, that the cause of this suffering is man's craving for earthly pleasures and possessions, that the suffering ceases upon his deliverance from this craving, and that he achieves this deliverance by following ''the noble eightfold path.'' The foundation of the Buddhist concept of morality and right behavior, the eightfold path, consists of right views, or sincerity in leading a religious life; right intention, or honesty in judgment; right speech, or sincerity in speech; right conduct, or sincerity in work; right livelihood, or sincerity in making a living; right effort, or sincerity in aspiration; right mindfulness, or sincerity in memory; and right concentration, or sincerity in meditation.

Buddhism spread first from China to Vietnam's Red River Delta region in approximately the second century A.D., and then from India to the southern Mekong Delta area at some time between

Children riding in a cyclo,
Ho Chi Minh City
Courtesy Bill Herod

the third and the sixth centuries. The Chinese version, Mahayana Buddhism, became the faith of most Vietnamese, whereas the Indian version, Theravada (or Hinayana) Buddhism, was confined mostly to the southern delta region. The doctrinal distinction between the two consists of their differing views of Gautama Buddha: the Mahayana school teaches that Gautama was only one of many "enlightened ones" manifesting the fundamental divine power of the universe; the Theravada school teaches that Gautama was the one-and-only enlightened one and the great teacher, but that he was not divine. The Mahayana sect holds further that laypersons can attain nirvana, whereas the Theravada school believes that only ordained monks and nuns can do so.

Few Vietnamese outside the clergy, however, are acquainted with Buddhism's elaborate cosmology. What appealed to them at the time it was introduced was Mahayana ritual and imagery. Mahayana ceremony easily conformed to indigenous Vietnamese beliefs, which combined folklore with Confucian and Taoist teachings, and Mahayana's "enlightened ones" were often venerated alongside various animist spirits.

Before the country was unified under communism, Buddhism enjoyed an autonomy from the state that was increasingly threatened once the communists gained power. For pragmatic reasons, however, the regime initially avoided overt hostility toward Buddhism or any other organized religion. Instead, it sought to separate

121

real and potential collaborators from opponents by co-optation and control. For example, within months after winning the South, the communist regime set up a front called the Patriotic Buddhist Liaison Committee. The committee's purpose was to promote the idea that all patriotic Buddhists had a duty to participate in building a new society liberated for the first time from the shackles of feudal and neo-colonialist influences. The committee also tried to show that most Buddhists, leaders and followers alike, were indeed rallying behind the new regime and the liaison committee. This strategy attempted to thwart the power of the influential, independent groups of Buddhist clergy, particularly the Unified Buddhist Church of Vietnam, which had been a major pre-1975 critic of the Saigon government and, of the roughly twenty Buddhist sects in Vietnam, the most vocal in opposing the war.

Communists also pressured monks and nuns to lead a secular life, encouraging them to take part in productive agricultural labor or to become actively involved in the work of the Patriotic Buddhist Liaison Committee. For their refusal to collaborate, some prominent clerical leaders in the South were placed under house arrest or imprisoned, their pagodas were converted to public use, and their holdings were confiscated. Such activity closely paralleled communist actions against Buddhists in the North in the 1950s. In addition, the party prevented Buddhist organizations from training monks and nuns in schools that previously had been autonomous. In April 1980, a national committee of Buddhist groups throughout the country was formed by the government. The government-controlled Vietnam Buddhist Church was established in November 1981, and it emerged as the only officially sanctioned organization authorized to represent all Buddhist groups both at home and abroad.

As a result of communist policy, the observance of Buddhist ritual and practice was drastically reduced. A 1979 study of a Red River Delta commune, reported to be "overwhelmingly Catholic," disclosed that the commune's two pagodas were "maintained and frequented regularly by the faithful (the majority of whom were old women), especially on the Buddhist feast days." No monks or nuns had been observed, however, and the study went on to note that pagodas had been eliminated entirely in nearby Hanoi. In 1987 occasional reports suggested that the observance of Buddhist ritual continued in some remote areas.

The communist government's attitude toward Buddhism and other faiths being practiced remained one of tolerance as long as the clergy and faithful adhered strictly to official guidelines. These guidelines inhibited the growth of religious institutions, however,

Chinese Buddhist temple, Cholon
Courtesy United States Army

by restricting the number of institutions approved to train clergy and by preempting the time of potential candidates among the youth whose daily routine might require study, work, and participation in the activities of communist youth organizations. In an apparent effort to train a new generation of monks and nuns, the Vietnam Buddhist Church reportedly set up one Buddhist academy in Hanoi in November 1981 and another in Ho Chi Minh City in December 1984 . These academies, however, served as an arm of the state.

Catholicism

Despite the Roman Catholic Church's rejection of ancestor worship, a cornerstone of the Confucian cultural tradition, Roman Catholicism established a solid position in Vietnamese society under French rule. The French encouraged its propagation to balance Buddhism and to serve as a vehicle for the further dissemination of Western culture. After the mid-1950s, Catholicism declined in the North, where the communists regarded it as a reactionary force opposed to national liberation and social progress. In the South, by contrast, Catholicism expanded under the presidency of Ngo Dinh Diem, who promoted it as an important bulwark against North Vietnam. Under Diem, himself a devout Catholic, Roman Catholics enjoyed an advantage over non-Catholics in commerce,

123

the professions, education, and the government. This caused growing Buddhist discontent that contributed to the eventual collapse of the Diem regime and the ultimate rise to power of the military. Roman Catholics in reunified Vietnam numbered about 3.0 million in 1984, of whom nearly 1 million resided in the North and the remainder in the South.

In 1955 approximately 600,000 Catholics remained in the North after an estimated 650,000 had fled to the South. That year the Liaison Committee of Patriotic and Peace-Loving Catholics was set up in the North by the communist regime in an attempt to win over those Catholics who had chosen to remain (but were slower than non-Catholics to embrace the regime) and to "reintegrate" them into northern society. The church was allowed to retain its link with the Vatican, although all foreign priests had either fled south or been expelled, and normal church activities were permitted to continue, albeit in the shadow of a campaign of harassment. The appearance of normalcy was misleading, however. The church was stripped of its traditional autonomy in running schools, hospitals, and orphanages. Its traditional right to own property was abolished, and priests and nuns were required to devote part of their time to productive labor in agriculture. Nevertheless, officials claimed that Catholics had complete freedom of worship as long as they did not question the principle of collective socialism, spurn manual labor, or jeopardize the internal and external security of the state.

In November 1977, the *Vietnam Courier* reported that the church in the North had changed from "opposition to acceptance and participation," but that the transformation had been difficult for Catholics. In the same month, the government unveiled a decree on religion that reaffirmed the constitution's position on religious freedom, but made it unequivocally clear that such freedom was conditional and depended on the compatibility of church activities with such higher imperatives as patriotism and socialism. The new decree not only prescribed the duties and obligations required of the clergy by the state but also imposed state control over the conduct of religious services, education, training, investitures, appointments, travels, and transfers.

Applicable to all religious communities in the North and South, the new law clearly introduced a period of more active state intervention in church affairs. The regime apparently acted out of concern that the church in the North, despite having coexisted with socialism for twenty-three years, was not progressive enough to lead in the socialist transformation of the Catholic community in the South. The *Vietnam Courier* suggested this link between the northern

Buddhist shrine with
portrait of Ho Chi Minh
Courtesy Bill Herod

and southern situations in November 1977, after noting that the northern Catholic church would have to shoulder the additional task of helping to reintegrate Vietnam's entire Catholic population into the national community.

Catholics in the South in 1975 officially numbered about 1.9 million, including 15 bishops, 3,000 regular and diocesan priests, 1,200 brothers, and 6,000 nuns. Four-hundred priests and lay brothers and 56,000 lay Catholics were estimated already to have fled the country in anticipation of the communist victory. At the time of the imposition of communist rule, the South had 870 parishes in 15 dioceses; Ho Chi Minh City alone had a half million Catholics, who were served by 600 priests and 4,000 lay brothers and nuns. The North's less than 1 million Catholics were served by about 3,500 churches attended by nearly 400 priests, 10 bishops, and 2 archbishops.

The government claimed that after April 1975 the religious activities of Roman Catholics were quickly stabilized, major services were held, and many cathedrals and churches that had been damaged or destroyed in the war were rebuilt. The regime claimed further that there was no religious persecution, or if there was persecution, that it was directed at the activities of "reactionary forces" bent on taking advantage of "the backwardness of a number of the faithful . . . ." Nevertheless, the authorities acted to isolate and to neutralize hard-core opposition to party policy and to persuade less strongly opposed factions to join a party-controlled "renovation and reconciliation" movement. A considerable number of Northern and Southern Roman Catholics, however, remained opposed to communist authority.

In 1980 the Unified Bishops' Council of Vietnam was established to enlist the aid of "patriotic" bishops in persuading recalcitrant elements of the Catholic community to cooperate with the regime. Three years later, in November 1983, a Committee for Solidarity of Patriotic Catholics was created to unite all Catholics and channel their energy into the building of socialism. This committee, which replaced the Liaison Committee of Patriotic and Peace-Loving Catholics, was formed at a time when the regime's surveillance of the Catholic community had been stepped up, reportedly due to the suspicion that some Catholics were involved in antistate activities. The regime's growing concern was further reflected in the establishment in March 1985 of a Religious Affairs Committee to coordinate and supervise religious organizations more effectively. Hanoi's increasing involvement in church affairs reportedly produced new strains in its relations with the Vatican. In 1987 it nevertheless appeared critical to Vietnam's leaders to convey to the public the impression that the Roman Catholic Church was active in the affairs of the nation and that church members were significant contributors to the socialist cause.

Other Faiths

Religions with less of a following than Buddhism or Catholicism were treated similarly by the regime, with the exception of those the regime considered merely superstitious, which incurred its outright hostility. Two religious movements that enjoyed considerable followings before 1975 were the Cao Dai (see Glossary) and the Hoa Hao (see Glossary). Both were founded in this century in the Mekong River Delta. The Cao Dai, the older of the two and a self-styled reformed Buddhist sect, flourished in the rural areas of the southern delta region. An amalgam of different beliefs derived from Confucianism, Taoism, and Christianity, among other sources, it claimed 1 million to 2 million adherents. The Hoa Hao, with more than 1 million followers, identified itself as a reformed Theravada Buddhist sect, but, unlike the Cao Dai, it preserved a distinctive Buddhist coloration. Based mostly in the southernmost areas of the delta, it stressed individual prayer, simplicity, and social justice over icon veneration or elaborate ceremonies. Before 1975 both faiths sought, with some success, to remain neutral in the war between Hanoi and Saigon. After 1975, however,

A painting at the Cao Dai Temple, Tay Ninh Province, depicting three of the Cao Dai movement's spiritual "fathers": founder of the Chinese Republic Sun Yat-sen, French poet and novelist Victor Hugo, and Vietnamese prophet Trang Thinh
Courtesy United States Army

like Buddhists and Roman Catholics, they were under heavy pressure from the communist regime to join its ranks.

Protestants, numbered between 100,000 and 200,000 in the early 1980s, and were found mostly among the Montagnard communities inhabiting the South's central highlands. Because of their alleged close association with American missionaries of the Christian and Missionary Alliance, Protestants were reported to have suffered more than Catholics after 1975.

In addition to organized religions, there existed a mélange of beliefs without institutional structure that nevertheless had an enduring impact on Vietnamese life well into the 1980s. These beliefs, which were derived partly from Confucianism, stressed the virtues of filial piety, loyalty, family solidarity, and ancestor veneration—all central to the family system of the old society. Taoism, another important system of belief introduced from China, emphasized the importance of an individual's relationship to nature and to the universe. Beliefs rooted in Taoism were condemned by the regime as superstitious.

Despite official disapproval of superstitious practices, most Vietnamese, regardless of their professed religion, level of education, or ideology, were influenced at one time or another by such practices as astrology, geomancy and sorcery. Diviners and other specialists in the occult remained in popular demand because they were believed to be able to diagnose supernatural causes of illness, establish lucky dates for personal undertakings, or predict the future. Moreover, many Vietnamese believed that individual destiny was guided by astrological phenomena. By consulting one's horoscope, one could make the most of auspicious times and avoid disaster. It was not unusual, for example, for a couple to consult an astrologer before marrying. He would determine if the betrothed were suitably matched and even fix the date of the ceremony.

The belief in good and evil spirits, or animism, antedated all organized faiths in Vietnam and permeated the society, especially in the rural areas and in the highlands. These beliefs held that all phenomena and forces in the universe were controlled by spirits and that the souls of the dead were instrumental in determining an individual's fate. If propitiated, they provided the living with protection; if ignored, they induced misfortune. Although officially condemned as "superstitious practices," these beliefs continued to proliferate in the rural and in the highland areas as well as in the cities in the 1980s.

Education

The Vietnamese inherited a high respect for learning. Under

Confucianism, education was essential for admission to the ruling class of scholar-officials, the mandarinate. Under French rule, even though Vietnamese were excluded from the higher echelons of the colonial power elite, education was a requisite for employment in the colonial civil service and for other white-collar, high-status jobs. In divided Vietnam, education continued to be a channel for social mobility in both the North and the South.

Before the 1950s, poverty was a major impediment to learning, and secondary and higher education were beyond the reach of all but a small number of upper class people. Subsequently, however, rival regimes in Hanoi and Saigon broadened educational opportunities. Both governments accomplished this despite the shortage of teachers, textbooks, equipment, and classrooms and despite the disruptions of war in the 1960s and early 1970s. The school system was originally patterned after the French model, but the curriculum was revised to give more emphasis to Vietnamese history, language, and literature and, in Hanoi, to the teaching of revolutionary ethics and Marxism-Leninism.

In the years after 1975, all public and private schools in the South were taken over by the state as a first step toward integration into a unified socialist school system. Thousands of teachers were sent from the North to direct and supervise the process of transition, and former teachers under the Saigon regime were allowed to continue their work only after they had completed "special courses" designed to expose "the ideological and cultural poisoning of which they had been victims for twenty years."

The educational system in 1987 was based on reforms announced in January 1979 that were designed to make education more relevant to the nation's economic and social needs. These reforms combined theory with practical application and emphasized the training of skilled workers, technicians, and managers. The reforms also stressed the need to develop the country's scientific and technological levels of achievement until they were comparable to international levels in order to assist Vietnam in expanding its technical cooperation with foreign countries in general and socialist countries in particular.

The 1979 reforms were implemented in stages beginning in the 1981–82 school year (September to August). By 1985 the northern and southern schools had been integrated into one system, new textbooks had been distributed throughout the country, and the curriculum had been made uniform for the first time. The government also tried to make the first nine years of general education compulsory, despite the continuing shortage of teachers, school buildings, and equipment, particularly modern equipment for

129

teaching applied sciences. The low morale of underpaid teachers with low job status complicated these attempts.

The perennial shortage of money presented another stumbling block in education. In order to address the problem, the 1979 reforms called on agricultural cooperatives and even "private citizens" to make contributions to local schools and to participate in "a movement for self-supply of teaching aids." In an apparent effort to utilize local resources for educational development, the government assigned "people's educational councils," set up at the grass-roots level, to undertake the task. Composed of representatives of the school, parents, local administration, and various mass organizations, these councils were designed to promote more productive relations between the school and the local community.

Education continued to be structured in a traditional manner, including preschool, vocational and professional schools, supplementary courses, and higher education. "General" education, however, was extended from ten to twelve years. The first nine years of general education formed the compulsory level, corresponding to primary and junior high schools; the last three years constituted the secondary level. Graduates of secondary schools were considered to have completed training in "general culture" and to be ready for employment requiring skilled labor. They were also eligible to apply to colleges or advanced vocational and professional schools. The general education category also covered the schooling of gifted and handicapped children. As part of the effort to foster "love and respect" for manual labor, students spent 15 percent of school time at the primary level and 17 percent at the secondary level in manual work.

Vocational schools at the secondary and college levels served to train technicians and skilled workers. Graduates of professional specialized schools at the college level primarily filled mid-level cadre positions in the technical, economic, educational, cultural, and medical fields. Senior cadres in these fields as well as members of the upper bureaucracy usually had graduated from regular universities. The 1979 educational reforms gave high priority to vocational and professional training in order to absorb a large number of general education students who were unable to proceed to colleges and secondary-level vocational schools. In 1980, for example, 70 percent of primary school students and 85 percent of secondary school students failed to matriculate either because of bleak prospects for employment after graduation or because the country's ninety-three institutions of higher learning could admit only 10 percent of all applicants.

130

Vocational schools continued to struggle to attract students. In a study of mass education in Vietnam, a Western scholar observed that "Vietnamese students aggressively avoided vocational schools and the specialized middle schools favored by the government." He also noted:

> The reason for the imbalance between the technical schools and the general middle schools was only too clear. The former were thought to foreclose entry to high-status occupations. The latter were thought to be an indispensable part of the ideal educational odyssey through university and into the upper bureaucracy—the modern equivalent of the old Vietnamese Confucian quest to become a metropolitan examination graduate . . . or imperial tribute student . . . as Vo Nguyen Giap bitterly acknowledged in January 1982.

Supplementary, or complementary, education served adults who had not completed a basic and secondary general education and who needed additional training in their specialties. Open to those under forty-five, supplementary courses were offered through correspondence, at worksites, or at special schools. Officials expected that participants in these courses could raise their "cultural level" to the equivalent of students who had completed ninth or twelfth grade.

The number of students in institutions of higher learning increased rapidly from about 50,000 (29,000 in the North and 20,834 in the South) in 1964 to 150,000 in 1980. Hanoi and Ho Chi Minh City served as the two major centers for universities and colleges; major provincial capitals were the sites of regional colleges; and the Ministry of National Defense and the Ministry of Interior sponsored an unspecified number of colleges. Of the 150,000 college students in 1980, approximately 23 percent were female.

In the mid-1980s, some Vietnamese observers believed that the college system needed reform to make it more diverse and flexible. They promoted change in order to accommodate more secondary school applicants and to improve the quality of college education. Students were perceived as spending too much time trying to earn diplomas and not enough time "in practical, creative activities."

Vietnam took part in international student exchange and cooperation programs in the fields of education and technical training, principally with the Soviet Union and with other communist countries (excluding China). *Nhan Dan* reported in 1983 that Vietnamese and

Soviet linguists had compiled textbooks for Vietnamese secondary general education schools and that they had also begun a similar project in Russian for use in Vietnamese colleges. The Soviets also assisted the Vietnamese in publishing scientific and technical dictionaries. In 1984 a Soviet source reported that, under the Soviet program of educational assistance that had begun in 1959, about 60,000 Vietnamese specialists and skilled workers had been trained in addition to 18,000 vocational students at the college and secondary school levels. As of mid-1986, Vietnam had "cooperative ties" with 15 Soviet universities.

In 1986 the reforms initiated in 1979 remained in the trial and error stage, but the educational system was considerably improved. Illiteracy was declining, and about 2.5 million children were being admitted to school annually. The Vietnamese report that in 1986 there were 3 million children enrolled in child-care centers and kindergartens, close to 12 million students in general education schools, and more than 300,000 students in vocational and professional schools and colleges. Scientific and technical cadres numbered more than 1 million. *Nhan Dan* reported in September 1986 that schools were shifting from literary education to literary, ethical, and vocational education, in accordance with the goals established by the 1979 reforms. The quality of education, however, remained low. Material and technical support for education were far from adequate, student absenteeism and the dropout rate were high, teachers continued to face difficult personal economic circumstances, and students and teachers in general failed to embrace the socialist ideals and practices the regime encouraged.

In April 1986, Reform Commission head Hoang Xuan Tuy related that two-thirds of preschool aged children had not yet enrolled in school, that elementary and junior-high-school education in the highlands and in the Mekong River Delta was inadequate, and that instruction in general was still oriented toward purely academic subjects and theory divorced from practical application. The majority of general education students, he added, were preoccupied with college entrance; and vocational schools, professional schools, and colleges had yet to restructure their curricula and training programs or to formulate plans for scientific research and experimentation. In Hoang's assessment, such shortcomings were symptomatic of a very low level of financial and human resource investment in education that was derived from the party and the government's failure to recognize the importance of "the human factor" and the fundamental role of education in socioeconomic development.

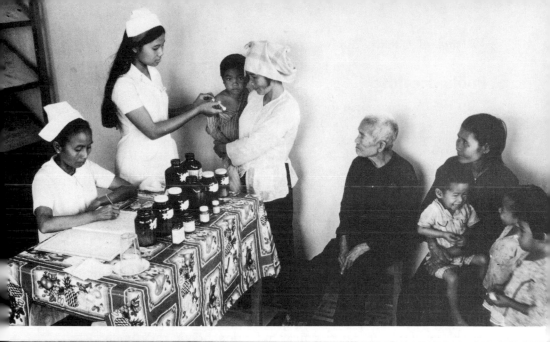

Top photo: Village medical clinic
Courtesy United Nations
Bottom photo: Agronomy students in a college near Can Tho
Courtesy United Nations

Public Health

In 1945 Vietnam had forty-seven hospitals with a total of 3,000 beds, and it had one physician for every 180,000 persons. The life expectancy of its citizens averaged thirty-four years. By 1979 there were 713 hospitals with 205,700 beds, in addition to more than 10,000 maternity clinics and rural health stations; the ratio of physicians to potential patients had increased to one per 1,000 persons, and the average life expectancy was sixty-three years.

Information concerning the health sector in the mid-1980s, although fragmentary, suggested that the country's unified health care system had expanded and improved in both preventive and curative medicine. Medical personnel totaled about 240,000, including physicians, nurses, midwives, and other paramedics. The quality of public health care and the level of medical technology remained inadequate, however, and authorities were increasingly concerned about such problems as nutritional deficiency, mental health, and old-age illnesses. Cardiovascular diseases and cancers were reportedly not widespread but had increased "in recent years." Information on AIDS was unavailable.

The most common diseases were malaria, tuberculosis, trachoma, intestinal infections, leprosy, diphtheria, tetanus, whooping cough, measles, poliomyelitis, chicken pox, typhoid fever, acute encephalitis, and acute meningitis. Hanoi claimed in 1970 that alcoholic cirrhosis and venereal diseases were "seldom found in North Vietnam because of the wholesome and temperate life of the population and the cadres." In November 1984, however, the government admitted that the incidence of these diseases had increased "significantly" since 1976, "especially in the major cities."

Vietnam claimed to have eliminated cholera, smallpox, and typhoid in the North as early as 1959 and poliomyelitis by 1961. Malaria, once endemic, was said to have been eradicated in many provinces of the North by 1965. Much progress was reported also in the containment of trachoma, tuberculosis, and other diseases, but an official assessment made public in November 1984 acknowledged that, except for smallpox, contagious and infectious diseases had yet to be brought under control and that the mortality rate associated with these diseases remained high. The high mortality rate associated with malaria was a matter of particular concern, especially in the provinces along the Vietnam-Laos border, the Central Highlands, the central region, and the northern border provinces. Tuberculosis, responsible for the death of about 1 percent of the national population, or nearly 600,000 persons annually, remained a major problem although the rate fell from the

1.7 percent reported in 1976. In 1984 as many as 92 percent of the people examined in many different localities were found to be afflicted with one or more diseases. Authorities judged from these results that as few as 48 to 60 percent of the people in the localities sampled were in good health. Gastroenteritis and such childhood diseases as diphtheria, and whooping cough accounted for the extremely high 35 percent mortality rate among children, but the annual death rate for the population as a whole in 1983 was 7.4 per 1000 persons, a decline from 26 per 1000 in 1945.

The prevalence of epidemics of bacterial, viral, and parasitic diseases was attributed to the unsanitary environment. For this reason the government introduced programs to improve hygiene habits. Sanitary stations emphasizing water and environmental purification were established in every district, and campaigns such as the Three Cleans movement (clean food, water, and living conditions) and the Three Exterminations movement (extermination of flies, mosquitoes, and rats) were instituted. In addition, officials encouraged district residents to dig wells and construct septic tanks. They recommended regular vaccinations and inoculations against diphtheria, tetanus, whooping cough, poliomyelitis, tuberculosis, and measles.

Although access to health care had improved by the mid-1980s, the shortages of funds, of qualified physicians, and of medicines prevented the Hanoi government from providing quality health care for more than a few. Minister of Public Health Dan Hoi Xuan acknowledged in November 1984 that the inadequacy of the public health system was responsible for the proliferation of private health services, the black market in medicines, and the consequent corruption of a number of doctors and pharmacists.

In 1987 the practice of traditional medicine remained an important part of the health care system. The Institute of Folk Medicine in Hanoi, a leading center devoted to the study of ancient theories and practices, utilized acupuncture and massage as an integral part of its treatment programs. Official sources maintained that traditional Vietnamese medicine had given rise to new therapeutic methods that called for the wider application of herbal medicine and acupuncture. The cultivation of medicinal plants and manufacture of drugs derived from these plants reportedly helped to overcome the shortage of Western medicines, which had to be imported in large quantities every year. Some of these traditional drugs were described as ''most effective'' in curing dysentery, arthritis, gastritis, stomach ulcers, heart diseases, influenza, blood clotting, and high blood pressure. In 1985 the Vietnamese press reported that many cooperatives were using folk medicines to satisfy 50 to 70 percent of their own needs for common drugs. Earlier in 1985, however, an official source had disclosed that efforts to develop Vietnamese medical science by integrating traditional and modern methods had not been systematic and had achieved minimal success.

In the mid-1980s, there were six medical and pharmacological colleges, one college-level institute for the training of managerial cadres in the health services, and more than forty secondary-level schools for mid-level paramedics and pharmacists. Physicians at "modern scientific and technical installations," according to the Vietnamese press, performed "sophisticated" heart, lung, kidney, and neurological surgery as well as microscopic eye surgery. Vietnamese doctors also were reported to be abreast of procedures in a number of other disciplines such as nuclear medicine and hematology.

Living Conditions

The improvement of living conditions has consistently been one of Hanoi's most important but most elusive goals. In the late 1970s and early 1980s, food, housing, medicines, and consumer goods were chronically scarce as agriculture and industry slowly recovered from the effects of prolonged wartime disruptions, corrupt and inept management, and the cost of the military occupation of Cambodia. Consequently, the Hanoi government was under tremendous pressure to address social problems such as urban unemployment, vocational training, homelessness, the care of orphans, war veterans, and the disabled, the control of epidemics, and the rehabilitation of drug addicts and prostitutes. These problems were complicated by rapid population growth, which tested the limits of the food supply and increased the need to import grains.

In December 1985, Vo Van Kiet, chairman of the State Planning Commission, nevertheless reported that farmers' lives had generally improved and that people employed in other economic sectors were adequately supplied with the basic necessities. The standard of living remained low, however, because of acute economic problems that arose between 1981 and 1985, including unemployment. During the 1981–85 period, a total of about 7 million young people reached working age (age 18), but up to 85 percent remained jobless. Among the unemployed of all ages nationwide, 80 percent were unskilled, while in Ho Chi Minh City, the figure rose to 95 percent.

For most Vietnamese having to face soaring inflation and a rapid drop in purchasing power, austerity was an inescapable fact of life. In the mid-1980s no one was starving, but the average diet was highly deficient in protein and amounted to only 1,940 calories per day, 23 percent below the level required for manual labor. Moreover, as much as an estimated 80 percent of a worker's monthly wage was spent on food. A reader complained to a Ho Chi Minh City newspaper in 1986 that the monthly salary and price subsidies paid to an ordinary worker or civil servant were barely enough to support his family for part of the month. The writer also noted that an increasing number of workers and public officials had succumbed to the lure of "outside temptations" and were misusing their functions and power to get rich illegally. "Because life is so difficult," a 1986 article in the military daily, *Quan Doi Nhan Dan* lamented, "even the most honest people must come up with schemes to earn a living and support the family."

In 1986 the standard of living was unstable, and cadres, manual workers, civil servants, armed forces personnel, and laborers experienced serious economic difficulties in their everyday lives. In March 1986, evidently as a stop-gap measure, the government reinstated rationing (discontinued since August 1985) in many parts of the country for such essential goods as rice, meat, sugar, and kerosene. In addition, the government granted more autonomy to commercial enterprises and even encouraged the development of small-scale private industry.

Although the state controlled the economy and most essential consumer goods, it lacked control of the free market, which accounted for more than 50 percent of retail trade volume (see Internal Commerce, ch. 3). In mid-1987 the free market flourished, although Vo Van Kiet had reported to the National Assembly in December 1986 that the government planned to "create conditions for stabilizing the market and prices step by step."

Meanwhile, Vo Van Kiet revealed that the new wage and allowance system put into effect in 1985 for state employees and members of the armed forces had failed to improve living conditions. Indexed to cost-of-living increases, the 1985 system had replaced the no-incentive egalitarianism of the past with a system that linked wages to productivity, quality, and efficiency of work performed.

Through the mid-1980s, the Vietnamese bureaucracy failed to act quickly enough to remedy the shortage of consumer goods in state shops. Shortages of raw materials and energy also continued, forcing manufacturing enterprises to operate at 50 percent of their production capacity. In 1987 it was hoped that the reform-minded leaders selected at the Sixth National Party Congress in December 1986 might begin to turn the economy around.

*　　*　　*

Reliable and current information on Vietnamese society remains relatively scarce. Among the most useful sources of information are *Indochina Chronology,* a quarterly of the Institute of East Asian Studies, of the University of California at Berkeley, which gives an informative summary of events, literature, and personalities relating to Vietnam, Cambodia, and Laos; and the *Southeast Asia Report,* of the Joint Publications Research Service, which contains translations of Vietnamese newspapers and periodicals. For a general understanding of the political and economic contexts in which Vietnamese society evolves, readers are advised to consult the annual summary articles on Vietnam contained in *Asian Survey, Far Eastern Economic Review Asia Yearbook,* and *Southeast Asian Affairs.* For official perceptions relating to various aspects of Vietnamese society, see *Vietnam Courier,* an English-language monthly of the Socialist Republic of Vietnam.

William J. Duiker's *Vietnam: Nation in Revolution* offers useful, well-balanced overviews on various aspects of contemporary Vietnam, with a brief annotated bibliography. Also useful is Nguyen Van Canh's *Vietnam Under Communism, 1975–1982,* which depicts life in post-1975 Vietnam as perceived and experienced by a number of Vietnamese expatriates. *Hai Van: Life in a Vietnamese Commune* by Francois Houtart and Genevieve Lemercinier provides a rare glimpse into the life of a Red River Delta commune in 1979; life in South Vietnamese rural communities in the early 1960s is given an excellent discussion in Gerald C. Hickey's *Village in Vietnam. We the Vietnamese: Voices from Viet Nam,* edited by Francois Sully, is useful for perspectives on various social aspects of South Vietnam in the 1960s. How Hanoi and Ho Chi Minh City appeared to visiting Western journalists in 1985 is presented in *Vietnam Ten Years After,* edited by Robert Emmet Long.

Graeme Jackson's "An Assessment of Church Life in Vietnam" is a balanced account of religious life; Alexander Woodside offers an informative analysis on education in his "The Triumphs and Failures of Mass Education in Vietnam." In "Vietnam 1975–1982: The Cruel Peace," Jacqueline Desbarats and Karl D. Jackson present their findings on the question of whether there were political executions in the years after the communist takeover in 1975. Ethnic minorities are the subject of scholarly treatment in Hickey's *Sons of the Mountains* and *Free in the Forest;* in *Southeast Asian Tribes, Minorities, and Nations,* edited by Peter Kunstadter; and in Ronald Provencher's *Mainland Southeast Asia: An Anthropological Perspective.* John DeFrancis's *Colonialism and Language Policy in Vietnam* is a scholarly analysis of the evolution of the national writing system, *quoc ngu;* also informative is *Language in Vietnamese Society: Some Articles by Nguyen Dinh-Hoa,* edited by Patricia Nguyen Thi My-Huong. (For further information and complete citations, see Bibliography.)

Chapter 3. The Economy

Farmers transporting goods to market

SINCE REUNIFICATION IN 1975, the economy of Vietnam has been plagued by enormous difficulties in production, imbalances in supply and demand, inefficiencies in distribution and circulation, soaring inflation rates, and rising debt problems. Vietnam is one of the few countries in modern history to experience a sharp economic deterioration in a postwar reconstruction period. Its peacetime economy is one of the poorest in the world and has shown a negative to very slow growth in total national output as well as in agricultural and industrial production. Vietnam's gross domestic product (GDP—see Glossary) in 1984 was valued at US$18.1 billion with a per capita income estimated to be between US$200 and US$300 per year. Reasons for this mediocre economic performance have included severe climatic conditions that afflicted agricultural crops, bureaucratic mismanagement, elimination of private ownership, extinction of entrepreneurial classes in the South, and military occupation of Cambodia (which resulted in a cutoff of much-needed international aid for reconstruction).

In the 1980s, the country was at a crossroads between economic liberalization and complete government economic control. It is possible that the leadership changes undertaken at the Sixth National Party Congress of the Vietnamese Communist Party (VCP, Viet Nam Cong San Dang) in December 1986 marked the beginning of the end of an era dominated by revolutionaries who emphasized security at the expense of social welfare and modernization. In 1987 Vietnam took practical steps to resolve chronic economic problems such as rapid inflation, slow and erratic economic growth, deteriorating living conditions, and severe trade imbalances. The new economic policy laid out at the Sixth National Party Congress addressed these issues while avoiding others such as high unemployment and substantial arrearage on foreign debt payments.

At the party's Second Plenum in April 1987, a new, reform-oriented leadership proposed measures that would give greater scope to the private sector, reduce the budget deficit, and boost the output of agricultural and consumer goods in order to raise market supplies and exports. Specifically, the government sought to make prices more responsive to market forces and to allow farmers and industrial producers to make profits. Barriers to trade were lowered; the checkpoint inspection system that required goods in transit to be frequently inspected was abolished; and regulations on private inflow of money, goods, and tourists from overseas were relaxed.

143

In the state-controlled industrial sector, wage raises were scheduled, and overstaffing in state administrative and service organizations was slated for reduction. Government leaders also planned to restructure the tax system to boost revenue and improve incentives.

Earlier efforts to reform the economy had employed methods similar to those proposed in 1987. These previous recovery policies, while achieving short-term gains toward economic recovery, eventually faltered because of poor implementation, lack of commitment, and decisions to industrialize and socialize the country regardless of cost. The 1987 effort to cure Vietnam's economic ills held more promise of being sustained, however. The power of the new reform-minded general secretary of the party, Nguyen Van Linh, appeared to strengthen as other reformers assumed key party Political Bureau positions. Moreover, Soviet pressure to improve economic performance increased markedly during 1987. A high Soviet official attending Vietnam's Sixth National Party Congress pointed out Vietnam's urgent need to reform and offered the Soviet Union's own reform efforts as a model for Vietnamese programs.

Economic Setting

In the 1980s, Vietnam was the world's third-largest communist country—ranking below China and the Soviet Union and above Poland—and the most densely populated. According to Vietnamese figures, the country's population in 1985 totaled more than 60 million, with an average density of 179 persons per square kilometer. In comparison, the German Democratic Republic (East Germany), ranking second in population density, averaged 154 persons per square kilometer. Vietnam's average annual population growth rate was reported to be 2.5 percent (see Population, ch. 2).

Demography

The 1979 census showed that more than 42 percent of the population at that time was younger than 15 years of age and nearly 5 percent was 65 or older. Furthermore, 71 percent of the Vietnamese population was 30 years of age or younger.

A population boom in the 1980s put pressure on food supplies and severely taxed the government's ability to create jobs. Harvest shortfalls were frequent, grain reserves remained low, and foreign exchange was extremely scarce. As a result, overcoming even a short-term food deficit was difficult for the government and costly for the people.

In 1984 a United Nations (UN) nutrition specialist calculated the daily average food consumption among Vietnamese to be only

1,850 calories per day, nearly 20 percent less than the generally accepted minimum daily standard of 2,300 calories. In 1985, the Vietnam Institute of Nutrition reported average daily intake at 1,940 calories. The institute also estimated that roughly 25 percent of the children suffered from malnutrition.

Labor

The Vietnamese labor force in mid-1985 was estimated at 31.2 million, having increased at the rate of 3.5 to 4 percent annually between 1981 and mid-1985. A 1987 Vietnamese estimate put unemployment at more than 20 percent. More than half of the work force was committed to agriculture; however, observers estimated that the unemployment level in the agricultural sector was very low because agricultural workers were more likely to be underemployed than unemployed. In contrast, the unemployment rate in the nonagricultural sector may have exceeded 40 percent, meaning that more than 2 out of every 5 Vietnamese workers were jobless. A similar calculation for the nonagricultural sector in 1981 yielded an estimate of 20 percent, or 1 out of 5.

Unemployment was particularly concentrated among younger workers living in urban areas. According to Vietnamese government statistics, of the 7 million persons who entered the work force between 1981 and 1985, about 33 percent lived in urban areas, and only 15 to 20 percent reportedly had found jobs. The actual ratio of jobs to unemployed people may not have been as grim as statistics indicate, however. According to some observers, the high rate of inflation during the period forced many people, especially state workers, to take a second job in order to make ends meet.

Vietnam's economic prospects for the late 1980s and early 1990s depended on resolving population and labor problems. Government population projections in 1987 showed that the gender imbalance, with females more numerous, probably would persist through the end of the century. National security concerns were unlikely to diminish, and the armed forces were expected to continue their high demand for males of service age. A similar demand also was expected to continue in the sectors and occupations in which males were employed during the 1980s: agriculture, fishing, mining, metallurgy, machine building, construction, and transportation. Female workers probably would remain concentrated in subsistence agriculture, light industry, and, perhaps, forestry. Education, training programs, and the wage structure were expected to continue to favor males and male-dominated occupations, while the absence of these incentives would cause productivity gains in female-intensive industries to remain low.

145

Economic recovery policies that emphasized austerity and postponed industrialization were unlikely to create sufficient new employment opportunities. In the short run, the government's discharge of surplus state employees during the mid-1980s in order to curb expenditures would tend to increase unemployment. The stress on boosting production in light industry was expected eventually to reduce unemployment, but only if expansion were supported with state investment and bank credit. The coincident removal of restraints on the labor-intensive informal economy, which was uncontrolled by the state, and the likely influx of labor into this sector could then be expected to expand the informal economy relative to the official economy.

Natural Resources

Although Vietnam is relatively rich in natural resources, the country's protracted state of war has precluded their proper exploitation. Coal reserves, located mainly in the North, have been estimated at 20 billion tons. With Soviet assistance, coal mining has been expanded somewhat. Commercially exploitable metals and minerals include iron ore, tin, copper, lead, zinc, nickel, manganese, titanium, chromite, tungsten, bauxite, apatite, graphite, mica, silica sand, and limestone. Vietnam is deficient, however, in coking coal, which, prior to the outbreak of hostilities with China in 1979, it traditionally imported from the Chinese. Gold deposits are small.

Vietnam's production of crude oil and natural gas was in very preliminary stages in the late 1980s and the amounts of commercially recoverable reserves were not available to Western analysts. With the cooperation of the Soviet Union, Vietnam began exploitation of a reported 1-billion-ton offshore oil find southeast of the Vung Tau-Con Dao Special Zone (see fig. 1). By early 1987, the Vietnamese were exporting crude oil for the first time in shipments to Japan. Production remained low, estimated at about 5,000 barrels per day, although Vietnam's minimum domestic oil requirements totaled 30,000 barrels per day. Despite optimistic plans for developing offshore fields, Vietnam was likely to remain dependent on Soviet-supplied petroleum products through the 1990s.

Vietnam's ability to exploit its resources diminished in the early 1980s, as production fell from the levels attained between 1976 and 1980. In the 1980s, the need to regulate investment and focus spending on projects with a short-term payoff pointed to continued slow development of the country's resource base, with the exception of areas targeted by the Soviet Union for economic assistance, such as oil, gas, coal, tin, and apatite.

Vietnam's fisheries are modest, even though the country's lengthy coast provides it with a disproportionately large offshore economic zone for its size. In the 1980s, Vietnam claimed a 1-million-square- kilometer offshore economic zone and an annual catch of 1.3 to 1.4 million tons. More than half the fish caught, however, were classified as being of low-quality. Schools of fish reportedly were small and widely dispersed.

As the 1990s approached, it seemed increasingly likely that Vietnam's economy would remain predominantly agricultural. This trend, however, did not necessarily limit attainable economic growth since Vietnam processed a significant amount of unused land with agricultural potential. According to Vietnamese statistics of the mid 1980s, agricultural land then in use theoretically could be expanded by more than 50 percent to occupy nearly one-third of the nation. Funds and equipment for expensive land-reclamation projects were scarce, however, and foreign economists believed that a projected increase in agricultural land use of about 20 to 25 percent was more realistic. Even if the reclaimed land were only minimally productive, an increase in land use would increase agricultural output substantially.

Both the availability of land and the density of settlement in traditional agricultural areas—about 463 persons per square kilometer in the Red River Delta and 366 persons per square kilometer in the Mekong Delta—explained much of the government's commitment to the building of new economic zones (see Glossary) in less-settled areas. During the period from 1976 to 1980, only 1.5 million out of the 4 million persons targeted for relocation actually were moved to new economic zones. The government's Third Five-Year Plan (1981–85) called for the relocation of 2 million people by 1985, and subsequent plans projected the resettlement of as many as 10 million by 1999. By the end of 1986, however, the Vietnamese reported that fewer than 3 million people had been resettled since the program began. Slow progress in bringing new land into production, low yields on reclaimed land, and hardships endured by resettled workers—particularly former city dwellers, many of whom chose to return home—testified to the problems inherent in the resettlement program.

Historical Background

Post-1975 developments, including the establishment of new economic zones, did not eradicate distinctions between North and South. North, South, and Central Vietnam historically were divided by ethnolinguistic differences, but until the mid-nineteenth century and the beginning of the French colonial period, they were all agrarian, subsistence, and village-oriented societies (see Early History, ch. 1). The French, who needed raw materials and a market for French manufactured goods, altered these commonalities by undertaking a plan to develop the northern and southern regions separately. The South, better suited for agriculture and relatively poor in industrial resources, was designated to be developed agriculturally; the North, naturally wealthy in mineral resources, was selected as the region in which industrial development was to be concentrated.

The separation distorted the basic Vietnamese economy by overly stressing regional economic differences. In the North, while irrigated rice remained the principal subsistence crop, the French introduced plantation agriculture with products such as coffee, tea, cotton, and tobacco. The colonial government also developed some extractive industries, such as the mining of coal, iron, and nonferrous metals. A shipbuilding industry was begun in Hanoi; and railroads, roads, power stations, and hydraulics works were constructed. In the South, agricultural development concentrated on rice cultivation, and, nationally, rice and rubber were the main items of export. Domestic and foreign trade were centered around the Saigon-Cholon area. Industry in the South consisted mostly of food-processing plants and factories producing consumer goods.

The development of exports—coal from the North, rice from the South—and the importation of French manufactured goods, however, stimulated internal commerce. A pattern of trade developed whereby rice from the South was exchanged for coal and manufactured goods from the North. When the North and South were divided politically in 1954, they also adopted different economic ideologies, one communist and one capitalist. In the North, the communist regime's First Five-Year Plan (1961–65) gave priority to heavy industry, but priority subsequently shifted to agriculture and light industry.

During the 1954–75 Second Indochina War (see Glossary), United States air strikes in the North, beginning in early 1965, slowed large-scale construction considerably as laborers were diverted to repairing bomb damage. By the end of 1966, serious strains developed in the North's economy as a result of war conditions. Interruptions in electric power, the destruction of petroleum storage facilities, and labor shortages led to a slowdown in industrial and agricultural activity. The disruption of transportation routes by U.S. bombing further slowed distribution of raw materials and consumer goods. In the North, all 6 industrial cities, 28 out of 30 provincial towns, 96 out of 116 district towns, and 4,000 out of 5,788 communes were either severely damaged or destroyed.

All power stations, 1,600 hydraulics works, 6 railway lines, all roads, bridges, and sea and inland ports were seriously damaged or destroyed. In addition, 400,000 cattle were killed, and several hundred thousand hectares of farmland were damaged.

The economy in the South between 1954 and 1975 became increasingly dependent on foreign aid. The United States, the foremost donor, financed the development of the military and the construction of roads, bridges, airfields and ports; supported the currency; and met the large deficit in the balance of payments. Destruction attributed to the Second Indochina War was considerable. Hanoi claimed that in the South, 9,000 out of 15,000 hamlets were damaged or destroyed, 10 million hectares of farmland and 5 million hectares of forest lands were devastated, and 1.5 million cattle were killed.

For Vietnam as a whole, the war resulted in some 1.5 million military and civilian deaths, 362,000 invalids, 1 million widows, and 800,000 orphans. The country sustained a further loss in human capital through the exodus of refugees from Vietnam after the communist victory in the South. According to the United Nations High Commission for Refugees, as of October 1982 approximately 1 million people had fled Vietnam. Among them were tens of thousands of professionals, intellectuals, technicians, and skilled workers.

Economic Roles of the Party and the Government

The Vietnamese economy is shaped primarily by the VCP through the plenary sessions of the Central Committee and national congresses. The party plays a leading role in establishing the foundations and principles of communism, mapping strategies for economic development, setting growth targets, and launching reforms.

Planning is a key characteristic of centralized, communist economies, and one plan established for the entire country normally contains detailed economic development guidelines for all its regions. According to Vietnamese economist Vo Nhan Tri, Vietnam's postreunification economy was in a "period of transition to socialism." The process was described as consisting of three phases. The first phase, from 1976 through 1980, incorporated the Second Five-Year Plan (1976–80)—the First Five-Year Plan (1960–65) applied to North Vietnam only. The second phase, called "socialist industrialization," was divided into two stages: from 1981 through 1990 and from 1991 through 2005. The third phase, covering the years 2006 through 2010, was to be time allotted to "perfect" the transition.

The party's goal was to unify the economic system of the entire country under communism. Steps were taken to implement this goal at the long-delayed Fourth National Party Congress, convened in December 1976, when the party adopted the Second Five-Year Plan and defined both its "line of socialist revolution" and its "line of building a socialist economy." The next two congresses, held in March 1982 and December 1986, respectively, reiterated this long-term communist objective and approved the five-year plans designed to guide the development of the Vietnamese economy at each specific stage of the communist revolution.

The Second Five-Year Plan (1976–80)

The optimism and impatience of Vietnam's leaders were evident in the Second Five-Year Plan. The plan set extraordinarily high goals for the average annual growth rates for industry (16 to 18 percent), agriculture (8 to 10 percent), and national income (13 to 14 percent). It also gave priority to reconstruction and new construction while attempting to develop agricultural resources, to integrate the North and the South, and to proceed with communization.

Twenty years were allowed to construct the material and technical bases of communism. In the South, material construction and systemic transformation were to be combined in order to hasten economic integration with the North. It was considered critical for the VCP to improve and extend its involvement in economic affairs so that it could guide this process. Development plans were to focus equally on agriculture and industry, while initial investment was to favor projects that developed both sectors of the economy. Thus, for example, heavy industry was intended to serve agriculture on the premise that a rapid increase in agricultural production would in turn fund further industrial growth. With this strategy, Vietnamese leaders claimed that the country could bypass the capitalist industrialization stage necessary to prepare for communism (see table 4, Appendix A).

Vietnam was incapable, however, of undertaking such an ambitious program on its own and solicited financial support for its Second Five-Year Plan from Western nations, international organizations, and communist allies. Although the amount of economic aid requested is not known, some idea of the assistance level envisioned by Hanoi can be obtained from available financial data. The Vietnamese government budget for 1976 amounted to US$2.5 billion, while investments amounting to US$7.5 billion were planned for the period between 1976 and 1980.

The economic aid tendered to Hanoi was substantial, but it still fell short of requirements. The Soviet Union, China, and Eastern Europe offered assistance that was probably worth US$3 billion to US$4 billion, and countries of the Western economic community pledged roughly US$1 billion to US$1.5 billion.

The Third Five-Year Plan (1981–85)

By 1979 it was clear that the Second Five-Year Plan had failed to reduce the serious problems facing the newly unified economy. Vietnam's economy remained dominated by small-scale production, low labor productivity, unemployment, material and technological shortfalls, and insufficient food and consumer goods.

To address these problems, at its Fifth National Party Congress held in March 1982, the VCP approved resolutions on "orientations, tasks and objectives of economic and social development for 1981–85 and the 1980s." The resolutions established economic goals and in effect constituted Vietnam's Third Five-Year Plan (1981–85). Because of the failure of the Second Five-Year Plan, however, the Vietnamese leadership proceeded cautiously, presenting the plan one year at a time. The plan as a whole was neither drawn up in final form nor presented to the National Assembly (see Glossary) for adoption.

The economic policies set forth in 1982 resulted from a compromise between ideological and pragmatic elements within the party leadership. The question of whether or not to preserve private capitalist activities in the South was addressed, as was the issue of the pace of the South's communist transformation. The policies arrived at called for the temporary retention of private capitalist activities in order to spur economic growth and the completion, more or less, of a communist transformation in the South by the mid-1980s.

The plan's highest priority, however, was to develop agriculture by integrating the collective and individual sectors into an overall system emphasizing intensive cultivation and crop specialization and by employing science and technology. Economic policy encouraged the development of the "family economy"; that is, the peasants' personal use of economic resources, including land, not being used by the cooperative. Through use of an end-product contract system introduced by the plan, peasant households were permitted to sign contracts with the collective to farm land owned by the collective. The households then assumed responsibility for production on the plots. If production fell short of assigned quotas, the households were to be required to make up the deficit the following year. If a surplus was produced, the households were to be allowed to keep it, sell it on the free market, or sell it to the state for a "negotiated price." In 1983 the family economy reportedly supplied 50 to 60 percent of the peasants' total income and 30 to 50 percent of their foodstuffs.

Free enterprise was sanctioned, thus bringing to an end the nationalization of small enterprises and reversing former policies that had sought the complete and immediate communization of the South. The new policy especially benefited peasants (including the overwhelming majority of peasants in the South) who had refused to join cooperatives, small producers, small traders, and family businesses.

The effort to reduce the capitalist sector in the South nevertheless continued. Late in 1983, a number of import-export firms that had been created in Ho Chi Minh City (formerly Saigon) to spur the development of the export market were integrated into a single enterprise regulated by the state. At the same time, the pace of collectivization in the countryside was accelerated under the plan. By the end of 1985, Hanoi reported that 72 percent of the total number of peasant households in the South were enrolled in some form of cooperative organization.

Despite the plan's emphasis on agricultural development, the industrial sector received a larger share of state investment during the first two years. In 1982, for example, the approximate proportion was 53 percent for industry compared with 18 percent for agriculture. Limiting state investment in agriculture, however, did not appear to affect total food production, which increased 19.5 percent from 1980 to 1984.

The plan also stressed the development of small-scale industry to meet Vietnam's material needs, create goods for export, and lay the foundation for the development of heavy industry. In the South, this entailed transforming some private enterprises into "state-private joint enterprises" and reorganizing some small-scale industries into cooperatives. In other cases, however, individual ownership was maintained. Investment in light industry actually decreased by 48 percent while investment in heavy industry increased by 17 percent during the first two years of the plan. Nonetheless, the increase in light-industry production outpaced that of heavy industry by 33 percent to 28 percent during the same two-year period.

The July 1984 Sixth Plenum (Fifth Congress) of the VCP Central Committee recognized that private sector domination of wholesale and retail trade in the South could not be eliminated until the state was capable of assuming responsibility for trade. Proposals therefore were made to decentralize planning procedures and improve the managerial skills of government and party officials.

These plans were subsequently advanced at the Central Committee's Eighth Plenum (Fifth Congress) in June 1985. Acting to disperse economic decision making, the plenum resolved to grant production autonomy at the factory and individual farm levels. The plenum also sought to reduce government expenditures by ending state subsidies on food and certain consumer goods for state employees. It further determined that all relevant costs to the national government needed to be accounted for in determining production costs and that the state should cease compensating for losses incurred by state enterprises. To implement these resolutions, monetary organizations were required to shift to modern economic accounting. The government created a new dong (D—for the value of the dong, see Glossary) in September 1985, and set maximum quotas for the amount permitted to be exchanged in bank notes. The dong also was officially devalued.

The Fourth Five-Year Plan (1986–90)

The central economic objectives of the Fourth Five-Year Plan were to increase production of food, consumer goods, and export goods. Increasing food production was of primary importance. Grain production was targeted to reach 22 to 23 million tons annually by 1990, and rice production was planned to total 19 to 20 million tons annually. Combined output for subsidiary crops was established at about 3 million tons annually. Planned annual per capita food production was set at 333 to 348 kilograms, and an effort was initiated to bring subsidiary food crops (corn, sweet potatoes, manioc, and white potatoes) into the people's diet.

Grain-production policy was accompanied by measures dealing with land use, water conservation, Mekong Delta irrigation works, Red River Delta dike consolidation, fertilizer imports, pest control, animal husbandry, tractor use, and seed production. The plan also stressed the cultivation and harvesting of marine products and the development of short-term industrial crops (crops that can be planted and harvested in a single growing season and that require some form of processing before being marketed, such as beans, peanuts, and oil-bearing crops) and long-term industrial crops (crops that also include a processing stage but that require a lengthy period of cultivation, such as coffee, tea, pepper, and coconuts). The government also identified forestry as an important sector of the economy to be developed.

Production of consumer goods was improved in order to meet the basic needs of the people, to balance goods and money, to create jobs, and to develop an important source of capital accumulation and export commodities. The volume of consumer goods produced

153

was expected to increase by an average annual rate of 13 to 15 percent, compared with the 11.3 percent average annual increase recorded during the Third Five-Year Plan.

Adequate incentive policies for raw materials production were deemed critical to the development of high-quality consumer goods for internal consumption and export. Priority in using foreign exchange was to be given to importers of needed raw materials. The plan also sought to protect domestic production of consumer goods and to emphasize local production of goods over imports.

In order to obtain the foreign exchange needed to fulfill import requirements and to carry out trade agreements with other countries, the government scheduled a major increase—70 percent above the previous plan's target—in the volume of exports. Under the Fourth Five-Year Plan, particular emphasis was to be given principal products such as processed agricultural goods, light industry, handicraft goods, and fish products (see table 5 and table 6, Appendix A).

Agriculture

Agricultural production, the backbone of Vietnam's development strategy, varied considerably from year to year following national reunification in 1975. A particularly strong performance in agriculture was recorded in 1976—up more than 10 percent from 1975—but production dropped back to approximately 95 percent of the 1976 level in 1977 and 1978 and recovered to a level higher than that of 1976 only in 1979 (see table 6 and table 7, Appendix A).

Vietnamese crop and livestock production offset agricultural performance during this period. For example, an 8-percent increase in the value of livestock production in 1977 balanced an 8-percent decrease in the value of crop production (mainly the result of a 1-million-ton decline in the rice harvest). In 1978 the reverse occurred: a steep decline in livestock output countered a significant increase in grain production. The value of crop production, however, averaged four times the value of livestock output at this time.

Foremost among Vietnam's agricultural troubles was exceptionally adverse weather, including a drought in 1977 and major typhoons and widespread flooding in 1978. The drought overtaxed Vietnam's modest irrigation systems, and the floods damaged them. In addition, the floods reportedly reduced cattle herds by 20 percent. The size of this loss was indirectly confirmed in Vietnamese statistics that showed a leveling off of growth in livestock inventories (particularly of cattle) between 1978 and 1980. Throughout the Second Five-Year Plan, and especially in the late 1970s, chemical fertilizers, pesticides, and spare parts for mechanical equipment were in short supply.

Despite their having occurred, for the most part, fairly early in the plan period, the severe reversals in the agricultural sector greatly diminished hopes of achieving self-sufficiency in food production by 1980. The 1980 grain target eventually was lowered from 21 million tons to 15 million tons, but even that amount proved unattainable.

The agricultural policies promulgated from 1976 through 1980 had mixed results. Pragmatic measures that encouraged the planting of more subsidiary food crops (such as sweet potatoes, manioc, beans, and corn) led to an increase of these crops from a level of less than 10 percent that of grain production in 1975 to a level that was more than 20 percent of grain output by the late 1970s. Improved incentives for farmers in 1978 and 1979 included efforts to boost availability of consumer goods in the countryside and to raise state procurement prices. They were reinforced by adoption of a contract system that sought to guarantee producers access to agricultural inputs in exchange for farm products. Even so, bureaucratic inefficiencies and shortages of agricultural supplies prevented complete success.

The program undertaken in mid-1977 to expedite unification of North and South by collectivizing Southern agriculture met with strong resistance. The reportedly voluntary program was designed to be implemented by local leaders, but Southern peasants were mainly freeholders—not tenants—and, aside from forming production teams for mutual assistance (an idea that won immediate acceptance), they resisted participation in any collective program that attenuated property rights.

Failure to collectivize agriculture by voluntary means led briefly to the adoption of coercive measures to increase peasant participation. It soon became apparent, however, that such harsh methods were counterproductive. Increased food shortages and heightened security concerns in late 1978 and 1979 caused the leadership once again to relax its grip on Southern agriculture.

In the North, formation of cooperatives had begun in 1959 and 1960, and by 1965 about 90 percent of peasant households were organized into collectives. By 1975 more than 96 percent of peasant households belonging to cooperatives were classified as members of "high-level cooperatives," which meant that farmers had contributed land, tools, animals, and labor in exchange for income.

Between 1976 and 1980, agricultural policy in the North was implemented by newly established government district offices in an effort to improve central control over planting decisions and farm work. The lax enforcement of state agricultural policies adopted during the war years gave way to a greater rigidity that diminished cooperative members' flexibility to undertake different tasks. Labor productivity fell as a result. A study by an overseas Vietnamese who surveyed ten rice-growing cooperatives found that, despite an increase in labor and area cultivated in 1975, 1976, and 1977, production decreased while costs increased when compared with production and costs for 1972 through 1974. Although the study failed to take weather and other variables into account, the findings were consistent with conclusions reached by investigators who have studied the effects of collectivization in other countries. Moreover, the study drew attention to the North's poor agricultural performance as a reason for Vietnam's persistent food problem.

State investment in agriculture under the Third Five-Year Plan remained low, and the sector was severely troubled throughout the plan period and into 1986 and 1987 as well. Only modest food-grain increases of 5 percent were generated annually. Although this was enough to outpace the 2.3 percent annual rate of population growth during the 1980s, it remained insufficient to raise average annual per capita food consumption much above the official subsistence level of 300 kilograms. One official Vietnamese source estimated in 1986 that farm families devoted up to 80 percent of their income to their own food needs.

At the conclusion of the Third Five-Year Plan, agricultural yields remained less than required to permit diverting resources to the support of industrial development. In 1986 agriculture still accounted for about 44 percent of national income (the figure for developed nations is closer to 10 percent). The agricultural sector also occupied some 66 percent of the work force—a higher percentage than in 1976 and 1980. Worse still, the output per agricultural worker had slipped during the plan period, falling even further behind the increasing output per worker in industry. In 1980 more than three agricultural workers were needed to produce as much national income as a single industrial or construction worker. By 1985 an industrial worker produced more than six times as much as an agricultural worker.

In December 1986, Vo Van Kiet, vice chairman of the Council of Ministers and member of the Political Bureau, highlighted most of the major problems of Vietnamese agriculture in his speech to the Twelfth Session of the Seventh National Assembly. While mentioning gains in fisheries and forestry, he noted that nearly all farming subsectors—constituting 80 percent of the agricultural sector—had failed to achieve plan targets for 1986. Kiet blamed state

Rice paddy dike construction
Courtesy Bill Herod

agencies, such as the Council of Ministers, the State Planning Commission, and the Ministry of Foreign Trade, for their failure to ensure appropriate "material conditions" (chiefly sufficient quantities of chemical fertilizers and pesticides) for the growth of agricultural production. Kiet also blamed the state price system for underproduction of key "industrial crops" that Vietnam exported, including jute, sugar, groundnut, coffee, tea, and rubber. Production levels of subsidiary food crops, such as sweet potatoes, corn, and manioc, had been declining for several years, both in relation to plan targets and in actual output as well. By contrast, livestock-output, including that of cattle, poultry, buffalo, and hogs, was reported by the government to have continued its growth and to have met or exceeded targets, despite unstable prices and shortages of state-provided animal feed.

Outside observers agreed that the problems noted in Kiet's speech had been exacerbated by the complexity of the pricing system, which included multiple tiers of fixed prices for quota and above-quota state purchases as well as generally higher free market prices. The removal of more orthodox leaders, the rise of moderate reformists such as Kiet to high party and government positions during the Sixth National Party Congress, and the cabinet changes in early 1987 seemed to indicate that the pricing system would be modified, although no change was evident in the fundamental structure of state-controlled markets or in the tension within the multiple-market system (see Internal Commerce, this ch.).

Industry

The pattern of Vietnamese industrial growth after reunification was initially the reverse of the record in agriculture; it showed recovery from a depressed base in the early postwar years. Recovery stopped in the late 1970s, however, when the war in Cambodia and the threat from China caused the government to redirect food, finance, and other resources to the military, a move that worsened shortages and intensified old bottlenecks. At the same time, the invasion of Cambodia cost Vietnam badly needed foreign economic support. China's attack on Vietnam in 1979 compounded industrial problems by badly damaging important industrial facilities in the North, particularly a major steel plant and an apatite mine (see The Armed Forces, ch. 5).

National leadership objectives during the immediate postwar period included consolidating factories and workshops in the North that had been scattered and hidden during the war to improve their chances of survival and nationalizing banks and major factories in the South to bring the financial and industrial sectors under state control. The government's continued use of wartime planning mechanisms that emphasized output targets and paid little heed to production or long term costs caused profits to erode, however, and increased the government's financial burdens. Economic reforms undertaken in 1977 gave factory management some independence in formulating production plans, arranging production resources, and containing production expenses. Such additional pragmatic steps as the adoption of incentive-structured wages and the realignment of prices better to reflect costs were also considered.

This first experiment with reform was relatively short-lived, partly because it ran counter to the overriding policy of socializing the South and integrating it with the North by reducing the centralized administrative control obviously needed to do the job. Some reform measures stayed on the books, however, and were revived in the 1980s.

Vietnamese statistics indicate that the gross value of industrial output in 1980 was not much higher than in 1976 and that the value of output per capita declined more than 8 percent. For example, cement production was relatively stagnant; it averaged 1.7 million tons annually during the Second Five-Year Plan, but only 1.4 million tons in 1985.

In general, fuel production increased at more than 10 percent annually. Coal output grew from 5.2 million tons in 1975 to

United States armored cars
converted into bulldozers, 1977
Production of small tractors

6 million tons in 1978 and fell to 5.3 million tons in 1980. According to official figures, 1985 coal production remained at, or somewhat below, the 1981 level of 6 million tons (see table 8, Appendix A). Coal accounted for about two-thirds of energy consumption in the 1980s. Coal mining remained handicapped by coordination and management problems at mining sites, incomplete rail connections to mines, equipment and materials shortages, and inadequate food and consumer goods for miners.

Some light industry and handicrafts sectors mirrored the difficulties experienced in agriculture because they used agricultural raw materials. By 1980 the Vietnamese press was reporting that many grain, food-product, and consumer-goods processing enterprises had reduced production or ceased operations entirely. Although detailed statistics on sector performance were insufficient to show annual results, the total value of light industry output peaked in 1978; by 1980 it was nearly 3 percent lower than it had been in 1976. Increasingly severe shortages of food (particularly grain and fish) and industrial consumer goods lessened workers' incentives.

Total industrial production during the Third Five-Year Plan reflected high levels of investment, averaging some 40 percent of total annual investment during the plan period. In 1985 the industrial sector accounted for some 32 percent of national income, up from approximately 20 percent in 1980.

From 1981 through 1985, industrial growth was unevenly distributed and in many instances simply restored production levels to their 1976 levels. The highest production growth rates were recorded in the manufacture of paper products (32 percent per year), and food processing (42 percent per year). Both sectors had declined in production during the Second Five-Year Plan. Production of processed sugar increased from 271,000 tons in 1981 to 434,000 tons in 1985, almost ten times the 1975 production level. The processing of ocean fish increased from 385,000 tons in 1980 to 550,000 tons in 1985, not quite reaching 1976 and 1977 levels, but clearly reversing the steady decline this sector had experienced in the late 1970s. (The decline had been generated in part by the use of fishing boats in the South as escape craft to flee the communist regime.) Other light industries grew at annual rates of 10 percent or more during the early 1980s, which essentially restored production to 1975 or 1976 levels. Brick production increased steadily to 3.7 billion bricks in 1985, after regular declines during the previous plan. Production of glass reached 41,000 tons in 1985, exceeding 1975 levels for the first time. Paper production in 1985 again reached the 1976 level of 75,000 tons, up from 42,000 tons at the beginning of the plan in 1981; and the textile subsector exhibited an

8 percent average annual growth rate during the plan period as cloth production more than doubled to 380 million square meters in 1985.

Among heavy industries, machine-building and chemical industries (including rubber) registered annual average production gains of approximately 25 percent. Chemical fertilizer production continued to exceed the 1975 level and, in 1985, reached 516,000 tons despite relatively underdeveloped mining and enrichment processes for apatite and pyrite ore and underutilization of the Lam Thao Superphosphate of Lime plant (Vinh Phu Province). Pesticide production also maintained a decade-long growth trend to reach 11.74 billion tons in 1985.

Fragmentary figures for iron and chromium ore production were discouraging and suggested a continuation of the decline from 1975 levels. Ferrous and non-ferrous metallurgical production actually declined overall, reflecting exhausted and obsolescent plants, low investment rates, and probably dwindling supplies of scrap left from the end of the Second Indochina War. Modest gains were reported annually in steel production, which reached 57,000 tons in 1985.

Electric power production, although handicapped by uncompleted projects and shortages of oil and spare parts, grew at an average of 8 percent per year. Vietnamese statistics on the annual output of primary products showed that production of electricity increased by almost 60 percent to nearly 3.8 billion kilowatt hours from 1976 through 1978, then declined to around 3.7 billion kilowatt hours in 1980. By 1985, however, production of electricity had increased to 5.4 billion kilowatt hours. Energy-producing industries generally remained stagnant, however, which caused tremendous difficulties for the other sectors of the economy. Power output grew very slowly, and power shortages forced many factories to operate at only 45 to 50 percent of capacity. The government planned that in the 1980s energy production would be tripled by the completion of three big Soviet-assisted projects: the 500-megawatt thermal plant at Pha Lai, Hai Hung Province; the 300-megawatt hydroelectric plant at Tri An, Dong Nai Province, and the giant, 1,900-megawatt hydroelectric plant at Hoa Binh, Ha Son Binh Province, which has been called the "Asian Aswan Dam."

Internal Commerce

The control and regulation of markets was one of the most sensitive and persistent problems faced by the government following the beginning of North-South integration in 1975. The government, in its doctrinaire efforts to communize the commercial, market-oriented Southern economy, faced several paradoxes. The first was the need both to cultivate and to control commercial activity by ethnic Chinese in the South, especially in Ho Chi Minh City. Chinese businesses controlled much of the commerce in Ho Chi Minh City and the South generally. Following the break with China in 1978, some Vietnamese leaders evidently feared the potential for espionage activities within the Chinese commercial community. On the one hand, Chinese-owned concerns controlled trade in a number of commodities and services, such as pharmaceuticals, fertilizer distribution, grain milling, and foreign-currency exchange, that were supposed to be state monopolies. On the other hand, Chinese merchants provided excellent access to markets for Vietnamese exports through Hong Kong and Singapore. This access became increasingly important in the 1980s as a way of circumventing the boycott on trade with Vietnam imposed by a number of Asian and Western Nations.

The second paradox lay in the role markets played in economic planning. State plans depended upon complex and interrelated flows of industrial and agricultural commodities, mediated by state markets at fixed prices. For example, predetermined amounts of food had to be produced and made available to coal miners, who were required to increase production of fuel for thermal power plants, which would in turn supply energy to fertilizer factories and machine shops. Production of fertilizer and small machines—for example, irrigation pumps and insecticide sprayers—would close the circle by providing planned levels of inputs necessary to increase agricultural production. Production campaigns under the guise of encouraging volunteerism—heroic efforts for the development of the fatherland—were to be used to keep production at quota levels at every part of the cycle. By the late 1970s, however, this plan had failed conspicuously. Although inhibited by controls and the exodus of numerous Chinese in the late 1970s, the private market remained active (see Ethnic Groups and Languages, ch. 2). Enterprises working under the Second Five-Year Plan found themselves competing for needed inputs in the private sector. Prices in the free market were usually well above those set by the plan, but private markets often were the only source for needed goods. Bottlenecks and shortages persisted, aggravated by the tendency of low-level managers to stockpile above-quota production against future levies or simply to sell production on the private market. Repeated failures to improve harvests caused food shortages to approach crisis proportions and forced the government to back away from its attempt to mold the South into the North's economic image. After 1978 the government moderated its crackdown on private commerce in the South to allow some commercial activity, including reinvestment of private profits. By 1979 the share of state-owned commerce in Ho Chi Minh City had declined to 27 percent, compared with 54 percent for the country as a whole.

A major problem for the leadership was the structure of the economy in the South. Nationalization had little effect on the small-scale manufacturing that characterized much of production. Moreover, commerce was a principal occupation in the major cities. While state stores were established as part of a new government-controlled distribution network, private vendors were able to compete effectively with them by offering to pay more to suppliers and by providing customers with better and otherwise unobtainable goods in exchange for higher prices. Hanoi's orthodox communist leaders viewed this activity in a time of shortage as speculation, hoarding, and monopolization of the market.

At roughly the same time that the government intensified the collectivization drive, it launched a campaign in the South to transform commerce into a largely public-sector activity. Private shops were closed, merchandise was redirected to state channels, and merchants were shifted to production work. At the peak of the transformation drive in 1978, state-sponsored commerce in Ho Chi Minh City reportedly accounted for 40 percent of retail sales. The government's crackdown on private traders initiated an unprecedented exodus of ethnic Chinese, who made up many of their number. The market dislocation also increased hardship in the South, which, along with unpopular resettlement policies, convinced many Southerners to flee. Not only did the government's program deprive the South of the services of some of the more capable members of the middle class, but the escape of many Southerners by sea provoked a shortage of fishing boats and a decline in the fish catch, a principal source of foreign-exchange income.

Through 1986 and 1987, official policy toward unofficial markets continued to alternate between restrictive and liberal approaches. Restrictions included licensing and tax regulations and proscriptions against reinvestment of profits. In periods of relaxation, these restrictions were eased; local organizations were given greater autonomy in setting prices for locally produced goods; and unofficial markets were permitted to flourish.

Lenient policies reflected official awareness that both production and distribution remained to some degree dependent on the unofficial market. In agriculture, for example, the "family economy" continued to account for an important share of peasant agricultural production. The state plan for industrial production recognized the existence and importance of the unofficial market in the "dual quota planning" system. Under this program,

Black market American goods, Ho Chi Minh City
Courtesy Bill Herod

introduced in 1985, enterprises that met plan quotas were allowed independently to plan, finance, produce, and privately market surplus goods on the unofficial market. In 1986 state enterprises in Hanoi reportedly were unable to meet their budget contribution quotas because of the high cost of purchasing goods on the unofficial market. Many organizations not authorized to trade continued to do so, however, and the available goods on the official, "organized" market remained well below quotas.

Foreign Trade and Aid

In the 1980s, the Vietnamese government, acting under party supervision, continued to regulate and control all foreign trade. The Ministry of Foreign Trade managed trade and was responsible for issuing of import and export licenses and approving any departures from the formal economic plan on an ad hoc basis. There was considerable division of responsibility, however, among high level agencies, financial institutions, state trading corporations, local export companies, and provincial and regional government bodies.

The role of planning in foreign trade became increasingly significant after June 1978, when the country formally joined the Soviet-sponsored Council for Mutual Economic Assistance (Comecon—see Glossary) and began to coordinate its five-year development and trade plans more closely with those of the Soviet Union

Scrambling to buy plastic water containers in Hanoi
Courtesy Bill Herod
Hanoi pen merchant uses hypodermic needle
to insert ink into used ballpoint pens
Courtesy Bill Herod

and other Comecon members. Planning officials set trade goals on the basis of the overall planning targets and quotas required by bilateral trade agreements with various Comecon countries. The 1978 Treaty of Friendship and Cooperation between the Soviet Union and Vietnam, the most important of numerous such agreements with Comecon members, established the basis for the two countries' "long-term coordination of their national economic plans" and for long-term Soviet development assistance in technology and other crucial sectors of the Vietnamese economy. A 1981 Soviet-Vietnamese protocol on coordination of state plans during the Third Five-Year Plan set specific targets for bilateral trade and for coordination of Soviet machinery and equipment exports with plans for development of Vietnam's fuel and energy sectors.

After approval by the Council of Ministers, major trade programs were announced at national party congresses (see Development of the Vietnamese Communist Party, ch. 4). The trade program announced in 1986 at the Sixth National Party Congress called for export growth of 70 percent during the Fourth Five-Year Plan (see table 9, Appendix A).

Closer linkages between trade and general economic planning in the 1980s had mixed effects. Fluctuating commodities prices at home and market-oriented trade with, and investment from, Western countries were too uncertain to plan. Consequently, the Second Five-Year Plan was crippled when hoped-for Western investment failed to materialize. The joint planning approach was designed to enable Vietnam to minimize risk because it could count on stable supplies of important resources and equipment at concessionary prices, especially from the Soviet Union. Any delays or bottlenecks in the plans or aid commitments of Comecon countries, however, could delay or disrupt Vietnam's planning effort. In the early 1980s, for example, announcement of the Third Five-Year Plan was delayed until the Fifth National Party Congress of March 1982 while Vietnam waited for the Soviet Union to confirm its aid commitment. Similarly, Vietnam in the mid-1980s endured first reduction, then elimination of Soviet price subsidies for purchases of Soviet oil. The reductions were in accordance with the then general Soviet practice of avoiding oil price subsidies in order to keep Comecon oil prices close to those of the world market. The volume of Vietnamese trade suffered increasingly from some of the recurring problems that troubled planners in other Comecon countries during this period, including overly optimistic targets, problems of regionalism, priorities often driven by ideology, and chronic shortages of domestically produced raw materials and industrial commodities. By 1987 observers had concluded that, despite Vietnam's financial ties with Comecon, increased investment and trade from Western countries and other non-Comecon sources would be required for a general Vietnamese economic recovery (following Vietnam's incursion into Cambodia in late 1978, numerous Western and regional aid donors had withdrawn their support and imposed a trade boycott).

Foreign Currency Management

In the 1980s, the Foreign Trade Bank, under the authorization of the State Bank of Vietnam (formerly the National Bank of Vietnam), made payments for imports. Headquartered in Hanoi, with a branch in Ho Chi Minh City, the Foreign Trade Bank managed Vietnam's foreign currency holdings and related matters, such as the resolution of debts owed foreign countries. The Foreign Trade Bank also conducted Vietnam's relationship with the World Bank (see Glossary), following Hanoi's assumption of the memberships held in the Asian Development Bank (see Glossary) and the International Monetary Fund (IMF—see Glossary) by the government of the Republic of Vietnam (South Vietnam) until 1975 (see Banking, this ch.).

Vietnam was, in addition, a member of the Comecon-affiliated International Investment Bank and the International Bank for Economic Cooperation in Moscow. Under the terms of Vietnam's Comecon membership, the International Bank for Economic Cooperation extended limited credit in transferable rubles (for value of ruble, see Glossary) for transactions not cleared through bilateral Soviet-Vietnamese trade agreements; the bank also maintained a convertible foreign exchange account for Vietnam.

In order to increase exports, the government used incentives. Bonuses for export production were introduced in 1980, and extended in 1985, to reward cooperatives and other collective entities that met their export production quotas. Incentives to increase exports also were applied through the government's manipulation of foreign exchange disbursement. In general, foreign exchange for import companies either was carefully allocated in the state plan or was determined by the relevant ministries on an ad hoc basis when the companies requested convertible currencies for their operations. The amount of foreign exchange allocated to a company for import operations, however, was determined by the amount of foreign exchange earned by the company's exports. Tying foreign exchange allocations to export earnings was intended to act as an incentive to boost export production. The government also required that most export companies turn in between 10 and 30 percent of their foreign exchange earnings. Beyond this general guideline, however, many enterprises were permitted to retain all or a portion of their hard currency earnings in the form of special credits against State Bank accounts. Companies operating in a developing region such as the highlands, for example, were granted a five-year holiday during which they could retain all foreign exchange earnings. Those exporting major commodities such as coal, rubber, and marine products were allowed to retain between 80 and 100 percent of their hard-currency earnings for use in necessary import purchases. Centrally controlled enterprises in the field of tourism were completely exempted from turn-in requirements, and companies that borrowed hard currencies from abroad received preferential status.

Under a system of procurement subsidies, export companies applied for funds to cover gaps between procurement costs and their export revenues. The Ministry of Finance, through its Export Support Fund, disbursed these subsidy payments to the centrally administered trading corporations. Local corporations could receive a subsidy mix based on profits from imports and payments made by local governments. All such subsidies were limited, and companies exceeding the limit could lose their export permits.

Decentralization of Trade

During the 1980s, there were variations in the level of decentralization of foreign trade that the government was willing to permit. A policy of giving local governments and export companies greater autonomy in making contractual and credit arrangements with foreign businesses and government organizations was attempted in 1981 without much success but was endorsed by the Sixth National Party Congress in December 1986. Decentralization was blocked initially by Hanoi's desire to bring the economically livelier southern region of the country, with its latent market-economy orientation, under fuller economic and political control. Such control—exemplified by a 1983 crackdown on the ethnic Chinese commercial community in Ho Chi Minh City— sometimes took precedence over trade promotion. In early 1987, however, city officials reportedly were again encouraging local companies to engage freely in foreign trade, joint ventures, acquisition of technology, and foreign currency borrowing. Provinces, as early as 1986, were permitted to set their own trade regulations and develop export strategies in order to draw sufficient revenue to pay for imports needed to fulfill provincial plan targets.

Some twenty-seven state trading corporations and twenty-two local trading companies conducted business directly or indirectly with companies abroad during the 1980s, either producing export goods or purchasing them from suppliers. Imexco, the central umbrella organization, handled general administrative matters, leaving detailed operations to specialized corporations such as Agrexport and Vegetexco (foodstuffs and animal products); Maranimex (marine products); Naforimex (forest products); and Machineimport and Technoimport (machinery, plants, and equipment). Two specialized corporations, the Vietnam Foreign Trade Corporation and the Vietnam Ocean Shipping Agency, administered all sea transport and cargo handling, respectively. The Soviet-Vietnamese joint venture Vietsovpetro conducted offshore petroleum exploration.

In their day-to-day operations, the specialized trading corporations independently arranged contracts with producers, coordinated in-country transportation, and even designed packaging (for example, of fresh fruit or marine products) to improve freshness and quality control. The Number One Frozen Seafood Export Company, a highly profitable corporation, regularly sent its officials abroad to negotiate trade contracts for its popular frozen prawns and other seafood. In 1986 the company reportedly earned a profit of around US$17 million, chiefly in trade with Japan and Hong Kong (see table 10, Appendix A).

Direction and Composition of Trade

Trading patterns from 1978 through 1986 reflected the growing importance of Vietnam's relationship with Comecon and its weakening ties with major Western economies and noncommunist regional trading partners. Total trade with non-Comecon countries peaked at a little more than US$1 billion in 1978, dropped to less than US$700 million in 1982 and 1983, then averaged some US$850 million per year through 1986 (all dollar figures are given in terms of 1987 conversion rates). Two-way trade with the Soviet Union, that totaled about US$550 million in 1977, reached US$1.2 billion in 1981. This trade, which averaged some 43 percent of total trade from 1977 through 1980, accounted for about 64 percent of the total during the period of the Third Five-Year Plan. According to export plans announced by the Sixth National Party Congress in December 1986, two-way trade with the Soviet Union would continue to account for the major share of the country's foreign trade under the Fourth Five-Year Plan (see table 11, Appendix A).

In the 1980s, Vietnam's trade deficits with non-Comecon countries declined as the country's deficit with the Soviet Union grew. In 1977 and for several years thereafter, Vietnamese exports to its non-communist trade partners averaged less than 20 percent of the value of its imports from them. Exports to these countries increased slowly throughout the mid-1980s as imports declined. Most of the improvement resulted from substantive reductions in imports from eight major trading partners: Canada, Australia, France, Italy, the Federal Republic of Germany (West Germany), Sweden, Britain, and India. The reduction in imports resulted as much from Vietnamese self restraint and loss of trade credit as from politically motivated boycotts on trade with Vietnam, such as that observed by a number of Western and Asian Nations including the United States and the member nations of ASEAN. Vietnam's exports to several Western countries, including West Germany and Britain, increased, however, and the Vietnamese occasionally showed small positive trade balances with Australia and Canada in the mid-1980s. By 1986 Vietnam had reduced its balance-of-payments deficit with non-Comecon countries to less than US$300 million (compared with more than US$700 million annually in the late 1970s) and was exporting products worth half the value of its import bill. Trade with the Soviet Union, however, followed the opposite pattern. Vietnamese exports were valued at an average of 49 percent of imports from the Soviet Union in 1977 and 1978, but at less than 25 percent of imports from 1981 through 1986.

Foreign Investment Policy

In December 1987, the National Assembly approved a new foreign investment code in an apparent effort to bypass boycott restrictions and deal directly with Western and regional businesses. The legislation, which was much more liberal than foreign investment laws in use in other communist states, gave more concessions to foreign investors than similar Vietnamese laws that had been enacted in 1977. The new code used low taxes—20 to 30 percent of profits—to encourage joint ventures and permitted wholly owned foreign enterprises in Vietnam. The code, which was designed to emphasize the development of export industries and services, also granted full repatriation of profits after taxes and guaranteed foreign enterprises against government expropriation. The new law also encouraged oil exploration and production contracts.

Major Trading Partners

By 1982 Vietnam's most important noncommunist trading partners were Japan, Hong Kong, and Singapore. In 1985 these three partners together accounted for US$576 million in trade, approximately 65 percent of Vietnam's trade with non-Comecon countries. In 1986 Japan and Hong Kong together conducted more than 50 percent of Vietnam's non-Comecon trade. Much of the trade with Hong Kong and Singapore, however, was in goods either

during the Second Five-Year Plan to a 2,000 hectare plantation managed by the Phu Rieng Rubber Company in Song Be Province suggested that preserving the long-term development of this important rubber source may have been a critical Soviet concern. Finally, Vietnamese vodka shipments to the Soviet Union enabled the Soviet Union to increase exports of its own higher quality product to the hard-currency markets of the West.

The Soviet-Vietnamese trade plan additionally included Vietnamese exports of nonferrous metals, although according to its practice of some years the Soviet Union did not report transactions in this category. In 1983 the Soviet Union claimed that Soviet-assisted projects, such as the Tinh Tuc Tin Mine in Cao Bang Province, accounted for 100 percent of Vietnam's tin production.

External Debt

Vietnam is one of only two communist countries—the Democratic People's Republic of Korea (North Korea) is the other—to default on its international debts. Vietnam's scheduled 1982 payments to Western creditors were estimated at US$260 million, well over the US$182 million value of Vietnam's exports that year to noncommunist countries with hard, or convertible, currencies. The Soviets cancelled some US$450 million of Vietnam's debts in 1975 and began a program of grant aid. As Vietnam-Comecon trade expanded in the 1980s, however, so did Vietnamese debts to Comecon countries. Comecon funds for project assistance and related equipment often were wasted because of mismanagement or remained frozen for years in projects not scheduled to become productive until the middle or late 1980s. Projected exports frequently fell short of expectations, widening trade deficits and requiring additional balance-of-payments aid. Taking the long view, the Soviet Union shifted its assistance during the Third Five-Year Plan to concessionary loans, repayable at 2 percent interest over a period of 20 to 30 years.

As Vietnam's international debt grew steadily through the 1980s, the debt owed to the Soviet Union and other Comecon countries accounted for larger portions of the total foreign debt. In 1982, according to estimates by the Organization for Economic Cooperation and Development (OECD), Vietnam's total foreign debt was US$2.8 billion. Of this debt, US$1.7 billion, or 60 percent, was owed to OECD member countries (advanced industrial Western countries) and their capital markets or to multilateral lenders. A large portion of Vietnam's international debt covered the balance of payments deficit with Comecon countries (see Foreign Economic Assistance, this ch.). In 1987 Le Hoang, deputy director of the

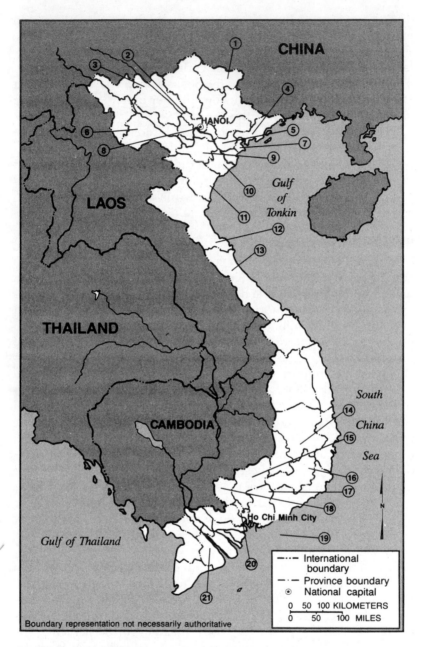

Source: Based on information from *Soren To Betonamu Tono Kyoryokukankei*, translated in Foreign Broadcast Information Service, *Southeast Asia Report*, March 19, 1985, 66–136.

Figure 12. Soviet Cooperation Projects, 1985

KEY TO SOVIET COOPERATION PROJECTS, 1985

1. Tinh Tuc Tin Mine and Plant

2. Lam Thao Superphosphate of Lime Plant
   Battery factory

3. Lao Cai Apatite Mine
   Thac Ba Hydroelectric Power Plant

4. Ha Tu Coal Mine
   Cao Son Coal Mine
   Mong Duong Coal Mine
   Vang Danh Coal Mine
   Quang Ninh Coal Mine
   Vang Dinh Coal Mine
   Uong Bi Hydroelectric Power Plant
   Uong Bi Vietnam-USSR Miners School
   Cam Pha Central Machine Plant
   Flour mill

5. Pha Lai Thermal Power Plant

6. Moc Chau Tea-Manufacturing Plant

7. Vietnam-USSR Farm Machinery Technicians School
   Truck repair workshop
   Haiphong port expansion

8. Dong Anh Electric Equipment Repair Workshop
   Giap Bac Automobile Servicing Plant
   Xuan Mai Prefab Housing Concrete Slab Factory
   Thang Long Bridge
   Branch of the Pushkin Russian Language School
   Meterological station
   Computer center
   USSR-Vietnam joint tropical weather research facility
   Ho Chi Minh Mausoleum
   Labor Cultural Center
   Ky An Scientific Research Center

9. Natural gas development
   Gas turbine power plant
   Hoa Binh Hydroelectric Power Plant
   Song Cong Diesel Engine Factory

10. Lotus One Inter-Sputnik Satellite Communications Ground Station

11. Bim Son Cement Factory
    Kien Chau Cement Factory

12. Vinh-Vientiane, Loas 500-kilometer oil pipeline

13. Dong Hoi diesel-powered electric generating plant

14. Farm machinery repair workshop

15. Phu Rieng Rubber Company

16. Bao Loc Tractor Servicing Plant
    Da Lat Nuclear Reactor

17. Tri An Hydroelectric Power Plant

18. Automobile servicing plant
    Trang Bang Tractor Repair Workshop

19. Vung Tau offshore: continental shelf oil and natural gas development

20. Automobile and tractor repair workshop
    Cu Chi Farm Machinery and Maintenance Workshop
    Meteorological radar observation post
    Lotus Two Inter-Sputnik Satellite Communcations Ground Station

21. Phung Hiep Farm Machinery Repair Plant

State Bank of Vietnam, told a Western correspondent that the country owed between US$5.5 and US$6 billion to Comecon member countries. Hoang stated that Vietnam's debts (both official and private) to hard-currency countries were about US$1 billion.

Creditors in convertible-currency areas included international organizations such as the IMF and the Asian Development Bank; national creditors such as Belgium, Denmark, France, India, Japan, and the Netherlands; and private creditors in numerous Western countries. In January 1985, the IMF suspended further credit when Vietnam failed to meet a repayment schedule on the amount owed to the fund. Talks to reschedule the obligation failed in 1987, making Vietnam ineligible for fresh funding. In 1987 Vietnam owed the fund some US$90 million. Its foreign exchange reserves in 1985 had been estimated at less than US$20 million.

Foreign Economic Assistance

In the late 1970s, Vietnam relied heavily on economic assistance from both Western and Soviet-bloc donors to finance major development projects, to underwrite its fledgling export industries, and to meet balance of payments deficits. Following Vietnam's acceptance of closer ties with the Soviet Union, its incursion into Cambodia in December 1978, and its border fighting with China in early 1979, aid from China and from Western countries and multilateral organizations dropped, slowing development.

Offshore oil exploration with the assistance of West German, Italian, and Canadian companies ended in 1981, but resumed subsequently with Soviet technical assistance. Aid from China, reportedly close to US$300 million in 1977 and 1978, dropped to zero in 1979, and Vietnamese recovery in coal production was profoundly affected by the accompanying loss of ethnic Chinese workers. In 1979 Japan suspended its Official Development Assistance funds (a mixture of grants and low-interest loans amounting to US$135 million) and made renewal contingent upon Vietnamese withdrawal from Cambodia. Loss of other Western aid in hard currencies crippled Vietnam's ability to continue importing needed modern machinery and technology from its West European trading partners. Following Vietnam's occupation of Cambodia, only Sweden continued to provide any significant amount of economic help. Some multilateral assistance, such as that for development of the Mekong River, was made available by the United Nations Economic and Social Commission for Asia and the Pacific, however. Western and multilateral assistance, therefore, did not stop entirely, although the yearly average of about US$100 million through 1986 provided only a fraction of the country's hard-currency needs.

In 1986 Vietnam's current account deficit with major industrial countries was some US$221 million. The conflicts with Cambodia and China in 1978 and 1979 proved particularly costly in terms of continuing economic ties with Western and neighboring Asian countries. As a result, Hanoi was forced to rely even more heavily on Soviet-bloc assistance.

The Soviet Union and other members of Comecon increased their aid commitments as their own planning became more closely coordinated with Vietnam's following Hanoi's entry into Comecon in June 1978. Soviet economic aid in 1978, estimated at between US$0.7 and 1.0 billion, was already higher than Western assistance. By 1982 it had increased to more than US$1 billion annually, close to US$3 million per day, and it remained at this level through the mid-1980s. The Soviet Union and other Comecon countries provided aid in all categories—project assistance, technical training, price subsidies, loans, and trade credits. Soviet publications emphasized the importance of project assistance to Vietnam's economic recovery, but about 75 percent of the value of aid disbursed during the Third Five-Year Plan was used to finance Vietnam's bilateral trade deficit with the Soviet Union, which averaged about US$896 million a year. Trade subsidies in the form of reduced prices for Soviet oil also declined sharply in the early 1980s as the Soviet Union brought Vietnam into the Comecon oil-pricing system based on world market values.

Although the details of Comecon assistance to Vietnam since the 1970s had not been made public as of late 1987, Soviet sources gave some indications of the type of project assistance provided and were quick to claim credit for production increases attributable to Soviet technical and plant assistance. Soviet-aid goals from 1978 to 1981 included helping with balance-of-payments problems, assisting with key projects, introducing industrial cooperation, accelerating scientific and technical cooperation, and assisting with the improvement of Vietnamese professional skills. During this period, the Soviet Union also signed numerous agreements calling for financial and technical assistance in matters ranging from traffic-improvement programs for the railroad from Hanoi to Ho Chi Minh City to completing construction of the Thang Long Bridge over the Red River (see Transportation, this ch.).

Overseas Remittances

During the 1980s, informal aid in the form of packages and remittances from overseas Vietnamese played an important role in improving the living standards of many families, maintaining the domestic economy, and boosting the country's holdings of hard

currency. Vietnamese customs officials in 1983 told a Western journalist that packages from overseas relatives—valued at some US$70
million annually in Western products—generated between US$10
million and US$20 million annually in customs revenues alone.
Remittances from overseas Vietnamese were believed to provide
an additional US$100 million or more in annual foreign exchange
earnings.

Finance

Budget

The government allocated resources through its annual plan,
which in the 1980s included the annual budget and credit plan.
The Ministry of Finance, in consultation with the State Planning
Commission, prepared the budget for approval by the Standing
Committee of the National Assembly. Both the fiscal year (FY—
see Glossary) and the annual plan year corresponded to the Western
calendar year.

The state budget included the revenues and expenditures of the
central government, 38 provincial governments, and more than
500 local governments. The state economic enterprises forwarded
the bulk of their profits to the state treasury. Tax revenue accounted
for about one-third of total budgetary revenue.

Tax measures introduced in 1983 included the imposition of new
agricultural levies based on the potential output of collectives rather
than actual per capita output and the actual output from private
plots (previously exempted from the agricultural tax). In addition,
more enterprises were made subject to taxation. Subsequently, total
tax revenue from agricultural as well as nonagricultural cooperatives and the private sector increased, reflecting higher official and
free-market prices, more efficient tax collection, and the continued
expansion of economic activity.

In the 1980s, Vietnamese authorities did not release budget
figures. Data prepared for the 1984 visit of IMF officials, however,
revealed a 1983 budget deficit of D20 billion (approximately US$2.2
billion), largely financed by increases in the money supply, the sale
of taxes paid in kind, the sale of government-enterprise products,
aid in kind, and the various taxes levied on the free market. These
revenues were offset by large outlays on employment in the state
sector and purchases (primarily of agricultural products) from
peasants and cooperatives. The payment of bonuses to production
workers, the attempt to match free-market prices, and the high level
of food subsidies to the urban population also constituted major
budget expenditures.

Money Supply

The increase in prices and wages, as well as a mismanaged devaluation of the dong in the early 1980s, contributed to increases in the demand for credit and in the actual amount of currency in circulation. Domestic credit subsequently increased to reflect the large price adjustments that were made, the increase in inventories, and the emergence of bank-financed budget deficits. Credit to the commercial sector accounted for nearly half the total outstanding capital-credit. The expansion of domestic credit was reflected in a proportional expansion in liquidity. Total deposits rose significantly, and the volume of cash in circulation increased. Interest rates were adjusted accordingly in order to restrain growth in credit and the amount of cash in circulation. The rate on savings deposits was raised, and lending rates were lowered to reflect higher deposit rates.

Inflation

The ill-conceived monetary-reform plan introduced in late 1985 set in motion unprecedented inflation. Hanoi replaced the old D10 note with a new D1 note and devalued the dong's foreign exchange rate from D1.20 to US$1 to D15 to US$1. A leak about the planned currency change and the unavailability of new notes of small denominations, however, defeated the goal of contracting the money supply by eliminating illegal cash holdings. As a result, inflation increased from about 50 percent in late 1985 to 700 percent by September 1986.

In implementing the reform, the government deprived both private and state-run enterprises of large amounts of cash they held for operating expenses. A Vietnamese economist estimated that half the cash in circulation was held by public enterprises for the purpose of expanding production. Most enterprises held their earnings in cash because the banking system encouraged only deposits and not withdrawals.

To curb inflation, the government directed its efforts at lowering prices by imposing state regulations. Price subsidies were reintroduced, and, in the face of widespread shortages and hoarding, the rationing of essential goods also was reinstituted.

Prices and Wages

During the early 1980s, the trend was toward greater price flexibility, but prices of both intermediate and consumer goods continued to be determined largely by the central government. Prices of agricultural and non-agricultural cooperative products were closely related to the government's procurement policy and the two-way contract system. Under this system, the government assigned production quotas. Production achieved in excess of the quota could then be sold either to the government at negotiated prices or to buyers in the free market. Negotiated prices normally were higher than quota prices but lower than free-market prices.

Prices of the products of state-owned enterprises were established on the basis of average cost norms, applicable taxes, and a fixed profit margin. Production in excess of quotas or from inputs not supplied by the state could be sold at higher prices, enabling producers to recoup input cost while providing an incentive for above-quota production.

Consumer prices for commodities distributed by the state were different from those for products distributed in the free market. Official consumer prices fell into three categories depending on the type of goods as well as on the type of consumer. The first two categories consisted of essential commodities, such as rice, pork, textiles, and soap, which were distributed under rations at two different price levels. Civil servants, workers in state enterprises, and selected groups of consumers, such as students, pensioners and welfare recipients, were permitted to purchase these goods at substantial subsidies. A third price category for the same commodities was based on cost and was reserved for members of cooperatives and for individuals associated with contract work for the government. The subsidized prices remained unchanged for twenty years, but the cost-based prices continued to rise.

Party leaders at the Central Committee's Eighth Plenum (Fifth Congress) in 1985 experimented with eliminating fixed prices and removing subsidies on staples, thus causing a price increase for basic items. At the Second Plenum (Sixth Congress) held in April 1987, a policy of rational pricing based on cost and projected consumer demand was implemented for industries.

Wage increases of between 90 and 110 percent were granted in mid-1981 to civil servants and employees of state enterprises. Before the wage increase, state employees had benefited from access to state-supplied commodities at subsidized prices. Afterwards, purchases of state-supplied commodities, as part of the total expenditures of civil servants and manual laborers, fell, a development that contributed to a decline in the real incomes of these workers.

Reform measures introduced in 1985 instituted major changes in wage policy. Beginning at that time, wages were determined on the basis of performance and paid in cash. Previously wages had been paid partly or entirely in kind. Government employees (including the military) received a further increase in salary but lost the supplements to their income that had previously included food subsidies. Wages for workers in state-run factories were increased at the April 1987 party plenum but any wage increases were directly translated into, and offset by, higher prices.

Banking

Following its reorganization in 1976, the State Bank of Vietnam (formerly the National Bank of Vietnam) became the central bank of the country. In addition to its national financial responsibilities, the State Bank also assumed some of the duties of a commercial bank. It maintained a head office in Hanoi, a division in Ho Chi Minh City, and numerous provincial branches. Other important banks operating in Vietnam in 1988 included the Foreign Trade Bank, which was charged with overseeing all aspects of foreign payments, and the Bank for Agricultural Development, which provided loans to agriculture and fishing.

The first solely commercial bank opened in Ho Chi Minh City in July 1987 to handle personal savings and to extend loans to enterprises and individuals. The bank was capitalized with D500 million (US$1.4 million) provided by the government and through stock issues. One objective in establishing Vietnam's first commercial bank was to limit inflation through the bank's ability to coordinate the extension of credit.

To attract more foreign exchange, the Foreign Trade Bank opened an account in 1987 for overseas Vietnamese remittances of foreign currencies to their relatives at home. The currencies dealt with were United States dollars, French francs, Swiss francs, Hong Kong dollars, Canadian dollars, British pounds, Japanese yen, Australian dollars, and West German marks. In 1987 the bank also agreed to establish a finance company in Tokyo in partnership with a Japanese bank. As the first joint venture between the two countries, the proposed company was intended to help settle bilateral trade accounts, but it was also expected to assist in technology transfers.

Transportation

As described by the Vietnamese government, the economy in the 1980s suffered from the "backwardness" of the transport system. The system's inadequate development constituted a major impediment to industrial development, created bottlenecks in the circulation of goods and supplies, and constrained domestic trade. The importance of transportation development was emphasized at the Sixth National Party Congress in December 1986, and confirmed at the Central Committee's Second Plenum in April 1987.

The plenum urged state cooperatives, private enterprises, and individuals to invest in expanding the transportation sector and to engage in transportation services that would benefit business (see fig. 13).

Damage to the transportation structure was extensive during the latter half of the Second Indochina War, particularly in the North, and the 1979 Chinese invasion severely interdicted rail transport near the Chinese border, but Vietnamese transportation statistics also indicated a lack of development from 1975 through 1980. In 1980 total cargo transported amounted to 42.3 million tons, an increase of only 4.2 percent over the 40.6 million tons transported in 1970. Cargo carried by rail totaled only 3.5 million tons in 1980, compared with 4.5 million tons in 1965. In terms of volume hauled over distance traveled, 758 million tons per kilometer were transported by rail in 1980, a figure not significantly greater than that measured in 1965 (749 million tons per kilometer). A 30-percent increase in the average rail distance traveled per shipment in 1980 (from 166 kilometers to 216 kilometers) was attributed to expanded shipments from the South to the North.

In 1987 Vietnamese road and railroad construction figures for the period of the Second Five-Year Plan were contradictory. Construction figures indicated that 1,500 kilometers of new roads were built and 137 kilometers of new railroad track were laid during this time, but the plan's fulfillment report cited 3,800 kilometers of road constructed and 2,000 kilometers of main and auxiliary track laid for the North-South railroad. Vietnamese reports to Comecon showed that total track increased by 837 kilometers to reach a total of 2,900 kilometers in 1980. Repair of war damage to the rail system and construction of new sidings, however, took up much of the effort that might otherwise have been directed toward expanding the rail system.

The profitability and efficiency of the railroad transportation system had declined even before the system was damaged by the Chinese invasion in 1979. According to a Vietnamese transportation economist, profit per dong of fixed-capital investment decreased from D0.17 in 1964 to D0.04 in 1978. The same source calculated that the productivity per railcar declined from 1,999 tons per kilometer per day in 1960 to 784 tons per kilometer per day in 1978. Comparable estimates for road transportation were not available; however, the aging truck stock and the severe parts shortages experienced in the late 1970s, which left trucks inoperable or cannibalized, suggested that road transportation was at least as problematic as rail transportation.

In 1985 Vietnam had approximately 85,000 kilometers of roads and 4,250 kilometers of railroad. According to Vietnamese officials, 238 kilometers of railroad and nearly 3,500 kilometers of road had been built in the ten years since reunification. The principal road and rail routes linked Hanoi to Ho Chi Minh City (1,730 kilometers), Hanoi to Haiphong (102 kilometers), Hanoi to Muc Quan (176 kilometers), Hanoi to Thanh Hoa (160 kilometers), and Hanoi to Lao Cai (295 kilometers). Railroads were in working order but needed substantial repair and restoration. Track running from Nha Trang, Phu Khanh Province, to Qui Nhon, Nghia Binh Province was completed between 1983 and 1984 by a French development-aid team.

Dozens of kilometers of bridges were constructed between 1975 and 1985. With Soviet assistance, Vietnam rebuilt the Thang Long bridge over the Red River, north of Hanoi. The country's longest bridge, extending 1,688 meters, it had been destroyed during the Second Indochina War. Other bridges were built on the national highway in central Vietnam and in the Mekong River Delta. The road system in the 1980s included 9,400 kilometers with a bituminous surface, 48,700 kilometers with a gravel or improved earth surface, and 26,900 kilometers with an unimproved earth roadbed.

Haiphong, Ho Chi Minh City, and Da Nang were the largest of nine major and twenty-three minor ports. Port capacity in the late 1970s and early 1980s increased greatly. Haiphong's wharves reportedly grew to 1,700 meters and were served by 3,600 meters of railroad track and 2,000 meters of crane track. Covered and open storage were increased to 90,000 square meters. Despite efforts to enlarge and equip the ports, however, they remained the weakest link in Vietnam's transportation system.

In early 1985, the Vietnamese portion of a 500-kilometer oil pipeline linking the seaport of Vinh in Nghe Tinh Province to Vientiane, Laos, was completed with Soviet assistance. The project was expected to provide Laos with an annual supply of 300,000 tons of petroleum and gas, some of which was to be used by Vietnamese army units stationed there.

The Vietnamese merchant fleet was upgraded with Soviet assistance. The Soviets installed and ran a sophisticated coastal freighter and barge system between Haiphong and Soviet Pacific Ocean ports. The system apparently was designed to transport military hardware in a secure manner. Vietnam also cooperated with Thailand and Laos in improving the navigability of the Mekong River under the auspices of the UN Mekong Committee. Navigable inland waterways totaled about 17,702 kilometers, of which more

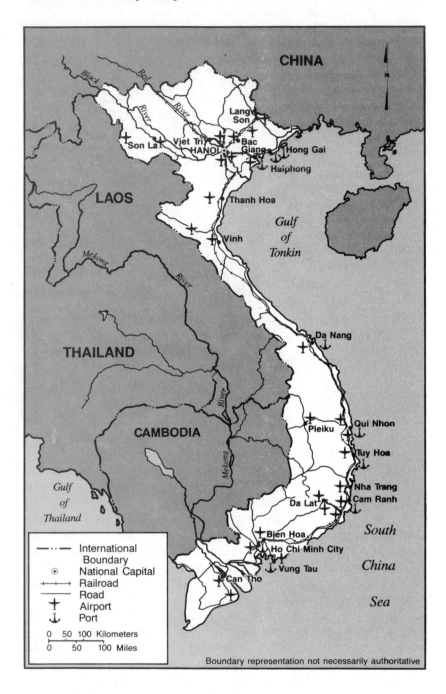

Figure 13. Transportation System, 1987

than 5,149 kilometers were navigable at all times by vessels of up to 1.8 meters in draft. According to Vietnamese statistics for the years 1984 and 1985, marine transport had increased by 2.2 times the level in 1976.

Civil aviation in the 1980s was controlled by the military and based primarily at two international airports, Noi Bai in Hanoi and Tan Son Nhut in Ho Chi Minh City. Domestically, Hanoi was linked by regular service to Phu Bai, Nha Trang, Da Nang, Pleiku, Da Lat, Buon Me Thuot, and Ho Chi Minh City. Ho Chi Minh City also was connected by regularly scheduled flights to Rach Gia, Phu Quoc, and Con Son Island. The aircraft used were Soviet-made.

In March 1983, commercial air service between Hanoi and Moscow was opened by Aeroflot. Air Vietnam, in the late 1980s, connected Hanoi with Vientiane, Phnom Penh and Bangkok, and Air France provided regular flights to Ho Chi Minh City from Bangkok. The number of airfields totaled 217, of which 128 were usable and 46 had permanently surfaced runways. Twelve had runways from 2,440 to 3,659 meters in length, and 28 maintained runways of 1,220 to 2,439 meters.

Telecommunications

By 1985 Vietnam possessed two satellite-ground stations constructed with the assistance of the Soviet Union. The Lotus One satellite communication station was located in Ha Nam Ninh Province, 100 kilometers south of Hanoi, and served to integrate Vietnam into the Soviet Intersputnik Communication Satellite Organization. Construction began in January 1979 and was completed in July 1980 in time for the Moscow Olympics. Lotus Two was inaugurated near Ho Chi Minh City in April 1985 to broadcast the ceremonies celebrating the tenth anniversary of the end of the Second Indochina War. The system linked Moscow, Hanoi, and Ho Chi Minh City, and the two stations were reportedly manned entirely by Soviet personnel. A French telecommunications company was installing a modern nationwide telephone system in 1987.

The installation of a national telephone system symbolized Hanoi's acknowledgement of the country's critical need to formulate an integrated development plan that would tap the country's economic potential on a national scale. It also demonstrated the pragmatic character of a new generation of leaders who had risen to power in the mid-1980s and appeared more willing than the nation's past leadership to risk economic and political reform for the sake of modernization. Reforms undertaken during this time were greeted by outside observers as a promising sign that the nation's economy might be moving at last out of its prolonged stagnation.

* * *

Information on Vietnam's economy can be found in Vietnamese newspaper and journal articles translated and published by the Foreign Broadcast Information Service and the Joint Publications Research Service of the United States government. Additional material is published by some of Vietnam's trading partners; especially useful is the *Statistical Yearbook of the Comecon Countries,* published annually by the Soviet government.

Another valuable source that combines data with some analysis is the *Quarterly Economic Review of Indochina* published by the Economist Intelligence Unit (EIU). Analytical articles are most readily found in the *Far Eastern Economic Review* and in the yearly summary issues published by *Asian Survey.* (For further information and complete citations, see Bibliography.)

Chapter 4. Government and Politics

Ho Chi Minh and General Vo Nguyen Giap plan Dien Bien Phu campaign, March 1954.

THE SOCIALIST REPUBLIC OF VIETNAM (SRV) is governed through a highly centralized system dominated by the Vietnamese Communist Party (VCP, Viet Nam Cong San Dang). As the force controlling the system, the party exercises leadership in all matters. The government manages state affairs through a structure that parallels the party's apparatus, but it is incapable of acting without party direction. All key government positions are filled by party members.

Society is ruled by the party's ubiquitous presence, which is manifested in a network of party cadres at almost every level of social activity. All citizens are expected to be members of one or another of the mass organizations led by party cadres, and all managers and military officials are ultimately answerable to party representatives.

The VCP in the mid-1980s was in a state of transition and experimentation. It was a time when a number of party leaders, who had been contemporaries of Ho Chi Minh (1890–1969), were stepping down in favor of a younger generation of pragmatists and technocrats, and a time when the prolonged poor condition of the economy sparked discontent among grass-roots party organizations as well as open criticism of the party's domestic policy. The party's political ethos, which had once seemed to embody the traditional Vietnamese spirit of resistance to foreigners and which had known great success when the country was overwhelmingly dominated by war and the issues of national liberation and reunification, appeared to have changed after the fall of the Republic of Vietnam (South Vietnam) in the spring of 1975 and the reunification of Vietnam in 1976. This ethos had been at the core of the VCP's rise to power during the struggles for independence and unification. To a large degree, the popularity of the communist movement remained tied to these causes; when victory over the South was achieved in 1975, it became apparent that some of the party's governing principles did not easily translate to peacetime conditions. In the absence of war, the ethos changed and the difference between what was communist and what was popular became increasingly noticeable.

Hanoi was apparently unprepared for the scale of its victory in the South, having anticipated that the path to complete power would require at the very least a transition period of shared power with the Southern communist infrastructure (the Provisional Revolutionary Government) and even elements of the incumbent order.

Two separate governments in North and South Vietnam were planned until the surprisingly swift disintegration of the South Vietnamese government eliminated the need for a lengthy transition. Following the establishment of communist control in the South, the government immediately was placed under a Military Management Commission, directed by Senior Lieutenant General Tran Van Tra with the assistance of local People's Revolutionary Committees. At a reunification conference in November 1975, the Party's plans for uniting North and South were announced, and elections for a single National Assembly—the highest state organ—(see Glossary) were held on April 26, 1976, the first anniversary of the Southern victory. The Socialist Republic of Vietnam was formally named at the first session of the Sixth National Assembly (the "Unification Assembly"), which met from June 24 to July 2, 1976.

After reunification, the focus of policy became more diffuse. Policy makers, absorbed with incorporating the South into the communist order as quickly as possible, were confronted with both dissension within the North's leadership and southern resistance to the proposed pace of change. The drive undertaken by party ideologues to eliminate all vestiges of capitalism and to collectivize the economy in the South was outlined in the Second Five-Year Plan (1976–80) and announced at the Fourth National Party Congress in December 1976. The plan, the first after reunification, stressed the development of agriculture and light industry, but it set unattainably high goals. The government expected that all industry and agriculture in the South would be state-controlled by the end of 1979. According to Vietnamese sources, however, only 66 percent of cultivated land and 72 percent of peasant households in the South had been organized into collectivized production by early 1985, and socialist transformation in private industry had led to decreased production, increased production costs, and decreased product quality. Meanwhile, the country's leaders were finding it necessary to divert their attention to a number of other equally pressing issues. Besides addressing the many problems of the country's newly unified economy, they also had to work out postwar relations with Cambodia, China, and the Soviet Union. The Sixth National Party Congress held in December 1986 was a watershed for party policy in the 1980s. The party's political mood was accurately reflected in the congress' candid acknowledgment of existing economic problems and in its seeming willingness to change in order to solve them. A new atmosphere of experimentation and reform, apparently reinforced by reforms initiated by the Soviet Union's new leadership, was introduced, setting the stage for a period of self-examination, the elimination of corrupt party officials, and new economic policies.

Development of the Vietnamese Communist Party

The state Constitution adopted in 1980 describes the party as "the only force leading the state and society and the main factor determining all successes of the Vietnamese revolution." The party's role is primary in all state activities, overriding that of the government, which functions merely to implement party policies. The party maintains control by filling key positions in all government agencies with party leaders or the most trusted party cadres and by controlling all mass organizations. Citizens belong to mass organizations appropriate to their status, such as the quasi-governmental Vietnam Fatherland Front, the Vietnam General Confederation of Trade Unions, or the Ho Chi Minh Communist Youth League (see Party Organization, this ch.). Party cadres leading such organizations educate and mobilize the masses through regular study sessions to implement party policies.

Although party congresses are rare events in Vietnam, they provide a record of the party's history and direction and tend to reflect accurately the important issues of their time. In February 1930 in Hong Kong, Ho Chi Minh presided over the founding congress of the VCP. At the direction of the Communist International (Comintern—see Glossary), the party's name was changed shortly afterwards to the Indochinese Communist Party (ICP). The designated First National Party Congress following the party's founding was held secretly in Macao in 1935, coincidentally with the convocation in Moscow of the Seventh Congress of the Comintern. At the Seventh Congress, the Comintern modified its "united front" strategy for world revolution chiefly to protect the Soviet Union from the rise of fascism. Member parties were instructed to join in popular fronts with noncommunist parties to preserve world socialism in the face of fascism's new threat. Although the Vietnamese party subsequently adopted the strategy, the timing of the two meetings dictated that the Vietnamese in Macao wait until after their meeting for directions from Moscow. Consequently, the resolutions enunciated at the ICP's first congress turned out to be only provisional because they stressed the older and narrower concept of the united front that divided the world into imperialist and socialist camps but failed to account for fascism. Under the new strategy, the ICP considered all nationalist parties in Indochina as potential allies. The Second National Party Congress was held in 1951 in Tuyen Quang, a former province in Viet Bac, a remote region of the North Vietnamese highlands controlled by the Viet Minh (see Glossary) during the First Indochina War (see Glossary—also known as the Viet Minh War). It reestablished the ICP, which had been officially dissolved in 1945 to obscure the party's communist affiliation, and renamed it the Vietnam Workers' Party (VWP, Dang Lao Dong Viet Nam). Nine years later in Hanoi, the Third National Party Congress formalized the tasks required to construct a socialist society in the North and to carry out a revolution in the South.

The Fourth National Party Congress, which convened in December 1976, was the first such congress held after the country's reunification. Reflecting the party's sense of rebirth, the congress changed the party's name from the Vietnam Workers' Party to the Vietnam Communist Party. This congress was significant for disclosing the party's plans for a unified Vietnam and for initiating the party's most widespread leadership changes up to that time. The delegates adopted a new party Statute, replacing one that had been ratified in 1960 when the country was divided. The new Statute was directed at the country as a whole but focused on the application of Marxist-Leninist principles in the South, stating that the party's goal was to "realize socialism and communism in Vietnam." It further described the VCP as the "vanguard, organized combat staff, and highest organization" of the Vietnamese working class, and a "united bloc of will and action" structured on the principle of democratic centralism (see Glossary). Democratic centralism is a fundamental organizational principle of the party, and, according to the 1976 Statute, it mandates not only the "activity and creativity" of all party organizations but also "guarantees the party's unity of will and action." As a result of unification, the Central Committee expanded from 77 to 133 members, the 11-member Political Bureau of the Central Committee grew to 17, including 3 alternate or candidate members, and the Secretariat of the Central Committee increased from 7 to 9. More than half of the members of the Central Committee were first-time appointees, many of whom came from the southern provinces.

Membership in the party doubled from 760,000 in 1966 to 1,553,500 in 1976, representing 3.1 percent of the total population. Comparable figures for China (4.2 percent) and the Soviet Union (6.9 percent) in 1986 suggest that the 1976 proportion of party membership to total population in Vietnam was small. Nevertheless, the doubling of the party's size in the space of a decade was cause for concern to Vietnam's leaders, who feared that a decline in the party's selection standards had resulted in increased inefficiency and corruption. They believed that quantity had been

Ho Chi Minh's tomb in Hanoi
Courtesy Bill Herod

substituted for quality and resolved to stress quality in the future. In an effort to purify the party, growth over the next decade was deliberately checked. Membership in 1986 was close to 2 million, only about 3.3 percent of the population. According to Hanoi's estimates, nearly 10 percent, or 200,000 party members, were expelled for alleged inefficiency, corruption, or other failures between 1976 and 1986.

Turning to the economy, the Fourth National Party Congress transferred the party's emphasis on heavy industry, initiated at the Third National Party Congress, to light industry, fishing, forestry, and agriculture. It directed attention to the Second Five-Year Plan, which was already a year old (see Economic Roles of the Party and the Government, ch.3). The Fourth National Party Congress also introduced a number of economic objectives, including establishment on a national scale of a new system of economic management, better use of prices to regulate supply and demand, budgets to implement economic development programs, tax policy to control sources of income, and banks to supply capital for production. Finally, differences over the role of the military surfaced at the congress, dividing party pragmatists, who saw the army as a supplement to the labor force, from the more doctrinaire theoreticians, who saw the military as a fighting force, the primary mission of which would be obstructed by economic tasks.

The Fifth National Party Congress, held in March 1982, confirmed Vietnam's alignment with the Soviet Union but revealed a breach in party unity and indecision on economic policy. An unprecedented six members of the Political Bureau were retired, including Vo Nguyen Giap, defense minister and former chief military strategist in the wars against France and the United States, and Nguyen Van Linh, future party general secretary who later returned to the Political Bureau in June 1985. The six who departed, however, were from the middle ranks of the Political Bureau. The topmost leaders—from General Secretary Le Duan to fifth-ranked member Le Duc Tho—remained in their posts. Thirty-four full members and twelve alternate members of the Central Committee also were dropped. The new Central Committee was increased from 133 members and 32 alternate members to 152 members and 36 alternate members. Party strength had grown to 1.7 million.

The Sixth National Party Congress, held in December 1986, was characterized by candid evaluations of the party and more leadership changes. There was an extraordinary outpouring of self-criticism over the party's failure to improve the economy. A new commitment was made to revive the economy but in a more moderate manner. The policy of the Sixth National Party Congress thus attempted to balance the positions of radicals, who urged a quicker transition to socialism through collectivization, and moderates, who urged increased reliance on free-market forces. Three of the country's top leaders voluntarily retired from their party positions: VCP General Secretary and President Truong Chinh, aged seventy-nine; second-ranked Political Bureau member and Premier Pham Van Dong, aged seventy-nine; and party theoretician and fourth-ranked Political Bureau member (without government portfolio) Le Duc Tho, aged seventy-five (see Appendix B). Afterwards, they took up positions as advisers, with unspecified powers, to the Central Committee. Chinh and Dong retained their government posts until the new National Assembly met in June 1987. Their simultaneous retirement was unusual in that leaders of Communist nations tend either to die in office or to be purged, but it paved the way for younger, better educated leaders to rise to the top.

Nguyen Van Linh, an economic pragmatist, was named party general secretary. The new Political Bureau had 14 members, and the new Central Committee was expanded to 173, including 124 full members and 49 alternate members. In continuing the trend to purify party ranks by replacing old members, the Sixth Party Congress replaced approximately one-third of the Central Committee members with thirty-eight new full members and forty-three

Ho Chi Minh addresses the Third National Party Congress (September 1960), flanked by Le Duan and Truong Chinh.
Courtesy Indochina Archives

new alternate members. It expanded the Secretariat from ten members to thirteen, only three of whom had previously served.

Party Organization

The Party Congress and the Central Committee

As stipulated in the party Statute, the National Party Congress (or National Congress of Party Delegates) is the party's highest organ. Because of its unwieldy size (the Sixth National Party Congress held in December 1986 was attended by 1,129 delegates), the infrequency with which it meets (once every 5 years or when a special situation arises), and its de facto subordinate position to the party's Central Committee, which it elects, the National Party Congress lacks real power. In theory, the congress establishes party policy, but in actuality it functions as a rubber stamp for the policies of the Political Bureau, the Central Committee's decision-making body. The primary role of the National Party Congress is to provide a forum for reports on party programs since the last congress, to ratify party directives for the future, and to elect a Central Committee. Once these duties are performed, the congress adjourns, leaving the Central Committee, which has a term of five years, to implement the policies of the congress.

The Central Committee—the party organization in which political power is formally vested—meets more frequently than the National Party Congress—at least twice annually in forums called plenums—and is much smaller in size (the Central Committee elected at the Sixth National Party Congress in December 1986 numbered 124 full members and 49 alternate members). Like the National Party Congress, however, it usually acts to confirm rather than establish policy. In reality, the creation of policy is the prerogative of the Political Bureau, which the Central Committee elects and to which it delegates all decision-making authority.

The Political Bureau, composed of the party's highest ranking members, is the party's supreme policy-making body; it possesses unlimited decision- and policy-making powers. At the Sixth National Party Congress, the Central Committee elected thirteen full members and one alternate member to the Political Bureau.

Acting in administrative capacities under the direction of the Political Bureau are a party Secretariat, a Central Control Commission, and a Central Military Party Committee. The Secretariat is the most important of these three bodies, overseeing the party and day-to-day implementation of policies set by the Political Bureau. In 1986 the Secretariat, headed by the party general secretary, was expanded from ten to thirteen members. Five of the Secretariat's members held concurrent positions on the Political Bureau: Nguyen Van Linh, Nguyen Duc Tam, Tran Xuan Bach, Dao Duy Tung, and Do Muoi. Among its roles are the supervision of Central Committee departments concerned with party organization, propaganda and training, foreign affairs, finance, science and education, and industry and agriculture. In 1986 there existed a seven-member Central Control Commission, appointed by the Central Committee and charged with investigating reports of party irregularities. A Central Military Party Committee with an undisclosed number of members, also appointed by the Central Committee, controlled the party's military affairs. In 1987, party committees throughout the armed forces were under the supervision of the People's Army of Vietnam's (PAVN—see Glossary) Directorate General for Political Affairs, which, in turn, was responsible to the Central Military Party Committee. These committees maintained close relationships with local civilian party committees (see fig. 14).

Other Party Organizations

Party caucuses operate throughout the government and mass organizations. Using assorted methods of persuasion and proselytization, they implement party lines, policies, and resolutions;

increase party influence and unity; and develop and propose guide-lines and programs for mass organizations and party committees at various administrative levels. Party caucuses are responsible for appointing political cadres to serve as delegates or to hold key posi-tions in such government organizations as the National Assembly and the people's councils, or in such party organizations as the party congresses and the mass organizations (see The System of Government, this ch.). In state agencies where the "manager sys-tem" is practiced—those in which party cadres have been appointed officially to management positions—the functions of party caucuses are assumed by coordination and operations committees.

The chapter is the basic party unit. It numbers from three to thirty members depending upon whether it represents a produc-tion, work, or military unit. Larger groups, such as factories or cooperatives, may have more than one party chapter. A chapter's chief responsibilities are to indoctrinate party members and to pro-vide political leadership for production units and the armed forces.

Cadres are party members in leadership positions. They func-tion at all levels of party organization but are most numerous at lower levels. The strength of the cadre system is its ability to mobi-lize the people quickly. Its weaknesses include abuse of power, which is facilitated by the absence of enforced standards of conduct, and over-reliance by the higher echelons on the lower. The higher party leaders tolerate the excesses of lower echelon cadres because the lower-level representatives tend to be well entrenched in local society and in the best position to influence the people. Higher officials simply lack the clout to motivate the people as well.

Front Organizations

The purpose of front organizations is to mobilize and recruit for the party and to monitor the activities of their members in coopera-tion with local security agents. Organizations may be segregated by sex, age, national origin, profession, or other traits designated by the party. From members of front organizations, such as the Red-Scarf Teenagers' Organization and the Ho Chi Minh Communist Youth League, the party is able to select potential party members.

The Vietnam Fatherland Front, because it unites a number of subordinate front organizations, is the most important. Its first uni-fied national congress took place in January 1977 when all national front organizations, including the National Front for the libera-tion of South Vietnam, informally called the National Liberation Front (NLF, Mat Tran Dan Toc Giai Phong Mien Nam Viet Nam), operating in the south, were merged under its banner. In the late 1980s, the Vietnam General Confederation of Trade

197

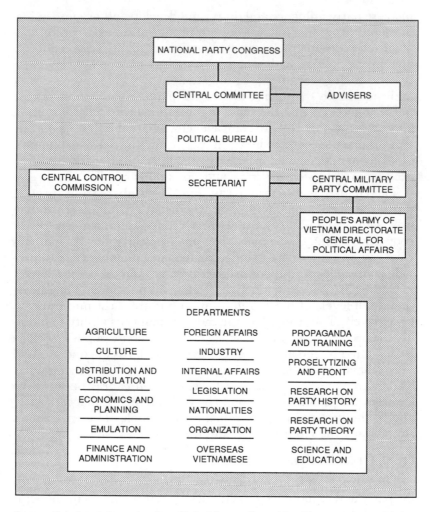

Source: Based on information from United States, Central Intelligence Agency, *Directory of Officials of Vietnam*, Washington, July 1985, 1–6; Nguyen Van Canh, *Vietnam under Communism 1975–1982*, Stanford, California, 1983, 57.

Figure 14. Organization of the Vietnamese Communist Party, 1987

Unions, described by the party as the "broadest mass organization of the working class," was also significant because its members, along with party members, state employees, and members of the Youth League, were included among the elite granted material privileges by the state. Finally, the Ho Chi Minh Communist Youth League was important because it acted to screen, train, and recruit party members.

In the mid-and late 1980s, the party increasingly viewed the front organizations as moribund and criticized them for being no longer representative of party policy. Party General Secretary Nguyen Van Linh, however, sought to revive and develop them as important avenues for controlled criticism of party abuses.

Political Dynamics

The VCP has been characterized by the stability of its leadership. According to Vietnam observer Douglas Pike, Hanoi's leadership was "forged of a constant forty-year association" in which individuals shared "the same common experience, the same development, the same social trauma." Because of their small number, Political Bureau members were able to arrive at agreement more easily than larger forums and hence were able to deal more effectively with day-to-day decisions. As individuals, they tended to take on a large number of diverse party and government functions, thus keeping the administrative apparatus small and highly personalized.

Decisions tended to be made in a collegial fashion with alliances changing on different issues. Where factions existed, they were differentiated along lines separating those favoring Moscow from those preferring Beijing or along lines distinguishing ideological hardliners and purists from reformists and economic pragmatists. The accounts of Hoang Van Hoan, a former Political Bureau member who fled to Beijing in 1978, and of Truong Nhu Tang, former justice minister of the NLF, verified the existence in the early 1970s of factions identified by their loyalty to either Moscow or Beijing. They asserted that the pro-Soviet direction taken following Ho Chi Minh's death in 1969, and particularly after the Fourth National Party Congress in 1976, was the result of the party's having progressively come under the influence of a small pro-Soviet clique led by Party Secretary Le Duan and high-ranking Political Bureau member Le Duc Tho, and including Truong Chinh, Pham Van Dong, and Pham Hung. Until Le Duan's death, these five represented a core policy-making element within the Political Bureau. Whether or not a similar core of decision makers existed in the Political Bureau of the mid-1980s, under Party Secretary Nguyen Van Linh, was not clear.

Differences within the Political Bureau in the mid-1980s, however, appeared focused on the country's economic problems. The line was drawn between reformists, who were willing to institute changes that included a free market system in order to stimulate Vietnam's ailing economy, and ideologues, who feared the effect such reforms would have on party control and the ideological purity of the society. The leadership changes that occurred in late 1986 and early 1987 as a result of the Sixth National Party Congress suggested that the reformers might have won concessions in favor of moderate economic reform. The scale of the infighting reportedly was small, however, and the changes that were made probably were undertaken on the basis of a consensus reached between the hardliners and the reformers. Nevertheless, the results demonstrated that Vietnam's leaders increasingly had come to the realization that rebuilding the country's war-torn economy was as difficult an undertaking as conquering the Saigon government.

Political Culture

Vietnam's political culture has been determined by a number of factors of which communism is but the latest. The country's political tradition is one of applying borrowed ideas to indigenous conditions. In many ways, Marxism-Leninism simply represents a new language in which to express old but consistent cultural orientations and inclinations. Vietnam's political processes, therefore, incorporate as much from the national mythology as from the pragmatic concerns engendered by current issues.

The major influences on Vietnamese political culture were of Chinese origin. Vietnam's political institutions were forged by 1,000 years of Chinese rule (111 B.C. to A.D. 939). The ancient Chinese system, based on Confucianism, established a political center surrounded by loyal subjects. The Confucians stressed the importance of the village, endowing it with autonomy but clearly defining its relationship to the center. Those who ruled did so with the "mandate of heaven." Although they were not themselves considered divine, they ruled by divine right by reason of their virtue, which was manifested in moral righteousness and compassion for the welfare of the people. A monarch possessing these traits received the unconditional loyalty of his subjects. Selection of bureaucratic officials was on the basis of civil service examinations rather than heredity, and government institutions were viewed simply as conduits for the superior wisdom of the rulers (see The Social System, ch. 2).

The Vietnamese adopted this political system rather than one belonging to their Southeast Asian neighbors, whose rulers were identified as gods. Nevertheless, Vietnamese interpretations of the system differed from those of the Chinese both in the degree of loyalty extended to a ruler and in the nature of the relationship between the institutions of government and the men who ruled. In Vietnam, loyalty to a monarch was conditional upon his success in defending national territory. A history of Chinese domination had sensitized the Vietnamese to the importance of retaining their territorial integrity. In China, territorial control did not arouse the same degree of fervor. In interpreting the role of government institutions, Vietnamese beliefs also conflicted with Confucian theory. Whereas the Confucians held that institutions were necessarily subordinate to the virtuous ruler, Vietnamese practice held the opposite to be true. Institutions were endowed with a certain innate authority over the individual, a trait manifested in the Vietnamese penchant for creating complex and redundant institutions. Despite Confucian influence, Vietnamese practice demonstrated a faith in administrative structures and in legalist approaches to political problems that was distinctly Vietnamese, not Confucianist.

Nevertheless, Confucian traits were still discernible in Vietnam in the mid-1980s. To begin with, many of the first-generation communist leaders came from scholar-official backgrounds and were well-versed in the traditional requisites of "talent and virtue" (*tai duc*) necessary for leadership. Ho Chi Minh's father was a Confucian scholar, and Vo Nguyen Giap and the brothers Le Duc Tho and Mai Chi Tho were from scholarly families. They cultivated an image of being incorruptible and effective administrators as well as moral leaders. The relationship between the government and the governed was also deliberately structured to parallel the Confucian system. Like the Confucians, leaders of the highly centralized Vietnamese communist government stressed the importance of the village and clearly defined its relationship to the center.

In this link between ruler and subjects, the Confucian and communist systems appeared to co-exist more readily among the disciplined peasants of the North than among their reputedly fractious brethren in the South, where the influence of India and France outweighed that of China. Searching for reasons to explain the phenomenon, some observers have suggested that the greater difficulty encountered in transforming Vietnam's southern provinces into a communist society stemmed, in part, from this region's having been the least Sinicized. In addition, Southeast Asian influences in South Vietnam, such as Theravada Buddhism, had created a cultural climate in which relations with a distant center of authority were a norm (see Religion, ch. 2). Moreover, the South's political systems had tended to isolate the center, in both symbolic and physical terms, from the majority of the people, who had no clear means of access to their government. The South had also been the first to fall to the French, who had extended their influence there by establishing colonial rule. In the North, however, the French had maintained only a protectorate and had allowed a measure of self-government. As a result, French influence in the

North was less than in the South and represented a smaller obstacle to the imposition of communism.

The influence of modern China, and particularly the doctrines of Mao Zedong and the Chinese Communist Party, on Vietnamese political culture is a more complicated issue. Vietnamese leaders, including Ho Chi Minh, spent time in China, but they had formed their impressions of communism in Paris and Moscow and through Moscow-directed Comintern connections. The success of the Chinese Communist Revolution in 1949, however, inspired the Vietnamese communists to continue their own revolution. It also enabled them to do so by introducing the People's Republic of China as a critical source of material support. The Second National Party Congress, held in 1951, reflected renewed determination to push ahead with party objectives, including reconstruction of the society to achieve communist aims and land reform.

The Soviet model, as well, can be discerned in Vietnamese political practice. In the areas of legal procedure, bureaucratic practice, and industrial management, the Vietnamese system more closely resembles the Soviet system than the Chinese. In the late 1950s and early 1960s, VCP leaders were attracted particularly by advances made in Soviet economic development. In the majority of cases, however, Vietnamese policies and institutions, rather than adhering strictly to either Chinese or Soviet models, have tended to be essentially Vietnamese responses to Vietnamese problems.

Traditional adversarial relationships with neighboring states have also helped to define Vietnam's political culture. The country's long-standing rifts with Cambodia and China, which developed into open conflicts in 1978 and 1979 respectively, suggest the need to view contemporary relationships in historical perspective (see Early History and The Chinese Millennium, ch. 1; Foreign Relations, this ch.). Hanoi's attitude regarding its relations with these two neighbors is grounded as much in accustomed patterns of interchange as in current concerns for national security. It is also firmly based in the Vietnamese tradition of resistance to foreign rule, which has been a theme of great appeal to Vietnamese patriots since the time of Chinese domination. The founding members of the VCP were the dissenting elite of a colonized country. They were attracted to Marxism-Leninism not only for its social theories but also because of the Leninist response to colonial subjugation. Ho himself was reported to have been more concerned with the problem of French imperialism than with that of class struggle.

Vietnam's agrarian economy also contributed to its political culture. As an agricultural people, the Vietnamese lacked an urban industrial proletariat to carry out their revolution. Leadership, therefore, necessarily passed into the hands of scholar-official intellectuals and peasants.

Vietnam's political culture, in turn, has contributed to the country's comparative isolation from noncommunist states. This isolation is partially a result of the ideology that has created self-imposed political barriers with the West, but it is also the result of the collective mentality of the nation's leadership, which views itself as set apart from communist as well as noncommunist nations. This view stems from years of preoccupation with the struggle for independence and the reunification of the country. Such an ethnocentric focus on domestic affairs resulted in a provincial outlook that continued in the late 1980s and was reinforced by the lack of international experience of many of Vietnam's leaders whose foreign travel was limited to official visits to other communist states. In addition, Vietnam's military victories over reputedly superior military forces, including those of France, the United States, and, in 1979, China, have created a sense of arrogance that a wider world view would not justify.

Communist ideology, particularly as manipulated by the Vietnamese leadership, has also helped to shape Vietnam's political culture. The country's communist leaders have been adept at stressing the continuity of Marxist-Leninist doctrine with Vietnamese history. The VCP successfully identified communism with the historical goals of Vietnamese nationalism and achieved leadership of Vietnam's independence struggle by accommodating the aspirations of a number of ethnic, religious, and political groups. The party has presented the myths and realities of the past in a manner that suggests that they led naturally to the present. In his writings, Ho Chi Minh used classical Vietnamese literary allusions to convey a sense of mystique about the past, and he cultivated the classical Vietnamese image of a leader who reflected *uy tin* (credibility), a charismatic quality combining elements of compassion, asceticism, and correct demeanor, which legitimized a leader's claim to authority. The communist regime additionally promoted the importance of archaeology, popular literature, and cultural treasures in order to emphasize its ties to Vietnam's classical traditions. VCP historiography views the French colonial period (1858–1954) as more an interruption than a part of Vietnamese history.

Despite the care taken to preserve Vietnamese identity, the party has hesitated to deviate from Marxist-Leninist doctrine even when its application resulted in failure. The planned rapid and total transformation of the South to communism in the 1970s failed because it was almost entirely ideologically inspired and did not sufficiently anticipate the scale of economic and social resistance that such a plan would encounter in the South. This failure paralleled the failure to collectivize the North rapidly in the 1950s. In both cases, however, the party maintained that the predominantly ideological programs had been instituted to attain nationalist goals and that nationalism had not been exploited for the purpose of furthering communism.

Vietnam's political culture represents, therefore, the steadfast survival of what is Vietnamese in the face of a long history of outside influence; integration of historical political ideals with an imported communist organizational model has created a communist identity that is no less Vietnamese.

The System of Government

Constitutional Evolution

The communist party-controlled government of Vietnam has ruled under three state constitutions. The first was promulgated in 1946, the second in 1959, and the third in 1980. Significantly, each was created at a milestone in the evolution of the VCP, and each bore the mark of its time.

The purpose of the 1946 constitution was essentially to provide the communist regime with a democratic appearance. The newly established government of the Democratic Republic of Vietnam (DRV) was sensitive about its communist sponsorship, and it perceived democratic trappings as more appealing to noncommunist nationalists and less provocative to French negotiators. Even though such guarantees were never intended to be carried out, the constitution provided for freedom of speech, the press, and assembly. The document remained in effect in Viet Minh-controlled areas throughout the First Indochina War (1946–54—see Glossary) and in North Vietnam following partition in 1954, until it was replaced with a new constitution in 1959.

The second constitution was explicitly communist in character. Its preamble described the DRV as a "people's democratic state led by the working class," and the document provided for a nominal separation of powers among legislative, executive, and judicial branches of government. On paper, the legislative function was carried out by the National Assembly. The assembly was empowered to make laws and to elect the chief officials of the state, such as the president (who was largely a symbolic head of state), the vice president, and cabinet ministers. Together those elected (including the president and vice president) formed a Council of Ministers, which constitutionally (but not in practice) was subject to supervision by the Standing Committee of the National Assembly. Headed by a prime minister, the council was the highest executive organ of state authority. Besides overseeing the Council of Ministers, the assembly's Standing Committee also supervised on paper the Supreme People's Court, the chief organ of the judiciary. The assembly's executive side nominally decided on national economic plans, approved state budgets, and acted on questions of war or peace. In reality, however, final authority on all matters rested with the Political Bureau.

The reunification of North and South Vietnam (the former Republic of Vietnam) in 1976 provided the primary motivation for revising the 1959 constitution. Revisions were made along the ideological lines set forth at the Fourth National Congress of the VCP in 1976, emphasizing popular sovereignty and promising success in undertaking "revolutions" in production, science and technology, culture, and ideology. In keeping with the underlying theme of a new beginning associated with reunification, the constitution also stressed the need to develop a new political system, a new economy, a new culture, and a new socialist person.

The 1959 document had been adopted during the tenure of Ho Chi Minh and demonstrated a certain independence from the Soviet model of state organization. The 1980 Constitution was drafted when Vietnam faced a serious threat from China, and political and economic dependence on the Soviet Union had increased. Perhaps, as a result, the completed document resembles the 1977 Soviet Constitution.

The 1980 Vietnamese Constitution concentrates power in a newly established Council of State much like the Presidium of the Supreme Soviet, endowing it nominally with both legislative and executive powers. Many functions of the legislature remain the same as under the 1959 document, but others have been transferred to the executive branch or assigned to both branches concurrently. The executive branch appears strengthened overall, having gained a second major executive body, the Council of State, and the importance of the National Assembly appears to have been reduced accordingly. The role of the Council of Ministers, while appearing on paper to have been subordinated to the new Council of State, in practice retained its former primacy (see Council of State and Council of Ministers, this ch.; Appendix A, table 12).

Among the innovative features of the 1980 document is the concept of "collective mastery" of society, a frequently used expression attributed to the late party secretary, Le Duan (1908–1986). The concept is a Vietnamese version of popular sovereignty that advocates an active role for the people so that they may become their own masters as well as masters of society, nature, and the nation. It states that the people's collective mastery in all fields is assured by the state and is implemented by permitting the participation in state affairs of mass organizations. On paper, these organizations, to which almost all citizens belong, play an active role in government and have the right to introduce bills before the National Assembly.

Another feature is the concept of socialist legality, which dictates that "the state manage society according to law and constantly strengthen the socialist legal system." The concept, originally introduced at the Third National Party Congress in 1960, calls for achieving socialist legality through the state, its organizations, and its people. Law, in effect, is made subject to the decisions and directives of the party.

The apparent contradiction between the people's right to active participation in government suggested by collective mastery and the party's absolute control of government dictated by "socialist legality" is characteristic of communist political documents in which rights provided the citizenry often are negated by countermeasures appearing elsewhere in the document. Vietnam's constitutions have not been guarantors, therefore, of the rights of citizens or of the separation and limitation of powers. They have been intended instead to serve the party-controlled regime.

The 1980 Constitution comprises 147 articles in 12 chapters dealing with numerous subjects, including the basic rights and duties of citizens. Article 67 guarantees the citizens' rights to freedom of speech, the press, assembly, and association, and the freedom to demonstrate. Such rights are, nevertheless, subject to a caveat stating "no one may misuse democratic freedoms to violate the interests of the state and the people." With this stipulation, all rights are conditionally based upon the party's interpretation of what constitutes behavior in the state's and people's interest.

Government Structure

The National Assembly

Constitutionally, the National Assembly is the highest government organization and the highest-level representative body of the people. It has the power to draw up, adopt, and amend the constitution and to make and amend laws. It also has the responsibility to legislate and implement state plans and budgets. Through its constitution-making powers it defines its own role and the roles of the Council of State, the Council of Ministers, the People's Councils and People's Committees, the Supreme People's Court, and the Supreme People's Organs of Control. The assembly can elect and remove members of the Council of Ministers, the chief justice of the Supreme People's Court, and the procurator general of the People's Supreme Organ of Control. Finally, it has the power to initiate or conclude wars and to assume other duties and powers it deems necessary. The term of each session of the National Assembly is five years, and meetings are convened twice a year, or more frequently if called for by the Council of State.

Despite its many formal duties, the National Assembly exists mainly as a legislative arm of the VCP's Political Bureau. It converts Political Bureau resolutions into laws and decrees and mobilizes popular support for them. In this role, the National Assembly is led by the Council of Ministers acting through the Council of State and a variable number of special-purpose committees. Actual debate on legislation does not occur. Instead, a bill originates in the Council of Ministers, which registers the bill and assigns a key party member to present it on the floor. Before presentation, the member will have received detailed instructions from the party caucus in the assembly, which has held study sessions regarding the proposed legislation. Once the legislation is presented, members vote according to party guidelines.

A general national election to choose National Assembly delegates is held every five years. The first election following the reunification of the North and South was held in April 1976 and the voters selected 492 members, of which 243 represented the South and 249 the North. In 1987 the Eighth National Assembly numbered 496 members. Because successful candidates were chosen in advance, the electoral process was not genuine. No one could run for office unless approved by the party, and in many cases the local body of the party simply appointed the candidates. Nevertheless, every citizen had a duty to vote, and, although the balloting was secret, the electorate, through electoral study sessions, received directives from the party concerning who should be elected. The elections in 1987, however, were comparatively open by Vietnamese standards. It was evident that the party was tolerating a wider choice in candidates and more debate.

The Council of State

The Council of State is the highest standing body of the National Assembly. Its members, who serve as a collective presidency for Vietnam, are elected from among National Assembly deputies. The Council of State is "responsible and accountable" to the National Assembly, according to Chapter VII of the 1980 Constitution. It plays a more active role than the titular presidency provided for in the 1959 constitution and, in addition, it has assumed the day-to-day duties of the former Standing Committee of the National Assembly under the old constitution. The council thus holds both legislative and executive powers, but in actuality it wields less power than the Council of Ministers. As stipulated in the Constitution, the Council of State comprises a chairman, several vice chairmen (there were three in 1987), a general secretary, and members (there were seven in 1987). Members of the Council of State cannot be concurrently members of the Council of Ministers. Its chairman concurrently commands the armed forces and chairs the National Defense Council, which controls the armed forces (see The Armed Forces, ch. 5). The Council of State nominally presides over the election of deputies to the National Assembly; promulgates laws and issues decrees; supervises the work of the Council of Ministers, the Supreme People's Court, the procurator general of the Supreme People's Organ of Control, and the People's Councils at all levels; decides, when the National Assembly is not in session, to form or dissolve ministries and state committees and to appoint or dismiss the vice chairmen of the Council of Ministers, ministers, and heads of state committees; declares a state of war, and orders general or local mobilization in the event of invasion. Such decisions, however, must be submitted to the next session of the National Assembly for ratification. The five-year term of the Council corresponds with that of the National Assembly, but the Council continues its functions until the new National Assembly elects a new Council of State.

The Council of Ministers

The Council of Ministers is entrusted by the 1980 Constitution with managing and implementing the governmental activities of the state. It is described in that document as "the Government of the Socialist Republic of Vietnam, the highest executive and administrative state body of the highest body of state authority." It is accountable to the National Assembly, and, more directly, to the Council of State when the National Assembly is not in session. Its duties include submitting draft laws, decrees, and other bills to the National Assembly and the Council of State; drafting state plans and budgets and implementing them following the National Assembly's approval; managing the development of the national economy; organizing national defense activities and assuring the preparedness of the armed forces; and organizing and managing the state's foreign relations. Its membership includes a chairman, vice chairman, cabinet ministers, and the heads of state committees, whose terms of office coincide with that of the National Assembly. The Council of Ministers includes its own standing committee, which serves to coordinate and mobilize the council's activities. In 1986 the standing committee was expanded from ten to thirteen members.

Each ministry is headed by a minister, who is assisted by two to twelve vice ministers. The number and functions of the ministries are not prescribed in the Constitution, but in 1987 there were twenty-three ministries, and a number of other specialized commissions and departments. In apparent response to the call by the Sixth National Party Congress in 1986 for a streamlined bureaucracy, several ministries were merged. The former ministries of agriculture, food, and food industry were joined in a newly created Ministry of Agriculture and Food Industry. The ministries of power and mines were merged to form the Ministry of Energy, and a newly created Ministry of Labor, War Invalids, and Social Welfare consolidated the duties of three former ministries. The addition of two new ministerial bodies also resulted from the 1986 Congress: a Ministry of Information to replace the Vietnam Radio and Television Commission, and a Commission for Economic Relations with Foreign Countries to act as a coordinating body for foreign aid.

People's Courts and People's Organs of Control

Vietnam's judicial bodies are the Supreme People's Court, the local People's Courts at the provincial, district, and city levels, the military tribunals, and the People's Organs of Control (see Internal Security, ch. 5). Under special circumstances, such as show-case trials involving breaches of national security, the National Assembly or the Council of State may set up special tribunals. Judges are elected for a term equivalent to that of the bodies that elected them, and trials are held with the participation of people's assessors, who may also act as judges. The Constitution guarantees defendants the right to plead their cases. Cases are prosecuted by a procurator.

The Supreme People's Court is the highest tribunal and is charged with the supervision of subordinate courts. As a court of first instance, it tries cases involving high treason or other crimes of a serious nature; and as the highest court of appeals, it reviews cases originating with the lower courts. Appeals are infrequent, however, because lower courts tend to act as final arbiters.

Local people's courts function at each administrative level except at the village level, where members of the village administrative committees serve in a judicial capacity. Proceedings of local courts are presided over by people's assessors.

The Supreme People's Organs of Control function as watchdogs of the state and work independently of all other government

209

agencies, although they are nominally responsible to the National Assembly. They are subordinate to the Supreme People's Organ of Control also known as the Supreme People's Procurate, which, in turn, is headed by a chief procurator or procurator general. These organs exercise extraordinary powers of surveillance over government agencies at every level, including the court system and agencies for law enforcement.

A new Penal Code was adopted in January 1986, replacing a 1950 code of justice based on the French Civil Code. Under the new code, crime is defined very broadly. Authorities interpret a wide range of antisocial behavior as potentially criminal, such as graft, petty corruption, hoarding, and currency malpractice (see fig. 15).

Local Government

Vietnam in 1987 remained divided into thirty-six provinces, three autonomous municipalities, and one special zone directly under the central government (see fig. 1). Provinces are divided into districts, towns, and capitals. The autonomous municipalities directly under central authority are divided into precincts, and these are subdivided into wards. Provincial districts are divided into villages and townships; provincial towns and provincial capitals are divided into wards and villages. Each administrative level has a people's council and a people's committee.

The people's councils represent the local authority of the state and are the top supervisory bodies at each level. They do not govern directly but instead elect and oversee people's committees that act as executive bodies and carry out local administrative duties. Council members are popularly elected—although candidates are screened by the party—and are responsible for ensuring strict local observance of the Constitution and laws and for ruling on local plans and budgets. Council members are further charged with overseeing the development and maintenance of local armed forces units (see The Armed Forces, ch. 5).

Following the Fourth National Party Congress in 1976, the districts became the basic administrative units of the government. The Congress had declared that the districts should become agro-industrial economic units, acting to orchestrate the reorganization of production. Formerly, they had functioned simply as intermediaries for channeling directives to the village level. After 1976 they functioned as agencies for economic planning, budgeting, and management, and as the chief political units of local government. Emphasis on this latter function has created an enormous bureaucracy. Many provincial people's committees have in excess of thirty separate departments, and each district people's committee has had to establish an equal number of counterparts.

The three autonomous municipalities in Vietnam are Hanoi, Haiphong, and Ho Chi Minh City (formerly Saigon). The government of an autonomous municipality consists of an elected people's council that in turn elects an executive committee headed by a mayor. The executive committee oversees numerous departments administering various activities.

The precinct wards of the three autonomous municipalities are divided into sectors, which are then further divided into neighborhood solidarity cells. As many as 28 to 30 cells, together numbering 400 to 600 households, may make up a sector, and 10 sectors may compose a ward. The administration of a village corresponds to that of an urban ward.

The ward executive committee ensures that government activities prescribed by the precinct committee are carried out. The precinct committee simply represents an intermediary level between the municipal government and the ward committees.

At the ward level, in addition to people's councils and executive committees, there are security departments with connections to the national security apparatus. The security departments monitor the activities of ward members, but the departments' decisions are kept secret from the chairpersons of the ward executive committees (see Internal Security, ch. 5).

A sector, instead of having an executive committee, has a residents' protective committee concerned with fighting fires and preventing petty crime. A sector security officer is charged with the suppression of dissent. Every head of household belongs to a subcell of only a few families and reports regularly to a neighborhood solidarity cell comprising twelve to twenty families. Party directives and policies reach the citizenry via the party's mass organizations or the hierarchy of the party and its representatives at the ward level.

Foreign Relations

Until the fall of the South Vietnamese government in 1975, the VCP considered foreign policy interests to be subordinate to the overriding issue of national liberation and reunification. Only with the end of the war did Hanoi turn its full attention to foreign policy concerns. Among the more pressing were its relations with Laos, Cambodia, China, the Soviet Union, the member nations of the Association of Southeast Asian Nations (ASEAN), and the West. Like domestic policy, foreign policy required the reconciliation of ideology and nationalism.

211

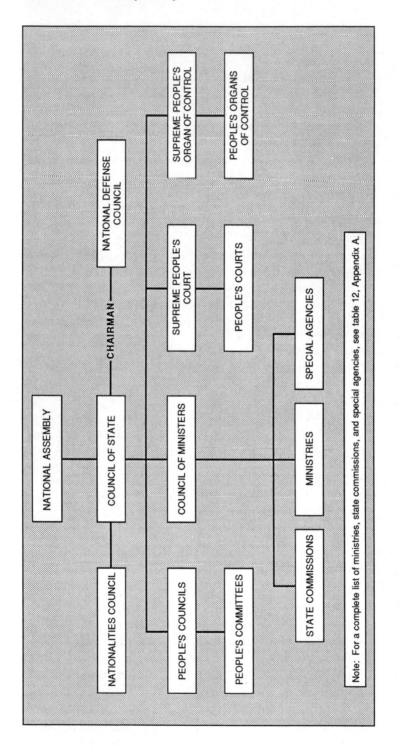

Figure 15. National Government Structure, 1987

From an ideological standpoint, the Vietnamese saw themselves as fulfilling their international socialist duty by defeating a major "imperialist" enemy and by carrying out a revolution that could be a model for the Third World. Communist ideology in turn served Vietnamese nationalism by providing a justification for the pursuit of its nationalist goals. A Marxist-Leninist historical view, for example, justified creating an alliance of the three Indochinese countries because such an alliance was instrumental in the struggle against imperialism. By the same reasoning, Hanoi's decision in 1978 to overthrow the Pol Pot regime in Cambodia was defensible on the grounds that a new government more closely dedicated to Marxist-Leninist principles was required in Cambodia in order to reestablish an effective alliance against imperialism. Ideological and nationalist goals thus were often interchangeable, and Vietnamese foreign policy could be construed as serving national interests and international communism at the same time. In the final analysis, however, nationalism and national security remained the primary foreign policy concerns.

Laos and Cambodia

In 1987 Vietnam's relationships with Laos and Cambodia did not differ substantially from their historic patterns. Contemporary Vietnamese attitudes reflected the conviction of cultural and political superiority that had prevailed during the nineteenth century when weaker monarchs in Laos and Cambodia had paid tribute to the Vietnamese court in a system modeled on Vietnam's own relationship to China (see The Chinese Millennium, Nine Centuries of Independence, ch. 1). In the 1980s, Laos and Cambodia had once more become Vietnam's client states. Laos, with a communist party long nurtured by the Vietnamese, entered the relationship with docility; Cambodia, however, under a ruthless, but anti-Vietnamese dictatorship of its own, resisted being drawn into the Vietnamese orbit. Tension between the two states escalated into open warfare and, in 1978, Hanoi launched an invasion that toppled the Pol Pot regime in Phnom Penh. In 1987 Cambodia remained a state governed precariously by a regime installed by Hanoi, its activities constrained by the presence of a substantial Vietnamese occupation force and a tenacious insurgency in the countryside. Repeated Vietnamese assurances that Hanoi would withdraw its troops from the beleaguered country by 1990 were received with skepticism by some observers.

The communist victory in Vietnam in 1975 was accompanied by similar communist successes in Laos and Cambodia. The impression of the noncommunist world at the time was that the three Indochinese communist parties, having seized control in their respective countries, would logically work together, through the fraternal bond of a single ideology, to achieve common objectives. What appeared to be a surprising deterioration in relations, however, was actually the resurfacing of historical conflict that ideological commonality could not override (see Early History, ch. 1). The victories of the Vietnamese communists and the Cambodian communist Khmer Rouge (see Glossary) in 1975 did not bring peace. Relations between the two parties had been strained since the close of the First Indochina War. The Geneva Agreements had failed to secure for the Khmer communists, as part of the first Cambodian national liberation organization, the United Issarak Front, a legitimate place in Cambodian politics. Some Khmer Communist and Issarak leaders subsequently went to Hanoi, but among those who stayed behind, Pol Pot and his faction, who later gained control of the Khmer (Kampuchean) Communist party, blamed Vietnam for having betrayed their party at Geneva. Pol Pot never lost his antipathy for Vietnam. Under his leadership, the Khmer Rouge adhered for years to a radical, chauvinistic, and bitterly anti-Vietnamese political line. Skirmishes broke out on the Cambodian-Vietnamese border almost immediately following the communist victories in Saigon and Phnom Penh, and in less than four years Vietnam was again at war, this time with Cambodia. Vietnam's offensive forces crossing the Cambodia border in December 1978 took less than a month to occupy Phnom Penh and most of the country.

When tensions between Cambodia and Vietnam broke into the open, the reason was ostensibly Cambodian demands that Hanoi return territory conquered by the Vietnamese centuries earlier. Vietnam's offers to negotiate the territorial issue were rejected, however, because of more urgent Khmer concerns that Hanoi intended to dominate Cambodia by forming an Indochina Federation (see Glossary) or "special relationship." In any event, Vietnamese interest in resolving the situation peacefully clearly came to an end once the decisison was made to invade Cambodia.

The invasion and the subsequent establishment of a puppet regime in Phnom Penh were costly to Hanoi, further isolating it from the international community. Vietnam's relations with a number of countries and with the United Nations (UN) deteriorated. The UN General Assembly refused to recognize the Vietnamese-supported government in Phnom Penh and demanded a total Vietnamese withdrawal followed by internationally supervised free elections. The ASEAN nations were unified in opposing Vietnam's action. Urged by Thailand's example, they provided support for

Statue representing Vietnamese and Cambodian solidarity,
Prey Veng, Cambodia
Courtesy Bill Herod

the anti-Phnom Penh resistance. In February 1979, China moved to retaliate against Vietnam across their mutual border (see China, this ch.).

The ensuing conflict in Cambodia pitted Vietnamese troops, assisted by forces of the new Phnom Penh government—the People's Republic of Kampuchea (PRK)—against a coalition of communist and noncommunist resistance elements. Of these elements, the government displaced from Phnom Penh by the Vietnamese, Pol Pot's communist Khmer Rouge (which had established the government known as Democratic Kampuchea in Cambodia in 1975), was the strongest and most effective military force, mainly because of support from the Chinese. The extremism and brutality of the Khmer Rouge's brief reign in Phnom Penh, where it may have been responsible for as many as 2 million deaths, made it infamous. ASEAN's concern that the reputation of the Khmer Rouge would lessen the international appeal of the anti-Vietnamese cause led it to press the Khmer Rouge and noncommunist resistance elements into forming a coalition that would appear to diminish the Khmer Rouge's political role. The tripartite Coalition Government of Democratic Kampuchea (CGDK) was formed on June 22, 1982. In addition to the Khmer Rouge, it comprised a noncommunist resistance force called the Kampuchean People's National Liberation Front (KPNLF)—under the leadership of a former official of Prince Norodom Sihanouk's government, Son Sann—and Sihanouk's own noncommunist force (the Armée Nationale Sihanoukiste—ANS). The Cambodian government in exile needed the added legitimacy that noncommunist factions and the prestige of Sihanouk's name could contribute. The Chinese were reluctant to withdraw their support from the Khmer Rouge, which they viewed as the only effective anti-Vietnamese fighting force among the three coalition members. They were persuaded, however, to support the coalition and eventually began supplying arms to Son Sann and Sihanouk as well as Pol Pot.

Despite an extensive record of internal squabbling, the coalition government in 1987 provided the international community with an acceptable alternative to the Vietnamese-supported Heng Samrin regime in Phnom Penh. From 1982 to 1987, the coalition survived annual Vietnamese dry-season campaigns against its base camps along the Thai-Cambodian border, and, by changing its tactics in 1986 to emphasize long-term operations deep in the Cambodian interior, increased its military effectiveness. The coalition's military operations prevented the Vietnamese from securing all of Cambodia and helped create a stalemate.

In 1987 the situation remained deadlocked. Despite the costs, Vietnam's negotiating position remained inflexible. Hanoi apparently perceived itself to have gained enormously in terms of national security. The "special relationship" it had futilely sought with Pol Pot was effected almost immediately with the new Phnom Penh government when, in February 1979, a Treaty of Friendship and Cooperation was signed. In 1982 and 1983 a substantial number of Vietnamese reportedly settled in Cambodia, although Vietnam did not seem to be making a concerted effort to colonize the country. Instead, Hanoi appeared to be striving to build an indigenous regime that would be responsive to general Vietnamese direction and become part of an Indochinese community under Vietnamese hegemony.

In contrast to its relationship with Cambodia, Vietnam's relations with communist Laos have been fairly stable. Historically, the ethnic tribes comprising present-day Laos had been less resistant to Vietnamese subjugation, and relations had never reached the level of animosity characteristic of the Vietnam-Cambodia relationship.

Although Hanoi was a signatory to the Geneva Agreement of 1962 that upheld the neutrality of Laos, it has failed to observe the agreement in practice. During the Second Indochina War (see Glossary), for example, the North Vietnamese obtained the cooperation of the Lao People's Revolutionary Party (Pathet Lao) in constructing and maintaining the Ho Chi Minh Trail (see Glossary), an unauthorized road communications network that passed through the length of Laos. Thousands of Vietnamese troops were stationed in Laos to maintain the road network and provide for its security. Vietnamese military personnel also fought beside the Pathet Lao in its struggle to overthrow Laos' neutralist government. Cooperation persisted after the war and the Lao communist victory. In 1976, agreements on cooperation in cultural, economic, scientific, and technical fields were signed between the two countries, followed in 1977 by a twenty-five-year Treaty of Friendship and Cooperation. The treaty was intended to strengthen ties as well as sanction Vietnam's military presence in, and military assistance to, Laos. Following Vietnam's invasion of Cambodia, Laos established links with the Vietnamese-supported PRK in Phnom Penh. Meanwhile, Hanoi maintained 40,000 to 60,000 troops in Laos. In 1985 the three governments discussed coordinating their 1986-90 five-year plans, and Vietnam assumed a larger role in developing Lao natural resources by agreeing to joint exploitation of Laotian forests and iron ore deposits. Nevertheless, such growth in cooperation prompted some debate on the Lao side over the country's growing dependence on Vietnam.

China

The deterioration of Sino-Vietnamese relations was gradual, commencing perhaps most dramatically with Richard M. Nixon's 1972 visit to China (which Hanoi later called the beginning of China's betrayal of Vietnam), but in the mid-1970s the signs of an impending breakdown were barely discernible. Until 1977 the Vietnam-Cambodia dispute appeared to the outside world to be purely bilateral, and China's strategic considerations seemed only distantly connected to the skirmishes taking place on the Vietnamese-Cambodian border. The Chinese in the 1976–77 period were preoccupied with internal affairs, including the deaths of Mao Zedong and Zhou Enlai, the arrest of Mao's widow, and the return to power of Deng Xiaoping. As the situation between Vietnam and Cambodia deteriorated, Cambodia's strategic importance to both China and Vietnam became more evident, and signs of a potential Sino-Vietnamese rift became clearer. Aside from risking the return of the Khmer Rouge, Vietnam viewed disengagement from Cambodia as tantamount to inviting China to establish a foothold on a second Vietnamese frontier. In China's view, Vietnam's sustained presence in Cambodia precluded such a development, but, more importantly, it placed Cambodia under the authority of an historic Asian adversary now closely allied with a superpower rival, the Soviet Union.

Vietnam's and China's shared modern experiences, namely their common exploitation by colonial powers and adaptations to communist ideology, did little to alter Vietnam's historical view of China, which was colored by lengthy periods of Chinese conquest and domination. During the Second Indochina War, China acted as North Vietnam's closest ally, but, according to later Vietnamese statements, the Chinese tried to dominate the relationship from the beginning. Vietnam's desperate need for Chinese assistance forced it to maintain good relations with Beijing for the duration of the war, despite Vietnamese suspicions that China's ultimate purpose was to weaken Vietnam (see The Chinese Millennium and Nine Centuries of Independence, ch. 1).

After the end of the Second Indochina War, underlying tensions between the two countries surfaced, and in 1978 a number of issues converged to bring the relationship to the breaking point. In addition to the growing dispute in Cambodia, these issues included territorial disagreements and Vietnam's treatment of its own largest minority group, the Hoa (see Glossary) or ethnic Chinese, who numbered nearly 2 million.

The territorial dispute involved primarily delineation of territorial waters in the Gulf of Tonkin and sovereignty over two archipelagos in the South China Sea, the Paracel and the Spratly Islands (the Xisha and the Nansha in Chinese; the Hoang Sa and Truong Sa in Vietnamese). A border dispute on land (over fewer than sixty square kilometers) was responsible for the relatively steady occurrence of low-level border clashes involving cross-border violations and the exchange of small-arms fire. In 1958 the two governments decided to defer settling their border differences until after victory had been achieved in the South.

Disagreement over territorial waters in the Gulf of Tonkin stemmed from agreements reached between China and France in 1887, stipulating a territorial limit of no more than three nautical miles. These agreements had been adequate until 1973, when Hanoi announced to Beijing its intention to negotiate contracts with foreign firms for the exploration of oil in the Gulf of Tonkin. The disputed islands in the South China Sea assumed importance only after it was disclosed that they were near the potential sites of substantial offshore oil deposits. In January 1974, Chinese military units seized islands in the Paracels occupied by South Vietnamese armed forces, and Beijing claimed sovereignty over the Spratlys. Following their conquest of South Vietnam in the spring of 1975, units of the People's Army of Vietnam (PAVN) nevertheless moved to occupy the Spratly Islands previously held by the Saigon regime.

Vietnam's treatment of the Hoa became an issue in 1978, when Hanoi instituted a crackdown on the Chinese community because of its pervasive role in domestic commerce in the South and its alleged subversive activities in the North. The government action forced an unprecedented exodus of thousands of Hoa across the border into China, prompting Beijing to accuse Vietnam of persecuting its Chinese community and of breaking a 1955 agreement that called for the gradual and voluntary integration of the Hoa into Vietnamese society. The situation was aggravated when Vietnam denied landing privileges to three Chinese ships dispatched to evacuate Hoa seeking voluntary repatriation to China. Beijing threatened Hanoi with unspecified retaliation, and Chinese activities on the Sino-Vietnamese border escalated.

The deterioration in bilateral relations became evident when China reduced in May 1978 and then cancelled on July 3 its remaining aid projects in Vietnam. The official announcement followed by only a few days Hanoi's admission on June 29 to the Soviet-dominated Council for Mutual Economic Assistance (Comecon—see Glossary).

A few months later, in November 1978, a new era in Soviet-Vietnamese relations began with the signing of a Treaty of Friendship and Cooperation that called for mutual assistance and consultation in the event of a security threat to either country. The document facilitated Soviet use of Vietnamese airports and port facilities, particularly the former United States military complex at Cam Ranh Bay (see The Armed Forces, ch. 5). In return, it assured Vietnam of economic and military aid for the anticipated invasion of Cambodia and established the Soviet Union as a deterrent to possible Chinese intervention in Cambodia.

Vietnam's decision to align with the Soviets, together with its invasion of Cambodia and mistreatment of the Hoa, provoked Beijing to "teach Hanoi a lesson." A "self-defense counterattack," mounted by China along the Sino-Vietnamese border on February 17, 1979, ended less than a month later, on March 5, when Chinese leaders announced that their objectives had been met and proceeded to withdraw their forces (see History, ch. 5). Despite the Chinese boast of having shattered the myth of Vietnam's invincibility, the invasion effected little more than the diversion of some Vietnamese troops from Cambodia. The bulk of the resistance reportedly was offered by local Vietnamese border units and regional forces. Outnumbered, they performed well, exposing significant weaknesses in Chinese tactics, strategy, logistics, equipment, and communications. In the final analysis, the results were far from conclusive. Peace negotiations were initiated following the disengagement of forces, but broke down several times before being discontinued in December 1979.

The Cambodian crisis, too, remained stalemated, and Vietnamese dependence upon the Soviet Union continued. In 1987 tensions along the Sino-Vietnamese border erupted in sporadic fighting. China believed that the Cambodian conflict would serve Chinese interests by draining the Vietnamese economically and weakening Hanoi. China's sustained pressure on Vietnam's northern border would also tax Vietnam militarily, while satisfying ASEAN's requests for Chinese assistance in the conflict and providing Chinese armed forces with invaluable combat experience. Consequently, Vietnam's dry-season campaigns to eliminate CGDK resistance base camps along the Thai-Cambodian border were generally matched by corresponding Chinese acts along the Sino-Vietnamese border. China issued vague threats to Vietnam of a "second lesson" in the mid-1980s but as of 1987 had not acted on these threats.

China imposed the removal of Vietnamese troops from Cambodia as a precondition to improved Sino-Soviet relations, and

Lang Son following 1979 Chinese invasion
Courtesy Bill Herod

diplomatic activity in late 1986 indicated that Vietnam might mend its differences with China in the event the Soviets moved closer to the Chinese. Despite Hanoi's desire to ease tensions with Beijing, however, it was not willing to do so at the expense of its position in Cambodia.

The Soviet Union

Since the earliest days of the VCP, when the party's primary mentor was the Comintern, the Soviet Union has played a complex role in VCP affairs. Many of Vietnam's leaders had trained in the Soviet Union and had formed personal ties with their Soviet contemporaries. Historically, however, the relationship between the two nations has been characterized by strain, particularly on the Vietnamese side, and the record suggests several instances of Soviet neglect or betrayal of Vietnamese interests. These included Moscow's indifference to the founding of the VCP in 1930; failure to support materially or otherwise the Vietnamese resistance war against the French in the 1930s and early 1940s; failure to recognize North Vietnam until five years after its founding; failure to support Vietnam's application for membership in the UN in 1948 and 1951; support for the partitioning of Vietnam at the Geneva Conference in 1954; and sponsorship of a proposal to admit both North and South Vietnam to the UN in 1956. These examples of

Soviet policy reminded the Vietnamese of the peril inherent in placing too much trust in a foreign ally.

The Sino-Soviet split in the late 1950s favorably altered the Soviet attitude toward Vietnam. Beginning in 1965, the Soviets initiated a program of military assistance to Hanoi that proved invaluable in carrying on the Second Indochina War. Hanoi, however, continued to suspect Soviet motives and perceived that Soviet aid, when offered, was insufficient and given only grudgingly after repeated appeals.

Following the conquest of South Vietnam in 1975, Hanoi sought to retain the equilibrium of its wartime relations with both China and the Soviet Union, but mounting tensions with Beijing, culminating in the loss of Chinese aid in 1978, compelled Hanoi to look increasingly to Moscow for economic and military assistance. Beginning in late 1975, a number of significant agreements were signed between the two countries. One coordinated the national economic development plans of the two countries, and another called for the Soviet Union to underwrite Vietnam's first postreunification Five-Year Plan. The first formal alliance was achieved in June 1978 when Vietnam joined Comecon. That organization, which facilitated the economic integration of the Soviet Union, six East European countries, Cuba, and Mongolia, was able to offer economic assistance for some of the projects abandoned by China (see Foreign Trade and Aid, ch. 3).

Vietnam's decision to invade Cambodia, which the leadership apparently made shortly after joining Comecon, required more than economic assistance from the Soviets (see Laos and Cambodia, this ch.). The possibility of a formal alliance between Hanoi and Moscow had apparently been discussed since 1975, but the Vietnamese had rejected the idea in order to protect their relationship with China. In 1978 that relationship had deteriorated to the point where protecting it was no longer a consideration, and circumstances in Cambodia confirmed the need for Vietnamese-Soviet military cooperation. In spite of Vietnam's needs, it is likely that the November 1978 Treaty of Friendship and Cooperation was imposed by the Soviets as a condition for military assistance. As a result of the treaty, the Vietnamese granted the Soviets access to the facilities at Da Nang and Cam Ranh Bay. Use of the bases represented a substantial regional strategic gain for Moscow, whose naval bases in the Pacific Ocean, until then, had been limited to the Soviet Far East.

Soviet support sustained Vietnamese operations in Cambodia. Military aid in 1978 approached US$800 million annually, but after the Vietnamese invasion of Cambodia and the Chinese attack on

Vietnam in February 1979, the figure rose to almost US$1.4 billion. The sharp increase, reflecting the Soviet effort to replace quickly Vietnamese equipment losses on the Sino-Vietnamese border, was subsequently reduced to between US$800 and 900 million in 1980 and between US$900 million and 1 billion in 1981. Military aid increased to 1.7 billion annually in the 1982–85 period and decreased to an estimated US$1.5 billion in 1985. Reported Soviet dissatisfaction with Hanoi's handling of Cambodia, stemming from the stalemated battlefield situation and its high costs, did not appear to affect Moscow's decision to continue to provide assistance for the war. At the end of 1987, there was no indication that the Soviets were pressing Vietnam to resolve the conflict.

In addition to its role as Vietnam's exclusive donor of military aid, the Soviet Union in 1987 was also Vietnam's largest contributor of economic aid and its biggest trade partner. During the Third Five-Year Plan (1981–85), the Soviets provided some US$5.4 billion in balance-of-payments aid, project assistance, and oil price subsidies. Total economic aid for 1986 was an estimated US$1.8 billion. The Soviets also have been a major supplier of food and commodity aid on a mostly grant-aid or soft-currency basis. By 1983 they were supplying 90 percent of Vietnam's petroleum, iron and steel, fertilizer, and cotton imports and 70 percent of its grain imports (see Foreign Trade and Aid, ch. 3).

Soviet-Vietnamese ties in the mid-1980s were sound, although troubled by some underlying strain. The Vietnamese distrusted Soviet intentions and resented Hanoi's dependent role; the Soviets in turn distrusted the Vietnamese for not confiding in them. Reportedly, on a number of occasions Moscow learned of major Vietnamese policy plans and changes only after the fact. According to some foreign observers, the Soviets were not entirely prepared for the sudden deterioration in Sino-Vietnamese relations in 1978, and they may not have been aware of the full extent of Vietnamese plans in Cambodia. Others believe the Soviet Union was aware of the deterioration and was allowing Vietnam to play the role of proxy in Moscow's own dispute with Beijing.

Friction was particularly evident in economic relations. The Soviets resented the enormous burden of their aid program to Vietnam and felt that much of it was wasted because of Vietnamese inefficiency. In turn, the Vietnamese were offended by Moscow's 1980 decision to reduce aid in the face of severe economic hardships in Vietnam. In the mid-1980s, aid continued at a reduced rate although Vietnam's economic situation had worsened.

The prospect of an improvement in the state of Sino-Soviet relations in the mid-1980s did not appear to threaten the Soviet

Union's ties with Vietnam. Although China demanded that Moscow ensure Vietnam's withdrawal from Cambodia as a condition to normalizing the Sino-Soviet relationship, Vietnamese leaders proceeded as if they were sure their existing policy in Cambodia would not be threatened. The Soviets even went so far as to promote improved relations between Hanoi and Beijing. At Vietnam's Sixth Party Congress in December 1986, the senior member of the Soviet delegation suggested that the normalization of relations between Vietnam and China would improve the situation in Asia and the world as a whole. The Vietnamese agreed with this premise but were unwilling to seek improved ties at the expense of weakening their position in Cambodia.

Eastern Europe

In addition to relations with the Soviet Union, Vietnam maintained close relations with other members of Comecon and the Warsaw Pact. Between 1965 and 1975, Eastern Europe provided Vietnam with some US$844 million in aid amounting to 18 percent of all aid received during that period. Between November 1976 and June 1977, Vietnam signed commodity and payments agreements with eight communist countries, cultural agreements with four, scientific cooperation agreements with eight, and separate agreements for economic, scientific, or technical cooperation with five. Its relations with Czechoslovakia, the German Democratic Republic (East Germany), and Hungary were particularly close.

The United States

The Communist victory in South Vietnam in 1975 abruptly concluded three decades of United States intervention in Vietnam and brought to a close a painful and bitter era for both countries. The war generated considerable social and political discord in the United States, massive disruption in Vietnam, and was enormously costly to both sides. Vietnam endured physical destruction—ravaged battle sites, leveled factories and cities, and untold numbers of military and civilian casualties. The United States escaped physical devastation, but it suffered the loss of 58,000 lives (2,400 unaccounted for) and spent roughly $150 billion in direct expenses to sustain the war. The war also divided and confused American society.

To the Vietnamese communists, the war against the United States simply extended the war for independence initiated against the French. In Hanoi's view, when the United States displaced the French in Indochina, it assumed the French role as a major-power obstacle to Vietnam's eventual reunification.

For the United States, intervention was derived from considerations that largely transcended Vietnam. In the closing months of World War II, the United States had supported the idea of an international trusteeship for all of Indochina. Subsequently, in spite of misgivings in Washington about French intentions to reimpose colonial rule in Indochina, the United States eventually tilted in support of the French war effort in the embattled region. Anticolonial sentiment in the United States after World War II thus failed to outweigh policy priorities in Europe, such as the evolving North Atlantic Treaty Organization (NATO) relationship. The formal creation of NATO and the communist victory in China, both of which occurred in 1949, led the United States to support materially the French war effort in Indochina. The perception that communism was global and monolithic led the administration of President Dwight D. Eisenhower to support the idea of a noncommunist state in southern Vietnam, after the French withdrawal under the Geneva Agreements of 1954. Although this goal arguably ran counter to two key features of the Geneva Agreements (the stipulation that the line separating North and South Vietnam be neither a political nor territorial boundary and the call for reunification elections), it was based on the United States assessment that the Viet Minh—which, contrary to the agreements, had left several thousand cadres south of the demarcation line—was already in violation. The first United States advisers arrived in the South within a year after Geneva to help President Ngo Dinh Diem establish a government that would be strong enough to stand up to the communist regime in the North.

Although Washington's advisory role was essentially political, United States policy makers determined that the effort to erect a non-communist state in Vietnam was vital to the security of the region and would be buttressed by military means, if necessary, to inhibit any would-be aggressor. Defending Vietnam's security against aggression from the North and from southern-based communist insurgency was a mission Washington initially perceived as requiring only combat support elements and advisers to South Vietnamese military units. The situation, however, rapidly deteriorated, and in 1965, at a time when increasing numbers of North Vietnamese-trained soldiers were moving into South Vietnam, the first increment of United States combat forces was introduced into the South and sustained bombing of military targets in North Vietnam was undertaken. Nearly eight more years of conflict occurred before the intense involvement of the United States ended in 1973.

An "Agreement Ending the War and Restoring Peace in Vietnam" was signed in Paris on January 27, 1973, by Washington,

225

Hanoi, Saigon, and the Provisional Revolutionary Government, representing the Vietnamese communist organization in the South, the Viet Cong (see Glossary—contraction of Viet Nam Cong San). The settlement called for a cease-fire, withdrawal of all United States troops, continuance in place of North Vietnamese troops in the South, and the eventual reunification of the country "through peaceful means." In reality, once United States Forces were disengaged in early 1973 there was no effective way to prevent the North from overwhelming the South's defenses and the settlement proved unenforceable. Following the fragile cease-fire established by the agreement, PAVN units remained in the South Vietnamese countryside, while Army of the Republic of Vietnam (ARVN— see Glossary) units fought to dislodge them and expand the areas under Saigon's control. As a result, the two sides battled from 1973 to 1975, but the ARVN, having to fight without the close United States air, artillery, logistical, and medevac (medical evacuation) support to which it had become accustomed, acquitted itself badly, losing more and more ground to the communists.

The surprisingly swift manner in which the South Vietnamese government finally collapsed in 1975 appeared to confirm that the Paris agreement had accomplished little more than to delay an inevitable defeat for the United States ally, South Vietnam, and that Washington had been impotent to avert this outcome.

Following the war, Hanoi pursued the establishment of diplomatic relations with the United States, initially in order to obtain US$3.3 billion in reconstruction aid, which President Richard M. Nixon had secretly promised after the Paris Agreement was signed in 1973. Under Article 21 of the agreement, the United States had pledged "to contribute to healing the wounds of war and to postwar reconstruction of the DRV . . ." but had specifically avoided using terminology that could be interpreted to mean that reparations were being offered for war damages. Nixon's promise was in the form of a letter, confirming the intent of Article 21 and offering a specific figure. Barely two months after Hanoi's victory in 1975, Premier Pham Van Dong, speaking to the National Assembly, invited the United States to normalize relations with Vietnam and to honor its commitment to provide reconstruction funds. Representatives of two American banks—the Bank of America and First National City Bank—were invited to discuss trade possibilities, and American oil companies were informed that they were welcome to apply for concessions to search for oil in offshore Vietnamese waters.

Washington neglected Dong's call for normal relations, however, because it was predicated on reparations, and the Washington political climate in the wake of the war precluded the pursuit of such an outcome. In response, the administration of President Gerald R. Ford imposed its own precondition for normal relations by announcing that a full accounting of Americans missing in action (MIAs—see Glossary), including the return of any remains, would be required before normalization could be effected. No concessions were made on either side until President Jimmy Carter softened the United States demand from a full accounting of MIAs to the fullest possible accounting and dispatched a mission to Hanoi in 1977 to initiate normalization discussions.

Although the Vietnamese at first were adamant about United States economic assistance (their first postwar economic plan counted on the amount promised by President Nixon), the condition was dropped in mid-1978 when Hanoi made additional gestures toward normal relations. At that time, Vietnamese Foreign Minister Nguyen Co Thach and the United States government reached an agreement in principle on normalization, but the date was left vague. When Thach urged November 1978, a date that in retrospect is significant because he was due in Moscow to sign the Treaty of Friendship and Cooperation with the Soviet Union, Washington was noncommittal. During this period, United States officials were preoccupied with the question of the Indochinese refugees, and they were in the process of normalizing relations with China. This was an action that could have been jeopardized had Washington concurrently sought a rapprochement with Vietnam, a nation whose relationship with Beijing was growing increasingly strained. Policy makers in Hanoi correctly reasoned that the United States had opted to strengthen its ties with China rather than with Vietnam, and they moved to formalize their ties with the Soviets in response. Their original hope, however, had been to gain both diplomatic recognition from the United States and a friendship treaty with Moscow, as a double guarantee against future Chinese interference.

In the United States, the issue of normalizing relations with Vietnam was complicated by Vietnam's invasion of Cambodia in December 1978, the continuing plight of Vietnamese refugees, and the unresolved MIA issue (see Ethnic Groups and Languages, ch. 2). In 1987, under President Ronald Reagan, the United States continued to enforce the trade embargo imposed on Hanoi in 1975 and barred normal ties as long as Vietnamese troops occupied Cambodia. Any efforts to improve relations remained closely tied to United States willingness to honor its 1973 aid commitment to Vietnam and to Hanoi's failure to account for the whereabouts of more than 2,400 MIAs in Indochina. From the signing of the Paris agreements in 1973 until mid-1978, the Vietnamese had routinely stressed the linkage between the aid and MIA issues. Beginning in mid-1978, however, Hanoi dropped its insistence that the MIA and aid questions be resolved as a precondition for normalization and stopped linking the MIA question to other unresolved matters between the two countries. Vietnamese leaders contrasted their restraint on the MIA issue with its alleged political exploitation by the United States as a condition for normal relations. As additional signs of goodwill, Hanoi permitted the joint United States-Vietnamese excavation of a B-52 crash site in 1985 and returned the remains of a number of United States servicemen between 1985 and 1987. Vietnamese spokesmen also claimed during this period to have a two-year plan to resolve the MIA question but failed to reveal details.

Although Vietnam's Sixth National Party Congress in December 1986 officially paid little attention to relations with the United States, the report of the congress noted that Vietnam was continuing to hold talks with Washington on humanitarian issues and expressed a readiness to improve relations. Although ambivalent in tone, the message was more positive than the 1982 Fifth National Party Congress report, which had attributed the stalemated relationship to Washington's "hostile policy." The improved wording was attributable to the influence of newly appointed Party General Secretary Nguyen Van Linh, who was expected to attach high priority to expanding Vietnam's links with the West.

Within a few months of the Sixth National Party Congress, however, Hanoi began to send conflicting signals to Washington. In mid-1987 the Vietnamese government, having determined that cooperation had gained few concessions from the United States, reverted to its pre-1978 position linking the aid and MIA issues. The resumption of its hardline stand, however, was brief. A meeting between Vietnamese leaders and President Reagan's special envoy on MIAs, General John W. Vessey, in August 1987 yielded significant gains for both sides. In exchange for greater Vietnamese cooperation on resolving the MIA issue, the United States agreed officially to encourage charitable assistance for Vietnam. Although the agreement fell short of Hanoi's requests for economic aid or war reparations, it marked the first time that the United States had offered anything in return for Vietnamese assistance in accounting for the MIAs and was an important step toward an eventual reconciliation between the two countries.

ASEAN

The Association of Southeast Asian Nations (ASEAN) was formed

*Ho Chi Minh City poster
portrays American and Chinese "aggressors," 1979.
Courtesy Bill Herod*

in 1967 as a regional, economic, cultural, and social cooperative organization. The original five member nations—Indonesia, Malaysia, the Philippines, Singapore, and Thailand (the sixth member, Brunei, was admitted in January 1984)—had little in common in their culture, history, or politics. Nevertheless, after a slow start the organization flourished; by 1987 it had the fastest growing GNP of all economic groups in the world and was a key force for regional stability.

ASEAN's charter declares that membership is open to all states in the region—a gesture toward Vietnam that Hanoi repeatedly rebuffed. Before Vietnam's invasion and occupation of Cambodia in December 1978, integration of the three Indochinese states and ASEAN into a larger regional organization was discussed within the ASEAN community as a possible solution to regional problems. The proposal surfaced at an ASEAN summit meeting held in Bali in January 1976, when, following reunification, Vietnam requested observer status at ASEAN meetings. It was understood at the time, however, that the inclusion of communist states within a grouping of free-market countries was unprecedented, and the idea was interpreted to be more a goodwill gesture than a serious proposition.

From 1976 to 1978, ASEAN's differences with Vietnam were both symbolic and real. ASEAN, for example, proposed establishing

Southeast Asia as a zone of peace, freedom, and neutrality and invited Vietnam to support the proposal. Hanoi refused but countered with its own proposal, calling instead for a region of peace, independence, and neutrality. Apparently, the Vietnamese objected to the term *freedom* because of their vulnerability to criticism on human rights issues. The term *independence,* on the other hand, was promoted by the Vietnamese as a concept opposing all foreign military bases in Southeast Asia, an idea that many of the ASEAN nations did not share.

During the Second Indochina War, each ASEAN state pursued its own Vietnam policy. Malaysia and Indonesia maintained strict neutrality, whereas Thailand and the Philippines contributed personnel and matériel to South Vietnam. Perceptions of Vietnam as a possible threat to the region also varied among member nations. Indonesia and Malaysia viewed Vietnam as a buffer against Chinese expansionism, whereas Thailand, wary of possible repetition of historic patterns of confrontation with Vietnam, turned to China for protection following the war's end and the subsequent withdrawal of United States forces from Thailand.

Following the 1978 invasion of Cambodia, however, the ASEAN nations were united in their condemnation of Hanoi. They took the lead in mobilizing international opinion against Vietnam, and, in the UN General Assembly, they annually sponsored resolutions calling for withdrawal of Vietnamese troops and for internationally supervised elections. The ASEAN nations also were instrumental in preventing the Vietnam-sponsored Heng Samrin regime in Phnom Penh from taking over Cambodia's UN seat. In June 1982, ASEAN was instrumental in persuading three disparate Cambodian resistance elements to merge into a coalition resistance government (see Laos and Cambodia, this ch.).

ASEAN's position on Cambodia was important to Hanoi, because it was through ASEAN's efforts at the UN that the world's attention continued to focus on Cambodia in the late 1980s. The Vietnamese thus saw ASEAN as having the power to confer upon them or to deny them legitimacy in Cambodia. Vietnamese diplomats sought to convince the ASEAN countries that the invasion of Cambodia was intended to eliminate the threat posed by Pol Pot's alignment with China. Rather than have its activity in Cambodia perceived as potentially damaging to ASEAN's security, Vietnam wanted to assure ASEAN members that it was in the group's interest to join with Vietnam in countering the Chinese threat to the region. Cultivating goodwill with key ASEAN members was an important part of this strategy. Thus, in 1978 Vietnam and the Philippines agreed to negotiate but failed to settle their conflicting claims to the Spratly Islands. Foreign Minister Thach, during a late-1982 visit to Indonesia, took a conciliatory position in discussing Vietnam's and Indonesia's competing claims to the Natuna Islands, and in 1984 Hanoi made a similar gesture to Malaysia in order to help resolve their conflicting claims over Amboyna Cay. In 1987, however, resolving the war in Cambodia remained the key to any further resolution of differences between Vietnam and ASEAN.

Thailand

As the ASEAN member most vulnerable to a Vietnamese attack, Thailand was foremost among the ASEAN partners opposing Vietnam's 1978 invasion of Cambodia. Thailand's suspicion of Vietnamese long-term objectives and fear of Vietnamese support for an internal Thai communist insurgency movement led the Thai government to support United States objectives in South Vietnam during the Second Indochina War. In 1979, after Vietnam's military occupation of Cambodia had raised these same concerns again, Bangkok was compelled once again to ally with an adversary of Vietnam and looked to Beijing for security assistance. In both instances, Thailand's actions hardened Hanoi's attitude toward Bangkok.

In 1973 a new civilian government in Thailand created a chance for some degree of reconciliation with Vietnam, when it proposed to remove United States military forces from Thai soil and adopt a more neutralist stance. The Vietnamese responded by sending a delegation to Bangkok, but talks broke down before any progress in improving relations could be made. Discussions resumed in August 1976. They resulted in a call for an exchange of ambassadors and for an opening of negotiations on trade and economic cooperation, but a military coup in October 1976 ushered in a new Thai government that was less sympathetic to the Vietnamese. Contact was resumed briefly in May 1977, when Vietnam, Thailand, and Laos held a conference to discuss resuming work on the Mekong Development Project, a major cooperative effort that had been halted by the Second Indochina War. Beginning in December 1978, however, the conflict in Cambodia dominated diplomatic exchanges, and seasonal Vietnamese military offensives that included incursions across the Thai border and numerous Thai casualties particularly strained the relationship.

Other Noncommunist Nations

Relations with noncommunist nations were still in the early stages of development in the mid-1970s to mid-1980s. Noncommunist aid, nevertheless, was a significant part of Hanoi's budget prior to

231

Vietnam's invasion of Cambodia in December 1978. In 1976 and 1977, for example, aid from noncommunist nations amounted to US$438.5 million, of which Sweden, France, Japan, and UN-related organizations accounted for 78 percent. With the exception of aid from Sweden, however, such aid was either significantly curtailed or terminated following the invasion.

Trade ties, after the invasion, suffered similarly. In 1976 four noncommunist trading partners—Japan, Hong Kong, France, and Sweden—accounted for 44 percent of Vietnam's imports, and more than half of Vietnam's exports went to noncommunist buyers such as Singapore, Hong Kong, Japan, and France. A decade later, in 1986, only 20 percent of Vietnam's imports were of noncommunist origin, and 40 percent of its exports were reaching noncommunist markets.

By the mid-1980s, however, Vietnam was actively seeking to improve its economic and political ties with the noncommunist world community in order to stimulate aid, trade, and investment. With few exceptions, noncommunist nations were prepared to reciprocate. The one obstacle preventing their doing so remained Hanoi's continued occupation of Cambodia and the absence of a resolution to the conflict.

International Organizations

In 1976 Vietnam was admitted to the UN and gained membership in a number of the organization's affiliated agencies, including the International Monetary Fund (IMF, see Glossary), the World Bank (see Glossary), and the Committee for Coordination of Investigations of the Lower Mekong Basin (see Glossary). Hanoi also successfully claimed the seat formerly occupied by South Vietnam in the Asian Development Bank (see Glossary). In the 1980s it was a member of Comecon, the Colombo Plan (see Glossary), the International Telecommunications Satellite Organization (INTELSAT, see Glossary), and actively participated in the Nonaligned Movement (see Glossary) and the Group of 77 (see Glossary).

The Media

Although an official description of the press, offered by the Sixth National Party Congress, defines the media's role as being ''the voice of the party and of the masses,'' and identifies its task as being to ''propagate the party's lines and policies,'' as well as to report and analyze the news, the Vietnamese press is much more a medium for educating the public and filtering information, than for reporting news. It is controlled by the VCP Central Committee's Propaganda and Training Department in accordance with guidelines established by the Ministry of Culture, and both agencies act to ensure that it reflects the policies and positions of the party. In mid-1987, however, there emerged increasing evidence within the media that a movement might be underway to change the character of the press. Articles stressing the importance of investigative reporting, calling for more journalistic freedom to report accurately, and defending the right of the people to be heard appeared in many of the leading newspapers. The movement appeared to be led by a small but influential group of journalists seeking to make the press more assertive by emphasizing accurate reporting and a more balanced reflection of public opinion.

In the late 1980s, there were approximately 350 national or local newspapers, magazines, journals, news bulletins, and newsletters published in Vietnam. Some local newspapers were published in the languages of tribal minorities and one, in Ho Chi Minh City, was published in Chinese. In addition, there were a small number of publications intended for distribution outside Vietnam.

The national press included publications intended for the general public (e.g., *Tap Chi Cong San,* Communist Review) as well as those aimed at specific audiences, such as women (*Phu Nu Vietnam,* Vietnamese Women) or trade union members (*Tap Chi Cong Doan,* Trade Union Review). Separate journals and newspapers covered sports, culture, economics, social sciences, the military, and science and technology. Each of the thirty-six provinces and the three autonomous municipalities, as well as the special zone, published a newspaper and one or more journals dealing with culture, education, and science and technology. Local newspapers covered local events and did not compete with national publications.

Party control of the press ensured the political correctness of a story and determined in which publication it would appear. Rarely was the same story covered in more than one national newspaper or magazine. *Nhan Dan* (People's Daily)—the VCP daily—and *Quan Doi Nhan Dan* (People's Army)—the armed forces daily—were normally limited to national and international stories. Articles on subjects like sports or art appeared in newspapers or journals devoted to those subjects. *Nhan Dan,* the leading national newspaper and the official organ of the VCP Central Committee, began publication in 1951. By 1987, as a four-page daily reporting domestic and international news, it published the full texts of speeches and articles by party and government leaders and included feature articles on the government, party, culture, and economy. *Quan Doi Nhan Dan,* published daily except Sunday by PAVN, was also four pages in length and included international and national news, but with an emphasis on military activities and training.

The principal national magazine was *Tap Chi Cong San* (Communist Review), a monthly journal. Formerly called *Hoc Tap* (Studies), its name was changed in January 1977, after the Fourth Party Congress. It was a theoretical and political journal and was considered to be the voice of the VCP. In 1987 its table of contents was published for international dissemination in English, French, Spanish, and Russian.

Publications intended specifically for foreign audiences in the 1980s were *Vietnam Courier,* in English and French—a monthly with articles on current events as well as Vietnamese culture and history; *Vietnam,* in Vietnamese, Lao, Cambodian, Russian, English, French, and Spanish—a monthly with pictorial essays on all aspects of Vietnamese life; *Vietnam Foreign Trade,* in English; *Vietnam Social Sciences,* in English, French, and Russian; *Vietnam Youth,* in English and French; *Vietnamese Scientific and Technical Abstracts,* in English; *Vietnamese Studies,* in English and French; *Vietnamese Trade Unions,* in English, French, and Spanish; *Women of Vietnam,* in English and French; and *Informado El Vjetnamio* (Information on Vietnam) in Esperanto.

The country's wire service, the Vietnam News Agency (VNA), was the principal source of domestic and international news for the nation's domestic and international media in 1987. It published, on a daily basis, a twelve-to-sixteen-page English-language compendium, *Vietnam News Agency,* which provided standard press-service coverage of the day's news events.

By 1986 international shortwave news reports were broadcast by the Voice of Vietnam in eleven languages (Cambodian, Chinese—both Mandarin and Cantonese, English, French, Indonesian, Japanese, Lao, Russian, Spanish, and Thai) as well as Vietnamese. The broadcast sites for these programs included five in Hanoi and fifteen in other locations throughout the country. Transmissions reached neighboring Southeast Asian countries and regions as distant as Latin America, Africa, and Europe. Domestic service was provided from fifty-one AM transmission sites, of which five were located in Hanoi, three in Ho Chi Minh City, and the rest in other cities and districts. In addition an FM station was located in Ho Chi Minh City, and an unspecified number of other FM stations were located elsewhere in Vietnam.

The Central Television network was created in 1970. By the mid-1980s, five channels were known to broadcast from twenty-one transmission sites in Vietnam. Viewers were served by two channels in Hanoi, one in Ho Chi Minh City and one in Da Nang;

Hue, Can Tho, and Qui Nhon were served by another channel. There may have been broadcasts from Nha Trang and Vinh as well. Television Vietnam offered programs in color and in black and white. Black and white daily national programming was broadcast from Hanoi, on Monday through Friday, for ninety minutes a day and, on Saturday and Sunday, for three hours a day.

* * *

Recent books on the political process in Vietnam are comparatively few in number, and even fewer detail the structure and the inner workings of the party and the government. Among works that are extremely informative, however, are *Vietnam since the Fall of Saigon* and *Vietnam: Nation in Revolution,* by William Duiker, and *Vietnamese Communism in Comparative Perspective,* the assembled views of a number of leading Vietnam scholars, edited by William Turley. Nguyen Van Canh's *Vietnam under Communism, 1975–1982* is useful because of its discussion of party and government structure both at the national and local level.

A legal discussion of the 1980 Constitution is provided in Chin Kim's article on "Recent Developments in the Constitutions of Asian Marxist-Socialist States." Party congresses are discussed in Ralph Smith's "Vietnam's Fourth Party Congress," Carlyle Thayer's "Development Strategies in Vietnam: The Fourth National Congress of the Vietnam Communist Party," An Tai Sung's "The All-Vietnam National Assembly: Significant Developments," and Thai Quang Trung's "The Fifth Congress of the Vietnamese Communist Party."

Vietnam's foreign relations, particularly the war in Cambodia and the Sino-Vietnamese conflict, have prompted a number of useful books and articles. First among these on the subject of the war in Cambodia is Nayan Chanda's *Brother Enemy,* a work also useful for its discussion of postwar United States-Vietnamese relations. *The Third Indochina Conflict,* edited by David Elliott, includes a number of informative chapters on the subject. The Chinese-Vietnamese border war in 1979 is discussed in a historical context in G.D. Loescher's "The Sino-Vietnamese Conflict in Recent Historical Perspective," and in Eugene Lawson's *The Sino-Vietnamese Conflict.* Vietnam's relations with Southeast Asia are covered in David Elliott's "Vietnam in Asia: Strategy and Diplomacy in a New Context," and Soviet-Vietnamese relations are discussed in Robert Horn's "Soviet-Vietnamese Relations and the Future of Southeast Asia," Douglas Pike's "The USSR and Vietnam: Into the

235

Swamp,'' and Leif Rosenberger's ''The Soviet-Vietnamese Alliance and Kampuchea.''

An overview of Vietnam since the end of the Second Indochina War is presented by Carlyle Thayer and David Marr in *Vietnam since 1975—Two Views from Australia* and by William Turley in ''Vietnam since Reunification.'' Additional articles focusing on Vietnam's domestic problems following unification include Carlyle Thayer's ''Vietnam's New Pragmatism,'' William Turley's ''Hanoi's Domestic Dilemmas,'' Stephen Young's ''Unpopular Socialism in United Vietnam'' and ''Vietnamese Marxism: Transition in Elite Ideology,'' and Jayne Werner's ''Socialist Development: The Political Economy of Agrarian Reform in Vietnam.''

To follow Vietnam's politics and government on a daily basis, some of the most useful reference sources are the *Daily Report: Asia & Pacific,* published by the Foreign Broadcast Information Service, and *Southeast Asia Report,* published by the Joint Publication Research Service. The *Indochina Chronology,* a quarterly published by the Institute of East Asian Studies, University of California at Berkeley, is also invaluable. (For further information and complete citations, see Bibliography.)

Chapter 5. National Security

National hero Ngo Quyen (A.D. 899–944), who defeated the Chinese fleet in A.D. 938 to end 1,000 years of Chinese domination

IN THE LATE 1980s, Vietnam's leaders continued to define national security in the same broad, all-encompassing terms used by other Marxist-Leninist societies. The basic precept was that any effort to alter the status quo was a threat to national security and was to be dealt with quickly and decisively. The threat could come from ideas as well as from invading armies. According to this doctrine, responsibility for maintaining security rested with all the people and was not simply vested in the police, armed forces, or other coercive elements of the system. Finally, the achievement of national security was regarded as a function of proper communication with, and motivation of, the people by various party and government organs. This approach, a careful mix of compulsion and persuasion, created in communist Vietnam a social discipline that contributed to the success of the Vietnamese Communist Party (VCP, Viet Nam Cong San Dang) in the North and was extended to the South after unification in 1976.

Overview of National Security

Official attitudes in Vietnam toward national security have arisen from an amalgam of the country's heritage, historical experience, internal sociopolitical strengths and weaknesses, and geopolitical position. They are also the product of a singular kind of leadership, which in 1987 was undergoing gradual change. The Vietnamese look back at the great events of their past and see themselves as victims of history. They perceive that Vietnam always has been threatened by formidable enemies, frequently has been beleaguered, and on occasion has only narrowly escaped destruction. For centuries China repeatedly sought to establish hegemony over Vietnam. A century of colonial control by the French was shaken off in 1954, following a long, bitter struggle that concluded by planting the seeds for still another struggle for complete unification of the country. In 1987 the Vietnamese perceived their country to be isolated, surrounded by hostile neighbors, and dependent on the Soviet Union in an intimate association that was a military alliance in all but name. Internally, the country was viewed as divided by geographic regionalism stemming from ancient cultural differences among the people of the North, Center, and South (see The Chinese Millennium, ch. 1). Regardless of their veracity, such perceptions were widely held in Hanoi and conditioned the leadership's thinking about national security.

The Tradition of Militancy

Vietnam's past is characterized by a strongly martial spirit tempered by war, invasion, rebellion, insurgency, dissidence, and social sabotage. In their view, the Vietnamese have always lived in an armed camp. The first "deities" of Vietnam, before the time of recorded history, were not gods but generals. Vietnam's naval fleet in the ninth century supposedly was the largest on earth. In the tenth century, when its population could not have numbered more than 2 million, its army purportedly stood at 1 million. Asia's first military academy was founded in Hanoi in the thirteenth century. The fourteenth century produced Tran Hung Dao (1230–1300), the greatest of all Vietnam's many military geniuses, who was consistently able to win battles against vastly superior forces. According to tradition Nguyen Hue (also known as Emperor Quan Trung, 1742–92), another great military leader, fielded an army so disciplined that for the battle of Dong Da in 1789 he force-marched his troops 600 kilometers to fight an uninterrupted five-day battle that left "mountains of enemy dead." Vietnamese of all political views take pride in these figures from antiquity and seem particularly fond of those most clever in combat, such as the general who persuaded his opponent that he had two armies when the second was only a phantom. Those who sacrificed themselves on some grand battlefield are also fondly remembered. For instance, the Hai Ba Trung legend, reminiscent of the story of Jeanne D'Arc, originated early in the first century A.D. It tells of the two Trung sisters, who led their army in a futile effort against a vastly superior Chinese force. Defeated, they drowned themselves in a Hanoi lake. Members of a thriving mystic cult continued to worship the lake in the 1980s despite official disapproval. Vietnam's standard histories depict the nineteenth and early twentieth centuries as times of continual rebellion predating the rise of post-World War II Asian nationalism. The century of French colonialism is described as one long, unbroken battle involving virtually all Vietnamese.

Contemporary Hanoi historians describe Vietnam's national tradition as one in which every Vietnamese is a soldier. They cite the famed historical record, *Annam Chu Luoc* (Description of Annam, by Le Tac, circa 1340): "During the Tran dynasty all the people fought the enemy. Everyone was a soldier, which is why they were able to defeat the savage enemy. This is the general experience throughout the people's entire history." This tradition is said to arise not from militarism, but rather from a spirit of *chinh nghia* (just cause), which connotes highly moral behavior rooted in rationality, compassion, and responsibility. The historians assert that the spirit of *chinh nghia* sustained the Vietnamese in their long struggle against the Sinicization (*Han-hwa*) efforts of the Han Chinese, and later against French colonialism and American neocolonialism. Drawn from this, then, is a special kind of martial spirit, both ferocious and virtuous. It is because of *chinh nghia* that the Vietnamese have been victorious, while usually outnumbered and outgunned. *Chinh nghia* is the mystique that imparts unique fighting capabilities to the Vietnamese: first, it mobilizes the people and turns every inhabitant into a soldier; second, it applies the principles of "knowing how to fight the strong by the weak, the great numbers by the small numbers, the large by the small."

Just as Prussia has been Europe's most fought-over ground, Vietnam is Asia's. For centuries the Vietnamese battled the Chinese, the French, the Americans, the Khmer, and again the Chinese. In between they battled the Thai, the Burmans, the Lao, the Cham, the Montagnards, and each other in regional and dynastic combat. In the view of Vietnam's neighbors, Vietnamese campaigns since the fifteenth century have been offensive rather than defensive. But Vietnamese school children are taught that in these wars the Vietnamese always were the victim, never the aggressor. With respect to Vietnam's national security, the point is not whether Vietnamese perceptions are factually correct, but that the Vietnamese act on them.

In Hanoi's view, Vietnam faced an extraordinarily difficult and complex geopolitical scene in the 1980s, one that was filled with both external and internal dangers; in meeting these threats the country suffered from some strategic weaknesses and enjoyed certain strategic strengths. The conclusion appeared to be that Vietnam could deal with these dangers because of its confidence that its strengths outweighed its weaknesses and that, regardless of the threat presented, the Vietnamese cause, as in the past, would prove triumphant. The ruling Political Bureau and the People's Army of Vietnam (PAVN—see Glossary) High Command long ago developed several firm policies to achieve this end: that Vietnam must remain more or less permanently mobilized for war; that it must maintain as large a standing army as the system can support; that, as far as it is able, it must be self-sufficient in protecting itself and not rely on outside assistance or alliance; and that internally it must maintain a tightly organized, highly disciplined society capable of maintaining a high level of militant spirit among the general population.

This threat perception, and the leadership's response to it, have had the net effect of creating in Vietnam a praetorian society dedicated to the preservation of the existing order. It makes the Vietnamese, as Premier Pham Van Dong observed to a Western journalist, ''incurable romantics.'' The society in the 1980s looked back at the First Indochina War (also known as the Viet Minh War—see Glossary) and Second Indochina War (see Glossary) as an era of high deeds and heroism contrasting unfavorably with humdrum postwar life.

Strategic Thinking

The central factor in Hanoi's strategic thinking, applicable to both external and internal threats, is the VCP's concept of *dau tranh* (struggle). Briefly stated, *dau tranh* strategy is the sustained application of total military and nonmilitary force over long periods of time in pursuit of an objective. Its chief characteristic is its conceptual breadth, for it is of greater scope than ordinary warfare and requires the total mobilization of a society's resources and psychic energies. The strategy, it is held, is unique to Vietnam because of its close association with the sources of Vietnamese national security strengths. Since the mid-1970s, journals published in Hanoi on military theory have defined these strengths as the heritage of unity and patriotism, the supportive collectivist state system, the technologically and ''spiritually'' developed armed forces, a superior strategy (the *dau tranh* strategy), the undeviating justice of Vietnam's cause, and the support of the world's ''progressive forces.'' The leadership's faith in these strengths emboldens it to take an implacable approach to world affairs and to treat external activities, such as diplomacy, like quasi-military campaigns.

The aim of the *dau tranh* concept is to put warfare into a new conceptual framework. Its essence is the idea of people not merely as combatants or supporters but as weapons of war to be designed, forged, and hurled into battle—hence the term *people's war*. All people, even children, are regarded as instruments of *dau tranh*. Operationally the strategy has two arms or pincers—armed *dau tranh* and political *dau tranh*. The two always work together to close on and crush the enemy. Political *dau tranh* is not politics but a mobilizing and motivating program operating in a gray area between war and politics. Specifically, it consists of three *van* (action) programs: the all-important *dich van* (action among the enemy) includes activities directed against the foreign enemy in his home country, the *dan van* (action among the people) includes activities conducted in a liberated area, and the *binh van* (action among the military) includes nonmilitary activities against the enemy's military forces. Of the three, the *dich van* program is particularly novel because it seeks to shape outside perception and, beyond this, to persuade outsiders not only that the Vietnamese will be successful in their struggle but that they deserve to be. Strategically, it seeks to undercut the enemy's war effort at home and its diplomacy worldwide. Tactically, it attempts to limit the enemy's military response by inhibiting the full use of his military potential.

Dau tranh strategy defines the enemy narrowly—imperialists, militarists, landlords—but does not tar all in the enemy camp. Some are considered merely to have been misled, while others are regarded as foreign patriots who nevertheless support Hanoi's cause. In this way, *dau tranh* not only changes the definition of a combatant but also revises the rules of warfare. It asserts that the final test need not be military, and that the decisive action may take place away from the battlefield.

The strategy requires the support of tremendous organizational resources as it seeks always to realize the ideal of total mobilization and motivation. It also requires meticulous attention to the mundane details of war and politics, such as logistics and administration.

The great utility of *dau tranh* strategy, as evidenced by forty years of use against the French, the Americans, and the Chinese, is twofold: it can cloud the enemy's perceptions and it can nullify his power. In the judgment of the Vietnamese leadership, it has proved to be highly effective in confounding the enemy's strategic response because it engenders misperception in the enemy camp. Vietnam's leaders have said that the nature of the Second Indochina War was never seen clearly either by the South Vietnamese or by the Americans. *Dau tranh* strategy, in effect, dictates the enemy's counterstrategy, even to the extent of forcing him to fight under unfavorable conditions. In circumscribing the enemy's military response by altering his perception of the war, *dau tranh*'s guiding principle is that military force must always be politically clothed. Every battle must be cast in terms of a political act. When this is not possible—as in a purely tactical engagement, such as that with United States forces at Khe Sanh in early 1968—the attack must be made to seem a military action for a political purpose (see The Second Indochina War, ch. 1). Theoretically, violence or military action defined or perceived as political becomes more acceptable to all parties, participant and onlooker alike.

After the Second Indochina War, the *dau tranh* concept served the Vietnamese less well. It was employed, more by accident than by design, against the invading Chinese during the brief border war in 1979 and worked fairly well. It did not prove workable in Cambodia, however, and was for the most part abandoned there. Interestingly, many of its techniques were borrowed by the

Cambodian resistance forces and used against the Vietnamese-supported Khmer People's Revolutionary Armed Forces (KPRAF), as well as against PAVN forces in Cambodia. Vietnam's experience in Cambodia inspired Hanoi to scrutinize the strategy more closely in order to assess its application to future needs. However, the strategy's past success weighed heavily in the assessment, and Vietnamese leaders in 1987 continued to place confidence in its viability.

PAVN generals, in 1987, were in the process of evaluating Vietnam's position in the world and reviewing the nature of its future strategic requirements. Vietnamese publications on the subject in the 1980s stressed continuity in strategic thinking and the need to treat the future as a logical extension of the past. The twin pillars with which the strategic planners sought to serve future national interests were, first, to exploit Vietnam's innate skill in strategic defense and, second, to capitalize on the party's ability to anchor the strategic process successfully in the people.

Four major themes could be discerned in Hanoi's strategic thinking in the mid-1980s. The first was the recognition that PAVN must be prepared to fight both limited, small-scale, orthodox wars and protracted, guerrilla wars. As a practical matter, renewed attention was given to preparing for warfare in mountainous terrain (Vietnam is 40 percent mountainous and 75 percent forested—see Geography, ch. 2).

The second theme was an increasing emphasis on military technology. This resulted from PAVN's experience with the United States military machine in the Second Indochina War and with the war in Cambodia, as well as from the influence of Soviet military advisers.

The third theme was a return to orthodox *dau tranh* strategy. This occurred partly as a result of the successes scored by Pol Pot's Cambodian guerrillas and partly as a result of the success of PAVN paramilitary forces against the invading Chinese. The counterinsurgency effort in Cambodia, for example, was regarded as simply a limited, small-scale, high-technology war. Another war against China, according to Vietnamese definitions, would require (as, indeed, the previous one had required) a mixture of orthodox limited-war strategy and elements of *dau tranh* strategy. The PAVN high command, in opposition to earlier practice, appeared increasingly to believe that high-technology warfare in the mountains was possible.

The fourth theme was the acknowledgment that the strategy in Cambodia and the strategy designed for use against China depended on continued support from the Soviet Union. In order to meet Vietnam's future external security needs, Hanoi's leadership probably will be led to conclude that it must eventually develop a new or revised strategic concept that is not overly dependent on past strategies or simple alliance with the Soviet Union. At the end of 1987, however, the leaders in PAVN and the Political Bureau appeared to have undiminished faith in the efficacy of their past doctrines and in the connection with Moscow. As long as they remained in power, a markedly new Vietnamese strategic approach to national security seemed unlikely.

Security Concerns

Victory did not bring Vietnam the security that Hanoi leaders had assumed would be theirs in the postwar world. Vietnam in the 1980s was beleaguered, in some ways more so than North Vietnam had been during the Second Indochina War. It feared invasion, which it had not feared then, and Vietnamese society in what was formerly North Vietnam was far more restive and dispirited than it had been even during the darkest days of the war. Newly acquired South Vietnam remained largely unassimilated. Hanoi's chief instrument for assuring internal security and tranquility, the VCP, had seriously declined in effectiveness, tarnished by a decade of failure. The party's wartime reputation for being virtually omnipotent was all but gone. In addition, Hanoi's victory in the spring of 1975 had radically altered geopolitics, not only for Vietnam and Indochina, but also for all of Asia. It had precipitated drastic changes in relations among several of the nations of the Pacific, and some of these changes had severe consequences for Vietnam.

In the 1980s, Hanoi regarded itself as a major force in Asia for the first time in history. Vietnam's population of about 60 million made it the thirteenth largest of the world's 126 nations, and the third largest of the communist nations (see Population, ch. 2). It was strategically located at a crossroads of Asia and had considerable natural wealth and economic potential. It also had a large, battle-hardened, and well-equipped army. Ironically, the strengthened Vietnamese geopolitical position that resulted from victory in war became something of a postwar weakness, for it thrust on an unprepared Hanoi leadership tasks in national security planning that it was ill-prepared to handle. For decades Hanoi's security planners had been totally preoccupied with their struggle within the Indochina peninsula and had ignored the world beyond. With victory they were required for the first time to look outward and examine their nation's strategic position; to estimate potential threats and determine possible enemies and allies; to think in terms of strategic manpower, fire power, and weapons systems; and to plan strategies accordingly. Despite their great experience in warfare, they were relative novices in peace; their performance in the first postwar decade did not prove impressive.

Vietnam suffered from other remediable liabilities, in addition to inexperienced strategic planners. These included an army still oriented toward guerrilla infantry; an inability to project air and naval forces over long distances; the lack of logistics and transport systems required by a modern armed force (particularly, lack of air transport); a low level of technical competence in the officer corps; and a shortage of good, reliable equipment and weapons. Hanoi's strategic planners, and their Soviet advisers, clearly recognized that new weapons systems were required for the vastly changed security conditions facing Vietnam. Efforts were undertaken to develop the Vietnamese navy, and new Soviet-built ships arrived to be added to the fleet captured in the South. Vietnam was also rumored to be creating a submarine force. Hanoi's vaunted military strongpoint, its divisions of light infantry, however, required conversion to a more orthodox high-technology force in order to become militarily credible in the region. Hanoi's military journals indicated that ambitious research and development projects were underway, but a significant upgrading of military technology was unlikely. In the late 1980s, Vietnam was at least a decade and a half away from a nuclear weapons delivery system—unless the Soviet Union were to provide a crash development program, which was considered unlikely.

In the meantime, Vietnam remained a nation fully mobilized for war. This was a condition that eventually would require a change to a peacetime mode, accompanied by some demobilization of PAVN and the reallocation of most resources to the task of economic development, if the country were to keep pace with its Asian neighbors. The fact that PAVN continued to grow, in fact to double in size in the decade after 1975, was a government concession to entrenched PAVN interests as well as to internal and external security fears, many of them brought on by the fact that Vietnam had not renounced warfare as a foreign policy option. In any event, hard decisions lay ahead for the Hanoi leadership concerning the armed forces' share of the annual governmental budget, the ultimate size and deployment of PAVN, the kind of air and naval power to be developed, the levels of military spending, and the development of indigenous sources of military hardware.

Vietnam in 1987 faced only one truly credible external threat— China (see The Chinese Millennium and Nine Centuries of Independence, ch. 1). The complex Sino-Vietnamese relationship, dating back two thousand years, is deeply rooted in the Confucian concept of pupil-teacher. Thus, any issues under contention or problems that exist between the two on the surface normally are transcended by this basic relationship. Much of the behavior demonstrated by the two since 1975—including Vietnam's invasion of Cambodia and China's subsequent "lesson" to Vietnam—is, in fact, traceable to the workings of this deep-rooted historic association (see Foreign Relations, ch. 4). Victory in the Indochina War left Hanoi leaders determined to change the centuries-old relationship. The Vietnamese sought to end the notion of the rimland barbarian's obligation to pay deference to the Middle Kingdom. They felt the tutelary relationship should give way to one of greater equality. The Chinese, however, considered that nothing significant had changed and that the original condition of mutual obligation should continue. For the Chinese, the touchstone would always be the Sino-Soviet dispute and the need to reduce Soviet influence in Hanoi. Most important for China was the nature and future of the Soviet presence in Indochina. Beijing tried several approaches to induce Hanoi to maintain its distance from Moscow. However, none was successful. In the 1980s it pursued what might be called a campaign of protracted intimidation—military, diplomatic, and psychological pressure—on the Vietnamese, calculating that eventually Hanoi would seek some accommodation.

In the minds of Hanoi's strategic planners, Vietnam's two Indochina neighbors posed nearly as large an external security threat as did China. Strategically, Cambodia and Laos represented weak flanks where internal anticommunist forces could challenge the local regimes and threaten Vietnam itself. Geography increased this threat. Vietnam is an extraordinarily narrow country—at its "waist" near Dong Hoi it is only forty kilometers across—and could be cut in half militarily with relative ease either through an amphibious landing on its coast or through an invasion from Laos. It is also a long country, with some 8,000 kilometers of border and coastline to defend. For these reasons Hanoi was prepared to do whatever was necessary to achieve a secure, cooperative, nonthreatening Laos and Cambodia.

External security threats to Vietnam from the Southeast Asia region were also possible. Just as the relationship with China was tied to Hanoi's Cambodian and Laotian policies, so the relationship with Cambodia and Laos was bound up with policies toward the six nations comprising the Association of Southeast Asian Nations (ASEAN). Vietnamese security goals in Southeast Asia in the 1980s appeared to be the elimination of any United States military presence; the diminution of American influence; a general balance of superpower activity in the region; and, possibly, the unified economic development of the region. PAVN dwarfed all of its ASEAN neighbors' armed forces and, in fact, was larger than all six combined. Its size and continued growth provided Hanoi's neighbors with legitimate cause for worry. PAVN, given the advantage of terrain, was sufficiently powerful to battle the Chinese army to a stalemate for a prolonged period, although not indefinitely. The composition of PAVN—large numbers of infantry with only guerrilla war experience, limited air power, and virtually no offensive naval capability—meant that Vietnam could not, however, project force over a long distance and could not, for instance, offer a credible threat even to Indonesia. Probably it could not even defend its holdings in the Spratly Islands against a determined Chinese assault (see fig. 1).

In strict strategic terms, PAVN was not as threatening to most of Vietnam's neighbors as its size suggested. Thailand, however, was a clear exception. PAVN had the military capability to crush Thailand's small, lightly equipped armed force in frontal battle. It could invade and occupy Thailand quickly, although most certainly that action would trigger the same kind of resistance encountered in Cambodia. Furthermore, such an invasion would incur the wrath of China and the displeasure of the Soviet Union, and would probably precipitate military support from the ASEAN states and the United States. In the long run, PAVN will be a credible threat to its remaining neighbors only when it develops adequate air and naval strength. Vietnam's acquisition of such a capability, however, will depend more on Moscow's inclinations than Hanoi's.

The Armed Forces

PAVN is a singular military establishment. (The full name is occasionally translated Vietnam People's Army, or VPA). Its singularity of purpose as well as form is a function of its Vietnamese cultural heritage, a centuries-old martial spirit, a history of messianic military leadership possessing extraordinary insight, and four decades of combat experience.

In the 1980s, PAVN was characterized by a sense of newly acquired destiny, a feeling of international prowess, and the real limitations imposed by economic stagnation, diplomatic isolation, and uncertainty regarding its closest ally, the Soviet Union. It was in the middle of a debate over the proper use of force (whether it should be applied nakedly as in Cambodia or in the more traditional manner prescribed by ''revolutionary force'' doctrine) and was determined to modernize its organization, including reforming the officer corps and renewing the never-ending internal battle against inefficiency and corruption. Finally, PAVN was faced with the prospect of an inevitable generational change of military leadership. In 1987 PAVN numbered about 2.9 million personnel, including its Paramilitary Force, making it the third largest armed force in the world. Nevertheless, it was well integrated into Vietnamese society and enjoyed a good working relationship with both the government and the VCP. It was tightly controlled, chiefly by various mechanisms in the hands of the VCP apparatus within it.

At the same time, PAVN was limited by critical weaknesses: it was technologically underdeveloped because it lacked various kinds of modern equipment, weapons, and training; its officer and noncommissioned officer corps were overaged; and it was highly dependent on outside military sources because there were no indigenous arms factories of any importance in Vietnam.

The purpose to which PAVN has been dedicated over the years has varied greatly and has turned chiefly on the demands of the party. Its basic functions are similar to those of armed forces everywhere: to defend Vietnam's territorial integrity, to support its foreign policy and strategic goals where appropriate, to contribute to the maintenance of its internal security, and to assist in its economic development. These aims are set forth in Section IV (Articles 50 through 52) of the 1980 Constitution.

In the first several years after the end of the Second Indochina War, PAVN's performance was tested twice—in Cambodia and along Vietnam's northern border with China. Its ability to maintain internal security has been tested continuously, although to a lesser degree.

History

PAVN's progenitor was a collection of guerrilla bands, many of them composed of ethnic minority highlanders, assembled in Indochina during World War II and armed and encouraged by the Allied Forces as opposition to the Japanese army, which had occupied much of Southeast Asia. A few of these guerrilla bands were organized by the Indochinese Communist Party (ICP), as the VCP was known at the time (see Development of the Vietnamese Communist Party, ch. 4).

Near the end of the war, the ICP began to experiment with a new kind of military force, called Armed Propaganda units. The first of these units was created in the mountains of northern Vietnam near the China border. The armed propaganda team was the brainchild of Ho Chi Minh (known then as Nguyen Ai Quoc) and a thirty-two-year-old Hanoi history teacher named Vo Nguyen Giap. It was designed both to engage in combat and to do organizational and mobilization work in the villages. Armed propaganda teams shaped the character of the subsequently formed PAVN.

On September 2, 1945, when Ho Chi Minh officially proclaimed the independence of the nation and announced the formation of the Democratic Republic of Vietnam (DRV), a Ministry of National Defense was created and the ministerial portfolio was given to a noncommunist, a measure that reflected the apparently broadly nationalistic composition of the new government. Giap, at the time the second most powerful communist figure, became minister of the interior. A year later the National Defense Council (NDC) was created, and Giap was made chairman, giving him more direct control of the Viet Minh armed force (see Glossary), the precursor to PAVN. When the French returned to Indochina, the newly formed Viet Minh—consisting of approximately 1,000 men in 13 infantry companies—was driven into the hills behind Hanoi.

The Viet Minh's military force, which fought the French for eight years, was a united-front army, meaning it was communist-influenced but was not entirely communist. For much of the First Indochina War, it was essentially an irregular force, growing to about 60,000 at the end of the first year of the war and to about 380,000 in 1954. Only about a third of these were considered regulars; the remainder were "regional" or "local" forces. This system was the forerunner of the three-elements concept of the armed forces—regulars, regionals (or territorials), and locals—which has been retained in PAVN. The regular force was organized into about 30 infantry battalions of 600 men each and 8 heavy-weapons battalions. Many of the early units were organized along ethnic lines. A preponderance of the day-to-day battles in the First Indochina War were fought by PAVN regional forces and local militia units. Regulars were used sparingly and were committed only to battles of strategic importance, such as the 1950 campaign to push French forces back from the China border region, the attempted capture of Hanoi in 1951, and the battle of Dien Bien Phu in 1954.

In 1954, at the end of the First Indochina War, PAVN was still a united-front military force. It remained for the party to "regularize" it. Control mechanisms were introduced gradually and perfected, reorganization was undertaken, military elements were enlarged, support units were added, and formal regulations on military service were developed. A tight system of party controls was introduced, military schools were opened and military assistance was solicited from abroad, chiefly from China. A directive of the Twelfth Plenum of the Central Committee (Second National Party Congress), issued in March 1957, established universal military conscription. By 1965 PAVN numbered 400,000; by 1975, 650,000. Of the approximately 2.9 million in uniform in 1987, about

Vo Nguyen Giap with Viet Minh troops, 1946
Courtesy Indochina Archives

1.1 million served in the PAVN Regular Force and 1.8 million served in the Paramilitary Force.

In 1959 the VCP (known at the time as the Vietnam Workers' Party—VWP, or Dang Lao Dong Viet Nam) decided to launch an armed struggle in the South in the name of unification of the fatherland. Part of the effort involved creation of a united-front organization, the National Front for the Liberation of South Vietnam (or Viet Cong, see Glossary) and a united-front armed force, initially called the People's Liberation Army (PLA) and later renamed the People's Liberation Armed Force (PLAF). The mission of the PLAF was to liberate the South in order to permit its unification with North Vietnam, and Hanoi began supplying this force with doctrinal know-how and key personnel. In keeping with a principle of people's war that called on combatants to be self-sustaining, North Vietnamese leaders also admonished the PLAF to be self-supporting and self-contained and not to rely on, or make requests of, Hanoi. Then and later, however, authorities always stood ready to meet any critical need of their southern brethren.

Until 1965 the war in the South was on the shoulders of the PLAF. Its rapid escalation in 1965, however, introduced PAVN troops to the South in ever-increasing numbers, and the burden of the war shifted to them. In 1972 in the so-called Easter offensive, about 90 percent of the combat was carried out by northern

251

regulars. The final campaign in April 1975 was fought almost entirely by PAVN troops. At the time, almost all PAVN infantry divisions were outside North Vietnam in Laos, in Cambodia, or, overwhelmingly, in South Vietnam. After the war, the remnant PLAF force was disbanded, and its members were either demobilized or transferred to PAVN units.

Throughout its developmental period, from the earliest protomilitary organizations of the 1930s until the late 1970s, PAVN was heavily influenced by China and by Chinese military thought and doctrine. The original party-led armed force, the Viet Minh army, was created by the Chinese Nationalist Party (Kuomintang) and fielded from China. Later, it was nurtured and funded largely by the Chinese Communist Party. Military manuals were of Chinese origin, first Nationalist then Communist, and in the early years nearly all imported logistic assistance came either directly from China or—if from the Soviet Union—through China and with Chinese cooperation. During the Second Indochina War, Chinese antiaircraft troops and Chinese railroad and warehousing personnel served in Vietnam.

Postwar Development

The chief changes in PAVN after April 1975 were enormous growth, augmented by increased war-making capability and fire power, and development away from a guerrilla-oriented infantry toward a more orthodox modern armed force. Hanoi's public statements indicated there would be a significant demobilization of PAVN immediately after the war and that many PAVN units would be converted into economic development teams. Within a few weeks, however, PAVN units were engaged in a border war in Cambodia with one-time ally the Khmer Rouge (see Glossary) and were preparing to defend Vietnam's northern border against China.

Following the end of the Second Indochina War, PAVN was in worse condition than was generally realized. Having been decimated by ten years of combat, it was in organizational disarray, with a logistics system that was nearly worn out. Both PAVN and the country were suffering from war weariness, and restructuring and rebuilding were hampered in part because the war's sudden ending had precluded planning for the postwar world. Vietnamese military journals acknowledged at the time that the new situation required the transformation of PAVN from an army of revolutionary soldiers fighting with guerrilla tactics into an orthodox armed force that could defend existing institutions and fixed installations from internal and external threats. It was a new and broader task, and Ho Chi Minh's observation made at the end of the First

South Vietnamese soldier guarding Viet Minh captive, First Indochina War
Courtesy New York Times, *Paris Collection, National Archives*

Indochina War was frequently quoted: "Before we had only the night and the jungle. Now we have the sky and the water."

Several problems had to be addressed. These included the dual-control system, i.e., the ill-defined division of authority between the military command structure and the party leadership within the armed forces, or between the military commander and the political commissar; the lack of esprit de corps among the rank and file, a general malaise termed "post-war mentality"; and the officer corps' inadequate military knowledge and insufficient military technological skills for the kind of war that had emerged in the 1970s. There were also policy conflicts over the conduct of large-scale combined or joint military operations and the nature of future military training, a lack of standardization of equipment, matériel shortages, administrative breakdowns, general inefficiency and lack of performance by basic military units, and an anachronistic party structure within PAVN stemming from an outmoded organizational structure and inappropriate or out-of-touch political commissars.

By 1978 the effort to restore PAVN had developed into the Great Campaign. This was a five-year program with five objectives: to increase the individual soldier's sense of responsibility, discipline, dedication, attitude toward solidarity, and mastery of weapons, equipment, and vehicles; to encourage more frugal expenditure of fuel, supplies, and matériel; to improve PAVN's officer corps, particularly at the basic unit level; to improve military-civilian

253

relations and heighten international solidarity; and to improve the material-spiritual life of soldiers. Of these, the most important was the program to improve the PAVN officer corps, the heart of which was a four-part statute called the Army Officers' Service Law, drafted in 1978 and officially promulgated in 1981. The Service Law, as it came to be called, established systematic new criteria for the selection and training of officers; defined PAVN officers' rights and military obligations; and overhauled, upgraded, and formally instituted a new PAVN reserve officer system. It also set up new regulations concerning officer promotions, assignments, and ranking systems.

The reorganization was a deliberate effort to professionalize the PAVN officer corps, in part by codifying the military hierarchy within PAVN, which had never been officially approved. Previous emphasis on egalitarianism had led to virtual denial of even the concept of rank. There were no officers, only cadres; no enlisted personnel; only combatants. Uniforms were devoid of insignia, and references to rank or title were avoided in conversation. With professionalization, distinctions emerged between officers and enlisted troops. Accompanying the basic law were directives from the Council of Ministers that dealt with PAVN ranks, uniforms, and insignia. A thirteen-rank officer system with appropriate titles was instituted. There were new designations for naval flag rank, which had previously carried generals' titles (although apparently naval officers below flag rank continued to bear army ranks). Under the new regulations, PAVN officers were distinguished as either line commanders, staff officers, political officers, administrative officers, or military-police officers. The new regulations additionally stipulated the use of unit insignia—bright red for infantry, sky blue for air force and air defense force, dark blue for navy, green for border defense, and light gray for specialist technicians—in all twenty-five separate services, each of which had its own emblem (see fig. 16).

Technological improvements for PAVN were instituted chiefly under the Great Campaign. Intensive technical training programs were begun. Heavy emphasis was placed on the training of surface-to-air missile (SAM) battery commanders, advanced air defense technicians, fighter pilots, radar technicians, communications-systems operators, and naval officers. The program was fully supported by the Soviet Union, which provided military aid and technical advisers and trainers. A costly developmental effort, it had not been long under way before events began to conspire against it.

Shortly after the Great Campaign was launched in 1978, Vietnam's disputes with Cambodia and China sharply intensified. On

March 5, 1979, the government issued a General Mobilization Order that established three "great tasks" for Vietnam: to enlarge the national defense structure, meaning to increase substantially the size of PAVN; to increase agricultural and industrial production in support of the war; and to develop better administrative systems in the party, PAVN, and the economic sector. The emphasis was on young Vietnamese, who were called to perform separate "great tasks," i.e., "annihilate the enemy, develop the paramilitary system, do productive labor, insure internal security, and perform necessary ideological tasks." The order required all able-bodied persons to work ten hours a day—eight hours in productive labor and two hours in military training. It also required universal participation in civil-defense exercises.

Conflict with Cambodia

Serious trouble between Hanoi and the Khmer Rouge under Pol Pot began at the end of the Second Indochina War when both PAVN troops and the Khmer Rouge engaged in "island grabbing" and seizures of each other's territory, chiefly small areas in dispute between Vietnam and Cambodia for decades. What goaded Hanoi to take decisive action was Pol Pot's determination to indoctrinate all Khmer with hatred for Vietnam, thus making Hanoi's goal of eventual Indochinese federation even more difficult to accomplish. Vietnam's Political Bureau had several options in "solving the Pol Pot problem," as it was officially termed. Vietnam's wartime relationship with the Khmer Rouge had been one of domination, in which control had been maintained through the intercession of native Khmers, numbering approximately five thousand, who had lived and trained in North Vietnam. The Political Bureau reasoned that by controlling the Khmer Rouge "five thousand" faction it could control the Khmer (Kampuchean) Communist Party, which in turn would control the Cambodian state and society. This strategy broke down when most of the Khmer communist cadres trained in Vietnam were executed by Pol Pot.

In another effort, the Political Bureau dispatched Le Duan to Phnom Penh soon after the end of the war for a stern meeting with Pol Pot, but his efforts to persuade or intimidate failed. A series of punitive military strikes followed with the objective of triggering the overthrow of Pol Pot. Some of these assaults, such as the one in the Parrot's Beak (see Glossary) region in 1977, involved as many as 90,000 PAVN troops, but they came to nothing. There also were covert Vietnamese attempts to eliminate Pol Pot by bribing his bodyguards to assassinate him.

COMMISSIONED OFFICERS

VIETNAM RANK 1	THIEU-UY	TRUNG-UY	THUONG-UY	DAI-UY	THIEU-TA	TRUNG-TA	THUONG-TA	DAI-TA	THIEU-TUONG	TRUNG-TUONG	THUONG-TUONG	DAI-TUONG
VIETNAM RANK 2									CHUAN DO DOC	PHO DO DOC	DO DOC	
ARMY, AIR FORCE AND NAVY												
ENGLISH TITLES 1	2D LIEUTENANT	1ST LIEUTENANT	CAPTAIN	SENIOR CAPTAIN	MAJOR	LIEUTENANT COLONEL	COLONEL	SENIOR COLONEL	MAJOR GENERAL	LIEUTENANT GENERAL	COLONEL GENERAL	SENIOR GENERAL
ENGLISH TITLES 2	ENSIGN	LIEUTENANT JUNIOR GRADE	LIEUTENANT	SENIOR LIEUTENANT	LIEUTENANT COMMANDER	COMMANDER	CAPTAIN	UPPER CAPTAIN	REAR ADMIRAL	VICE ADMIRAL	ADMIRAL	SENIOR ADMIRAL

ENLISTED PERSONNEL

VIETNAM RANK	BINH NHI	BINH NHAT	HA-SI	TRUNG-SI	THUONG-SI
ARMY, AIR FORCE AND NAVY					
ENGLISH TITLES 1	BASIC PRIVATE / AIRMAN BASIC	PRIVATE / AIRMAN	PRIVATE 1ST CLASS / AIRMAN 1ST CLASS	SERGEANT / STAFF SERGEANT	SERGEANT 1ST CLASS / MASTER SERGEANT
ENGLISH TITLES 2	SEAMAN RECRUIT	APPRENTICE SEAMAN	SEAMAN	PETTY OFFICER 2D CLASS	CHIEF PETTY OFFICER

CAP INSIGNIA

ALL SERVICES WEAR THE SAME EMBLEM: A GOLD STAR SURROUNDED BY TWO SHEAVES OF RICE AND ONE HALF OF A GOLD WHEEL ON A RED BACKGROUND.

VIETNAM OFFICER RANKS: UP TO THUONG-TA HAVE SILVER STARS, STRIPES AND BUTTONS. THIEU-TUONG/CHUAN DO DOC TO DAI-TUONG HAVE GOLD STARS AND BUTTONS. DAI-TA HAS SILVER STARS AND STRIPES AND GOLD BUTTON. ALL BACKGROUNDS ARE GOLD WITH PIPING IN RED FOR ARMY, BLUE FOR AIR FORCE, AND DARK BLUE FOR NAVY.

VIETNAM ENLISTED RANKS: ALL HAVE SILVER BUTTONS. ARMY HAS GREEN BACKGROUND WITH RED STRIPES AND PIPING. AIR FORCE HAS BLUE SHOULDERBOARDS WITH GOLD STRIPES. NAVY HAS DARK BLUE SHOULDER BOARDS WITH GOLD STRIPES.

WITH THE EXCEPTION OF NAVAL FLAG RANK OFFICERS, VIETNAM'S OFFICER AND ENLISTED PERSONNEL USUALLY HAVE ARMY RANKS REGARDLESS OF THEIR SERVICE AFFILIATION. THUS AN ARMY PRIVATE 1ST CLASS, AN AIR FORCE AIRMAN 1ST CLASS, AND A NAVY SEAMAN COMMONLY SHARE THE ARMY DESIGNATION HA-SI; SIMILARLY AN ARMY COLONEL AND A NAVY CAPTAIN BEAR THE SINGLE ARMY RANK THUONG-TA.

1 ARMY AND AIR FORCE
2 NAVY

Figure 16. Rank Insignia of the People's Army of Vietnam (PAVN), 1987

Finally, in early 1978, Hanoi returned to tested methods of revolutionary guerrilla warfare. Special PAVN teams recruited volunteers for a future Khmer liberation army from Khmer refugee camps in southern Vietnam. About 300 of the most promising were taken to Ho Chi Minh City (formerly Saigon), installed in the former Cambodian embassy building, and organized into armed propaganda teams, with Khmer Rouge defector Heng Samrin in charge of training. The plan, according to program defectors, was to send armed propaganda teams, like the Kampuchea Liberation Front, into Cambodian provinces along the Vietnamese border to infiltrate Khmer villages and begin organization and mobilization work. A Radio Liberation broadcast unit would be established, a liberated area would be proclaimed, and eventually a Provisional Revolutionary Government of Kampuchea would be formed that would then dispatch emissaries abroad in search of support. In late 1978, however, this revolutionary guerrilla war strategy was suddenly abandoned in favor of a full-scale, blitzkrieg-style attack on Cambodia. Later it became evident that the idea for the attack had come from young PAVN officers, many of whom had been trained in Moscow, who had assured the Political Bureau that the matter could be resolved in a maximum of six months. The Political Bureau's decision to attempt a military solution in Cambodia was taken against the advice of General Giap and probably most of the other older PAVN generals.

PAVN struck across the Cambodian border from the Parrot's Beak area of Vietnam on Christmas Day 1978. The drive was characterized by a highly visible Soviet-style offensive with tank-led infantry that plunged suddenly across the border, drove to the Thai border, and then fanned out to occupy Cambodia within days. Heng Samrin and his 300 Khmer cadres proceeded to form a new government, called the People's Republic of Kampuchea, in Phnom Penh, and began building an army to take over from the occupying PAVN by 1990. The first indication to the PAVN high command in Hanoi that it was in fact trapped in a protracted conflict came in the summer of 1979, when a major pacification drive, launched by PAVN forces using some 170,000 troops, proved to be inconclusive. It was only in the wake of that drive that PAVN settled down to the slow task of pacifying Cambodia.

Officially, PAVN troops in Cambodia were volunteers, performing what were called their "internationalist duties." The number involved decreased over the years, from 220,000 in January 1979 to 140,000 in January 1987. As the war progressed, Hanoi officials increasingly portrayed it as a struggle against China and labeled the Khmer insurgent forces as Chinese surrogates. By late 1982, they had begun to portray the war as a thing of the past, claiming that Vietnamese dominance had become irreversible, with only mopping up of scattered pockets of opposition yet to accomplish. The Cambodian resistance, however, continued, never able to challenge PAVN seriously, certainly not able to drive it from the country, but still gaining in strength. By 1987 the resistance was stronger than it had been at any time since 1979. To reduce strain on its system and to quiet outside criticism, PAVN lowered the profile of the war. There were fewer military sweeps into guerrilla lairs and greater use of artillery, more static guard duty, and less road patrolling. Military forces concentrated on keeping open the lines of communication, guarding the towns, and building up Phnom Penh's fledgling army—the Khmer People's Revolutionary Armed Forces (KPRAF). At the same time, increments of PAVN forces were withdrawn from Cambodia each year in what the Chinese press labeled the ''annual semi-withdrawal performance.'' By 1986 Hanoi was stating that all PAVN forces would be withdrawn from Cambodia by 1990, a decision officials insisted was ''absolute and without conditions.'' In retrospect, Vietnam's invasion of Cambodia appears to have been a serious mistake. Apparently it was a decision hastily taken in the belief that a quick, successful takeover would force the Chinese to accept the new situation as a fait accompli. The undertaking was also based on the estimate that Pol Pot had neither the political base nor the military power to resist a traumatic assault, which would shatter his capability to govern and cause the Khmer people to rally overwhelmingly to the new government. Assumptions proved wrong, and the strategy failed. The invasion did not solve the Pol Pot problem, but rather bogged Vietnam down in a costly war that tarnished its image abroad and undermined relations with China that might otherwise have been salvaged. The war drained the economy and continued to be one of Vietnam's unsolved national security problems in late 1987.

Conflict with China

China has posed a far more serious challenge to Vietnam's national security since the Second Indochina War, especially because of its twenty-nine-day incursion into Vietnam in February 1979, which, according to the Vietnamese, has continued as a ''multifaceted war of sabotage.'' China's 1979 invasion was a response to what China considered to be a collection of provocative actions and policies on Hanoi's part. These included Vietnamese intimacy with the Soviet Union, mistreatment of ethnic Chinese (Hoa—see Glossary) living in Vietnam, hegemonistic

Vietnamese soldiers returning from duty on the Chinese border
Courtesy Bill Herod

"imperial dreams" in Southeast Asia, and spurning of Beijing's attempt to repatriate Chinese residents of Vietnam to China. The Chinese attack came at dawn on the morning of February 17, and employed infantry, armor, and artillery. Air power was not employed then or at any time during the war. Within a day, the Chinese People's Liberation Army (PLA) had advanced some eight kilometers into Vietnam along a broad front. It then slowed and nearly stalled because of heavy Vietnamese resistance and difficulties within the Chinese supply system. On February 21, the advance resumed against Cao Bang in the far north and against the all-important regional hub of Lang Son. Chinese troops entered Cao Bang on February 27, but the city was not secured completely until March 2. Lang Son fell two days later. On March 5, the Chinese, saying Vietnam had been sufficiently chastised, announced that the campaign was over. The PLA withdrawal was completed on March 16.

Hanoi's post-incursion depiction of the border war was that Beijing had sustained a military setback if not an outright defeat. Nevertheless, the attack confirmed Hanoi's perception of China as a threat. The PAVN high command henceforth had to assume, for planning purposes, that the Chinese might come again and might not halt in the foothills but might drive on to Hanoi. By 1987 China had stationed nine armies (approximately 400,000

259

troops) in the Sino-Vietnamese border region, including one along the coast. It had also increased its landing craft fleet and was periodically staging amphibious landing exercises off Hainan Island, across from Vietnam, thereby demonstrating that a future attack might come from the sea.

In the early 1980s, China began pursuing what some observers have described as a semi-secret campaign against Vietnam that was more than a series of border incidents and less than a limited small-scale war. The Vietnamese called it a "multifaceted war of sabotage." Hanoi officials have described the assaults as comprising steady harassment by artillery fire, intrusions on land by infantry patrols, naval intrusions, and mine planting both at sea and in the riverways. Chinese clandestine activity (the "sabotage" aspect) for the most part was directed against the ethnic minorities of the border region (see Ethnic Groups and Languages, ch. 2). According to the Hanoi press, teams of Chinese agents systematically sabotaged mountain agricultural production centers as well as lowland port, transportation, and communication facilities. Psychological warfare operations were an integral part of the campaign, as was what the Vietnamese called "economic warfare"—encouragement of Vietnamese villagers along the border to engage in smuggling, currency speculation, and hoarding of goods in short supply.

The Vietnamese responded to the Chinese campaign by turning the districts along the China border into "iron fortresses" manned by well-equipped and well-trained paramilitary troops. In all, an estimated 600,000 troops were assigned to counter Chinese operations and to stand ready for another Chinese invasion. The precise dimensions of the frontier operations were difficult to determine, but its monetary cost to Vietnam was considerable.

The Legal-Constitutional Basis of the Military

The 1980 Constitution establishes the legal basis for PAVN in Section IV (Articles 50 through 52), titled Defense of the Socialist Homeland. Supervision of the armed forces is vested in the Council of State (see The System of Government, ch. 4). The Council of State, newly formed under the 1980 Constitution, assumes the equivalent authority of the previous National Assembly Standing Committee in that it can declare war and mobilize the country if the assembly is not in session. The Council chairman (Truong Chinh in 1987), according to the Constitution, concurrently chairs the National Defense Council (NDC)—retained from the 1959 constitution—and serves as commander in chief of PAVN. The latter function, however, is ceremonial. Under the Constitution, the role of the NDC is "to mobilize all forces and potentials of the country to defend the homeland." It thus is made explicitly responsible for what is the National Assembly's implicit duty, mobilization in the broadest sense. By comparison with the previous constitution, the 1980 document gives the National Assembly (see Glossary) legal authority with respect to PAVN that is perhaps broader but is less clearly defined. For example, "The National Assembly has the duty and power . . . to decide on matters of war and peace," but its chairmanship (under Nguyen Huu Tho in 1987) is a merely nominal position.

The highest operational authority over PAVN is exercised by the Council of Ministers, equivalent to a cabinet, which is responsible for "organizing national defense activities and building the people's armed forces." In 1987 the chairman of the Council of Ministers was Premier Pham Van Dong.

Basic national defense policy is fixed by the NDC, then transmitted first to the Ministry of National Defense and second to the PAVN High Command. As is common throughout the Vietnam ruling apparatus, there is a great deal of overlap because of "two hat" (or concurrent) assignments. The chairman of the NDC is the president of the State Council; the vice chairman is the prime minister. NDC members include the VCP secretary general, the chairman of the National Assembly Standing Committee, the PAVN chief of staff, the minister of national defense, the minister of foreign affairs, the minister of interior, and the chairman of the State Planning Commission. In time of war, the NDC acts as a supreme headquarters for mobilizational purposes and is vested with the authority to command all manpower and other resources in the country (see fig. 17).

The Military's Place in Society

PAVN exerts a great deal of complicated direct and indirect influence both on party and government policy-making and on everyday non-military life. It is so well integrated into the social system that there is no precise point at which it can be said that the military ends and the civilian world begins.

By official definition, Vietnam is an egalitarian, proletarian-based classless society. This means that PAVN is not an army of the people—although it must serve all of the people—but that it is an army of the proletariat. Society is supposed to support PAVN as well as police it to assure that the armed forces meet the requirements of the new social order. Conversely, PAVN is charged with assuming, in alliance with the party, the leadership of the proletariat and of society in general. PAVN is expected to be all things to the people and special things to the party. It must both lead the people and serve them. It must be loyal both to the political line and to the military line, even when these conflict. It must act as the vanguard of the party yet be scrupulously subservient to it.

Despite the praetorian qualities of Vietnamese society—the result of centuries of martial cultural influence—PAVN, like its predecessors, is not militaristic in the sense the term is understood in the West. Nor is there in Vietnam what might be called a military-industrial complex, that is, a coalition of military and political vested interests that are distinctly separate from the rest of the social system. Rather, the relationship of the military and the rest of the society is symbiotic, marked by a strong sense of material and psychological dependence. Society's responsibility to PAVN, which is rooted in the Constitution, requires that all of the people support the armed forces in all ways. PAVN's duties to society, in turn, incorporate political and economic responsibilities as well as defense of the country. Complicating this relationship is the party, which is neither civilian nor military but has some of the characteristics of both.

The chief obligation of the average citizen to PAVN is military service, which is universal and compulsory. This duty long predates the advent of communism to Vietnam. Conscription in traditional Vietnam was carried out in a manner similar to the requisitioning of corvée labor. Village councils were required to supply conscripts according to population ratio (one *linh* or soldier for every three to seven villagers, depending on the section of the country). The 1980 Constitution stipulates that "citizens are obliged to do military service" and "take part in the building of the national defense force." Article 52 mandates compulsory military service as part of the state's efforts to "stimulate the people's patriotism and revolutionary heroism." In December 1981, the National Assembly promulgated a new Military Obligation Law stating that "military obligation is mandated by law and is a glorious task for a citizen. . . . All male citizens from all rural areas, city districts, organs, state enterprises, and vocational schools from elementary to college level, regardless of the positions they hold, if they meet the induction criteria of the annual state draft plan, must serve in the armed forces for a limited time in accordance with the draft law." Under the law there are no exemptions to military service, although there can be deferments. This practice has led to charges that extensive corruption allows the sons of influential party and state officials one deferment after another.

The draft is administered by PAVN itself and is conducted chiefly by a corps of retired officers stationed in district offices throughout the country. The process begins with registration, which is voluntary for all males at age sixteen and compulsory at seventeen. A woman may register if she is a member of the Ho Chi Minh Communist Youth League. The draft age is from eighteen to twenty-seven. The enlistment period is three years for ordinary enlistees, four years for technical specialists and naval personnel, and two years for certain ethnic minorities. Youths who do not enlist and await the draft receive a military service classification, of which there are six. Draft calls are issued twice a year.

Since the beginning of the war in Cambodia, the draft call has been accompanied by enlistment campaigns to persuade youths to volunteer rather than wait for conscription. Recruitment drives have been conducted by PAVN veterans of the Cambodian war who have met with prospective soldiers in school yards, where they have presented lectures or shown films. A quota was set for each province, by village and urban ward, but often was not met. To make military service more equitable and attractive, a system of options was established, which included the "three selects program" and the "six opens program." The three who could "select," or have a voice in the draft process, were the family, the local mass organization (Vietnam Fatherland Front), and the production unit, such as a commune or factory. The "six opens program" involved the unrestricted posting of six elements of military conscription information in which there was a high level of public interest. This information included highlights of draft procedures, lists of draftees and deferments, and names of party officials, their children and their draft status. The purpose was to allow everyone to know who was and was not being drafted and why. A system of perquisites also was established as an inducement for families whose sons joined PAVN. The families were offered assistance in resolving their legal or class-status problems, in getting work papers or added food rations, and in obtaining permission to return from new economic zones (see Glossary).

The General Mobilization Order of March 5, 1979, in the wake of the Chinese invasion, suspended the voluntary enlistment periods. In 1987 the period of PAVN service was indefinite. The mobilization order also eased some restrictions on drafting southerners, such as the requirement that each draftee have a "clear history," meaning a proletarian background with no strong ties to the previous government or to its army, the Army of the Republic of Vietnam (ARVN—see Glossary). After 1979 certain ARVN enlisted men and noncommissioned officers, chiefly technicians and military specialists (but not ex-ARVN officers) were drafted. Increasingly, draftees sent to Cambodia were from the South. The mobilization order also cracked down on draft resistance, which

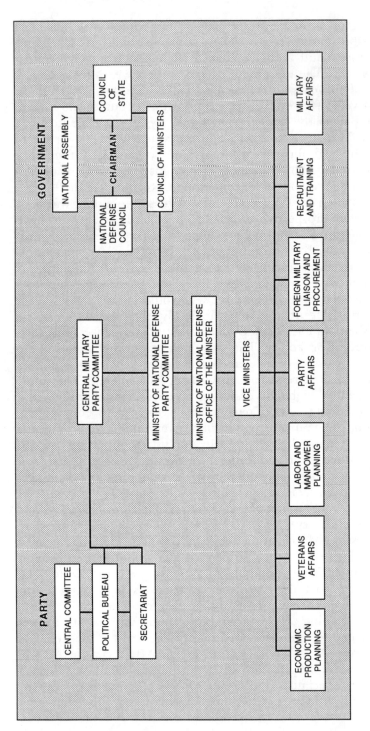

Source: Based on information from Douglas Pike, *PAVN: People's Army of Vietnam*, London, 1986, 88.

Figure 17. Military Organization, 1987

appeared to be widespread and even socially acceptable, especially in the South. A common method of draft avoidance was use of counterfeit military discharge papers, the fabrication of which was an extensive and lucrative enterprise; in 1981 two of five persons convicted of producing counterfeit discharges were sentenced to death in Haiphong. A common form of draft evasion was termed irregular compliance, i.e., the failure of a young man to register in the hope that the cumbersome bureaucracy would fail to catch up with him. In 1985 it was estimated that 20 percent of male youths in the South, and perhaps as many as 5 percent in the North, had not registered. Communes or factories, which did not want to lose the services of draftable individuals, may have tried to protect them from the local draft board. Because a quota system was employed, a common avoidance tactic was to supply a substitute known to be in bad health, who would then fail his physical examination. The People's Security Service (PSS) continually rounded up draft dodgers and deserters. Special teams called bandit hunters raided coffee shops, noodle stands, and other likely hangouts. Draft evaders faced a mandatory five-year jail sentence; deserters were returned to their military units for punishment. Measures were also taken against the families of inductees who failed to report. For instance, a draftee's family could be jailed, and the family's home or other property could be impounded until he reported for duty.

PAVN's chief function is to defend the homeland. Its second, equally important, function is to ensure the perpetuation of the existing sociopolitical system. It also has economic responsibilities and acts as a role model for the general population. PAVN's behavior is expected to instill the basic tenets of a Leninist system among the populace. It is expected to engage in class struggle and to eliminate antiproletarian sentiment in its ranks and in society in general. Individual soldiers are expected to set an example of proper socialist behavior by being dedicated, hard-working, incorruptible, and highly skilled in the performance of their duty. Above all, PAVN is expected to be a model of loyalty to the party and to Vietnam.

PAVN also is expected to bear a material responsibility in the economic sector. It is commonplace in Marxist-Leninist systems for the armed forces to contribute in some way to the economy. In Vietnam during the First Indochina War, PAVN units, mostly guerrilla bands, were forced to fend for themselves by living off the countryside and on the charity of friendly villagers. During the Second Indochina War, PAVN had a weak quartermaster system in the South and adopted what was called the "three-nine system," under which a PAVN unit was supplied with food for nine months of the year but supported itself for the remaining three, usually by gardening or bartering (lumber traded for food, for example). Implicit in this system was the notion that it was proper for a soldier to engage in nonmilitary economic production activities, an idea that was increasingly challenged with the growth of professionalism in PAVN's ranks. After the Second Indochina War, PAVN was instructed to assume a greater economic role. The Fourth National Party Congress (December 1976) called on the military to "dedicate itself to the single strategic mission of carrying out the socialist revolution and building socialism." PAVN not only accepted this challenge but proceeded to stake out a central claim in the economic life of the country. PAVN's soldiers, said General Giap, would fight the "bloodless war" of economic development as the "shock troops" of the economic sector. Military units began operating state farms, mining coal, building roads and bridges, repairing vehicles, engaging in commercial fishing, and participating in countless other economic ventures. Although the invasion of Cambodia in 1978 followed by China's invasion of Vietnam in 1979 necessitated heavy reinforcement of the China border region and the allocation of resources for combat, an enlargement of PAVN in 1983 made it possible for the troops to resume most of their economic activities.

It was clear from the discussion of economic duties in Vietnam's military journals that not all PAVN generals were enthusiastic about the idea. The chief criticism was that it detracted from what was seen as the central PAVN mission—defense of Vietnam—which was regarded as a full-time task. Some military critics complained that economic duty "dissipate[d] the thoughts" of the soldiers, undermined military discipline, and was a cause of corruption. Troops themselves also complained of the arduous work involved, such as digging miles of irrigation ditches, the most hated assignment of all.

The armed forces, nevertheless, engaged in the production of weapons and military hardware, undertakings identified in the press as "national defense enterprises" and defined by PAVN as "production establishments of the armed forces." These included vehicle assembly plants, ordnance plants, and explosives factories. As in other societies with large standing armies, the question in Vietnam was whether it made sense economically for a military unit to engage in production: whether, for instance, it could grow rice more productively or build a bridge more efficiently than a civilian counterpart. Vietnamese officials appear to have decided in favor of military participation, for they incorporated PAVN production potential into long-range economic planning (see Economic Roles of the Party and the Government, ch. 3). Contingency plans existed that called for PAVN units to sign production contracts with central-level ministries or provincial-level agencies, just as agricultural collectives or construction enterprises were required to do. Tapping the skilled manpower pool represented by PAVN may very well be the key to significant long-range economic development in Vietnam.

Party Control in the Military

It is a fundamental tenet of any Marxist-Leninist system that the communist party must dominate the system's military. Lenin, it is said, coined the slogan, ''the party controls the gun,'' reflecting a deep and abiding fear that political power can be lost to the armed forces.

The party's relationship with PAVN in Vietnam is one of neither coercion nor repression. Instead, the VCP and the armed forces are integrated and mutually dependent. Control is exercised by means of parallel military and party hierarchies that are both part of the overall political system. These parallel hierarchies may best be depicted by two pyramids: the VCP organization within PAVN, represented by the smaller pyramid, enclosed within the organization of the armed forces, represented by the larger pyramid. These two hierarchical pyramids may also be divided horizontally into levels of command. At each level, from the Ministry of National Defense to the infantry company, there is a military command structure and a corresponding party apparatus consisting of a political officer and party committee. VCP control of the military thus is not from the outside, but from within.

PAVN and the VCP worked together harmoniously over the years, more so perhaps than their counterpart institutions in China or the Soviet Union. Party-military relations in the early days of the First Indochina War were clear and unequivocal. Indochinese patriots faced a highly visible, commonly hated enemy, and the single goal that united all—to expel the French—was something each could understand and approve. Party representatives led the cause because they seemed to possess an inherent superiority. Young Viet Minh recruits, mostly from the villages, willingly deferred to the well-traveled, more experienced, better educated party cadres, who understood the complicated relationship between war and politics and always seemed to know what to do. Eventually, however, these perceptions changed, and by the 1980s the unquestioned acceptance of VCP superiority by the PAVN rank and file had dissipated. In its place there emerged a growing ambivalence fueled by resentment, not only of the party's postwar failures, but also of the privileged status enjoyed by party cadres and the party's exclusive authority over both the military leadership in place and the manpower pool from which future officers were drawn. To some degree the PAVN high command shared this ambivalence, but senior PAVN leaders were in a difficult position. Although permitted to exercise great influence within the party, preservation of their privileged status at times required them to put party interests over those of the armed forces. In the postwar years, relations with the party increasingly placed a severe strain on the high command. Factionalism, however, a condition that existed both within the ranks of PAVN's military leadership and within PAVN's party apparatus, apparently did not create a problem between the two.

Divisive Issues

During the postwar years, a number of nettlesome issues arose to trouble the generally symbiotic relationship between the armed forces and the party. A point of major contention was the dual command system, in which responsibility for a military unit was shared between its commander and political officer. During the First Indochina War, the military had been directed entirely by the party. What had counted chiefly in a leader was not military knowledge but political acumen, organizational skills, and the ability to persuade and motivate. However, as the war had increased in intensity, a need had developed for experienced combat officers. When the demand soon exhausted manpower pools, the party had been obliged to turn to large numbers of officers with military rather than party credentials to fill PAVN officer ranks. Fearing it would lose control, the party in 1952 introduced in PAVN the position of political commissar or political officer (borrowed from the Soviet Union and China), thereby creating the so-called two-commander system. It was dogma at the time, however, that even with two commanders neither was a purely military officer. A large part of officer training consisted of political orientation to military activity. Nevertheless, the division of power between the two officers was not clearly defined. In theory, they shared authority in tactical matters, but in reality they competed for power over the years. The system generated party-military friction, bitter jurisdictional disputes, sharp personality clashes, and confusion in authority. Despite its many flaws it endured for nearly three decades, surviving the Second Indochina War. As that conflict intensified in the early 1960s, however, the balance of power between the two figures began to favor the military officer.

Pressure to revise the role of the political officer and to end the dual command structure developed only after the Second Indochina War. Selected PAVN units were experimentally restructured in

1977 in such a way that the functions of military commander and political officer were combined in a single officer. Gradually, this system was extended throughout PAVN, but as a concession to the party, PAVN agreed that the authority formerly wielded by the political officer in company-, battalion-, and regimental-level units should be vested in the party committee at each level. The chief difficulty encountered in this plan was that a dual command became a multiple command. Party committees sending orders directly to specific military, logistic, or technical officers in a unit could bypass the military commander, with the result that PAVN units were run by committee. When this system was taken into Cambodia, it proved totally unworkable. In 1980 the arrangement was supplanted by a "one-man-command system." Authority was vested in the unit commander, who was responsible to higher authorities, including the party committee at his level, but who exercised actual control of his unit. A March 1982 party resolution endorsed this change but added a new arrangement that supported retaining the position of political officer as an institution but spelled out its subordinate status to the military commander. Still in the developmental stage in 1987, this new arrangement clearly established the authority of the military commander over the political officer, but left his authority with respect to the party committee somewhat ambiguous. The military commander was permitted greater latitude in initiating decisions, but remained ultimately accountable to the party for whatever actions he took.

A second major divisive issue between the party and PAVN was commonly termed the "red versus expert" argument. This doctrine, imported from China and reflective of Mao Zedong's thinking about the conduct of war, began with the assumption that warfare was a test of all adversarial strengths—ideological, economic, psychological, and spiritual, as well as military. It then asked successively which ranked higher in such a test—the material or the immaterial, men or weapons, and whether it was more important for the individual soldier to be ideologically motivated ("red") or technologically skilled in combat ("expert"). As expressed, the choice raised a false dichotomy, but it was an argument that raged within PAVN for decades. It was not simply a philosophical question, but a question that manifested itself in party-PAVN personnel relations, in strategic and tactical military planning, in officer selection, assignment, and promotion, and in training programs designed to produce the ideal soldier. The debate surfaced in Vietnam after the First Indochina War when a PAVN modernization program was launched. Part of that effort involved creating a series of specialized military schools and academies. Planning the course

269

work for these new institutions triggered a spirited dispute over the relative value and importance of military expertise and revolutionary consciousness. In 1987 an easy resolution of this dichotomy was still beyond reach. Even in a politicized military organization such as PAVN, nonprofessional influences, whether political, ideological, or social, were limited by the demands of the work itself. New technology, requiring the mastery of complicated weapons and military processes, increasingly demanded the soldier's attention and time.

The Model Soldier

At a fundamental level, the "red-expert" debate concerned Vietnam's military ethos, the basic qualities and virtues of the model soldier. The prototypical, or composite, PAVN soldier in the 1970s and 1980s was twenty-three years old, had been born and raised in a village, was a member of the *ban co* class (poor for many generations), was unmarried, and had less than five years' formal education. His rural, agrarian background was the dominant influence in his thinking. He was one of five children and had lived his pre-army life in an extended family that included several generations of his immediate family as well as collateral relatives. He tended to resent outsiders as well as city people. His limited schooling made it difficult for him to cope with certain aspects of army life, for example, technical duties. He was raised as a nominal Buddhist but had always been subject to many direct and indirect Confucianist and Taoist influences. He was uninformed about the outside world, even other parts of Vietnam. He firmly believed in the importance and collective strength of the *ho* or extended family, and seldom questioned its demands on him, an attitude that served him well in his military career.

At the age of nine, the model future soldier joined the Ho Chi Minh Young Pioneers and spent much time involved in its activities. At sixteen, if he impressed his elders as being worthy, or if his family had influence, he became one of four youths (on an average) in his village to join the Ho Chi Minh Communist Youth League, participation in which led more or less automatically to admittance to the party as an adult. At twenty or twenty-one he was drafted, received two months' basic training, and was assigned to a unit. He did not particularly want to enter the army, nor did his parents wish it. However, he was obedient and accepted discipline easily. He had faith that PAVN and the state would treat him in a generally fair manner, which chiefly meant to him that they would assist him or his family if he was disabled or killed in battle. He was nonmaterialistic, got along easily on the bare necessities of life, and regarded simplicity as a great virtue—a fortunate coincidence as he received little material reward; his pay per month averaged the price of a dozen bottles of beer. Despite extensive indoctrination by the party, the soldier was not politically conscious. Much of what he knew about politics consisted of slogans he had been obliged to memorize, the meanings of which he only dimly comprehended. Beyond his brief basic training he received little military training, but, if he was illiterate, he was taught to read. He was a survival-oriented, tough, disciplined combat fighter, who persevered with stubborn determination, often against hopeless odds. He could be stubbornly hostile, even rebellious on occasion, without regard to consequences. He knew little about strategy or tactics, but believed that warfare consisted largely of careful planning, meticulous preparation, and then sustained, intensive mass attack.

The party's contribution to this ethos of the model Vietnamese soldier was ideological. To his innate virtues of courage, tenacity, boldness, and cleverness, the party sought to add a commitment to revolutionary ideals. The party thus stimulated an ongoing debate, encompassing sociological, philosophical, psychological, and technological arguments over the fundamental relationship of ideology to technology in modern warfare, an understanding of which was the key to understanding the mind of the Vietnamese soldier. Over the years, the party debate pitted the revolutionary model, that is, the peasant soldier—perhaps ill-equipped but nevertheless infused with revolutionary zeal—against the expert model, the superbly trained but ideologically neutral military technician. The revolutionary model always dominated the debate and found many allies , some transient and some permanent, both inside and outside PAVN. Supporting the expert model, on the other hand, was a small, shifting collection of technologically minded military professionals and civilians. In late 1987, the "experts" in PAVN's general officer corps remained outnumbered, but they had gained the support of a powerful ally—the Soviet military advisers in Vietnam. In reality, the debate between preserving the revolutionary character of PAVN and building a thoroughly modern professional armed force was overtaken by the imperatives of military technology, and the issue became obsolete.

Finally, there were the PAVN-party vested-interest conflicts, in which what was best for the party was not always interpreted as best for PAVN. Subjects of conflict included party and state security controls over PAVN personnel, party use of the military for economic and other nonmilitary tasks, party use of political criteria in selecting generals and senior staff officers who planned grand strategy or directed major military campaigns in the field, the role of the paramilitary, officer-enlisted relations and command authority of the militia within PAVN, and intermilitary and military-civilian relations.

Mechanisms of Control

The VCP controls PAVN through an organizational and motivational mechanism that can monitor, guide, influence, and if necessary coerce. Its interest in the process is to ensure ideological purity and to improve military efficiency. Party cadres and members who are part of PAVN are charged with imparting to the ranks the proper ideological spirit and are responsible for ensuring good individual military performance. At their command is a set of impressive institutional instruments that promote loyalty and dedication to the party and work against deviationism, personalism (selfishness), and other negative phenomena. Essentially the effort is one of indoctrination, which can be divided into three specific functions.

The first of these functions is "information-liaison group" work and consists of discussion group meetings or lectures by political officers, who shore up existing beliefs and behavioral patterns and explain new party lines. The second is the *kiem thao* (self-criticism) session, which has no counterpart in noncommunist armies. *Kiem thao* requires "criticism and self-criticism from below to expose and eliminate shortcomings in work and to fight against a show of complacent well-being." Rooted in group dynamics, it is aimed at harnessing peer pressure. Thematic material in indoctrination sessions tends to focus on whatever is of major concern to the leadership at the moment (in 1987 it was the China threat). The *kiem thao* weekly session usually lasts about two hours and requires the individual to be constructively critical of himself, his peers, and his superiors. As such it gives the leadership insights into PAVN morale and provides a means of signaling present or potential problems. It also acts as a release valve, a means of reducing pressure, in circumstances for which no other remedy is available.

The third function is the "emulation movement," a party control mechanism used in PAVN and in Vietnamese society at large. It was borrowed from the Soviet Union and China and also has no counterpart in noncommunist systems. The "emulation movement" campaigns incite people to imitate standards established by the party. Most are short-run mobilization efforts, although some are semipermanent, having been in existence for a decade or more. Each is designed to serve a specific purpose. In PAVN the campaigns seek to heighten vigilance against spies and counterrevolutionaries, reduce logistic expenditures, improve weapon and vehicle maintenance, or increase the individual soldier's sense of international solidarity. The "emulation movement" in PAVN is viewed as "an essential means of advancing the Revolution," which in practice means increasing unit solidarity, increasing the sense of discipline in the individual soldier, and improving military-civilian relations. The institution that runs these campaigns is a vast enterprise that requires the services of thousands of cadres who expend millions of man-hours in labor.

All of these control devices are supervised by the PAVN political officer, the figure who breathes life into the abstraction of the party. The political officer has no exact counterpart in noncommunist armies; some of his functions may be performed by the chaplain, the troop information and education officer or the special services officer in the armed forces of other nations, but his role in some respects is far more tangibly authoritative and significant. His duties are many and varied but chiefly involve political indoctrination, personal-problem solving, and maintenance of his unit's morale. He mobilizes the emotions and will through intensive moralistic exhortation, and he personalizes the impersonal party by representing the distant Political Bureau to the individual soldier. He is a figure of consequence who over the years has acquired a mystique of legendary proportions.

Within PAVN, party control of a different type is exercised through control of party membership. Party membership can be granted, denied, suspended, or removed permanently. The success or failure of a soldier's career is almost always determined by his having gained or failed to gain party membership. Weeding out of party members in PAVN takes place annually and averages about 1 percent of the total PAVN party membership, although in some units it can run as high as 6 percent. At the same time, intensive recruitment drives are held to induce soldiers to join the party. Prior to 1987, party members constituted 5 percent of PAVN; in 1987 the figure was between 10 and 20 percent.

Organization

PAVN (People's Army of Vietnam) is the formal name given to all elements of the Vietnamese armed forces; hence the designation PAVN (or People's) Navy and PAVN (or People's) Air Force. This usage is traceable to the 1954 Geneva Agreements under which the Democratic Republic of Vietnam (DRV) was permitted to keep such armed forces as it already possessed. To adhere to the letter of the agreements, DRV leaders immediately created a navy and air force, but listed these new services as part of PAVN.

Separate naval and air forces with distinct military identities evolved over the years, however, and traditional interservice rivalries quickly began to assert themselves (see fig. 18).

From their earliest days, the Vietnamese communists organized their armed forces into three basic categories described informally as "types of troops." Within the first category, the PAVN Regular Force ("main force troops"), are the army, the navy, and the air force. In 1987 the army consisted of about 1.2 million officers and enlisted personnel; the navy, about 15,000; and the air force, about 20,000. The second grouping, the Regional Force (or "territorial troops"), is organized geographically and consists chiefly of infantry units with limited mobility. In 1987 it totaled about 500,000. The third category, the PAVN Militia/Self-Defense Force (or "local troops"), is a semi-mobilized element organized by community (village, urban precinct) or economic enterprise (commune, factory, worksite). In 1987 it numbered about 1.2 million.

Military writers in Hanoi have tended to refer to the Regional and Militia/Self-Defense forces collectively as the Strategic Rear Force. The Regional Force is deployed at the provincial level and has units headquartered in each provincial capital, at the very least. The Militia/Self-Defense Force fulfills combat, combat support, and police functions from the district to the village level. The Regional and Militia/Self-Defense forces are two of about a dozen separate military organizations that constitute the Paramilitary Force, which is an integral part of PAVN.

The Paramilitary Force has four functions: to defend its local area in time of war and to delay, not to halt, the enemy; to support PAVN regular units in combat; to maintain local security in peace and in wartime; and to engage in economic activity, chiefly food production and road-building. In the deployment of troops during wartime for the purpose of repelling a full-scale invasion, PAVN strategists make a doctrinal distinction between the Regular Force, which would use conventional tactics, and the Paramilitary Force, which would employ guerrilla tactics in "local people's warfare."

Backing up the Regular and Paramilitary Forces is a reserve of about 500,000 personnel designated the Tactical Rear Force. This semi-mobilized body is composed mainly of veterans and overage males, who in time of emergency would replace personnel in the Militia/Self-Defense Force. The latter would move up to the Regional Force, whose units might in turn be upgraded into the Regular Force.

Augmenting the Regular and Paramilitary Forces are two other military bodies whose status or functions appear anomalous. In the North, a "super" paramilitary force called the People's Guerrilla Force was created in 1979. It was described as a special combat organization with units deployed in villages along the China border and seacoast. However, in late 1987, little more was known about it. In the South, a somewhat better-known organization, designated the Armed Youth Assault Force (AYAF) or Youth Assault Force (YAF), is reported to perform paramilitary functions. The AYAF is organized along military lines (from platoon to brigade) and usually is commanded by retired PAVN officers. However, it appears to be more a party organization than a military body reporting through defense channels. Units at various echelons are under the supervision of local district party committees, and the chain of command apparently leads to Hanoi. AYAF strength in 1986 was estimated at 1.5 million.

In 1986 the PAVN chain of command was headed by the party-government military policy-making apparatus: the National Assembly, the Ministry of Defense, and the National Defense Council on the government side; and the Political Bureau of the VCP Central Committee and the Central Military Party Committee on the party side. Because of overlapping Political Bureau and Central Military Party Committee membership, the Central Military Party Committee could be regarded as the ultimate power for all military matters. It was reorganized in 1982 and consisted of a secretary, a first deputy secretary, two deputy secretaries, and six members. Under guidance from the Political Bureau or the Central Committee, the Central Military Party Committee translated the will of the party—expressed in broad political terms—into specific instructions for the military.

The Ministry of Defense Party Committee, at the very top of the Ministry of Defense, had an entirely military membership. It was the highest operational party arm that dealt directly with PAVN, and consisted of a secretary, the PAVN commander in chief, the chiefs of the five military general-directorates (Military General Staff Directorate, General Political Directorate, General Rear Services Directorate, General Technical Directorate, and General Economic Construction Directorate), and the senior political commissars of the major subordinate commands, that is, the air force, the navy, and the four theaters of operation (the China border, the coast from the China border to below Da Nang, Northern Vietnam and Northern Laos, and Cambodia). Its secretariat was composed of a secretary general, two deputies, and ten members. The committee administered other party committees from

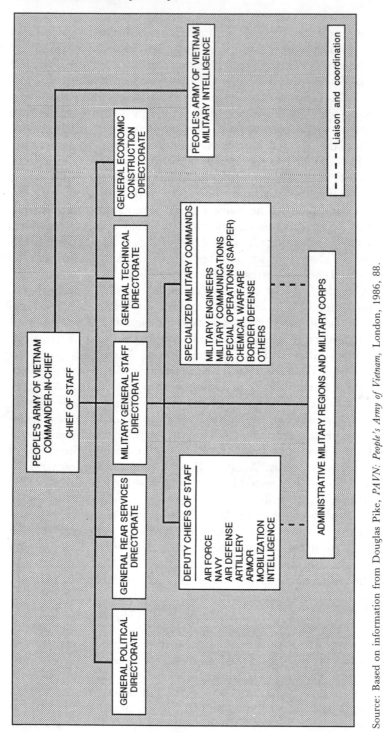

Source: Based on information from Douglas Pike, *PAVN: People's Army of Vietnam*, London, 1986, 88.

Figure 18. Organization of the People's Army of Vietnam (PAVN), 1987

the military-theater level to the basic party-unit level. At the division level and above, party committees were sizable permanent institutions whose function was to interpret Political Bureau and Central Committee directives for their respective organizations.

The major services, such as the air force and navy, had at headquarters level a Command Party Committee with a secretariat headed by the top political officer for the service and including the heads of all departments. At the company level was the party chapter, or *chi bo* (see Glossary), run by an executive committee of two or three full-time officials and made up of a collection of party cells (*to dang*, see Glossary), each run by a cell leader. The leaders of party chapters communicated the party line, indoctrinated both party and nonparty members within PAVN, directed "emulation movement" drives and other motivational programs, recruited and purged the membership, and generally ensured the party's participation in all military matters.

The Ministry of Defense, organizationally, consisted of the Office of the Minister of Defense and offices of seven vice ministers of defense. These vice ministries were fairly small and for the most part coordinated the activities of the Ministry of Defense with other ministries and state organs whose activities concerned the armed forces (see fig. 17).

The highest level of authority for military operations in PAVN was the PAVN High Command, an institution encompassing the Office of the Commander in Chief, the five military directorates, and the offices of seven deputy chiefs of staff. The most important element of the High Command, under the chief of staff, was the Military General Staff Directorate, which can be likened to the Joint Chiefs of Staff in the United States Department of Defense. At the next lower echelon were four other Military General Directorates that functioned roughly as staff sections of the high command. Also under the chief of staff were seven deputy chiefs of staff, whose purpose was liaison rather than command, and a number of specialized military commands. The PAVN Military Intelligence Department reported directly to the commander in chief (see fig. 18). It had personnel at lower levels of PAVN, and its chief responsibility appeared to be military intelligence activities within Vietnam and in Cambodia, where it reportedly had a large staff. It is not known whether this department operated outside Indochina.

The PAVN command structure was divided geographically into four military theaters and nine military regions or zones, including a Capital Military Region around Hanoi and Quang Ninh Province Special Region (see fig. 19). It was also divided tactically into military units ranging in descending order from corps to divisions, brigades, regiments, battalions, companies, platoons, and squads. The military-theater designation was introduced in the midst of a postwar buildup when PAVN increased its regular force from 400,000 to about 1.2 million members and its divisions from 25 to 51 (38 infantry divisions and 13 support or economic construction divisions). The number of PAVN corps was also increased from six to eight. Creation of the military theater and the military corps was designed to facilitate what was called the combined arms strategy, meaning larger and more complex military operations that might include use of indigenous military forces from Cambodia and Laos.

A corps ranged in size from 30,000 to 50,000 troops and normally consisted of 4 infantry divisions plus service and support elements. A PAVN infantry division normally was composed of 3 infantry regiments (2,500 men each), 1 artillery regiment, 1 tank battalion, and the usual support elements. A regiment in turn was divided into battalions (600 men each) and the battalion into companies (200 men each).

As of mid-1986, the thirty-eight PAVN regular infantry divisions were assigned thus: nineteen in Cambodia, sixteen in Vietnam (ten in northern Vietnam, six in central and southern Vietnam), and three in Laos. Most of the thirteen economic construction divisions were in the China border region. A construction division was made up of older soldiers, including many who had fought in the South during the Second Indochina War. Each construction division was fully armed, had a specific tactical purpose, and continued to carry out its military training in addition to economic tasks, usually road building (see The Military's Place in Society, this ch.). These units carried the burden of the brief 1979 war with China and generally acquitted themselves well.

In 1987 PAVN's major combat services—artillery, armor, air defense, and special operations—were organized along standard lines, similar to armies elsewhere. Each consisted of a force whose commanding officer reported to the Military General Staff Directorate. A mystique surrounded the PAVN Special Operations Force, successor to the legendary Sapper Combat Arm of the First and Second Indochina Wars that specialized in sabotage and clandestine military operations. In 1987, the Special Operations Force consisted of two elements, the Sapper Command and the Airborne Command (the 305th Airborne Brigade). Reportedly there was a third element, an amphibious commando unit, about which little was known.

The Army in 1986 was estimated to maintain 1,600 Soviet-made T-34/-54/-55/-62, Type-59 tanks and 450 PT-76 and Type 60/63 light tanks. It was also equipped with an estimated 2,700 reconnaissance vehicles; approximately 600 artillery guns and howitzers; an unknown number of rocket launchers, mortars, and antitank weapons; and 3,000 air defense weapons.

The PAVN Navy, begun in 1955 as the PAVN Riverine and Maritime Force, in 1959 became the Coastal Defense Force. Its "tradition day" is celebrated annually on August 5 to mark the 1964 Gulf of Tonkin incident in the Second Indochina War. The PAVN Navy began a buildup in the mid-1960s with the arrival of twenty-eight gunboats from China and thirty patrol torpedo boats from the Soviet Union. At the end of the Second Indochina War, it assumed the normal dual missions of a navy, that is, coastal defense and sea surveillance.

In 1986 the PAVN Navy continued to receive Soviet assistance and encouragement and was the largest naval force in Southeast Asia. Including some 1,300 former United States and South Vietnamese naval vessels, naval and civilian junks, and coasters, the PAVN Navy had a total of about 1,500 vessels. Its inventory contained two principal combat vessels, 192 patrol boats, 51 amphibious warfare ships, 104 landing ships, and 133 auxiliary craft.

The command structure of the PAVN Navy originated in Hanoi, where the commander in chief of naval forces was located. His office, the Naval Directorate, reported to the Military General Staff Directorate, i.e., the high command. The top operational Commander was the Commander, Vietnam Naval Forces, headquartered in Haiphong. The two posts were usually held by the same individual. Regulations issued in April 1982 established three flag-rank officers: rear admiral, equivalent to a major general; vice admiral, equivalent to a lieutenant general; and full admiral, equivalent to a colonel general.

Five naval regions made up the operational command. Headquartered at Haiphong, Vinh, Da Nang, Vung Tau, and Rach Gia, each region had two or more naval installations or facilities for which it was responsible. Within this structure were the naval fleets or naval groups, in turn divided into naval brigades. In 1987 the Ham Tu Fleet patrolled the northern Gulf of Tonkin as a strategic deterrent to China; its Chuong Duong Brigade was designed to oppose amphibious landings; its Kiet Brigade was assigned to defend the offshore islands and to perform troop transport duties. The Bach Dang Fleet served in the South. Its Ham Tu Naval Brigade (with 80 percent of its personnel South Vietnamese Navy veterans) operated almost entirely in Cambodian waters.

The PAVN Air Force fixed April 3, 1965, as its tradition day, the day when its pilots supposedly first engaged their United States

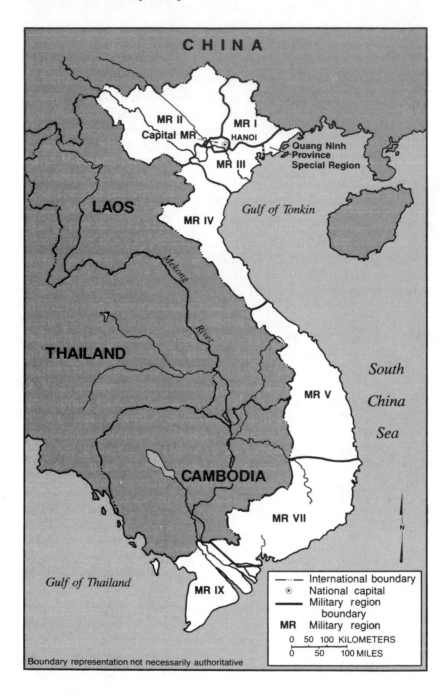

Figure 19. Military Regions, 1986

counterparts in a dogfight over North Vietnam, and celebrates it annually. The Soviet Union increased the PAVN air inventory late in the Second Indochina War and again in 1979 after the Chinese attack. As of 1985 it was estimated that the PAVN Air Force consisted of about 1,600 planes and 20,000 personnel, making it the largest air force in Southeast Asia (somewhere between China's and India's in size). The operational element of the PAVN Air Force was the air regiment, of which there were seventeen in 1987 grouped into air divisions and headquartered at Noi Bai (Hanoi), Da Nang, Tho Xuan, and Tan Son Nhut (Ho Chi Minh City). The air regiments included 7 attack fighter-plane regiments (450 planes); 4 basic and advanced training regiments (225 trainers); 3 cargo-transport regiments (350 planes); and 3 helicopter regiments (600 helicopters). One light bomber force (60 planes) existed separately from the air regiments. The commander of the Air Force, headquartered at Bac Mai Air Base outside Hanoi, reported to the General Staff Directorate of PAVN. Strategic use of the Vietnamese Air Force, from its inception until 1979, was entirely defensive. During the Second Indochina War it existed to defend North Vietnam from United States air attack, but after the war, and especially in 1979, it existed to defend Vietnam from attack by China. Although defense remained its primary strategic function, the air force increasingly developed an offensive capability after 1979— chiefly through its attack-helicopter regiments—for use in Cambodia and presumably, should the need arise, against China. The PAVN Air Force made a first tentative venture into space flight in 1981, when Lt. Col. Phan Tuan (son of former defense minister Vo Nguyen Giap) took part in the Soviet Union's Soyuz 37 mission, a linkup with the orbiting Soviet space laboratory, Salyut 6.

In 1987, the PAVN Border Defense Command was the newest military organization. Until 1979, responsibility for border security was vested in the People's Armed Public Security Force (PAPSF), under the control of the Ministry of Interior, and paramilitary units acted collectively as a border patrol. Border defense became a full-time task only with the rise of the China threat. As a result, the Border Defense Command was transferred to the Ministry of Defense in 1979 and divested of such responsibilities as dealing with smugglers and illegal border crossings so that it could devote full attention to border defenses. The command was organized into battalions and included a mixture of PAVN and paramilitary units. Their duties included operating border checkpoints, patrolling the border, operating boats in the coastal waterway network, maintaining security on nearby islands, and operating roving border-area units (mostly composed of Montagnards) to guard against incursions by Chinese patrols.

Leadership

PAVN's officer corps and its underlying concept of command have changed significantly since the first officer corps was formed in the 1930s. The initial leaders were a few dozen individuals chosen primarily for their ability to mobilize villagers and motivate troops, rather than for their tactical knowledge. As the corps developed, its lack of trained and experienced battlefield commanders was made the best of, and a premium was placed on collective military decision making (the dual command system) and on a military strategy that did not require a large number of military tacticians. Hierarchy among officers was played down, and the concept of "officer" was not applied. Leaders were cadres, and were required to guide the revolution, but it was not necessary that leaders be distinguished from one another, only from those they led (combatants). Cadres were either military, nonmilitary, or a mix of the two—it did not matter which; only cadre status was important. Gradually, military cadres evolved into PAVN officers, a trend that was intensified following the Second Indochina War when PAVN moved to develop a military structure to conform with other armed forces around the world. The influence of Soviet advisers and the growing importance of military technology accelerated the trend. Military professionalism, as a result, became one of the chief characteristics of the PAVN officer and soon distinguished him from military cadre, such as the political officer.

Although the exact size of the PAVN officer corps was not known in 1987, various estimates suggested it comprised about 180,000 officers, or roughly 15 percent of a force of approximately 1.2 million. In 1955 the officer corps reportedly had accounted for only 9.5 percent of a force of about 210,000.

The general officer corps in 1987 included the ranks of senior general, colonel general, lieutenant general, major general, and, in some cases, senior colonel, depending on the command held. The number of general officers totaled at least 450. The central feature of their interaction with one another was based on the Chinese political custom of *bung di* or faction-bashing, which highlighted factional infighting and reflected a broader power struggle within the party and within the system as a whole. Senior generals, colonel generals, and some lieutenant generals had their own constituencies, which in part they controlled and which in part controlled them. There were political alliances, some permanent and

Women militia members in Hanoi just after the Chinese invasion, 1979 Courtesy Bill Herod

some temporary, as well as relations based on familial ties, past associations, common interests, and personalities.

The end of the Second Indochina War found the PAVN officer corps seriously debilitated. Its ranks had been thinned by battle casualties, and the remaining officers were for the most part over-aged and undereducated. An ambitious officer development program was launched as part of the "Great Campaign" (see History, this ch.). The officer training system was overhauled, modernized, and greatly expanded with the assistance of Soviet military advisers. The curriculum in officer-training schools was revised to introduce new leadership methods, modern managerial techniques, and greater use of technology in administering the armed forces. The age bulge was addressed by encouraging retirements, and, for the first time, specific retirement ages were established: for company-grade officers the age was set at thirty-eight; for majors, forty-three; for lieutenant colonels, forty-eight; for colonels, fifty-five; and for senior colonels and general officers, sixty. Modern military administration and management methods were introduced, especially in personnel matters, and greater attention was directed toward such concerns as officers' pay, benefits, career development, uniforms, commendations, and intangible honors.

PAVN leaders were commonly believed to be men of implacable determination, indifferent to reverses and failures, enormously self-confident, and confident in their chosen strategy and their cause.

If there was a weakness in the ability of the individual PAVN officer, it was compensated for by the collective decision-making process that put several minds to work on a single problem. The net effect was a military leadership that could mobilize the Vietnamese soldier and instill in him the necessary discipline to fight repeatedly against overwhelming odds.

Administration

PAVN's systems for dealing with administrative, managerial, logistic, and manpower problems remained rudimentary in 1987. Vietnam's two major military operations, against Cambodia and China, caused serious administrative difficulties to surface. Many were traceable to the condition of the Vietnamese economy, which in the late 1970s and 1980s had declined in virtually every sector (see Economic Setting, ch. 3). As more than one observer noted, Vietnam had stayed in the bicycle age while the rest of Asia had moved into the computer age. PAVN's logistic requirements suffered accordingly.

Vietnam's military budget remained a closely guarded secret and was doubly difficult to estimate because it was largely covered by Soviet military assistance that reportedly did not need to be repaid. According to a generally accepted estimate, about 50 percent of the state budget was devoted to national defense. Soviet military assistance to Vietnam has varied greatly from year to year depending on PAVN's precise needs. In the mid-1980s, it was authoritatively estimated to be the equivalent of at least US$350 million per year.

Vietnam's manpower resources are relatively extensive. In 1987 its population was about 62 million, with approximately 6.5 million males of military-service age and 650,000 reaching draft age each year. Normally, 60 percent of those screened for military duty were found to be physically and mentally fit for full service. Other restrictions, such as those based on class, race, religion, and place of origin (i.e., the South), reduced the manpower pool somewhat. In 1986 PAVN was conscripting at the rate of about 300,000 annually.

To reassert discipline within PAVN ranks, a system of "military inspection and control" was instituted that served both judicial and police functions within PAVN. Under this system, the activities of enlisted men and officers were monitored to prevent wrongdoing (such as corruption) and to ensure continued discipline, obedience to orders, and adherence to PAVN regulations and state laws. This system was backed by a new code of military justice that regulated personal conduct. For enlisted personnel the code specified, in ascending order of severity, the following punishments for misconduct: censure, restriction to camp on days off (denial of shore-leave in the case of naval personnel), warning, disciplinary detention of from one to ten days (not applied to female military personnel), assignment to a lesser position, demotion, discharge, and dismissal from military service. Officers were not subjected to disciplinary detention as noncommissioned officers and enlisted men were. The seven punishments for officers (in ascending order of severity) were censure, warning, assignment to a lesser position, dismissal from position, reduction in rank, deprivation of officers' insignia, and dismissal from military service.

The new regulations also established commendations and a series of incentive awards. Approximately 100,000 PAVN officers and enlisted men received medals and other commendations each year. PAVN pay has always been notoriously low. Although pay was increased in the 1978 overhaul of the armed forces, it remained below comparable income levels elsewhere in the society and was constantly undercut by high inflation. Pay was based on rank, length of service, size of family, and honors and awards received. Seniority pay (1 percent of base pay times years of service), family allowances, a 30-percent hardship-service bonus for those assigned to Cambodia, and a 10-percent cost-of-living bonus for those assigned to the South were added to base pay.

A veteran PAVN soldier who was discharged, retired, or demobilized became a "revolutionary retiree." In 1987 at least 50 percent and possibly 60 percent of all adult males in Vietnam had served in the armed forces.

The veteran in Vietnam has become a figure of increasing importance. Officially he has been viewed with a mixture of appreciation and obligation, but privately leaders have worried that the socioeconomic isolation of veterans could lead to the formation of a vested interest bloc. In general, veterans have been treated well by the society and have been provided with social welfare benefits. Vietnamese women were assigned a major place in the revolution by VCP cadres quite early. Several of the early PAVN military cadres were women, including the legendary Ha Thi Que, a military theorist who adapted Maoist guerrilla war strategy to Vietnam. The principle that women represent a potent source of support continued to be upheld in the 1980s. Military service for women was voluntary and was open to those over eighteen who were members of the VCP or party youth organizations. Estimates of the number of women in PAVN ranged from 5 to 15 percent of the 2.9-million-member force. Most held technical or administrative assignments, although, in earlier years, combat assignments in guerrilla units were common and command assignments were not unknown. For instance, the third-ranking general officer in the

PLAF during the war in the South was a woman. There were no confirmed reports of women in PAVN engaged in combat duty in Cambodia, although it is possible that some were there; and there was no general conscription program for women, although they were encouraged to volunteer and the VCP asserted that it was their duty to do so.

Foreign Military Relations

In the 1950s and 1960s, the primary influence on PAVN was Chinese (see Foreign Relations, ch. 4). Early military thinking, organization, and strategy drew heavily on the Chinese, and particularly the Maoist, example, although Hanoi later officially denied Chinese influence and military assistance.

PAVN's dependence on the Soviet Union in the 1970s and 1980s for weaponry, military hardware, and technical training assured the Soviets an influential role, if not always a dominant one, in the Vietnamese military's activity and development. At the end of the Second Indochina War, the Soviet Union was supplying about 75 percent of North Vietnam's military hardware (China about 15 percent and Eastern Europe about 10 percent). Without Soviet assistance, Vietnam would have been unable to defend itself against China in 1979. By the 1980s, the estimate was that the Soviets provided 97 percent of such equipment and that the German Democratic Republic (East Germany), Poland, and Czechoslovakia together supplied the remaining 3 percent (see Appendix A, table 9). Military aid to PAVN in 1987 was almost exclusively Soviet in origin. In the mid-1980s, the Soviets contributed some 15,000 military advisers and military aid estimated to range from US$1.3 to US$1.7 billion annually.

The Soviet Union's relations with PAVN allowed Moscow to establish a military presence on the Indochina Peninsula. Access to the naval and air facilities at Cam Ranh Bay and Da Nang provided transit facilities for the Soviet Pacific Fleet and boosted Soviet intelligence-collecting efforts. The effect was to augment Moscow's military strength and facilitate global deployment of its forces.

The value of the relationship for Vietnam was logistic, not geopolitical. Hanoi had no arms factories, although it could make explosives and small armaments such as bullets, shells, and hand grenades. Sophisticated weaponry and equipment, mandatory for modern warfare, however, had to be imported.

The kind of Soviet military aid provided in the postwar years varied. In the first year or so, the Soviet Union routinely resupplied and replaced PAVN military inventories. After PAVN invaded Cambodia, the Soviets provided counterinsurgency aid, such as helicopters, and after the Chinese invaded Vietnam, Moscow gave Hanoi military hardware for conventional limited warfare. An analysis of the weapons supplied reveals that the Soviets were interested not only in enhancing Vietnam's defensive capability against China but also in developing a joint Soviet-Vietnamese offensive capability. Soviet generals, determined to pass on to the Vietnamese some of the burden of containing China, assigned PAVN specific strategic missions and provided the military hardware required to perform them. In late 1987, PAVN had no significant military relations with any nation except the Soviet Union.

Internal Security

Internal security was never much of a problem in North Vietnam; it was probably somewhat more tenuous in unified Vietnam. Unification, understandably, introduced new internal threats, which the regime in the 1980s was able to keep in check. As perceived in Hanoi theoretical journals, the most significant internal threat was the danger of counterrevolution, a possibility that had both internal and external implications. Hanoi feared that a resistance effort in Vietnam would mount an effective guerrilla war aided by outsiders who sought either to roll back communism in Indochina or to effect change in Hanoi's leadership. These outsiders might include not only foreign governments but also émigré Vietnamese seeking to destroy the ruling system.

There was widespread latent opposition to the regime, particularly in the South. In general it was low-level, widely scattered, and poorly organized and led. Opposition activities ranged from graffiti and similar token gestures to fairly large-sized guerrilla attacks in the Central Highlands. In the early 1980s, an active militant resistance force was estimated by observers abroad to number about 25,000 combatants. That figure tended to dwindle later in the decade. Given the extraordinary amount of social control in Vietnam, as in other Marxist-Leninist societies, it would be difficult for a resistance force to achieve sufficient size, strength, and cohesiveness to present a serious challenge to the existing system. The regime's strategy, therefore, was to keep the opposition off balance and prevent it from organizing.

Police, crime-detection, and law-enforcement activities tended to be treated collectively under the heading of "public security." These activities were conducted by overlapping, but tightly compartmentalized, institutions of control, separated by only hazy lines of jurisdiction. In particular, there was no sharp division between the internal security duties of PAVN forces and those of the civilian elements of the Ministry of Interior. This amorphous organization

287

of law enforcement and internal security work can be traced to the
VCP's early heritage and its experiences in the First Indochina
War when functional distinctions within the party organization were
less pronounced. Contributing to it is the clandestine character of
such activity and the penchant for secrecy and covert action endemic
in Vietnamese culture. Both party and state have paid enormous
attention to the maintenance of public order. Perhaps it is for this
reason that internal security has always been well managed and
security threats have always been contained. The methods employed
are sophisticated, often subtle, and there is less use of naked repression than many outsiders believe.

Four clusters of agencies were responsible for crime prevention
and the maintenance of public order and internal security under
the 1985 Criminal Code. The enforcement bodies were the People's
Security Force (PSF) or People's Police, operating chiefly in urban
areas; the People's Public Security Force (PPSF), called the People's
Security Service or PSS at the village level; the plain-clothes or
secret police; and the People's Armed Security Force (PASF), a
quasi-military organ, including some PAVN personnel, operating
chiefly in the villages and rural areas and concerned both with crime
and antistate activities. These agencies of control had the broad
responsibility of mobilizing the general population to support
internal security programs, in addition to performing internal
auditing, inspection, and general monitoring of both party and state
activity. The judiciary promoted security and law enforcement.
The courts, i.e., the investigative elements of the judicial system,
were charged with uncovering evidence in addition to prosecuting
the accused.

These institutions were charged under the Criminal Code with
protecting the public from crime, broadly defined as "any act dangerous to society." Supporting them, although independent of
them, was the party apparatus, which reached to the most remote
hamlets of the country. In the mid-1980s, both urban and rural
geographic areas were divided into wards, sub-wards, and blocks
and were administered by security cadres, who were aided and supported by the mass organizations. Each of the basic units (generally
the ward or block) had a security committee. In addition, in key
or sensitive areas, there was a special party unit (called Red Flag
Security) also organized at the ward or block level. The philosophy
of this internal security system was that self-implemented, self-
motivated, social discipline was required for true internal security
and that this was both the duty and the right of the individual
citizen. An important characteristic of the public security sector
was that, although it extended equally across the civilian (the

Ministry of Interior) and the military (PAVN, especially its paramilitary forces) sectors, the dominant influence was civilian and, ultimately, the party.

Problems

North Vietnam, before and during the Second Indochina War, experienced few serious internal security challenges. Disorders were recorded, however, the most famous being the so-called Quynh Luu uprising in 1956, in which farmers in predominantly Roman Catholic Nghe An Province demonstrated and rioted against the agricultural collectivization program. During the war, however, and despite South Vietnamese and American clandestine efforts to provoke resistance to the Hanoi regime, little internal opposition resulted. After the war, security problems were experienced in the newly occupied South, and a rise in dissidence was recorded in the North. As far as can be determined, however, in neither case were the problems serious enough to be considered a challenge to the regime. In 1987 public attitudes in the south remained widely anticommunist and there was greatly increased antipathy for the party in the North. In official circles, these conditions were labeled negative phenomena and were explained in the press as rising criminal and counterrevolutionary activity caused by a decline in social responsibility.

The most dangerous negative phenomenon was organized internal resistance to the regime that occurred chiefly in, but was not limited to, the South. For the most part this resistance found expression in graffiti, antiparty poetry, outlaw theater, rumor mongering, and general disinformation efforts. Less common, but still in evidence, were more militant resistance elements, who attempted, but rarely succeeded in, sabotaging the transportation and communication systems, party and state facilities, and economic enterprises. Finally, there were the armed resistance groups, which engaged in guerrilla war. By far the most challenging resistance effort was carried on by the people of the Central Highlands in the South, who are usually called Montagnards (see Ethnic Groups and Languages, ch. 2). Many were associated with the organization known as the Unified Front for the Struggle of Oppressed Races (Front Unifié pour la Lutte des Races Opprimées—FULRO) and operated in the region known in the Hanoi press as the "nameless front," that is, the area between Buon Me Thuot and Da Lat. They were supplied and supported by Khmer Rouge forces in Cambodia and, through them, by the Chinese. Hanoi handled the Montagnards in the South after the Second Indochina War far less skillfully and effectively than it had managed the northern

Montagnards a generation earlier. The primary reason appeared to be that in the North in the mid-1950s the problem had been handled by trained party cadres, some of them Montagnards themselves, who had dealt carefully with their ethnic brethren. In the South in 1975 (because the war ended so unexpectedly), responsibility was given to combat troops, who were ill-prepared to handle such a sensitive problem. Since the war's end, large battles reportedly have taken place occasionally in the Highlands, some involving as many as 1,000 resistance fighters.

The Montagnard resistance has not represented a revolutionary movement in the modern sense because it has not tried to overthrow or change the government in Hanoi. Rather, the upland dwellers of southern Vietnam have sought autonomy, and they would settle for being left alone. In 1987 a stabilized condition of local accommodation appeared to have been achieved between local PAVN commanders in the "nameless front" region and indigenous Montagnard tribes.

The second most important resistance elements were the militant southern socioreligious sects called the Hoa Hao (see Glossary) and Cao Dai (see Glossary), whose total membership was more than a million (see Religion, ch. 2). The Hoa Hao sect is concentrated in Chau Doc Province and adjacent provinces. The Cao Dai is headquartered in Tay Ninh Province, and most of its followers live in this region. In the early years after the Second Indochina War, the two sects offered considerable armed resistance to the new government. By the mid-1980s, however, resistance had fallen off because it was widely believed local accommodation had been achieved.

A third resistance element comprised various nationalistic and patriotic groups, many of whom came under the generic term *chu quoc* or "national salvation." The bulk of these were members of the Dai Viet and the Viet Nam Quoc Dan Dang, two militant anticommunist nationalist organizations dating from the 1930s, or were ARVN holdouts in the far south. Other resistance groups, with more exotic names, reported by émigrés included the Black Sail Group (Catholics in the Ho Nai region); the Black Dragon Force (ex-ARVN 7th-Division Catholic soldiers in the My Tho vicinity); the Yellow Crab Force (Cao Dai in Tay Ninh Province); the White Tigers (Hoa Hao in An Giang Province); the Laotian National Cobra Force (Vietnamese and Lao along the Laos-Vietnam border); and the Cambodian Border Force (a similar group in the Cambodia-Vietnam border region). Armed resistance, as practiced by these groups, commonly consisted of attacks on reeducation camps, remote military installations, and VCP offices. Reported resistance activities during the 1980s included launching rocket attacks on a Phan Rang reeducation camp and on a Xuan Loc camp (during which 6,000 inmates escaped), dynamiting a Ho Chi Minh City water pumping station, detonating a bomb near that city's Continental Hotel, and throwing a grenade into the yard of the former United States ambassador's residence, which had been transformed into living quarters for several PAVN generals. There were also reports of road mining incidents and booby-trapped railroad switching equipment.

Catholics in Vietnam, who number almost 3 million, have represented a significant potential resistance force of increasing concern to Hanoi officials. Initial policy was to control the church as an institution, while allowing free religious expression. In the late 1970s, however, all religious groups increasingly were harassed, and attendance at religious services was discouraged. A few well publicized trials of clergy followed. By the mid-1980s, it was apparent that the initial tolerance for religion had waned. Some observers, including church officials in the Vatican, speculated that Hanoi officials were concerned because of the growing appeal of religion to the young.

Intellectual dissent also was reported to be increasing in the mid-1980s. Fueled by the obvious failure of the party and state to solve the country's more pressing economic problems, intellectual dissent took the form of psychological warfare conducted by literary and cultural figures and ordinary people alike. There had been a similar outbreak of intellectual dissent in North Vietnam in the 1956-58 period, when the regime experimented, to its regret, with a "hundred flowers movement" similar to that in China. In the late 1980s, the most common medium was graffiti such as "Born in the North to Die in Cambodia" and "Nothing is More Precious than Independence and Liberty—Ho Chi Minh" (a famous Ho quotation used as an ironic commentary by southerners). The slogan *Phuc quoc,* or "restore national sovereignty," was reported to have been seen on walls in Ho Chi Minh City and in Hue. Propaganda leaflets also were scattered along city sidewalks at night or left in schoolroom desks, and underground literary societies were founded, including the Hanoi Barefoot Literary Group, the Danang Han River Literary Society, the Ho Literary Society of Hue, and the Stone Cave and Literary Flame societies of Ho Chi Minh City. According to editorials in the official press, the writings of these subversive groups "depict resentment and incite antagonism" through the use of "ambiguous symbolism and double entendres." An example cited by *Lao Dong* (August 22, 1985) was the following excerpt from a poem: "Biting our lips, hating the North wind/We lay with aching bones/Lamenting the West wind.'' Poets have been incarcerated for their works. A cause célèbre in 1984 was the arrest of a leading novelist, Doan Quoc Sy, of the Danang Han River Literary Society.

Resistance activity is supported by the nearly 1 million Vietnamese émigrés living abroad. There is a welter of supportive organizations—more than fifty in California alone—about which little reliable information is available. The broadest-based group is the Overseas Free Vietnam Association, which has chapters in the United States, Europe, and Australia.

Development of the Internal Security System

During the First Indochina War, police and internal-security functions were regarded as a single activity. Security cadres and personnel had three duties: guarding Viet Minh facilities, high-level personnel, lines of communication, and troop movements; insuring public safety in the Viet Minh-controlled areas; and conducting counterintelligence and antisabotage work.

At the time of the DRV's formation in 1945, all of this activity was vested in the Ministry of Interior. Within the ministry was a large sub-element called the Directorate General for Security, concerned with counterrevolution. This arrangement was abolished in 1954, when the police and internal-security functions were separated and the Ministry of Public Security was created. After the takeover of the South in 1975, which imposed new internal security tasks, the two functions were again combined, this time into the Ministry of Interior, which was then vastly enlarged.

By the mid-1980s, the ministry was composed of seven major departments: the People's Police Department, responsible for general law enforcement; the Traffic Police Department, responsible for traffic control; the Public Security Department, responsible for general internal security; the Social Order Department, responsible for detention, the family registration system, immigration-emigration, border control, and port-of-entry security; the Public Security Forces, responsible for both law enforcement and internal security in the rural areas; the Counterespionage Department, chiefly responsible for investigative work and dossier compilation; and the Counterreactionary Department, chiefly responsible for investigation of religious organizations in the South.

Also in the ministry were smaller, more specialized offices under vice ministers, including those concerned with counterintelligence, foreign intelligence coordination (shared with PAVN intelligence agencies and primarily concerned with Cambodia and Laos), official communication systems operations (including mail censorship), political indoctrination of ministry personnel, and ethnic minorities' activities.

The Ministry of Interior was again enlarged and restructured in 1979, when, according to Hanoi, China launched its "multi-faceted war of sabotage." This brought increased and more systematic coordination with PAVN, especially in the China border region. The restructuring moved the ministry closer to the Soviet model of internal security organizations, a development undoubtedly encouraged by Soviet Komitet Gosudavstvennoy Bezopasnosti (KGB, Committee of State Security) advisers. It is possible that in these shifts the ministry gained a certain degree of autonomy from the VCP.

Tran Quoc Hoan created Hanoi's state security system in the 1940s and ran it until he stepped down or was forced out in 1982. He then served as a director of the Central Committee's Proselytizing and Front Department. Hoan continued to publish extensively on security problems, and he remained an influential figure in the field until his death in late 1986. Pham Hung replaced Hoan as Minister of Interior in 1982 and served until December 1986, when he relinquished the post to Mai Chi Tho. Before his elevation to the ministry and the Political Bureau, Tho was in charge of security in southern Vietnam as the mayor of Ho Chi Minh City.

The Police

Police functions, such as routine crime detection, apprehension of suspects, and enforcement of judicial orders, were vested in two elements that differed both conceptually and functionally. The PSF was a law enforcement agency in the same sense as the term is used in the West. It operated chiefly in urban rather than in rural areas and was first established in 1962. Its purpose was "to execute the laws of the state, maintain public order and security, protect public property, protect the lives and property of individuals, and prevent juvenile delinquency." These functions were expanded and made more specific in 1972, and again in 1976, by National Assembly directives authorizing the PSF to "arrest, temporarily detain, and temporarily release suspects; search people, homes, belongings, and mail; temporarily hold evidence; issue identification certificates, travel permits, and other documents; motivate citizens to observe the law and security measures; stop acts of sabotage; prevent juvenile delinquency; give aid to victims of accidents, including commandeering transportation to perform this function; and punish or carry out other compulsory measures against those who infringe on public order and security regulations." Fire fighting was also administered by the PSF. Members of the PSF were admonished to "serve the people wholeheartedly, show bravery, and constantly demonstrate responsibility, revolutionary vigilance, and political and military professionalism."

The second unit was the PASF, a combination of gendarmerie and police field force, which operated chiefly in the villages and rural areas. The PASF had a broader security function than the PSF, since its concern extended beyond criminal and illegal political activity to insurgency threats and transprovincial organized counterrevolutionary activity. It was a hybrid security institution composed of party security cadres and PAVN personnel whose duties were in a gray area between ordinary police work and guerrilla warfare. The PASF was similar to the militia of the Soviet Union, with a domain described as "inland security," and functioned both as a protective and investigative body. PASF units guarded defense-industry installations, state and party offices, communication facilities, and important economic centers and supplied bodyguards for high-level officials. It was also charged with handling antigovernment conspiracies requiring sensitive political investigations and with investigating interprovincial crimes such as counterfeiting, smuggling, and hijacking.

PASF was created in March 1959 by combining several small party-security and PAVN special units. From the start it had a semimilitary character. In 1960, the Third National Party Congress assigned it the "leading mission of defense against counterrevolution" and stressed the political character of its work, which in part meant activities designed to make security measures more acceptable to the general public through what was termed PASF's "people-motivating mission." Its formation also relieved PAVN regular forces of certain border and coastal static-defense duties. In the decade that followed unification in 1976, it became something of a catch-all security institution.

The structure of the PASF was quasi-military—that is, it was organized by battalions and companies with administrative centers in provincial capitals. In 1987 the PASF was estimated to have at least 500 personnel in each province, with a total strength of at least 21,000. It was more heavily armed and more mobile than ordinary police.

The PASF headquarters in Hanoi was in a Ministry of Interior building, once the Don Thuy French Military Barracks on Hang Bai Street. It was divided into eight bureaus. The first handled administration, including personnel, supply, and housing. The second maintained criminal records and handled correspondence. The third was responsible for the Hanoi capital area and supervised crime detection, fire fighting, traffic control, and issuance of identity cards. The fourth conducted investigations, including interrogations. The fifth handled incarceration of persons under arrest, including their detention while awaiting trial. The sixth controlled political and indoctrination training, as well as internal police affairs. The seventh handled budget and fiscal matters for the organization, and the eighth managed communication surveillance, censored mail, and controlled unauthorized publications.

PAVN's function is dual in nature, having been derived from the French concept of police duty, introduced in the colonial period, and the Soviet Union's idea of militia. It rests on the belief that all challenges to the regime should be treated as law-enforcement rather than military problems. Even in the suppression of insurgency movements such as FULRO, PAVN's responsibilities were carried out as an exercise in law enforcement rather than as a military enterprise.

PAVN shared command responsibilities with the Ministry of Interior over a host of specific police organizations, including Regional Police Force units operating out of the country's forty provincial capitals; the Border-Control Police or Port-of-Entry Police, established by the Ministry of Interior in 1981; and Naval Security units, which used armed civilian fishing boats to apprehend persons illegally leaving the country. In theory, all such organizations functioned under the jurisdiction of the Ministry of Interior. Their place in PAVN's organizational structure, however, remained ambiguous.

Deputized, nonprofessional law-enforcement units were reportedly numerous, but they were only vaguely described in press reports. They included the People's Protection Squads (active in both street-patrol work and fire fighting), the Enterprise Protection Force (active in factories, government buildings, and communes), the Municipal Security Protection Force (active in major cities), the Neighborhood Protection Civil Guard Agency, the Capital Security Youth Assault Units, the Township Public Security Force, and the Civil Defense Force. Many of the personnel in these units served concurrently with the Paramilitary Force.

In addition, PAVN elements were detailed to police duty, usually on a temporary basis, and assigned chiefly in the South and along the China border. Their primary responsibilities in these areas were the prevention of smuggling and of illegal departures or entries.

The Ministry of Interior divided Vietnam into "security interzones," and the major cities—Hanoi, Haiphong, and Ho Chi Minh City—were allotted separate security status. The interzone headquarters coordinated law enforcement and internal security work with the judiciary, local military commanders, and provincial party officials. Each of the interzone directors (as well as the director of the Hanoi Security Service) reported directly to the Ministry of Interior and the Political Bureau Secretariat.

The villages, which normally experienced little crime, had only rudimentary law enforcement, usually in the hands of a deputized nonprofessional working part-time and often without a regular salary. If a major crime occurred—for example, a murder—it was investigated by an official sent from the provincial capital.

The function of the nonprofessional deputized law-enforcement officer, indeed even his existence, was not formally established or codified. The position of the village deputy was conceived as a means by which local authority could organize the village to police itself. Crime prevention and security became the responsibility of all, under the guidance of a local figure backed by the local party committee. This made for a pervasive surveillance system. It could also result in inept law enforcement and the accruing of enormous power by the deputy, who was privy to information gathered through the surveillance system.

Public Security

Vietnam did not have a secret police force of the same kind as Nazi Germany's Gestapo. The PPSF (or PSS at the village level), a plainclothes internal security organization charged with handling sensitive security threats, bore the closest resemblance.

Actually, the secret police function in Vietnam appeared to be distributed among the Ministry of Interior, the party, PAVN, and the Paramilitary Force, with the PPSF as the pivotal element. The PPSF was more a party than a state organization, and observers believe that its chain of command ran from the district level through a hierarchy to the Political Bureau Secretariat in Hanoi. In its reporting responsibilities as an organ of the party, the PPSF largely bypassed or coordinated only laterally with the minister of interior, its nominal superior in the government hierarchy. This organizational arrangement was instituted in the early 1950s by two top party security figures, Le Giang and Tran Hieu, at the time the director and deputy director respectively of what was then the First Directorate for Security of the Ministry of Public Security. Some observers believe that the PPSF was in reality an institution of professional police and trained security agents disguised as ordinary party administrative cadres.

During the First Indochina War, the PPSF supervised the issue of travel permits and identification cards, checked on the movements of marine fishermen, identified strangers in the villages, and maintained family census and travel records. At one point it also monitored and reported on public health, apparently in the belief that North Vietnam was to be subjected to chemical warfare attacks.

The PPSF assumed new importance in the late 1970s with the rise of the China threat and the increased prospect of a serious sabotage and espionage effort by outsiders. In order to cope with these developments, authorities in 1980 enlarged the hamlet-village-level structure. A nationwide system was instituted, with a PSS chief and two cadres detailed to every hamlet and a chief and five cadres assigned to each village. In many instances, they replaced PASF personnel. At the same time, higher recruitment standards were established (for education and age), a six-month training program was introduced, and an effort was made to create a more professional service with more sophisticated operations. In 1983 plans for putting the PPSF into uniform were announced, but in 1987 they had yet to be acted upon.

In the South, the PPSF (or PSS) was more or less under direct party control. Members wore yellow armbands with a red inscription, *Order and Security Control,* to differentiate them from PAVN security units, whose members wore red armbands with a yellow inscription, *Military Control,* and from the PASF forces, whose red and blue arm bands bore the yellow legend *Order.*

The rise of the China threat highlighted certain weaknesses in the security system related to the proper division of labor between the Ministry of Interior and the Ministry of National Defense. In 1981 a concerted effort was launched to increase and improve coordination between the two ministries: they signed two interministerial directives, one establishing the mechanism for systematic, joint security work and the other spelling out the respective duties of each in "the three tasks of maintaining political security, strengthening social discipline, and insuring public safety."

Under the new arrangement, there was unified recruiting for the two services. A recruit could choose the service he would enter and, in many instances, the province to which he would be assigned. PAVN made available to the Ministry of Interior some of its military hardware, including such highly desirable items as equipment used by special weapons and tactics teams. The Ministry of Interior relieved the Defense Ministry of its responsibility for guarding foreign missions in Hanoi and for supplying guards to the country's prisons. Personnel also were transferred, most from the Ministry of Interior to PAVN, and a new PAVN unit called the Police Protection Regiment was formed. Transfers from this ministry to strengthen PAVN units along the China border were probably due to the growing China threat, the nature and size of which was perceived as simply beyond Ministry of Interior capabilities. Some PASF units were converted into PAVN Border Defense Command regiments, although their duties, like those of the Police Protection regiments, were not known in 1987.

Some observers noted that the net effect of the security reorganization initiated in 1981 was the Ministry of Interior's improved ability to check on the actions and loyalties of high-ranking PAVN generals. Others observed that PAVN authority now extended deeper into the civilian sector. The new arrangement also highlighted the underlying competition between the Ministry of Interior and the Ministry of National Defense with respect to security responsibilities and authority.

One other dimension of security activity was the use of youth and youth organizations for internal security purposes. Hanoi appeared to have calculated that young people tended to have greater loyalty to the existing order than their elders, and that they represented a vast manpower pool ideally suited to mass surveillance work. The mass media commonly referred to Vietnam's three security forces as PAVN, public security, and "fourth generation" youth (that is, the fourth generation since the founding of the VCP). The security role of youth was stressed more in southern Vietnam, where, through an umbrella youth group called the Revolutionary Action Movement (RAM), the energies of the young were harnessed in the name of social improvement. Much of this activity was economic and related to various nation-building programs; some, however, concerned political security, social order, and safety, areas of activity commonly given the collective label of "revolutionary action against negativism."

RAM had a large corps of organizations from which to draw. In the mid-1980s, the total party youth force was about 4.5 million; this included the Ho Chi Minh Communist Youth League (2 million) and the organizations for those younger in age—the Vanguard Teenager Organization, the Ho Chi Minh Young Pioneers, and the Ho Chi Minh Children's Organization (2.5 million). A front organization called the Vietnam Youth Federation included about 10 million party and nonparty youth.

The most important RAM subgroup was the Ho Chi Minh Assault Youth Force (usually termed the AYF), the core of an amorphous organization called the Young Volunteers Force or Volunteer Service. The AYF was open to males seventeen to twenty-five years of age and females seventeen to twenty, who volunteered for two years' service (the males thus could escape the military draft). The AYF was organized along quasi-military lines and was assigned chiefly economic duties, mostly in the rural areas of the South.

Within the AYF were smaller organizations, such as the Assault Security Team and the Assault Control Team, which had security assignments. Some teams focused on ordinary crime; others were engaged in covert surveillance, particularly of other youth. The most elite of these were the Youth Union Red Flag teams, which were made up entirely of Ho Chi Minh Communist Youth League members. (AYF teams, by contrast, were a mix of party and non-party youth.) Red Flag teams were entrusted with the most sensitive assignments given to the young. The high point of AYF security activity apparently came in the few years immediately following the 1979 China incursion. After that, vigilance in security matters tapered off somewhat.

Law Enforcement

Vietnamese legal thought with regard to the treatment of criminals is the result of three major influences: classic Confucianism, the Napoleonic Code, and Marxism-Leninism. The relevant Confucian concept is that society is to be governed not by law but by moral men and that crime is symptomatic of an absence of virtue that engenders conflict and disharmony. Most important, the Confucian ethic provides no principle of judicial administration. In imperial China, justice was an interpretation of the moment by the emperor and his mandarins, meaning that in every instance imperial will was superior to the law. The spirit of the law the French brought to Vietnam was that guilt should be determined by fair and impartial means and should be assigned appropriate punishment. However, French colonialism inculcated a view of the law as something to be manipulated and the courts as institutions to be bribed or subverted. The result was a general lack of respect for the judicial process. Marxism-Leninism added to this attitude the perspective that crime is a reflection of environmental factors that victimize the individual by turning him into a criminal. The proper remedy for this condition is to eliminate the causal factors while rehabilitating the criminal. The combination of the three legacies has produced in Vietnamese society a legal philosophy that is inquisitional rather than adversarial, seeking reform rather than punishment. The system imposes on the individual and the state the responsibility of bringing all members of society to a condition of self-imposed moral rectitude in which behavior is defined in terms of collective, rather than individual, good. In contrast to the West, where law is the guarantor of rights that all may claim, in Vietnam the law concerns duties that all must fulfill.

Vietnamese law seeks to give the prisoner the right to reformation. In theory, at least, there are very few incorrigibles. It also permits a relativist approach in fixing sentences, much more so than do the precedent-based systems of the West. Mitigating circumstances, such as whether the accused acted out of passion or premeditation, loom large as a factor in sentencing. Murder by stabbing is treated more leniently than murder by poison, for example, because the latter is perceived to require a greater degree of premeditation than the former. The personal circumstances of the accused are also a factor in determining punishment. In the administration of criminal justice in Vietnam, an effort is made to understand the criminal, his crime, and his reasons; and the notion of permanent or extended incarceration is rejected in favor of an effort to determine whether or not and, if so, how the criminal can be rehabilitated and restored to society.

Political crimes are treated less liberally, however. In such cases, the administration of justice can be arbitrary and harsh. Politics clearly plays a role in the arrest, trial, and sentencing procedures. The rationale for this policy, which is openly acknowledged, is that the revolution must be protected and that the individual may be sacrificed, perhaps even unjustly, for the common cause. The courts also take a more jaundiced view of the rehabilitation of political prisoners than of common criminals.

The court system was reorganized in 1981 into four basic levels: the Supreme People's Court; the provincial/municipal courts reporting to Hanoi; the local courts, chiefly at the district/precinct levels, reporting respectively to provincial or municipal governments; and military courts. In addition, a number of specialized courts were created. In judicial procedure the courts still owed much to the French example, particularly with respect to the role of the procurator, who had much broader responsibilities than the prosecutor or district attorney under the Anglo-Saxon system.

On January 1, 1986, a new Penal Code officially went into effect after nearly five years of preparation. It contained 280 articles divided into 12 chapters or sections. Unlike earlier laws, the new code included detailed sections on juvenile and military offenders. The first eight chapters defined jurisdiction and judicial procedures; distinguished among infractions, misdemeanors, and felonies; and outlined sentencing procedures. The last section, consisting of four chapters, defined specific crimes and fixed penalties. The code identified seven categories of legal punishment: warning, fine, reform without detention, house arrest, imprisonment, life imprisonment, and death. There was no parole, but remission of punishment was possible and the conditions for it appeared to be lenient (eligibility for remission of a life-imprisonment sentence began after seven years). In general, definitions of crime were broad, vague, and could be interpreted so that virtually any antisocial word or deed was indictable. Penalties were stern and included capital punishment for a lengthy list of crimes. In 1986 Minister of Justice Phan Hien defended in writings and interviews the new code's long list of capital crimes, arguing that in general the code was liberal. He cited as evidence that polygamy was a crime, whereas adultery was not. Most serious crimes (all drawing the death penalty) were crimes endangering the national security, i.e., treason, "taking action to overthrow the people's government," espionage, rebellion, sabotage, terrorism, "undermining unity," spreading "anti-socialist" propaganda, "disrupting security," obstructing or inciting to obstruct state agencies' activities, hijacking, destroying important national security projects and property, and "crimes against humanity."

Upon arrest, an individual was taken first to a Ministry of Interior records office where he was fingerprinted and interrogated, and where his record was checked. He was then remanded to a detention cell to be held until his trial. Posting bail to obtain temporary release was not practiced, although in some instances release on one's own recognizance was permitted.

Trials themselves were brief, businesslike, and conducted in an informal, somewhat nonjudicial atmosphere. All participants were expected to seek justice rather than simply to observe the letter of the law. The defense was supposed to proceed in an objective manner, meaning it was expected to pursue the truth and not to engage in courtroom tactics "that distort the truth or conceal the guilty person's faults." The defendant was expected to confine his efforts to presenting facts that proved his innocence or that supported his plea to the tribunal for reduction of the gravity of the charge. In most trials, defense strategy was not directed toward exoneration but toward a sentence of reform without detention.

Sentences for nonpolitical crimes, and particularly for less serious felonies, tended to fall into three categories: reform without detention, reform with detention, and detention (i.e., an ordinary prison sentence). Perhaps half of the sentences imposed for these crimes were of the first category, and the remaining half were divided more or less equally between the other two categories. The system rested on the assumption that most criminals could be rehabilitated, but the procedure required that the individual petition the court for rehabilitation. The court might also sentence a person to loss of civil rights, an auxiliary penalty that deprived the individual of certain rights for a specific period of time (see Social Control, this ch.). Formal incarceration that resulted from judicial proceedings might be either in a prison or a work-reform camp (detention with labor). Vietnamese prisons imposed confinement in a manner more or less like prisons anywhere in the world. Work reform camps incarcerated prisoners as well, but also required them to perform outside physical labor, constructing roads, clearing brush, and similar tasks on contract for the state. Beyond confinement arising from judicial proceedings, there was also administrative detention that did not involve the courts and was usually the result of action by party officials. Eligible for this type of incarceration was a host of offenders that included juvenile delinquents, foreigners (chiefly Laotians), northerners who had defected to the South during the war, and "enemies of the people" (those judged to be dangerous to society by virtue of their social, political, economic, or family background). The largest and best known facilities for administrative detention were the re-education camps and social-labor camps. Both were "educative" in purpose and both were designed for "social negatives." The difference between the two, insofar as there was any, was that the re-education camp was for those whose attitudes, ideas, and beliefs required correction, while the social-labor camps were for those of "backward behavior," such as draft dodgers, tax evaders, and persons who "spread social negativism."

In official Hanoi thinking, there was a sharp difference between confinement as a result of judicial proceedings and administrative detention. Those who were incarcerated in a prison or a work-reform camp as the result of a court sentence were considered incorrigible or without social value. Prisoners confined under administrative detention were those for whom there was some hope of rehabilitation. While the individual inmate caught up in the system might find the distinction meaningless, it was important for an observer of the Vietnamese judicial and internal security system to bear in mind the distinction between the two institutions.

Detailed information on Vietnam's prison system—the number and location of its prisons and the size of its prison population—has always been extraordinarily difficult to obtain, and much of the information available in 1987 was questionable. Hanoi had not published anything of consequence on the subject. Credible available data tended to combine statistics on prison, work-reform camps, and administrative detention facilities. Each of the forty Vietnamese provinces had at least one prison with a capacity ranging from about 1,000 to 5,000 inmates. Some provinces also had what were called model prisons, which resembled new economic zones in that, in the spirit of modern penology, they offered the prisoners financial incentives to engage in agricultural production. Most of the district capitals had small prisons or detention centers, and the PPSF (or PSS) operated detention cells in most villages and some hamlets. In addition, there were perhaps a dozen central (or national) prisons that could hold as many as 40,000 inmates. The largest of these were the Hoa Lo prison in Hanoi (with a branch in Haiphong) and the Chi Hoa prison outside Ho Chi Minh City. The major cities also had detention centers (Hanoi had 18, which could hold 500 prisoners each) where individuals were held awaiting trial.

Life in a Vietnamese prison, as reported by ex-prisoners, was harsh. There were work details for those in prisons, as well as in the work-reform camps, that chiefly involved agricultural production for prison use. Rehabilitation lectures were held daily, and prisoners spent much time describing past behavior and thoughts in detail in their dossiers. Visitors were permitted only infrequently in most prisons. Discipline was strict, and prisons in particular were well guarded; usually there was 1 guard for every 250 prisoners. In general, the use of torture, corporal punishment, and what might be termed police brutality were no longer legal but were still condoned by officials and even accepted by the general public.

Social Control

Under the Hanoi government, "control" was a legal term used both as a verb and a noun. "Control" meant use of state power to deal with individuals who committed either civil or political crimes judged not serious enough to warrant imprisonment, but serious enough to deserve reform without detention. "Control" referred also to the status of an individual under such sentence (also one released from prison but considered not fully reformed). Hence it combined the condition of being on parole with that of being in the custody of the court or under state surveillance. A person under "control" had to report periodically to local authorities to account for his activities and detail his efforts to reform. He was proscribed from certain occupations, including teaching, publishing, practicing medicine or pharmacy, and operating a restaurant, hotel, or bookstore. Such restrictions were deemed legal because one under "control" was considered to have already forfeited some of his civil rights, at least temporarily.

The mechanism of "control," called the People's Organ of Control, was hierarchically organized and formally defined by the 1980 Constitution (Articles 127, 138, and 141). At the top was the Supreme People's Organ of Control, and at the bottom were the district and precinct organs of control. These institutions functioned to "control the observance of the law by the ministries, armed forces, state employees and citizens; to exercise the right of public prosecution; and to insure strict and uniform observance of the law." Their purview was "any act encroaching upon the interests of the State, the collective, or the lives, property, freedom, honor, and dignity of citizens." The underlying justification for their existence was that major internal security problems developed because of a breakdown in social discipline and that restoration of discipline was best achieved with a system of self-control or self-discipline. The system was composed of many activities: physical control; re-education and reform; indoctrination, emulation, and motivation; and education. Its essence was organization and motivation, and in the hands of skilled cadres it could harness social pressure to induce new attitudes and ways of thinking.

Population Relocation

Massive relocation of the population, blandly called the "state redistribution of labor" program, began after reunification in 1976 and has been an integral part of the security effort. At least 5 million people have been uprooted in this process, known as "breaking the machine." While partly economic in its motivation, the relocation's main purpose has been to break up the existing social structure. In assigning individuals to new economic zones, for instance, care has been taken to scatter those from a single urban area or village to separate locations. The formation of new associations by these people was then supervised by the VCP, which used various mass movements and proletarian social organizations—augmented by communication and education programs intended to raise class consciousness—to help foster class struggle and to turn the middle and upper classes into social pariahs. This social ostracism was one of the reasons that many middle-class Vietnamese left the South after 1975 as "boat people" (see Glossary).

Re-education Camps

The re-education camp remained the predominant device of social "control" in the late 1980s. It was used to incarcerate members of certain social classes in order to coerce them to accept and conform to the new social norms. This type of camp was one feature of a broader effort to control the social deviant and to campaign against counterrevolution and the resistance. The concept of re-education was borrowed from the Chinese communists and was developed early in the First Indochina War, at least in part because the nomadic government of North Vietnam was unable to maintain orthodox prisons. The process was continued in the North in 1954, but it came fully to the world's attention only after North Vietnam's takeover of the South in 1975. The camps were administered by PAVN or the Ministry of Interior, but they were not regarded as prisons and indeed were separate from the prison system. They were considered to be institutions where rehabilitation was accomplished through education and socially constructive labor. Only those who "deserved rehabilitation" (as opposed to those who deserved jail) were sent to the camps, where their political attitudes, work production records, and general behavior were closely monitored.

The re-education camp system, as it developed in the South, was both larger and more complex than its counterpart in the North. Three types of camps were created to serve three purposes—short-term re-education, long-term re-education, and permanent incarceration. The system was also organized into five levels.

There were two levels of short-term re-education. The first was the study camp or day study center which was located in or near a major urban center, often in a public park, and allowed attendees to return home each night. Courses, chiefly lectures to "teach socialism and unlearn the old ways lasted about thirty days." They were attended mostly by southern proletarians and juvenile delinquents. These level-one camps, which instructed perhaps 500,000 people, were the most common kind in the South in the first few years after the end of the Second Indochina War, but were phased out near the end of the 1970s. The level-two camps were similar in purpose to level one camps, but they required full-time attendance for three to six months, during which time the inmate was obliged to supply his own food. Security was minimal, and it was possible simply to walk away from the camp, although later arrest was likely. During the 1970s, there were some 300 of these level-two camps in the South, with at least 200,000 inmates. Some level-two camps remained in the 1980s, although most had been phased out.

Long-term re-education was undertaken at level-three camps. Termed the collective reformatory, level three had thought reform as its purpose. Whereas re-education of individuals in the first two levels of camps was regarded chiefly as a matter of informing them of the "truth" and making them aware of facts about the new social order, reforming the thought of those in level-three camps required a process of deeper examination and analysis. The orientation was both more psychological and more intellectual. Although the inmate was apt to be better educated, and thus less susceptible to manipulation, than most Vietnamese, the system considered him salvageable. The level-three camps at their most prevalent, in the late 1970s, were found in every province in southern Vietnam and dealt with at least 50,000 persons. Although the camps were still in use both in the North and South, by 1987 the number had decreased.

The third type of re-education camp, the socialist-reform camp, was intended for permanent incarceration, and re-education involved indoctrination and forced labor. When these camps were first established in the South, individuals were assigned according to the probable time that each person's re-education would require. Level-four camp inmates were said to require three years and level-five camp inmates, five years. For this reason the two were commonly termed "three-year-sentence" and "five-year-sentence" camps. Their true purpose, it became apparent eventually, was to incarcerate certain southern individuals—including educators, legislators, province chiefs, writers, and supreme court judges—until the South was judged stable enough to permit their release. In 1987 at least 15,000 were still incarcerated in level-four and level-five camps. When the three-year or five-year period expired, they were simply sentenced to three or five more years of re-education.

Initially, the five levels of re-education were structured in ascending order of perceived individual recalcitrance and ascending length of incarceration. In 1987, however, only the level-three camp remained dedicated to its original purpose. The level-four and level-five camps were simply detention centers for those judged potentially dangerous to the system. Camp conditions were reportedly poor, with little food, no medicine, and a high death rate.

Surveillance

Perhaps the most effective instrument of social control in the 1980s was the "revolutionary vigilance" surveillance system, commonly called "the warden method." In theory at least, every hamlet, city block, state farm, factory, school, and state and party office had its own Revolutionary Vigilance Committee headed by a warden and made up of a team of neighbors, usually 25 to 40 households (120 to 300 persons). Institutionally, the Vigilance Committee was described as neither party nor state, but a form of alliance. Its purpose was to "help the government in all ways and aspects," specifically by monitoring the behavior of its members, reporting public opinion to higher authorities, and promoting various state and party policies and programs locally. The committee's authority was shored up by the *Ho Khau* registration system, which required each individual to have an identity card and each family to have a family registration certificate or residence permit (listing the names of all persons authorized to live at one address). Both identification cards and family registration certificates were checked frequently by security cadres.

It is historical fact that social "control" as administered by the Vietnamese party and government worked impressively over the years to organize, mobilize, and motivate the society to serve the interests of national security. It produced an implacably determined military force and an internal security system that virtually policed itself. However, it was evident by the late 1980s that the system no longer worked as well as it once had. The Political Bureau acknowledged the influence of "negativism" that endangered the "quality of socialist life," and military and security service professional journals emphasized the need to improve security methods, including "techniques for suppressing rebellions." Although the spread of full-scale social unrest in Vietnam was not likely, the idea was no longer unthinkable.

What developed in Vietnam in the 1980s was not so much a rise in internal security consciousness on the part of the government as a change in public attitudes toward security problems. Military and public alertness to the dangers of counterrevolution, crime, and antisocial behavior diminished to the point of indifference. Nguyen Van Linh, before his appointment as VCP general secretary in 1986, complained that the "spirit of vigilance" was lagging in Vietnam and that "some individuals suffer[ed] from revolutionary vigilance paralysis." Massive indoctrination campaigns, undertaken to correct this shortcoming by arousing public concern, apparently met with indifferent results. The condition was symptomatic of a society that was beginning to be buffeted by the winds of change.

* * *

The major source of research materials for this chapter was the Indochina Archive at the University of California at Berkeley. The archive has 2.5 million pages of documentary material, 15 percent of which relates directly to Vietnam's armed forces, internal security, law, and judiciary. Much of the archive is original source material from Vietnam, including official newspaper and journal articles translated and published by the Foreign Broadcast Information Service and the Joint Publications Research Service of the United States Government.

PAVN: People's Army of Vietnam, by Douglas Pike, is the only book-length study of Vietnam's armed forces; William Turley has written several lengthy articles on the subject. Human rights violations in Vietnam have been dealt with in journal articles by Karl Jackson and Jacqueline Desbarats. (For further information and complete citations, see Bibliography.)

Appendix A

Table 1. *Metric Conversion Coefficients and Factors*

When you know	Multiply by	To find
Millimeters	0.04	inches
Centimeters	0.39	inches
Meters	3.3	feet
Kilometers	0.62	miles
Hectares (10,000 m²)	2.47	acres
Square kilometers	0.39	square miles
Cubic meters	35.3	cubic feet
Liters	0.26	gallons
Kilograms	2.2	pounds
Metric tons	0.98	long tons
....	1.1	short tons
....	2,204	pounds
Degrees Celsius	9	degrees Fahrenheit
(Centigrade)	divide by 5 and add 32	

Table 2. Population, 1979, 1984, and 1988
(in thousands)

Place	1979 Census Population	Estimated 1984 Population	Estimated 1988 Population
Municipalities			
Hanoi	2,571	2,878	3,170
Haiphong	1,279	1,397	1,500
Ho Chi Minh City	3,420	3,564	3,685
Provinces			
An Giang	1,532	1,765	1,980
Bac Thai	815	903	980
Ben Tre	1,042	1,164	1,275
Binh Tri Thien	1,902	2,020	2,120
Cao Bang	480	540	595
Cuu Long	1,504	1,686	1,850
Dac Lac	490	611	735
Dong Nai	1,305	1,502	1,690
Dong Thap	1,183	1,314	1,430
Gia Lai-Kon Tum	596	692	785
Ha Bac	1,663	1,892	2,110
Ha Nam Ninh	2,781	3,061	3,315
Ha Son Binh	1,537	1,705	1,850
Ha Tuyen	782	881	975
Hai Hung	2,145	2,396	2,625
Hau Giang	2,233	2,495	2,735
Hoang Lien Son	778	866	950
Kien Giang	995	1,123	1,245
Lai Chau	322	378	432
Lam Dong	397	487	580
Lang Son	485	534	580
Long An	957	1,081	1,195
Minh Hai	1,220	1,550	1,900
Nghe Tinh	3,112	3,398	3,655
Nghia Binh	2,095	2,355	2,600
Phu Khanh	1,189	1,332	1,465
Quang Nam-Da Nang	1,530	1,678	1,810
Quang Ninh	750	812	870
Son La	488	562	635
Song Be	659	734	805
Tay Ninh	684	758	830
Thai Binh	1,506	1,653	1,790
Thanh Hoa	2,532	2,780	3,010
Thuan Hai	938	1,085	1,220
Tien Giang	1,265	1,388	1,505
Vinh Phu	1,488	1,656	1,805
Special Zone			
Vung Tau-Con Dao	92	94	98
TOTAL	52,742	58,770	64,385

Table 3. Ethnic Composition, 1979

Ethnic group	Alternate names	Principal areas of residence (provinces)	Population [1]
Viet	Kinh	Throughout the nation	46,065,400
Hoa (Han, Chinese)	Trieu Chau, Phuc Kien, Quang Dong, Hai Nam, Ha, Xa Phang	Ho Chi Minh City, Hanoi, Hau Giang, Dong Nai, Minh Hai, Kien Giang, Haiphong, Cuu Long	935,100
Tay	Tho, Ngan, Phen, Thu, Lao, Pa Zi	Cao Bang, Lang Son, Ha Tuyen, Bac Thai, Hoang Lien Son, Quang Ninh, Ha Bac, Lam Dong	901,800
Thai	Tai, Tai Khao (White Thai), Tay Dam (Black Thai), Tai Moui, Tai Thanh (Man Thanh), Hang Tong (Tai Muong), Pu Thay, Tho Da Bac	Son La, Nghe Tinh, Thanh Hoa, Lai Chau, Hoang Lien Son, Ha Son Binh, Lam Dong	766,700
Khmer	Cur, Cul, Cu, Tho, Khmer-Vietnamese, Khmer Krom	Hau Giang, Cuu Long, Kien Giang, Minh Hai, Ho Chi Minh City, Song Be, Tay Ninh	717,300
Muong	Mol, Mual, Moi, Moi Bi, Ao Ta (Au Ta)	Ha Son Binh, Thanh Hoa, Vinh Phu, Hoang Lien Son, Son La, Ha Nam Ninh	686,100
Nung	Xuong, Giang, Nung An, Phan Sinh, Nung Chao, Loi, Quy Rin, Khen Lai	Cao Bang, Lang Son, Bac Thai, Ha Tuyen, Ha Bac, Hoang Lien Son, Quang Ninh, Ho Chi Minh City, Lam Dong	559,700

313

Table 3.—*Continued.*

Ethnic group	Alternate names	Principal areas of residence (provinces)	Population [1]
Hmong (Meo)	Meo Hoa, Meo Xanh, Meo Do, Meo Den, Na Mieo, Man Trang	Ha Tuyen, Hoang Lien Son, Lai Chau, Son La, Cao Bang, Lang Son, Nghe Tinh	411,100
Zao	Man, Dong, Trai, Xa, Ziu Mien, Kiem Mien, Quan Trang, Zao Do, Quan Chet, Lo Gang, Zao Tien, Thanh Thah Y, Lan Ten, Dai Ban, Tieu Ban, Coc Ngang, Coc Mun, Son Dau	Ha Tuyen, Hoang Lien Son, Cao Bang, Lang Son, Bac Thai, Lai Chau, Son La, Ha Son Binh, Vinh Phu, Ha Bac, Thanh Hoa, Quang Ninh	346,800
Jarai	Giorai, Chorai, Tobuan, Hobau, Hdrung, Chor	Gia Lai-Kon Tum	184,500
Ede	Rhade, De, Kpa, Adham, Krung, Ktul, Dlie Rue, Blo, Epan, Mdhur, Bih	Dac Lac, Phu Khanh	140,900
Bahnar	Golar, Tolo, Gho long (Y-lang) Rengao, Ro Ngao, Kren, Roh, Kon Kde, A-la Kong, Kpang Kong, Bo Man	Gia Lai-Kon Tum, Nghia Binh, Phu Khanh	109,100
San Chay (Cao Lan-San Chi)	Cao Lan, Man Cao Lan, Hon Ban, San Chi (also called Son Tu but excludes the San Chi of Bao Lac and Cho Ra)	Bac Thai, Quang Ninh, Ha Bac, Cao Bang, Lang Son, Ha Tuyen	77,100
Cham	Chiem Thanh, Hroi	Thuan Hai, An Giang, Ho Chi Minh City, Nghia Binh, Phu Khanh	77,000

Table 3.—Continued.

Ethnic group	Alternate names	Principal areas of residence (provinces)	Population [1]
Sadang	Xo Teng, Hdang, To Trah, Mo Nam, Ha Lang, Ka Dong, Km Rang, Con Lan, Bri La, Tang	Gia Lai-Kon Tum, Quang Nam-Da Nang	73,100
Kohor	Xre, Nop (Tu-lop), Codon Chil, Lat (Lach), Trinh	Lam Dong, Thuan Hai	70,500
Hre	Cham Re, Chom, Kre, Luy	Nghia Binh	66,900
San Ziu	San Zeo, Trai, Trai Dat, Man Quan Coc	Bac Thai, Vinh Phu, Ha Bac, Quang Ninh, Ha Tuyen	65,800
Raglai	Ra Clay, Rai, Noang, La Oang	Thuan Hai, Phu Khanh	58,000
Mnong	Phong, Nong, Pre, Bu Zang, Di Pri, Biat, Gar, Ro-lam, Chil	Dac Lac, Lam Dong, Song Be	46,000
Stieng	Xa dieng	Song Be, Tay Ninh	40,800
Bo Ru Van Kieu	Bru, Van Kieu, Mang Cong, Tri, Khua	Binh Tri Thien	33,100
Kho Mu	Khmu, Xe Cau, Mun Xen, Pu Thenh, Tenh, Tay Hay	Nghe Tinh, Son La, Lai Chau, Hoang Lien Son	32,100
Giay	Nhang, Dang, Pau Thin Pu, Na, Cui Chu, Xa	Hoang Lien Son, Ha Tuyen, Lai Chau	27,900
Ko Tu	Ka tu, Cao, Ha, Phuong, Ka Tang	Quang Nam-Da Nang, Binh Tri Thien	27,000

Table 3. —Continued.

Ethnic group	Alternate names	Principal areas of residence (provinces)	Population [1]
Tho	Keo, Mon, Cuoi, Ho, Dan Lai, Ly Ha, Tay Pong, Con Kha, Xa La Vang	Nghe Tinh, Thanh Hoa	24,900
Ta Oi	Toi Oi, Pa Co, Pa Hi (Ba Hi)	Binh Tri Thien	20,500
Ma	Chau Ma, Ma Ngan, Maxop Ma To, Ma Krung	Lam Dong, Dong Nai	20,300
Jehtrieng	Jeh, Gie, Dgieh, Tareh, Giang Ray, Pin, Trieng, Treng, Ta Rieng, Ve (Veh), La Ve, Ka Tang	Quang Nam-Da Nang, Gia Lai-Kon Tum	16,800
Co	Cor, Col, Cau, Trau	Nghia Binh, Quang Nam-Da Nang	16,800
Ha Nhi	U Ni, Xa U Ni	Lai Chau, Hoang Lien Son	9,400
Cho Ru	Chru, Che-ru, Chu	Lam Dong, Thuan Hai	7,700
Cho Ro	Zo Ro, Chau Ro	Dong Nai	7,100
Xing Mun	Puoc, Pua	Son La, Lai Chau	7,000
Phu La	Bo Kho Pa, Mu Zi Pa, Xa Pho, Pho, Va Xo Lao, Pu Zang	Hoang Lien Son, Lai Chau	6,900
Lao	Lao Boc, Lao Noi	Lai Chau, Son La, Thanh Hoa, Hoang Lien Son	6,800

Table 3.—Continued.

Ethnic group	Alternate names	Principal areas of residence (provinces)	Population [1]
La Chi	Cui Te, La Qua	Ha Tuyen	5,900
La Hu	Khu Xung, Co Xung, Kha Qay	Lai Chau	4,300
La Ha	Xa Khao, Khla Phlao	Lai Chau, Son La	3,200
Lu	Nhuon (Zuon)	Lai Chau	3,000
Chut	Sach, May, Ruc, Ma Lieng, A Rem, Tu Yang, Pa Leng, Xo Lang, To Hung, Cha Cu, Tac Cui, U Mo, Xa La Vang	Binh Tri Thien	3,000
Lo Lo	Mun Zi	Cao Bang, Lang Son, Ha Tuyen	2,700
Mang	Mang U, Xa La Vang	Lai Chau	2,400
Khang	Xa Khao, Xa Sua, Xa Don, Xa Dang, Xa Hoc, Xa Ai, Xa Bung, Quang Lam	Lai Chau, Son La	2,300
Pathen	Pa Hung, Tong	Ha Tuyen	2,200
Ngai	Xin, Le, Dan, Khanh Gia	Quang Ninh, Cao Bang, Lang Son	1,300
Boy	Chung Cha, Trong Gia, Tu Zi, Tu Zin	Hoang Lien Son, Ha Tuyen	1,300
Co Lao	none	Ha Tuyen	1,200

Table 3.—Continued.

Ethnic group	Alternate names	Principal areas of residence (provinces)	Population [1]
Cong	Xan Khong, Mong Nhe, Xa Xeng	Lai Chau	800
Si La	Cu De Xu, Kha Pe	Lai Chau	400
Pu Peo	Ka Beo, Pen Ti, Lo Lo	Ha Tuyen	300
Brau	Brao	Gia Lai-Kon Tum	100
O Du	Tay Hat	Nghe Tinh	100
Romam	n.a.	Gia Lai-Kon Tum	100
Other (including foreign residents)			43,400
Total			52,742,000

[1] 1979 census figures rounded to the nearest 100.

Source: Based on information from *Vietnam Courier*, [Hanoi], June 1987, 28–31; and Committee for Social Sciences, Socialist Republic of Vietnam, *Vietnam Social Sciences*, [Hanoi], March and April 1986, 172–76.

Table 4. *Economic Growth Rate, 1976–90*
(in percentages)

Five-Year Plans	National Income		Agricultural Production		Industrial Production	
	Projected	Actual	Projected	Actual	Projected	Actual
Second Five-Year Plan (1976–80)	13–14	0.4	8–10	1.9	16–18	0.6
Third Five-Year Plan (1981–85)	4.5–5	6.4	6.0–7	4.9	4.0–5	9.5
Fourth Five-Year Plan (1986–90)*	8.0	4.3	6.2	1.4	9.0	5.6

*Projected figures through 1987; actual figures for 1986.

Source: Based on information from Tetsusaburo Kimura, *Vietnam: International Relations and Economic Development,* Tokyo, 1987, 164–65.

Table 5. *National Income by Sector, Selected Years, 1975–85*
(in percentages)

Sector	1975	1980	1982	1984	1985
Agriculture	46.8	50.1	57.2	42.4	44.6
Industry	24.0	19.9	25.3	32.8	32.4
Commerce	13.5	18.2	10.5	12.8	17.9
Construction	6.2	3.4	2.4	4.5	2.4
Transport and services	4.0	4.1	2.2	2.8	0.9
Other	5.5	4.3	2.4	4.7	1.8
TOTAL	100.0	100.0	100.0	100.0	100.0

Source: Based on information from *Statisticheskii ezhegodnik stranchlenov Soveta Ekonomicheskoi Vzaimopomoshchi* (Statistical Yearbook of Member Countries of the Council for Mutual Economic Assistance), Moscow, 1986, 42–43.

Table 6. *Agricultural and Industrial Production, 1975–84*
(in millions of dong)*

Year	Agriculture	Industry
1975	6,429.5	7,288.4
1976	7,087.8	8,208.9
1977	6,740.2	9,028.9
1978	6,743.6	9,520.1
1979	7,204.1	9,089.9
1980	7,622.5	8,218.4
1981	7,867.1	9,463.0
1982	81,135.6	72,095.0
1983	84,116.3	82,999.8
1984	89,331.8	88,995.2

*1975–81 based on fixed 1970 prices; 1982–84 based on fixed 1982 prices.

Source: Based on information from Tong Cuc Thong Ke, *So Lieu Thong Ke, 1930–1984*
(Statistical Data, 1930–1984), Hanoi, March 1985, 40–82; *Thong Ke* (Statistics),
Hanoi, March 1985, 31–33; and Foreign Broadcast Information Service, *Southeast
Asia Report,* JPRS-SEA-85-100, June 1985, 96–97.

Table 7. *Rice Production, 1975–85*

Year	Production (million tons)	Area Cultivated (1,000 hectares)	Yield (100 kilograms/hectare)
1975	10.54	4,940	21.3
1976	11.87	5,314	22.3
1977	10.89	5,409	20.1
1978	10.04	5,442	18.5
1979	10.76	5,483	19.8
1980	11.68	5,544	21.1
1981	12.55	5,645	22.2
1982	14.17	5,709	24.8
1983	14.73	5,603	26.3
1984	15.61	5,671	27.5
1985*	16.50	5,750	28.7

*Estimated.

Source: Based on information from Tong Cuc Thong Ke, *So Lieu Thong Ke, 1930–84*
(Statistical Data, 1930–84), Hanoi, March 1985, 93.

Table 8. Electricity and Coal Production, Selected Years, 1975–85

	1975	1978	1980	1983	1984	1985
Electricity [1]	2428	3846	3680	4184	4853	5400
Coal [2]	5.20	6.00	5.30	6.20	4.90	6.00

[1] Millions of kilowatt hours.
[2] Millions of tons.

Source: Based on information from *Statisticheskii ezhegodnik stranchlenov Soveta Ekonomicheskoi Vzaimopomoshchi* (Statistical Yearbook of Member Countries of the Council for Mutual Economic Assistance), Moscow, 1986, 73, 74. Translation of Hanoi, Statistical General Department, Statistics Publishing House, *So Lieu Thong Ke, 1930-84,* 1985, in Foreign Broadcast Information Service, *Southeast Asia Report, Reference Aid, Vietnam, Statistical Data 1930-84,* JPRS-SEA-86-108, June 25, 1986, 44.

Table 9. Soviet Economic and Military Assistance to Vietnam, 1978–86
(in millions of United States dollars)

Year	Economic Assistance	Military Assistance	Total	Military Assistance as Percentage of Total
1978	700–1,000	600–800	1,300–1,800	46.1–44.4
1979	800–1,100	900–1,400	1,700–2,500	52.9–56.0
1980	2,900–3,200	800–900	3,700–4,100	21.6–22.0
1981	900	900–1,000	1,800–1,900	50.0–52.6
1982	1,200	1,000	2,200	45.4
1983	1,300	1,200	2,500	48.0
1984	1,400	1,300	2,700	48.1
1985	1,600	1,700	3,300	51.5
1986*	1,800	1,500	3,300	45.4

*Estimated.

Source: Based on information from Douglas Pike, *Vietnam and the Soviet Union,* Boulder, Colorado, 1987, 139.

Table 10. Foreign Trade, 1976–86
(in millions of United States dollars)

Year	Imports	Exports	Trade Balance
1976	825.9	215.0	– 610.9
1977	1,044.1	309.0	– 735.1
1978	1,465.8	406.7	– 1,059.1
1979	1,653.0	383.1	– 1,269.9
1980	1,576.7	398.6	– 1,178.1
1981	1,697.3	388.3	– 1,309.0
1982	1,599.6	479.7	– 1,119.9
1983	1,689.2	534.5	– 1,154.7
1984	1,802.5	570.5	– 1,232.0
1985	2,046.3	660.3	– 1,386.0
1986	2,506.9	739.5	– 1,767.4

Source: Based on information from International Monetary Fund, *Direction of Trade Statistics Yearbook*, Washington, 1987, 412–13.

Table 11. Trade with the Soviet Union, 1976–86
(in millions of United States dollars)

Year	Imports	Exports	Trade Balance	Total	Trade with Soviet Union as Percentage of Total Foreign Trade
1976	308.4	84.4	– 224.0	392.8	37.7
1977	372.0	176.1	– 195.9	548.1	40.5
1978	446.4	222.5	– 223.9	668.9	35.7
1979	680.3	225.0	– 455.3	905.3	44.5
1980	700.1	242.4	– 457.7	942.5	47.7
1981	1,006.4	232.2	– 774.2	1,238.6	59.4
1982	1,107.4	284.4	– 823.0	1,391.8	66.9
1983	1,213.9	315.3	– 898.6	1,529.2	68.8
1984	1,230.1	316.0	– 914.1	1,546.1	65.2
1985	1,410.9	339.3	– 1,071.6	1,750.2	64.7
1986	1,878.1	419.2	– 1,458.9	2,297.3	70.8

Table 12. Ministries, State Commissions, and Special
Agencies of the Council of Ministers, 1987

Ministries

Agriculture and Food Industry	Home Trade
Building	Information
Communications and Transportation	Interior
Culture	Justice
Education	Labor, War Invalids, and Social Welfare
Energy	Light Industry
Engineering and Metals	Marine Products
Finance	National Defense
Foreign Affairs	Public Health
Foreign Trade	Supply
Forestry	Water Conservancy
Higher and Vocational Education	

State Commissions

Capital Construction Commission	State Planning Commission
Commission for Economic Relations with Foreign Countries	State Price Commission
State Inspection Commission	State Prize Commission
State Law Commission	State Science and Technology Commission
State Nationalities Commission	State Bank of Vietnam

Special Agencies

Commissions

Vietnam News Agency	Social Science Commission
Government Organization Commission	

Departments

Chemicals General Department	Oil and Natural Gas General Department
Civil Aviation Department	Physical Education and Sports General Department
Food Administration Department	Political Tasks Department
Forestry Administration Department	Posts and Telecommunications Department
General Information Department	Railway General Department
General Rubber Department	Statistics General Department
Geography Department	Vocational Training General Department
Geology Department	
Land Management General Department	
Metereorology and Hydrology General Department	

Source: Based on information from United States Central Intelligence Agency Directorate of Intelligence, *Directory of Officials of Vietnam,* Washington, July 1985, 27–52.

Party Leaders in the 1980s

The Political Bureau elected during the Sixth National Party Congress in December 1986 consisted of thirteen full members and one alternate member. Five were new, one was appointed in June 1985, and the remainder were carried over from the previous Political Bureau, elected at the Fifth National Party Congress in 1982. The Political Bureau elected in 1982 numbered thirteen full and two alternate members. Between 1982 and 1986, one member died, three were voluntarily retired, three were removed, and one was promoted from alternate to full membership. Top party leadership during this period was therefore restricted to twenty-one individuals. The inner circle of party leadership, however, extended to a secondary, but nevertheless critical, tier of leadership represented by members of the Secretariat of the Central Committee who were not simultaneously members of the Political Bureau. In 1986 there were nine.

Political Bureau Members in December 1986
(Members listed in decreasing order of political importance.)

Nguyen Van Linh, elected Vietnamese Communist Party (VCP, Viet Nam Cong San Dang) general secretary in 1986, had been a rising political star since the end of the Second Indochina War. Born in the North in 1915, he had spent most of his political career in the South and much of that time underground in Saigon, where he worked closely with Le Duan in 1956. In 1960, because of his underground role in the South, he was elected secretly to the VCP's Central Committee. At war's end in 1975, Linh was appointed party secretary for Ho Chi Minh City (formerly Saigon) for a brief period, only to be replaced by Vo Van Kiet at the Fourth National Party Congress in 1976. In 1976 he was elected for the first time to the Political Bureau and ranked twelfth. He was dropped from the Political Bureau in 1982, however, apparently for his opposition to the rapid socialization of the South after the 1975 victory. He was renamed party secretary for Ho Chi Minh City in December 1981, where the success of his reformist economic policies gained the attention of the Political Bureau. Linh's reappointment in 1985, when he was ranked sixteenth, may have resulted from the intercession of then-party general secretary Le Duan and had the effect of strengthening the reform contingent of the VCP's leadership.

325

Following Le Duan's death in July 1986, he was returned to the Secretariat where he ranked immediately behind Duan's heir apparent, Truong Chinh. Before assuming the party's top position in December 1986, Linh advocated an end to discrimination against intellectuals who had served the former regime in South Vietnam and better treatment for Vietnam's Roman Catholics and the Chinese minority. He publicly thanked representatives of the Chinese community for their contribution to Vietnam.

Pham Hung, formerly ranked fourth in the Political Bureau, was promoted to the second-ranked position in December 1986. In June 1987, he was named to succeed Pham Van Dong as premier. Hung had been minister of interior from 1980 to 1986, and a vice premier since 1958. He began his career fighting the French in the South and directed the political campaign in the South during the Second Indochina War as head of the Central Office for South Vietnam (COSVN) and the Political Bureau's chief representative in South Vietnam from 1967 to 1975. His deputy during this period was Nguyen Van Linh. He was the first native South Vietnamese to attain senior party and government rank and was considered a hard-liner not because he was an ideologue but because he believed communist orthodoxy promoted better security. Although Hung was associated with the implementation of unpopular economic policies on money, prices, and wages, his career apparently suffered no lasting damage. He was born in 1912 and died on March 10, 1988, after having held the post of premier for only nine months.

Vo Chi Cong, who was ranked seventh in the 1982 Political Bureau and was promoted to third in 1986, was appointed to the largely ceremonial post of president in place of Truong Chinh in June 1987. His previous experience had been mainly in the field in Central Vietnam, and during the Second Indochina War he was a formal communist representative on the Hanoi-sponsored National Liberation Front central committee. From 1976 to 1980 Vo Chi Cong held the government posts of vice premier, minister of agriculture, and minister of fisheries, but reportedly he was fired from each post for administrative incompetence. A strong advocate of liberalization in agriculture, he was counted as being among Nguyen Van Linh's reform advocates on the Political Bureau and was an advocate for openness in the party. Cong was born in 1912.

Do Muoi, ranked eleventh on the Political Bureau in 1982 and fourth in 1986, directed the party's failed effort to socialize southern industry and commerce rapidly. Nevertheless, in 1986 he was identified with the reform program and subsequently was named to the Secretariat of the Central Committee as a resident economic expert. In 1984 he was called upon to explain the party's Sixth

Plenum resolution on reforming industrial management, and he has since spoken on behalf of agricultural reform. Following the death of Pham Hung in March 1988, he was named to replace Hung as premier. He was born in 1920 and established his career in Haiphong.

Vo Van Kiet, vice premier and chairman of the State Planning Commission in 1986, moved from the tenth to the fifth position on the Political Bureau. During the Second Indochina War, he worked with the Hanoi-controlled People's Revolutionary Party in the South; after the war, he became Ho Chi Minh City party secretary. In this capacity, Kiet initiated liberalized local trade and commerce policies that became the models for later national economic reforms. His rise in the party was comparatively rapid. Until the Fourth National Party Congress in 1976, when he appeared as an alternate member on the Political Bureau and as a member of the Central Committee, he had not been listed on any list of senior party officials. In company with Nguyen Van Linh, however, Kiet was initially elected to the Central Committee in 1960. Because of their sensitive positions in the South at the time, their Central Committee memberships were not revealed until after the war in 1976. He was an advocate of pragmatic economic reform, such as decentralized planning, loosened central controls, and socialization of the South without production disruption. The youngest Political Bureau member in 1986, he was born in 1922.

Le Duc Anh, formerly ranked twelfth on the Political Bureau and promoted to sixth in 1986, was appointed Minister of National Defense in early 1987. He was almost totally unknown until given full Political Bureau status in 1982. During the Second Indochina War, he worked closely with Vo Van Kiet and was deputy commander of the Ho Chi Minh City campaign; afterwards, he was appointed commanding general and political commissar of the military region bordering Cambodia. He commanded the Vietnamese task force that invaded Cambodia in 1978.

Nguyen Duc Tam, previously ranked thirteenth on the Political Bureau, was promoted in 1986 to seventh despite his position as head of the Organization Department of the Central Committee, which was the target of heavy criticism at the Sixth National Party Congress. His department was blamed for an unprecedented decline in the quality of party cadres. A protégé of Le Duc Tho, whom he replaced as head of the Organization Department, he built his career in his native Quang Ninh Province.

Nguyen Co Thach, promoted from alternate to full Political Bureau membership in 1986, was Vietnam's Minister of foreign affairs and ranked eighth on the Bureau. Immediately following the Sixth National Party Congress, he was promoted to vice premier (deputy chairman of the Council of Ministers). Thach had been a career diplomat serving in diplomatic posts until his election to the Political Bureau as an alternate member in 1982, marking the first time that an official from a diplomatic background had entered the top party leadership. A protégé of Le Duc Tho, Thach was apparently a political moderate, although his support of Vietnam's occupation of Cambodia demonstrated his alignment with official policy. Once a specialist on American affairs (he participated in the Paris negotiations to end the Second Indochina War with then-United States national security adviser Henry Kissinger), Thach became increasingly associated with Soviet and East European affairs and traveled to Moscow in 1978 with other top Vietnamese officials to sign the Treaty of Friendship and Cooperation. He was the first Political Bureau member after Ho Chi Minh to speak English, having learned it while serving in India in the late 1950s. According to one Western author, Thach's greatest value to the leadership may have been his ability to interpret the views of the English-speaking world. He was born in 1920.

Dong Sy Nguyen, promoted from alternate to full Political Bureau membership in 1986, was a cadre of surprising resilience. His election to the Political Bureau in 1982 was a surprise to most outsiders. Previously, Nguyen had been known as a middle-ranking communist and an unspectacular member of the Quartermasters and Engineers Corps of the armed forces. He was removed as minister of communications and transportation in June 1986 because of his alleged involvement with widespread corruption in that ministry.

Tran Xuan Bach, a relatively unknown official newly elevated to the Political Bureau in 1986, formerly headed the secret Vietnamese organization code-named "B-68," which supervised the administration of Cambodia. Bach was in Phnom Penh in 1979 as the personal secretary of Le Duc Tho, the Political Bureau member in charge of Cambodia at that time. In the early 1960s he led the Vietnam Fatherland Front, and from 1977 to 1982 he chaired the Central Committee cabinet. In 1982 he was elected a full member of the Central Committee and secretary of the Secretariat of the Central Committee. Following the Sixth National Party Congress in December 1986, he ranked third on the Secretariat and tenth on the Political Bureau.

Nguyen Thanh Binh, newly elected to the Political Bureau, was elected secretary of the Hanoi municipal party committee in 1986. Before that he had been a Central Committee secretary. A forceful advocate for the party's agricultural reforms and for the gradual rather than rapid socialization of southern agriculture, Binh was a strong critic of the party's failure to revise agricultural policies.

Doan Khue, a new member of the Political Bureau in 1986, was first elected to the Central Committee in 1976, but was virtually unknown except for his military background. He was former commander and political officer of Military Region V (central Vietnam) of the People's Army of Vietnam (PAVN), and in 1987 was appointed PAVN chief of staff.

Mai Chi Tho, the lowest ranking of the new full Political Bureau members, was appointed minister of interior in early 1987. He was a former Ho Chi Minh City deputy secretary and mayor and was believed to have overall responsibility for security in southern Vietnam. Having been a past subordinate of Nguyen Van Linh and Vo Van Kiet, Tho was a strong supporter of economic reform and increased openness in the party. He was born in 1916 and is a brother of Le Duc Tho.

Dao Duy Tung, named as an alternate member of the Political Bureau in 1986 and a full member in 1988, was criticized, nevertheless, in the political report of the Sixth National Party Congress for his leadership of the Propaganda and Training Department. During his tenure, the department was faulted for failing to meet the party's goals in carrying out propaganda and training work. First appointed deputy chief of the Propaganda and Training Department in 1974, he was promoted to chief in 1982. In 1976 he was elected an alternate member of the Central Committee, and he attained full membership in 1982. He was named editor-in-chief of *Tap Chi Cong San* (Communist Review) in 1977 and director of the Vietnam News Agency (VNA) in 1982. In 1986 he ranked fourth on the Secretariat of the Central Committee.

Political Bureau Members Voluntarily Retired in 1986

Truong Chinh retired at age 79 as the incumbent VCP general secretary, having held the position for some five months following the death of Le Duan. Previously Chinh had ranked second on the Political Bureau and was chairman of the Council of State and of the National Defense Council, as well as chief of state. He stepped down as president in June 1987 and was succeeded by Vo Chi Cong. A founding member of the Indochinese Communist Party (ICP), Chinh was viewed by party colleagues as a theoretician and as the leader of the party ideologues. He initially opposed economic and liberal agricultural reforms and was firm in seeking to maintain Vietnam's "special relationship" with Laos and Cambodia. He suffered a brief eclipse from 1956 to 1958 for his leading role in the failed agrarian reform program in the North, but he retained a strong following among party cadres. A firm believer in such Maoist theories as relying on poor and landless peasants to carry out revolution, he was the leader of a pro-Chinese element in the party hierarchy in the early 1970s. But after 1979 Chinh strongly condemned the Chinese, rejected the idea of emphasizing the role of the peasantry and ignoring the role of the working class, and supported Hanoi's alliance with Moscow as essential. As early as 1985 he publicly endorsed reform, but by 1986, nevertheless, he appeared out of step with the direction the party was beginning to take. He died September 30, 1988.

Pham Van Dong, the only one of the three retirees known to be ill when he stepped down, resigned from his number-two Political Bureau position, but retained his prime ministership until June 1987, when he was replaced by Pham Hung. Like Chinh, Dong was a founding member of the ICP, but he was a political moderate and probably the most popular of his generation of leaders. He was born in 1906.

Le Duc Tho was ranked fourth on the Political Bureau when he retired, but his rank belied his true power. Tho was a protégé of Le Duan and before Duan's death was arguably the most influential Political Bureau member and possibly the party chief's preferred successor. As an adviser to the Central Committee after his retirement, his influence probably remained considerable. Tho was also a founding member of the ICP; he apparently was at Pac Bo for the formation of the Viet Minh in 1940 and with Ho Chi Minh when the provisional government was established in Hanoi in August 1945. Like many of his generation of communists, he spent much of his early adulthood in prison. In 1950 Tho was sent south by the party, and in 1951 he helped establish the VCP's Central Office for South Vietnam (COSVN), where he assisted Le Duan. Later, he played the role of trouble-shooter for Duan, representing the party secretary in the South during the final offensive in 1975, on the Cambodian border when fighting erupted there in 1978, and on the Chinese border immediately before and after the Chinese invasion in 1979. Vietnam's occupation of Cambodia was apparently Tho's responsibility after 1978, and he headed Commission Sixty-Eight, the VCP special commission handling Cambodian affairs. In 1982 he emerged as a supporter of economic reform. His birth date is variously given as 1911 or 1912.

Political Bureau Members Removed in 1986

Van Tien Dung was one of the most prominent casualties of the Sixth National Party Congress in 1986. He was minister of national defense and ranked sixth on the Political Bureau before being dropped for his or his family's involvement in corruption scandals. He was, nevertheless, permitted to retain his seat on the Central Committee. PAVN had earlier given Dung a vote of no-confidence when it failed to elect him as one of the seventy-two delegates chosen for the Sixth Party Congress. Considered a government lame duck following the loss of his Political Bureau seat, he lost his defense post to his protégé, Le Duc Anh, shortly afterward. Dung had commanded the forces that won Hanoi's final victory over the Saigon government in 1975 and is credited with the "blooming lotus" technique of warfare, which was used to take Saigon and was used again in Cambodia four years later. The technique calls for troops first to assault the heart of a city in order to seize the enemy command center and then to proceed to occupy suburban areas at leisure. He was a formidable conservative, vocal in stressing the need for a strong defense, and an adamant supporter of the continued Vietnamese occupation of Cambodia. He was born in 1917.

To Huu, fired as vice chairman of the Council of Ministers in June 1986, was reported to be responsible for a currency change in September 1985 that led to disastrous inflation. He had ranked ninth on the Political Bureau before his removal and had held more truly significant party and government positions than virtually any other senior Political Bureau member. As a protégé of Truong Chinh, Huu was a leader among the ideologues and an opponent of economic reforms. He had been in charge of party propaganda when tapped to be vice premier and, in the early 1980s, was a leading candidate to succeed Premier Pham Van Dong. Huu was born in 1920.

Chu Huy Man ranked eighth when removed from the Political Bureau and the Central Committee. Prior to the Sixth National Party Congress, he had headed the army's political department and reportedly was severely criticized by PAVN for his autocratic leadership style. Like Van Tien Dung, he was not initially elected to represent PAVN at the Sixth Party Congress. Man was a protégé of former Minister of National Defense Vo Nguyen Giap and one of the most important battlefield commanders during the Second Indochina War, most notably in the Central Highlands. He was born in 1920.

Political Bureau Members Deceased in 1986

Le Duan, until his death in July 1986, was VCP general secretary; he had been elevated to the post following the 1969 death of Ho Chi Minh, who had groomed Duan as his successor beginning in the late 1950s. Under Duan's leadership, the war in the South was successfully concluded, the country was reunified,

Cambodia was invaded and occupied, relations with China were severed, and dependence upon the Soviet Union for economic and military aid increased dramatically. After initially supporting overly ambitious policies that worsened Vietnam's economic condition, he encouraged gradual political change coupled with moderate economic reforms. These included financial incentives for peasants and workers, some decentralization in planning, and a broadening of economic relations with the rest of the world. Le Duc Tho, Nguyen Van Linh, Pham Hung, and Vo Van Kiet were close colleagues. During his career, Duan was considered to be colorless, more an organizer than a diplomat. He never held a government position. In the spring of 1985, a year before his death, he was described in a series of articles in the party newspaper, *Nhan Dan (People's Daily)*, as the architect of the 1975 victory in the South and as the dominant figure in Vietnamese communist history next to Ho Chi Minh. He was born in 1908.

Central Committee Secretariat Members in 1986

Membership on the Secretariat of the Central Committee stood at thirteen in 1986. The four highest ranking members—Nguyen Van Linh, Nguyen Duc Tam, Tran Xuan Bach, and Dao Duy Tung—held concurrent positions on the Political Bureau and are described above. The remaining nine are listed below in order of decreasing political importance.

Tran Kien, also known as Nguyen Tuan Tai, was formerly secretary of party chapters in Haiphong, Gia Lai Kon Tum, Dac Lac Province, and Nghia Binh Province. He was first appointed secretary of the Secretariat of the Central Committee and chairman of the Central Control Commission in 1982 and reappointed in 1986. He was minister of forestry from 1979 to 1981.

Le Phuoc Tho was elected an alternate member of the Central Committee in 1976 and a full member in 1982. He was appointed a member of the Secretariat of the Central Committee in 1986. At the Fifth National Party Congress in 1982, he was selected to address the congress on the subject of agriculture, and in 1987, he was listed in Soviet sources as head of the party's agriculture department.

Nguyen Quyet, a lieutenant general in PAVN in 1986, was appointed to full membership on the Central Committee at the Fourth National Party Congress in 1976 and reappointed in 1982 and 1986. In December 1986, at the Sixth National Party Congress, he was appointed to the Secretariat of the Central Committee. Previously he had been commander of the Capital Military Region, Hanoi, and commander of Military Region III. In 1986 he was a member of the Central Military Party Committee and deputy head of the General Political Department. He replaced Chu Huy Man as director of the General Political Department in February 1987.

Dam Quang Trung, an ethnic Tay, was a major general and commander of Military Region I (the Sino-Vietnamese border region) at the time of the Chinese invasion in 1979. He was promoted to lieutenant general in 1981. In 1976 he was elected to the Central Committee, and in 1982, while still commander of Military Region I, became a member of the Central Military Party Committee. He was a member of the National Assembly from 1976 to 1981 and in 1981 was appointed to the Council of State.

Vu Oanh was elected an alternate to the Central Committee at the Fourth National Party Congress in 1976. He was elevated to full membership in 1982 and assumed the directorship of the VCP's Agriculture Department, a position he continued to hold until 1987. IIe was elected to the Secretariat at the Sixth National Party Congress in December 1986.

Nguyen Khanh, elected as an alternate to the Central Committee in 1982, gained full membership and a seat on the Secretariat in 1986. Appointed chief of the Central Committee cabinet (replacing Tran Xuan Bach) and director of the General Affairs and Administration departments of the Central Committee in 1982, he assumed similar duties in the government when appointed general secretary and a vice chairman of the Council of Ministers in February 1987.

Tran Quyet, when appointed to the Secretariat at the Sixth National Party Congress in December 1986, had been a full member of the Central Committee since 1976. As a vice minister of Public Security from the mid-1960s and vice minister of Interior from 1975, he specialized in security matters. A northerner, he was sent to Ho Chi Minh City in 1976 to establish the Ministry of Interior's Permanent Office for South Vietnam as a measure to more firmly impose North Vietnamese control. Between 1975 and 1980, he was commander and political officer of the Ministry of Interior's People's Public Security Force and held the rank of lieutenant general.

Tran Quoc Huong, also known as Tran Nach Ban and Muoi Huong, was elected to full membership on the Central Committee in 1982, under the name Tran Nach Ban. A southerner, he was formerly a standing member of the Ho Chi Minh City Party Committee and head of its Organization Department. In 1983, under the name Tran Quoc Huong, he was appointed deputy secretary of the Hanoi Party Committee, and in 1986 was named to the Secretariat of the Central Committee of the VCP. His government positions have included vice chairmanship of the State Inspection Commission, to which he was appointed in 1985, and chairmanship of the Vietnam Tourism General Department, which he assumed in 1986.

Pham The Duyet, previously a coal mine director in Quang Ninh Province and vice chairman and general secretary of the Vietnamese Confederation of Trade Unions, was elected a Central Committee alternate member at the Fifth National Party Congress in 1982. At the time of his election to full Central Committee membership at the Sixth National Party Congress in 1986 and his succeeding appointment to the Secretariat of the Central Committee, he was also acting chairman of the Confederation. In 1987 he was promoted to chairman.

Bibliography

Chapter 1

Bowman, John S. (ed.). *The Vietnam War: An Almanac*. New York: World Almanac Publications, 1985.

Burchett, Wilfred. *Catapult to Freedom*. London: Quartet Books, 1978.

Buttinger, Joseph. *Vietnam: A Dragon Embattled*. 2 vols. New York: Praeger, 1967.

_____. *Vietnam: A Political History*. New York: Praeger, 1968.

_____. *Vietnam: The Unforgettable Tragedy*. New York: Horizon Press, 1977.

Cady, John Frank. *The Roots of French Imperialism in Eastern Asia*. Ithaca, New York: Cornell University Press, 1954.

Duiker, William J. *The Communist Road to Power in Vietnam*. Boulder, Colorado: Westview Press, 1981.

_____. *The Rise of Nationalism in Vietnam, 1900–1941*. Ithaca, New York: Cornell University Press, 1976.

Fall, Bernard B. *The Two Viet-Nams: A Political and Military Analysis*. New York: Praeger, 1967.

Fall, Bernard B. (ed.). *Ho Chi Minh on Revolution: Selected Writings, 1920–66*. New York: Praeger, 1967.

Gruening, Ernest, and Herbert Wilton Beaser. *Vietnam Folly*. Washington: National Press, 1968.

Gurtov, Melvin. *The First Vietnam Crisis*. New York: Columbia University Press, 1967.

Halberstam, David. *The Making of a Quagmire*. New York: Random House, 1964.

Hall, David George Edward. *A History of South-East Asia*. New York: St. Martin's Press, 1968.

Hammer, Ellen J. *The Struggle for Indochina, 1940–1955*. Stanford, California: Stanford University Press, 1965.

Hejzlar, J. *The Art of Vietnam*. London: Hamlyn Publishing, 1973.

Hickey, Gerald Cannon. *Free in the Forest: Ethnohistory of the Vietnamese Central Highlands, 1954–1976*. New Haven: Yale University Press, 1982.

Hodgkin, Thomas Lionel. *Vietnam: The Revolutionary Path*. New York: St. Martin's Press, 1981.

Huynh Kim Khanh. *Vietnamese Communism, 1925–1945*. Ithaca, New York: Cornell University Press, 1982.

Kahin, George McTurnan. *Intervention*. New York: Knopf, 1986.

Karnow, Stanley. *Vietnam: A History*. New York: Viking Press, 1983.

Knoebl, Kuno. *Victor Charlie: The Face of War in Viet-Nam.* New York: Praeger, 1967.

Komer, Robert W. *Bureaucracy at War.* Boulder, Colorado: Westview Press, 1986.

Lacouture, Jean. *Ho Chi Minh: A Political Biography.* New York: Random House, 1968.

Lawson, Eugene K. *The Sino-Vietnamese Conflict.* New York: Praeger, 1984.

McAleavy, Henry. *Black Flags in Vietnam.* London: George Allen and Unwin, 1956.

McAlister, John T. *Viet-Nam: The Origins of Revolution.* New York: Alfred A. Knopf, 1969.

Marr, David G. *Vietnamese Anticolonialism, 1885–1925.* Berkeley: University of California Press, 1971.

Neher, Clark D. "The Bronze Drum Tradition," *Asian Studies Professional Review,* 14, Nos. 1 and 2, 1974–75, 186.

Pike, Douglas. *A History of Vietnamese Communism, 1925–1976.* Stanford, California: Hoover Institution Press, 1978.

_____. *Viet Cong: The Organization and Techniques of the National Liberation Front of South Vietnam.* Cambridge: M.I.T. Press, 1966.

_____. *War, Peace, and the Viet Cong.* Cambridge: M.I.T. Press, 1969.

Porter, Gareth (ed.). *Vietnam. A History in Documents.* New York: New American Library, 1981.

Shaplen, Robert. *The Lost Revolution.* New York: Harper and Row, 1955.

Sheehan, Neil. *A Bright Shining Lie.* New York: Random House, 1988.

Smith, Ralph B. *An International History of the Vietnam War.* 2 vols. New York: St. Martin's Press, 1985.

_____. *Viet-Nam and the West.* Ithaca, New York: Cornell University Press, 1968.

Spector, Ronald H. *Advice and Support: The Early Years, 1941–1960.* Washington: United States Army Center of Military History, 1983.

Taylor, Keith Weller. *The Birth of Vietnam.* Berkeley: University of California Press, 1983.

Thayer, Thomas C. *War Without Fronts: The American Experience in Vietnam.* Boulder, Colorado: Westview Press, 1985.

Turley, William S. *The Second Indochina War: A Short Political and Military History, 1954–75.* Boulder, Colorado: Westview Press, 1986.

United States. Congress. 98th, 2d Session. Senate. Committee on Foreign Relations. *The U.S. Government and the Vietnam War:*

Executive and Legislative Roles and Relationships. Washington: GPO, 1984.

Van Dyke, Jon M. *North Vietnam's Strategy for Survival*. Palo Alto, California: Pacific Books, 1972.

Whitfield, Danny J. *Historical and Cultural Dictionary of Vietnam*. Metuchen, New Jersey: Scarecrow Press, 1976.

Woodside, Alexander Barton. *Community and Revolution in Modern Vietnam*. Boston: Houghton Mifflin, 1976.

_____. *Vietnam and the Chinese Model*. Cambridge: Harvard University Press, 1971.

Chapter 2

American University. Cultural Information Analysis Center. *Minority Groups in the Republic of Vietnam*. (Ethnographic Study Series.) Washington: GPO, 1966.

Anh Phong. "Catholicism in Vietnam and Catholic Reintegration into the National Community," *Vietnam Courier* [Hanoi], No. 66, November 1977, 24–30.

Anh Thu. "Family Planning in Vietnam and Prospects," *Vietnam Courier* [Hanoi], No. 5, 1985, 26–27.

Chanda, Nayan. "The New Revolution: The South Leads the Way Away from Subsidized Socialism," *Far Eastern Economic Review* [Hong Kong], 132, No. 15, April 10, 1986, 24–28.

Che Viet Tan. "A Major Question of the Second Five-Year Plan (1976–1980): Population Growth, Labor Redeployment, and Population Relocation," *Vietnam Courier* [Hanoi], No. 58, March 1977, 9–11.

"Climatic Evolution in Vietnam," *Vietnam Courier* [Hanoi], No. 2, 1979, 25.

Communist Party of Vietnam. "General Resolution of the Fourth National Congress of the Communist Party of Vietnam," *Vietnam Courier* [Hanoi], No. 56, January 1977, 5–7.

Crawford, Ann Caddell. *Customs and Culture of Vietnam*. Rutland, Vermont: Charles E. Tuttle, 1966.

Crossette, Barbara. "Vietnam Punishing Party Corruption: Unusually Detailed Accounts in Press Tell of Crackdown," *New York Times*, March 27, 1987, A1.

"Cultural and Social Achievements in Five Years (1976–1980): From the Fourth to the Fifth Congress of the Communist Party of Vietnam," *Vietnam Courier* [Hanoi], No. 3, 1982, 5–6.

Dang Nghiem Van. "Sketch of the Ethnic Composition of Reunified Vietnam," *Vietnam Courier* [Hanoi], No. 58, March 1977, 28–29.

Dao Hung. "Ethnographical Notes: The Tay and the Nung," *Vietnam Courier* [Hanoi], No. 3, 1985, 29–31.

DeFrancis, John Frances. *Colonialism and Language Policy in Vietnam.* The Hague: Mouton, 1977.

Democratic Republic of Vietnam. *The Democratic Republic of Vietnam.* Hanoi: Foreign Languages Publishing House, 1975.

Desbarats, Jacqueline, and Karl D. Jackson. "Vietnam 1975–1982: The Cruel Peace," *Washington Quarterly,* 8, No. 4, Fall 1985, 169–82.

"The DRVN Advances: Transfer of Population to New Economic Areas," *Vietnam Courier* [Hanoi], No. 27, August 1974, 14–15.

Duc Uy, and Vu Van Thao. "New Features of Family Structure in Vietnam's Rural Areas," *Vietnam Courier* [Hanoi], No. 8, 1980, 12–13.

Duiker, William J. "The Legacy of History in Vietnam," *Current History,* 83, No. 497, December 1984, 409–12.

––––––. "Vietnam Moves Toward Pragmatism," *Current History,* 86, No. 519, April 1987, 148–51.

––––––. *Vietnam: Nation in Revolution.* Boulder, Colorado: Westview Press, 1983.

Elliott, David W. P., et al. *Vietnam: Essays on History, Culture, and Society.* New York: Asia Society, 1985.

The Europa Year Book, 1986: A World Survey. London: Europa Publications, 1986.

"The Fifth National Congress of the Communist Party of Vietnam: Socio-Economic Problems as seen by the Congress," *Vietnam Courier* [Hanoi], 2, No. 5, 1982, 6–10.

Fisher, Charles A. *South-East Asia: A Social, Economic, and Political Geography.* London: Methuen, 1964.

Foreign Broadcast Information Service—FBIS (Washington). The following articles are from the FBIS *Daily Report* series:

Asia and Pacific

"AFP Cites 'Observers' on Economic Difficulties." Agence France Presse (AFP) [Hong Kong], broadcast in English 0154 GMT, September 15, 1986. (FBIS–APA–86–178.) September 15, 1986, K6–K8.

"All the People Participate in Building the Draft Marriage and Family Law," *Nhan Dan* [Hanoi], July 30, 1986. (FBIS–APA–86–153.) August 8, 1986, K1–K2.

"Renovation and Progress," *Nhan Dan* [Hanoi], January 1, 1987. (FBIS–APA–87–009.) January 14, 1987, K2–K5.

"The Outcome of the Sixth CPV Congress, *Nhan Dan* [Hanoi], December 24, 1986. (FBIS–APA–87–005.) January 8, 1987, K1–K21.

Fraser, Stewart E. "The Four R's of Vietnamese Education: Revolution, Reunification, Reconciliation, and Redevelopment," *Phi Delta Kappan*, 58, June 1977, 730–34.

———. "Vietnam Struggles with Exploding Population," *Indochina Issues*, No. 57, May 1985, 1–7.

"From the Paris Agreement to Vietnam's Major Internal and External Problems," *Vietnam Courier* [Hanoi], No. 6, 1985, 7–15.

"General Education in the Socialist Republic of Vietnam: Interview with Education Minister Nguyen Thi Binh," *Vietnam Courier* [Hanoi], No. 10, 1984, 16–18.

"A Glimpse at Modern Medicine in Vietnam, 1945–1980," *Vietnam Courier* [Hanoi], 16, No. 9, 1980, 16–17.

Hawthorne, Lesleyanne. *Refugee: The Vietnamese Experience*. Melbourne: Oxford University Press, 1982.

Hickey, Gerald Cannon. *Free in the Forest: Ethnohistory of the Vietnamese Central Highlands, 1954–1976*. New Haven: Yale University Press, 1982.

———. *Sons of the Mountains: Ethnohistory of the Vietnamese Central Highlands to 1954*. New Haven: Yale University Press, 1982.

———. *Village in Vietnam*. New Haven: Yale University Press, 1964.

"Ho Chi Minh City: A Turning Point (An Interview with Dr. Nguyen Khac Vien)," *Vietnam Courier* [Hanoi], No. 4, 1981, 10–13.

"Ho Chi Minh City Ten Years after Liberation," *Vietnam Courier* [Hanoi], No. 6, 1985, 18–19.

Hoang Bao Chau. "Vietnamese Traditional Medicine," *Vietnam* [Hanoi], No. 309, September 1984, 19.

Hoang Mai. "Family Planning in Vietnam," *Vietnam Courier* [Hanoi], No. 7, 1981, 20–22.

Hoang Van Chi. *From Colonialism to Communism: A Case History of North Vietnam*. New York: Praeger, 1964.

Houtart, François, and Geneviève Lemercinier. *Hai Van: Life in a Vietnamese Commune*. London: Zed Books, 1984.

Hung, G. Nguyen Tien. *Economic Development of Socialist Vietnam, 1955–80*. (Praeger Special Studies in International Economics and Development.) New York: Praeger, 1977.

"Implementation of the 1984 State Plan and Socio-Economic Tasks for 1985," *Vietnam Courier* [Hanoi], No. 2, 1985, 6–8.

"An Important Question for the Advancement of Women in Vietnam," *Vietnam Courier* [Hanoi], No. 4, 1983, 18–19.

Jackson, Graeme. "An Assessment of Church Life in Vietnam," *Religion in Communist Lands*, 10, Spring 1982, 54–68.

Jenkins, David. "A Country Adrift," *Far Eastern Economic Review* [Hong Kong], 126, No. 45, November 8, 1984, 25–32.

Joint Publications Research Service. *Southeast Asia Report: Vietnam Fact Book.* (JPRS–SEA–85–121.) Washington, August 1985.

Kaylov, Robert. "Vietnam Firmly on Course but Losing the Peace," *U.S. News and World Report*, 100, No. 25, June 30, 1986, 30–31.

Khong, Dien. "Population Distribution in Urban and Rural Areas of Vietnam," *Vietnam Courier* [Hanoi], No. 10, 1983, 27.

Kunstadter, Peter (ed.). *Southeast Asian Tribes, Minorities, and Nations.* Princeton, New Jersey: Princeton University Press, 1967.

Le Dan. "Vietnam's Ethnic Minorities—Pawns in Beijing's Game?" *Vietnam Courier* [Hanoi], No. 3, 1982, 14–17.

Le Duan. "The New Woman in the Socialist Society," *Vietnam Courier* [Hanoi], No. 24, May 1974, 8–9.

_____. "The Present Tasks of the Vietnamese Youth," *Vietnam Courier* [Hanoi], No. 12, 1980, 3–6.

Le Hong Tam. "Vietnam's Revolution, Hard Work, Not Miracles," *Southeast Asia Chronicle*, No. 76, December 1980, 22–25.

Le Van Hao. "Hue, A Center of Culture and Tourism," *Vietnam Courier* [Hanoi], No. 2, 1981, 20–21.

Le Van Khue. "The Hoa People in Southeast Asia," *Vietnam Courier* [Hanoi], No. 5, 1981, 3–5.

Long, Robert Emmet (ed.). *Vietnam Ten Years After.* New York: H.W. Wilson, 1986.

Mai Quang. "A Glance at Some Major Ethnic Groups in Vietnam," *Vietnam Courier* [Hanoi], No. 59, April 1977, 25–29.

Mai Thi Tu. "Educational Problems: Professional Orientation for General School Students," *Vietnam Courier* [Hanoi], No. 2, 1982, 22–24.

_____. "Vietnamese Women in the 80's," *Vietnam Courier* [Hanoi], No. 10, 1981, 19–23.

McAlister, John T., Jr., and Paul Mus. *The Vietnamese and Their Revolution.* New York: Harper and Row, 1970.

McWilliams, Edmund. "Vietnam in 1982: Onward into the Quagmire," *Asian Survey*, 23, No. 1, January 1983, 62–72.

Marr, David G. *Vietnamese Tradition on Trial, 1920–1945.* Berkeley: University of California Press, 1981.

Mole, Robert L. *The Montagnards of South Vietnam: A Study of Nine Tribes.* Rutland, Vermont: Charles E. Tuttle, 1970.

"Nationalities in Vietnam and the Nationality Policy of the Communist Party of Vietnam," *Vietnam Courier* [Hanoi], No. 11, 1984, 30–31.

Netter, Thomas W. "Vietnam's Deforestation Brings New Alarm," *New York Times,* May 21, 1983, 63.

Nghiem Chuong Chau. "Thirty-five Years of Educational Development," *Vietnam Courier* [Hanoi], No. 10, 1980, 13–15.

Ngo Nhat Quang. "From One Region to Another: Haiphong City," *Vietnam Courier* [Hanoi], No. 5, 1985, 20–21.

Nguyen Cong Thang and Nguyen Thi Xiem. "Population Growth and Family Planning," *Vietnam Courier* [Hanoi], No. 10, 1983, 22–24.

Nguyen Duy Hinh and Tran Dinh Tho. *The South Vietnamese Society.* Washington: United States Army Center of Military History, 1981.

Nguyen Huu Chung. "Catholicism and the Revolution," *Vietnam Courier* [Hanoi], No. 8, 1980, 14–16.

Nguyen Huu Thuy. *Chinese Aggression: Why and How It Failed.* Hanoi: Foreign Languages Publishing House, 1979.

Nguyen Khac Kham. *An Introduction to Vietnamese Culture.* (East Asian Cultural Studies Series, No. 10.) Tokyo: The Center for East Asian Cultural Studies, 1967.

Nguyen Khac Thuat. "Health for All by the Year 2000: Caring for Patients at Their Homes," *Vietnam Courier* [Hanoi], No. 12, 1983, 22–25.

Nguyen Khac Vien. "Meo Country," *Vietnam Courier* [Hanoi], No. 66, November 1977, 14–16.

_____. *Tradition and Revolutions in Vietnam.* Berkeley, California: Indochina Resource Center, 1974.

_____. "Writing About Vietnam," *Vietnam Courier* [Hanoi], No. 57, August 1976, 8–9, 28–29.

Nguyen Khac Vien (ed.). *Données Ethnographiques.* (Etudes Vietnamiennes, No. 36), Hanoi: Xunhasaba, 1973.

Nguyen Long. *After Saigon Fell: Daily Life under the Vietnamese Communists.* Berkeley: Institute of East Asian Studies, University of California, 1981.

Nguyen Thi My Huong, Patricia (ed.). *Language in Vietnamese Society: Some Articles by Nguyen Dinh Hoa.* Carbondale, Illinois: Asia Books, 1980.

Nguyen Thi Xiem. "Family Planning in Vietnam: Fifteen Years' Birth Control by Contraception," *Vietnam Courier* [Hanoi], No. 71, April 1978, 19–20.

Nguyen Van Canh (with Earle Cooper). *Vietnam Under Communism, 1975–1982.* Stanford, California: Hoover Institution Press, 1983.

Nguyen Van Chien. "Compiling the National Atlas," *Vietnam Courier* [Hanoi], No. 12, 1983, 19–21.

Nguyen Van Huong. "Women's Rights in the Democratic Republic of Vietnam," *Vietnam Courier* [Hanoi], No. 35, April 1975, 8-12.

Nong Quoc Chan. "Cultural Work among Ethnic Minorities in Southern Vietnam: Problems and Tasks," *Vietnam Courier* [Hanoi], No. 53, October 1976, 23-24.

Ognetov, S. Divilkovsky I. *The Road to Victory: The Struggle for National Independence, Unity, Peace and Socialism in Vietnam.* Moscow: Progress Publishers, 1980.

Oliver, Victor L. *Cao Dai Spiritism: A Study of Religion in Vietnamese Society.* Leiden: E.J. Brill, 1976.

Pfeiffer, Egbert W. "The Conservation of Nature in Vietnam," *Environmental Conservation* [Geneva], 11, No. 3, Autumn 1984, 217-21.

Phan Quang. "The MeKong Delta," *Vietnam Courier* [Hanoi], No. 8, 1983, 23-26.

_____. "The MeKong River Delta: The MeKong River in Nam Bo," *Vietnam Courier* [Hanoi], No. 7, 1983, 14-17.

Pham Van Dong. "Two Objectives: Building the Material and Technical Foundations of Socialism and Improving the Living Conditions of the Working People Step by Step," *Vietnam Courier* [Hanoi], No. 53, October 1976, 2-4.

Pham Van Hoan. "On Educational Reform: The New Educational System," *Vietnam Courier* [Hanoi], No. 11, 1979, 10.

Pike, Douglas (ed.). *Indochina Chronology,* 5, No. 3, July-September 1986, 3-28.

Provencher, Ronald. *Mainland Southeast Asia: An Anthropological Perspective.* Pacific Palisades, California: Goodyear, 1975.

Quinn-Judge, Paul. "Hanoi's Bitter Victory," *Far Eastern Economic Review* [Hong Kong], 128, No. 17, May 2, 1985, 30-34.

_____. "Vietnam: Acceptable Face of Capitalism," *Far Eastern Economic Review* [Hong Kong], 130, No. 44, November 7, 1985, 32-33.

Quinn-Judge, Sophie. "Tailoring Education to Meet Vietnam's Needs," *Indochina Issues,* No. 61, October 1985, 1-7.

Rambo, A. Terry. *A Comparison of Peasant Social Systems of Northern and Southern Vietnam: A Study of Ecological Adaptation, Social Succession, and Cultural Evolution.* (Monograph Series III.) Carbondale, Illinois: Center for Vietnamese Studies, Southern Illinois University at Carbondale, 1973.

Ramsay, Ansil. "Thailand: Surviving the 1980s," *Current History,* 86, No. 519, April 1987, 164-167.

"Recent Ethnological Works in North Vietnam," *Vietnam Courier* [Hanoi], No. 18, November 1973, 22.

"Resolution of the Political Bureau of the Communist Party of Vietnam on Educational Reform," *Vietnam Courier* [Hanoi], No. 10, 1979, 6–7.

Richards, Paul W. "The Forests of South Vietnam in 1971–72: A Personal Account," *Environmental Conservation* [Geneva], 11, No. 2, Summer 1984, 147–53.

Rosner, Sara. "Vietnam's Revolution, Hard Work, Not Miracles: Those Who Have Stayed," *Southeast Asia Chronicle,* 76, December 1980, 26–28.

"Rural Medicine and Preventive Medicine in the DRVN," *Vietnam Courier* [Hanoi], No. 5, October 1972, 24–25.

Sagan, Ginetta, and Stephen Denney. *Violations of Human Rights in the Socialist Republic of Vietnam, April 30, 1975–April 30, 1983.* Atherton, California: Aurora Foundation, 1983.

Schonberg, Andre. *Social Structure and Political Order: Traditional and Modern Vietnam.* Jerusalem: The Hebrew University, Magnes Press, 1979.

Schrock, Joann L., et al. *Minority Groups in North Vietnam.* (DA Pamphlet 50–110 Ethnographic Study Series.) Washington: GPO, 1972.

Socialist Republic of Vietnam. *Vietnam Social Sciences* [Hanoi], March and April 1986, 172–76.

"Some Data on Economic and Cultural Achievements in the DRVN, 1945–1975," *Vietnam Courier* [Hanoi], No. 40, September 1975, 16–17.

"Some Data on Marriages in a Highland Area of Vietnam," *Vietnam Courier* [Hanoi], No. 3, 1980, 8–9.

"South Vietnam '76," *Vietnam Courier* [Hanoi], No. 48, May 1976, 3–7.

Spinks, Charles N., John C. Durr, and Stephen Peters. *The North Vietnamese Regime: Institutions and Problems.* Washington: Center for Research in Social Systems, The American University, April 1969.

Stern, Lewis M. "The Overseas Chinese in the Socialist Republic of Vietnam, 1979–82," *Asian Survey,* 25, No. 5, May 1985, 521–36.

Sully, Francois (ed.). *We the Vietnamese: Voices from Vietnam.* New York: Praeger, 1971.

Ta Xuan Linh. "Armed Uprisings by Ethnic Minorities along the Truong Son," *Vietnam Courier* [Hanoi], No. 28, September 1974, 15–20.

Thanh Tung. "A Pharmaceutical Factory," *Vietnam Courier* [Hanoi], No. 12, 1983, 26–27.

Thuy, Vuong G. *Getting to Know the Vietnamese and Their Culture.* New York: Frederick Ungar Publishing, 1976.

To Lan. "The Dinh and the Traditional Vietnamese Village," *Vietnam Courier* [Hanoi], No. 17, June 1981, 28-29.

Tran Dang Van. "Re-deployment of the Labor Force in Vietnam," *Vietnam Courier* [Hanoi], No. 69, February 1978, 10-12.

Tran Van Ha. "Food and Population by the Year 2000," *Vietnam Courier* [Hanoi], No. 11, 1983, 25-26.

Truong Chinh. "Strengthening the Proletarian Dictatorship State in Order to Build Socialism Successfully," *Vietnam Courier* [Hanoi], No. 58, March 1977, 4-8.

"Twenty Years of the Law on Marriage and the Family (1960-1980): The Application of the Law on Marriage and the Family in Vietnam over the Past Twenty Years," *Vietnam Courier* [Hanoi], No. 3, 1980, 8-9.

Ululff, Erich. "Vietnam's Revolution, Hard Work, Not Miracles: Must We Make All the Old Mistakes Again?" *Southeast Asia Chronicle,* No. 76, December 1980, 19-21.

Whitfield, Danny, J. *Historical and Cultural Dictionary of Vietnam.* Metuchen, New Jersey: Scarecrow Press, 1976.

Woodside, Alexander Barton, "The Triumphs and Failures of Mass Education in Vietnam," *Pacific Affairs* [Vancouver], 56, No. 3, Fall 1983, 401-27.

Chapter 3

Bekaert, Jacques. "Eye on Indochina: Scant Progress Achieved in Ho Chi Minh City," *Bangkok Post,* October 17, 1986, 6.

_____. "Eye on Indochina: Vietnam 'Serious' about Revitalizing Economy," *Bangkok Post,* November 28, 1986, 4.

Bogatova, Y., and M. Trigubenko. "The Sixth CPV Congress on the Strategy of Vietnam's Socio-Economic Development," *Far Eastern Affairs* [Moscow], March 1987, 1-13.

"Bottom of Marx's League: Mr. Gorbachev Can't Go On Ignoring Vietnam's Self-Ruination," *The Economist,* No. 301, 7470, November 1, 1986, 15.

Chanda, Nayan. "The New Revolution: The South Leads the Country away from Subsidized Socialism," *Far Eastern Economic Review* [Hong Kong], 132, No. 15, April 10, 1986, 24-28.

Conboy, Kenneth. "Hanoi's Newest Friend, Tokyo," *Executive Memorandum, Heritage Foundation,* 160, May 6, 1987.

Dejevsky, Mary. "Vietnam Radical Reform Encourages Profits in Return of Free Enterprise," *Times* [London], April 18, 1987, 6.

Duiker, William J. "Vietnam in 1985: Searching for Solutions," *Asian Survey,* 26, No. 1, January, 1986, 102–11.

_____. "Vietnam Moves Toward Pragmatism," *Current History,* 86, No. 519, April 1987, 148–51.

Esterline, John H. "Vietnam in 1986: An Uncertain Tiger," *Asian Survey,* 27, No. 1, January 1987, 92–103.

"First in, First Served in Vietnam," *Asiaweek* [Hong Kong], 12, No. 48, November 30, 1986, 54–55.

Foreign Broadcast Information Service—FBIS (Washington). The following articles are from the FBIS *Daily Report* series:
Asia and Pacific

Dawson, Alan. "Eye on Indochina: Vietnam's Money Troubles Pile Up," *Bangkok Post* [Bangkok], August 4, 1982. (FBIS–APA–82–150.) August 4, 1982, J1–J2.

"Further Reportage on National Assembly Session: Vo Van Kiet Report, Installment 1," Hanoi Domestic Service, 1100 GMT, December 26, 1986. (FBIS–APA–250.) December 30, 1986, K5–K12.

East Asia

Bertinetto, Gabriel. "Interview with Communist Party of Vietnam General Secretary Nguyen Van Linh," *L'Unita* [Milan], June 21, 1987, 13. (FBIS–EAS–87–122.) June 25, 1987, N2–N8.

Campion, Gilles. "AFP Gives Details of New Investment Code," Agence France Presse (AFP) [Hong Kong] broadcast in English 0515 GMT, June 25, 1987. (FBIS–EAS–87–123.) June 26, 1987, N5–N6.

"Details of 1986–90 Export Development Plan," Vietnam News Agency (VNA) [Hanoi] broadcast in English 1456 GMT, November 10, 1987. (FBIS–EAS–87–219.) November 13, 1987, 48–49.

"Foreign Currency Transactions," Hanoi International Service [Hanoi], broadcast in English, 1000 GMT, June 29, 1987. (FBIS–EAS–87–127.) July 2, 1987, N9.

"Fruit, Vegetable Exports to USSR Increase," Hanoi Domestic Service [Hanoi], broadcast in Vietnamese 1000 GMT, September 10, 1987. (FBIS–EAS–87–180.) September 17, 1987, 40.

"Further on Eighth National Assembly Session," Hanoi Domestic Service [Hanoi], broadcast in Vietnamese 1430 GMT, June 22, 1987. (FBIS–EAS–87–120.) June 23, 1987, N2–N12.

Vo Chi Cong, "Some Basic Issues Concerning the Renovation of the Economic Management Mechanism in Our Country," *Nhan Dan* [Hanoi], September 18, 1987. (FBIS–EAS–87–190.) October 1, 1987, 31–42.

Foreign Broadcast Information Service—FBIS. *Analysis Report-Vietnam: Party Plenum Boosts Economic Reform Agenda.* (FBIS-87-10011.) Washington, May 22, 1987.

"Hanoi's Saigon Solution," *Asiaweek* [Hong Kong], 14, No. 6, February 5, 1988, 42–43.

International Monetary Fund. *Annual Report on Exchange Arrangements and Exchange Restrictions, 1987.* Washington: 1987.

_____. *Direction of Trade Statistics Yearbook, 1981.* Washington: 1987.

Jenkins, David. "A Country Adrift," *Far Eastern Economic Review* [Hong Kong], 126, No. 45, November 8, 1984, 25–27.

Joint Publications Research Service—JPRS (Washington). The following articles are from the JPRS series:

Southeast Asia Report

"Agricultural Production Statistics Reported as of 5 February," Hanoi Domestic Service [Hanoi], broadcast in Vietnamese 1100 GMT, February 10, 1987. (JPRS-SEA-87-034.) March 11, 1987, 114–16.

Dang Van Tiep. "About Export Policy," *Nhan Dan* [Hanoi], January 13, 1987. (JPRS-SEA-87-048.) April 6, 1986, 86–87.

"The Industrial Sectors in Recent Years: Production Capabilities Have Increased; Results, Productivity, and Product Quality Have Declined," *Nhan Dan* [Hanoi], December 8, 1986. (JPRS-SEA-87-037.) March 16, 1987, 110–12.

So Lieu Thong Ke, 1930–1984 (Vietnam Statistical Data, 1930–1984) [Hanoi], 1985. (JPRS-SEA-86-108.) June 25, 1986.

Tong Cuc Thong Ke. *Thong Ke* (Statistics) [Hanoi], No. 3, March 1985, 31–33. (JPRS-SEA-85-100.) June 1985, 96–97.

Kimura, Tetsusaburo. *Vietnam: International Relations and Economic Development.* Tokyo: Tokyo Institute of Developing Economics, 1987.

_____. "Vietnam—Ten Years of Economic Struggle," *Asian Survey*, 26, No. 10, October 1986, 1039–55.

Kurian, George Thomas. *Encyclopedia of the Third World.* New York: Facts on File, 1986, 1987.

Luong Dan. "Hanoi in Early 1987: Facts and Reflections," *Vietnam Courier* [Hanoi], No. 4, April 1987, 16–18.

Marr, David G. "Central Vietnam Rebuilds: An Eyewitness Account," *Indochina Issues*, No. 59, July 1985.

Nivolon, Francois. "Interview/Tran Phnong: Rescheduling, Rethinking," *Far Eastern Economic Review* [Hong Kong], 130, No. 50, December 1985, 98–99.

"Oil for the Lamps of Vietnam," *Pacific Defense Reporter*, 14, No. 2, August 1987, 7.

Organization for Economic Cooperation and Development. *External Debt Statistics: The Debt and Other External Liabilities of Developing, CMEA, and Certain Other Countries and Territories.* Paris: 1987.

——. *Geographical Distribution of Financial Flows to Developing Countries, 1982–1985.* Paris: 1987.

——. *Geographical Distribution of Financial Flows to Developing Countries, 1986.* Paris: 1987.

Petrov, M. "Vietnam's Cooperation in the Comecon Framework," *Foreign Economic Affairs* [Moscow], 1, 1983, 168–79.

Pike, Douglas. *Vietnam and the Soviet Union: Anatomy of an Alliance.* Boulder, Colorado: Westview Press, 1987.

Quinn-Judge, Paul. "Acceptable Face of Capitalism: Changes to Economic System Bewilder Party Faithful," *Far Eastern Economic Review* [Hong Kong], 130, No. 44, November 7, 1985, 32–33.

——. "Hanoi's Bitter Victory," *Far Eastern Economic Review* [Hong Kong], 128, No. 17, May 2, 1985, 30–36.

——. "Policies Weather Criticisms: Major Economic Problems Still Dog Vietnam," *Far Eastern Economic Review* [Hong Kong], 130, No. 50, December 19, 1985, 98–99.

Richburg, Keith. "A Glimmer of Light in the East," *The Guardian* [Manchester], August 15, 1987, 6.

——. "In South of Vietnam, It's Business as Usual," *Washington Post,* July 14, 1987, A1.

Sherwell, Chris. "Hanoi Takes Steps to Come in from the Cold," *Financial Times* [London], April 12, 1985, 6.

Statisticheskii ezhegodnik stran-chlenov Soveta Ekonomicheskoi Vzaimopomoshchi (Statistical Yearbook of Member Countries of the Council for Mutual Economic Assistance). Moscow: Finansy i statistika, 1986.

Stern, Lewis M. "The Overseas Chinese in the Socialist Republic of Vietnam, 1979–82," *Asian Survey,* 25, No. 5, May 1985, 521–36.

——. "The Scramble Toward Revitalization: The Vietnamese Communist Party and the Economic Reform Program," *Asian Survey,* 27, No. 4, April 1987, 477–93.

——. "The Vietnamese Communist Party During 1984 and 1985: Economic Crisis Management, Organizational Reform and Planning for the Sixth National Party Congress," *Asian Profile,* 15, No. 3, June 1987, 267–79.

Thai Quang Trung. "The Moscow-Hanoi Axis and the Soviet Military Buildup in Southeast Asia," *Indochina Report,* 8, October 1986.

"Thousand of Citizens Sent to Uncertain East Block Future," *Insight*, 3, No. 30, July 27, 1987, 30–31.

Tong Cuc Thong Ke. *So Lieu Thong Ke, 1930–1984* (Statistical Data, 1930–1984) [Hanoi], March 1985, 40–82.

Trigubenko, M. "On the Participation of the Soviet Union's Far Eastern Areas in the USSR's Trade and Economic Cooperation with Vietnam," *Far Eastern Affairs* [Moscow], 4, 1983, 28–36.

United Nations. *Quarterly Bulletin for Asia and the Pacific.* New York: June 1984.

United States: Arms Control and Disarmament Agency. *World Military Expenditures and Arms Transfers.* Washington: GPO, 1986.

_____. Central Intelligence Agency. *Handbook of Economic Statistics.* Washington: September 1987.

USSR. Ministry of Foreign Trade. *Vneshniaia togovlia SSSR v 1986* (Foreign Trade of the USSR in 1986). Moscow: Finansy i Statistika, 1987.

"Vietnam Stresses Need for Reforming Its Economy," *Asian Wall Street Journal* [Hong Kong], April 20, 1987, 5.

Vo Nhan Tri. "Vietnam: The Third Five-Year Plan, 1981–1985." *Indochina Report*, 4, October–December 1985.

Wain, Barry. "Popular Outcry Brings Vietnam Reforms," *Asian Wall Street Journal* [Hong Kong], May 27, 1987, 1.

_____. "Vietnam Eases Foreign Investment Rules," *Asian Wall Street Journal* [Hong Kong], May 29–30, 1987, 1.

_____. "Vietnam Turns to Its Capitalists for Help," *Asian Wall Street Journal* [Hong Kong], May 28, 1987, 1.

World Bank. *World Development Report, 1987.* Oxford: Oxford University Press, 1987.

Chapter 4

An Tai Sung. "The All-Vietnam National Assembly: Significant Developments," *Asian Survey*, 17, No. 5, May 1977, 432–39.

Bekaert, Jacques. "Hanoi Willing to Talk to All," *Bangkok Post*, January 21, 1987, 1.

_____. "VN Continues to Ignore Voice of World Assembly," *Bangkok Post*, October 23, 1986, 4.

Bonavia, David. "The Climax of a Bad Dream," *Far Eastern Economic Review* [Hong Kong], 99, No. 2, January 13, 1978, 13.

Buszynski, Leszek. "Vietnam's Asian Diplomacy: The Assertion of a Fait Accompli," *World Today* [London], 42, No. 4, April 1986, 63–66.

Carney, Timothy. "Kampuchea in 1982: Political and Military Escalation," *Asian Survey,* 23, No. 1, January 1983, 73–83.

Chanda, Nayan. "Anatomy of the Conflict," *Far Eastern Economic Review,* [Hong Kong], 99, No. 2, January 13, 1978, 11–16.

——. *Brother Enemy: The War after the War.* New York: Harcourt Brace Jovanovich, 1986.

——. "Clash of Steel among the Comrades," *Far Eastern Economic Review* [Hong Kong], 99, No. 2, January 13, 1978, 10–11.

——. "Not Soft on Cambodia," *Far Eastern Economic Review* [Hong Kong], 135, No. 1, January 1, 1987, 11–13.

——. "Vietnam in 1983: Keeping Ideology Alive," *Asian Survey,* 24, No. 1, January 1984, 28–36.

Chang Pao-min. "The Sino-Vietnamese Conflict over Kampuchea," *Survey* [London], 27, Autumn–Winter 1983, 177–206.

"China, Vietnam 'Exploit Clashes'," *Bangkok Post,* October 28, 1986, 7.

"Congress Casualties," *Far Eastern Economic Review* [Hong Kong], 134, No. 52, December 25, 1986, 9.

Crossette, Barbara. "Many Top Leaders Shifted in Vietnam," *New York Times,* February 18, 1986, A7.

——. "Vietnam Punishing Party Corruption: Unusually Detailed Accounts in Press Tell of Crackdown," *New York Times,* March 27, 1987, A1.

Doan Van Toai and David Chanoff. "Learning from Vietnam: The Pattern of Liberation Movements," *Encounter* [London], 59, No. 3-4, September–October 1982, 19–26.

Draguhn, Werner. "The Indochina Conflict and the Positions of the Countries Involved," *Contemporary Southeast Asia* [Singapore], 9, No. 1, June 1983, 95–116.

Duiker, William J. *The Comintern and Vietnamese Communism.* Athens, Ohio: Center for Southeast Asia Studies, Ohio University Center for International Studies, 1975.

——. *The Communist Road to Power in Vietnam.* Boulder, Colorado: Westview Press, 1981.

——. "Ideology and Nation-building in the Democratic Republic of Vietnam," *Asian Survey,* 17, No. 5, May 1977, 413–31.

——. "The Legacy of History in Vietnam," *Current History,* 83, No. 497, December 1984, 409–12.

——. *The Rise of Nationalism in Vietnam, 1900–1941.* Ithaca, New York: Cornell University Press, 1976.

——. "Vietnam in 1984: Between Ideology and Pragmatism," *Asian Survey,* 25, No. 1, January 1985, 97–105.

——. "Vietnam in 1985: Searching for Solutions," *Asian Survey,* 26, No. 1, January 1986, 102–11.

349

————. *Vietnam: Nation in Revolution.* Boulder, Colorado: Westview Press, 1983.

————. *Vietnam since the Fall of Saigon.* Athens, Ohio: Center for Southeast Asian Studies, Ohio University Center for International Studies, 1985.

Elliott, David, W.P. (ed.). *The Third Indochina Conflict.* Boulder, Colorado: Westview Press, 1981.

————. "Vietnam in Asia: Strategy and Diplomacy in a New Context," *International Journal* [Toronto], 38, No. 2, Spring 1983, 287–315.

Esterline, John H. "Vietnam in 1986: An Uncertain Tiger," *Asian Survey,* 27, No. 1, January 1987, 92–103.

Gates, John M. "Vietnam: The Debate Goes On," *Parameters: Journal of the US Army War College,* 14, No. 1, Spring 1984, 15–25.

Hamilton-Smith, M.L.J. "The Development of Revolutionary Warfare Strategy, Vietnam 1946–64, Part I," *Army Quarterly and Defense Journal* [Tavistock, United Kingdom], 113, No. 3, July 1983, 329–39.

"Hanoi's Displeasure Stalls MIA Talks," *Muslim* [Islamabad], March 25, 1987, 4.

Hellmann, John. *American Myth and the Legacy of Vietnam.* New York: Columbia University Press, 1986.

Hiebert, Murray. "A New Gerontocracy," *Far Eastern Economic Review* [Hong Kong], 135, No. 1, January 1, 1987, 10–11.

————. "Vietnam Holds Elections for National Assembly," *Washington Post,* April 20, 1987, A19.

Hodgkin, Thomas. *Vietnam: The Revolutionary Path.* New York: St. Martin's Press, 1981.

Horn, Robert C. "Soviet-Vietnamese Relations and the Future of Southeast Asia," *Pacific Affairs* [Vancouver], 51, No. 4, Winter 1978–79, 585–605.

Kahin, George McTurnan. *Intervention: How America Became Involved in Vietnam.* New York: Alfred A. Knopf, 1986.

Kendall, Harry H. "Vietnamese Perceptions of the Soviet Presence," *Asian Survey,* 23, No. 9, September 1983, 1052–61.

Kiernan, Ben. "Vietnam's New Broom Targets Economic Errors," *Guardian* [Manchester], February 13, 1987, 10.

Kim Chin. "Recent Developments in the Constitutions of Asian Marxist-Socialist States," *Case Western Reserve Journal of International Law,* 13, No. 3, Summer 1981, 483–500.

Kulkarni, V.G. "Under the Counter Trade," *Far Eastern Economic Review* [Hong Kong], 124, No. 14, April 5, 1984, 54–56.

Lawson, Eugene K. *The Sino-Vietnamese Conflict.* New York: Praeger, 1984.

Leifer, Michael. "The Balance of Advantage in Indochina," *World Today* [London], 38, No. 6, June 1982, 232–38.

Leighton, Marian Kirsch. "Perspectives on the Vietnam-Cambodia Border Conflict," *Asian Survey*, 18, No. 5, May 1978, 448–57.

_____. "Vietnam and the Sino-Soviet Rivalry," *Asian Affairs* 6, No. 1, September–October 1978, 1–31.

Lewy, Guenter. "Some Political-Military Lessons of the Vietnam War," *Parameters: Journal of the US Army War College,* 14, No. 1, Spring 1984, 2–14.

Loescher, G.D. "The Sino-Vietnamese Conflict in Recent Historical Perspective," *Survey* [London], 24, Spring 1979, 129–41.

"Long-Term Program for Vietnamese-Soviet Economic Cooperation," *Vietnam Courier* [Hanoi], No. 12, December 1983, 4–7.

"The Longest War," *Asiaweek* [Hong Kong], 11, No. 18, May 3, 1985, 12–42.

McWilliams, Edmund. "Vietnam in 1982: Onward into the Quagmire," *Asian Survey,* 23, No. 1, January 1983, 62–72.

Marr, David G. *Vietnamese Tradition on Trial, 1920–1945.* Berkeley: University of California Press, 1981.

Moise, Edwin E. "Land Reform and Land Reform Errors in North Vietnam," *Pacific Affairs* [Vancouver], 49, No. 1, Spring 1976, 70–92.

Myers, Michael J. "How Vietnam Negotiates: A Personal Glimpse," *Asia Record,* 2, No. 9, December 1981, 26.

Nguyen Van Canh (with Earle Cooper). *Vietnam under Communism, 1975–1982.* Stanford, California: Hoover Institution Press, 1983.

Pike, Douglas. *PAVN: People's Army of Vietnam.* Novato, California: Presidio Press, 1986.

_____. "The USSR and Vietnam: Into the Swamp," *Asian Survey,* 19, No. 12, December 1979, 1159–70.

_____. *Vietnam and the Soviet Union: Anatomy of an Alliance.* Boulder, Colorado: Westview Press, 1987.

_____. "Vietnam During 1976: Economics in Command," *Asian Survey,* 17, No. 1, January 1977, 34–42.

Porter, Gareth. "Hanoi's Strategic Perspective and the Sino-Vietnamese Conflict," *Pacific Affairs* [Vanouver], 57, No. 1, Spring 1984, 7–25.

_____. "The Sino-Vietnamese Conflict in Southeast Asia," *Current History,* 75, No. 442, December 1978, 193–96.

_____. *Vietnam: The Definitive Documentation of Hunan Decisions.* Stanfordville, New York: Earl M. Coleman Enterprises, 1979.

Rees, David. *The New Vietnam: Hanoi's Revolutionary Strategy.* London: Institute for the Study of Conflict, 1977.

Rees, Jacqueline. "Partners on the Quiet," *Far Eastern Economic Review* [Hong Kong], 124, No. 14, April 5, 1984, 56–57.

Richburg, Keith B. "Cambodians Fight Poverty Through Free Enterprise," *Washington Post,* April 9, 1987, A1.

_____. "Vietnam Reshuffles Government; Changes Likely to Spur Reform," *Washington Post,* February 18, 1987, A12.

Rosenberger, Leif. "The Soviet-Vietnamese Alliance and Kampuchea," *Survey* [London], 27, Autumn–Winter 1983, 207–31.

Schonberg, Andre. *Social Structure and Political Order: Traditional and Modern Vietnam.* Jerusalem: The Hebrew University, Magnes Press, 1979.

Shaplen, Robert. "A Reporter at Large: Return to Vietnam," Pt. 1, *New Yorker,* April 22, 1985, 104–25.

_____. "A Reporter at Large: Return to Vietnam," Pt. 2, *New Yorker,* April 29, 1985, 92–108.

Simons, William B., and Stephen White (eds.). *The Party Statutes of the Communist World.* The Hague: Martinns Nijhoff, 1984.

Smith, Ralph B. "Vietnam's Fourth Party Congress," *World Today* [London], 33, No. 5, May 1977, 195–202.

Spector, Ronald H. *Advice and Support: The Early Years of the United States Army in Vietnam, 1941-1960,* New York: Collier Macmillan, 1985.

Stern, Lewis M. "The Overseas Chinese in the Socialist Republic of Vietnam, 1979–82," *Asian Survey,* 25, No. 5, May 1985, 521–36.

Szulc, Tad. "The War We Left Behind," *New York,* 11, No. 3, January 16, 1978, 30.

Thai Quang Trung. *Collective Leadership and Factionalism: An Essay on Ho Chi Minh's Legacy.* Singapore: Institute of Southeast Asian Studies, 1985.

_____. "The Fifth Congress of the Vietnamese Communist Party," *Contemporary Southeast Asia* [Singapore], 4, No. 2, September 1982, 236–45.

Thayer, Carlyle A. "Development Strategies in Vietnam: The Fourth National Congress of the Vietnam Communist Party," *Asian Profile,* 7, No. 3, June 1979, 275–86.

_____. "Vietnam: Beleaguered Outpost of Socialism," *Current History,* 79, No. 461, December 1980, 165–69.

_____. "Dilemmas of Development in Vietnam," *Current History,* 75, No. 442, December 1978, 221–25.

_____. "Vietnam's New Pragmatism," *Current History,* 82, No. 492, April 1983, 158–61.

Thayer, Carlyle A., and David G. Marr. *Vietnam since 1975—Two Views from Australia.* Nathan, Australia: Centre for the Study of Australian-Asian Relations, Griffith University, 1982.

Tong Cuc Thong Ke, *So Lieu Thong Ke, 1930–1984* (Statistical Data, 1930–1984) [Hanoi], 1985. Joint Publications Research Service, *Southeast Asia Report*. (JPRS–SEA–86–108.) June 25, 1986.

"Top Posts Shuffled in Hanoi," *Times* [London], February 18, 1987, 7.

Truong Nhu Tang (with David Chanoff and Doan Van Toai). *A Vietcong Memoir*. New York: Harcourt Brace Jovanovich, 1985.

Turley, William S. "Hanoi's Domestic Dilemmas," *Problems of Communism*, 29, No. 4, July–August 1980, 42–61.

————. *The Second Indochina War: A Short Political and Military History, 1954–1975*. Boulder, Colorado: Westview Press, 1986.

————. "Urban Transformation in South Vietnam," *Pacific Affairs*, 49, No. 4, Winter 1976–77, 607–24.

————. "Vietnam since Reunification," *Problems of Communism*, 26, No. 2, March–April 1977, 36–54.

Turley, William S. (ed.). *Vietnamese Communism in Comparative Perspective*. (Special Studies on South and Southeast Asia.) Boulder, Colorado: Westview Press, 1980.

Turner, Robert F. *Vietnamese Communism: Its Origins and Development*. Stanford, California: Hoover Institution Press, 1975.

United States. Central Intelligence Agency. Directorate of Intelligence. *Directory of Officials of Vietnam*. (CR85–12955.) Washington: July 1985.

Van Der Kroef, Justus M. "Hanoi and ASEAN: A New Confrontation in Southeast Asia?" *Asia Quarterly* [Brussels], No. 4, 1976, 245–69.

"Vietnam's Aging Leaders Step Down," *Bangkok Post*, December 18, 1986, 1.

"Vietnam's Economic Growth and Debt Problem," *Indonesian Observer* [Jakarta], September 4, 1984, 7.

Watts, David. "Three Top Communist Party Leaders Quit Vietnamese Hierarchy," *Times* [London], December 18, 1986, 12.

————. "Vietnam Leader Admits Mistakes," *Times* [London], December 16, 1986, 10.

————. "Vietnam Party Picks Reformer in a Rout for the Old Guard," *Times* [London], December 19, 1986, 12.

Werner, Jayne. "Socialist Development: The Political Economy of Agrarian Reform in Vietnam," *Bulletin of Concerned Asian Scholars*, 16, No. 24, April–June 1984, 48–55.

"What Future?" *Asiaweek* [Hong Kong], 12, No. 14, April 6, 1986, 31–38.

Whebell, C.F.J. "Empire on the Mekong: Does Vietnam Have Further Territorial Ambitions," *Canadian Defence* [Toronto], 14, No. 4, Spring 1985, 39–42.

Woodside, Alexander Barton. *Community and Revolution in Modern Vietnam.* Boston: Houghton Mifflin, 1976.

_____. "Problems of Education in the Chinese and Vietnamese Revolutions," *Pacific Affairs* [Vancouver], 49, No. 44, Winter 1976-77, 648-66.

Young, Stephen B. "Good Government in Hanoi: The Dubious Harvest of Uncle Ho," *The American Spectator,* 15, No. 4, April 1982, 20-24.

_____. "Unpopular Socialism in United Vietnam," *Orbis,* 21, No. 1, Summer 1977, 227-34.

_____. "Vietnamese Marxism: Transition in Elite Ideology," *Asian Survey,* 19, No. 8, August 1979, 770-79.

Chapter 5

Aurora Foundation. *Re-education Camps and Prisons in the Socialist Republic of Vietnam.* Atherton, California: March 1985.

Bardain, Ernest F., et al. *Profile of North Vietnam Prisoners of War.* 4 vols. Washington: Advanced Research Projects Agency, 1971.

Beck, Carl, and Karen Eide Rawling. "The Military as a Channel of Entry into Positions of Political Leadership in Communist Party States," *Armed Forces and Society,* 3, No. 2, Winter 1977, 199-218.

Bernstein, Alvin H. "The Soviets in Cam Ranh Bay," *National Interest,* No. 3, Spring 1986, 17-29.

Boudarel, George (ed.). *Banner of People's War: The Party's Military Line.* Praeger: New York, 1970.

Bowman, John S. (ed.). *The Vietnam War: An Almanac.* New York: World Almanac Publications, 1985.

Butterfield, Fox. "Veterans Issue Troubling Hanoi," *New York Times,* October 28, 1971, 7.

_____. "Who Was This Enemy?" *New York Times Magazine,* February 4, 1973, 8-9.

Chanoff, David, and Doan Van Toai. *Portrait of the Enemy.* New York: Random House, 1986.

_____. *Vietnamese Gulag.* New York: Simon and Schuster, 1986.

Conley, Michael Charles. *The Communist Infrastructure in South Vietnam: A Study of Organization and Strategy.* 2 vols. Washington: Center for Social Systems, American University, 1967.

Dang Vu Hiep. "Basic Problems in the New Mechanism of Party Leadership over the Army and National Defense," *Nhan Dan* [Hanoi], April 23, 1984. Foreign Broadcast Information Service, *Daily Report: Asia and Pacific.* (FBIS-APA-84-108.) June 4, 1984, K8-K15.

Desbarats, Jacqueline, and Karl D. Jackson. "Political Violence in Vietnam: The Dark Side of Liberation," *Indochina Report* [Singapore], No. 6, April–June 1986.

Duiker, William J. *China and Vietnam: The Roots of Conflict.* (Indochina Research Monograph 1, IEAS.) Berkeley: University of California, 1986.

———. *The Communist Road to Power in Vietnam.* Boulder, Colorado: Westview Press, 1981.

———. *The Rise of Nationalism in Vietnam, 1900–1941.* Ithaca, New York: Cornell University Press, 1976.

Duncanson, Dennis J. *Government and Revolution in Vietnam.* New York: Oxford University Press, 1968.

Dunstan, Simon. *Vietnam Tracks: Armor in Battle, 1945–75.* Novato, California: Presidio Press, 1982.

Fall, Bernard B. *Breaking Our Chains: Documents on the Vietnamese Revolution of August 1945.* Hanoi: Foreign Languages Publishing House, 1960.

———. *The Two Viet-Nams: A Political and Military Analysis.* New York: Praeger, 1967.

———. *The Viet Minh Regime.* New York: Institute of Pacific Relations, 1956.

Garrett, Banning N., and Bonnie S. Glaser. *War and Peace: The Views from Moscow and Beijing.* (Policy Papers in International Affairs, No. 20.) Berkeley: Institute of International Studies, University of California, 1984.

Gurtov, Melvin. *Viet Cong Cadres and the Cadre System.* (Rand Memorandum 5414.) Rand: Santa Monica, California, 1967.

Heinzig, Dieter. *Sowjetische Interessen in Indochina* (Soviet Interests in Indochina). Cologne: Bundesinstitut Fur Ostwissenschaftliche und Internationale Studien, 1980.

Hoang Van Thai. *Aspects of Guerrilla Warfare in Vietnam.* Hanoi: Foreign Languages Publishing House, 1965.

Horn, Robert C. "Soviet-Vietnamese Relations and the Future of Southeast Asia," *Pacific Affairs* [Vancouver], 51, No. 4, Winter 1978–79, 585–605.

Huynh Kim Khanh. *Vietnamese Communism, 1925–1945.* Ithaca, New York: Cornell University Press, 1982.

Jacobs, G. "Vietnam's Potential Threat to ASEAN," *Asian Defence Journal* [Kuala Lumpur], May 1982, 16–27.

Joint Publications Research Service—JPRS (Washington). The following articles are from the JPRS series:
Southeast Asia Report
Haubold, Erhard. "Their Job is to Shoot, Breed Pigs, and Build Power Plants—Vietnam's Armed Forces as the Nation's Big

Classroom," *Frankfurter Allgemeine* [Frankfurt], March 1, 1984. (JPRS-SEA-84-054.) April 12, 1984, 80-82.

Khanh Van. "The Han River Literary Society Case," *Lao Dong* [Hanoi], August 22, 1985; August 29, 1985; September 12, 1985; September 19, 1985. (JPRS-SEA-85-191.) December 17, 1985, 120-37.

Le Duc Anh. "The Vietnam People's Army and Our Noble International Mission in the Friendly Country of Cambodia," *Tap Chi Quan Doi Nhan Dan* [Hanoi], December 1984. (JPRS-SEA-85-056.) April 2, 1985, 78-94.

Le Duy Luong. "Some Legal Terms," *Giao Duc Ly Luan* [Hanoi], October 1985. (JPRS-SEA-86-084.) May 16, 1986, 62-69.

"Military Academies, Military Colleges, and Advanced Schools." *Nhan Dan* [Hanoi], December 17, 1984. (JPRS-SEA-85-037.) February 22, 1985, 93-96.

Pham Hung. "Building People's Armed Forces That Are Worthy of Being the Reliable Tool of the Party, the Effective Instrument of the Proletarian Dictatorship State, the Beloved Sons and Daughters of the People," *Tap Chi Cong San* [Hanoi], October 1984. (JPRS-SEA-84-170.) December 11, 1984, 13-26.

Phan Hien. "Understanding Our State's Criminal Code," *Nhan Dan* [Hanoi], July 2-3, 1985. (JPRS-SEA 85-138.) September 12, 1985.

_____. "The Party's Leadership Is the Decisive Factor in Each Victory Won in the Struggle to Maintain National Security and Social Order," *Tap Chi Cong San* [Hanoi], September 1985. (JPRS-SEA-85-186.) December 5, 1985, 33-44.

"Rank Changes for Colonels, Naval Officers Cited," *Quan Doi Nhan Dan* [Hanoi], January 14, 1983. (JPRS83068.) March 15, 1983, 78.

"SRV Criminal Code." *Nhan Dan* [Hanoi], July 12,15-17, 1985. (JPRS-SEA-85-135.) September 3, 1985.

"SRV Criminal Code on Crimes Against State, Economic Crime, Articles 74-278," *Nhan Dan* [Hanoi], November 8, 1984. *Quan Doi Nhan Dan* [Hanoi], November 9, 1984. (JPRS-SEA-84-178.) December 26, 1984, 93-158.

"SRV Draft Constitution Contents, Terminology Explained." (JPRS-75213.) February 27, 1980.

"Terminology of Criminal Code Explained." (JPRS-SEA-86-220.) December 18, 1986.

Tran Le. "Twenty-Five Years of Activities and Growth of the People's Control Sector," *Tap Chi Cong San* [Hanoi], July 1985. (JPRS-SEA-85-148.) September 27, 1985, 22-30.

Tran Van Tra. *Vietnam: History of the Bulwark B-2 Theater. Vol. 5: Concluding the Thirty Years War.* Ho Chi Minh City: Van Nghe Publishing House, 1982. (Report No. 1247, JPRS-SEA 82-783.) 1983.

Lao Dong Party. *Historic Documents of the Lao Dong Party.* Hanoi: Foreign Languages Publishing House, 1970.

Lawson, Eugene K. *The Sino-Vietnamese Conflict.* New York: Praeger, 1984.

Le Duan. *Hold High the Revolutionary Banner.* Hanoi: Foreign Languages Publishing House, 1964.

_____. *This Nation and Socialism Are One.* Chicago: Vanguard Books, 1976.

_____. *The Vietnamese Revolution.* Hanoi: Foreign Languages Publishing House, 1970. Reprint. New York: International Publishers, 1971.

Lent, Michael. *Decision Making in the DRV.* Kensington, Maryland: American Institute for Research, July 1973.

Luxmoore, Jonathan. *Vietnam: The Dilemmas of Reconstruction.* (Conflict Studies Monograph 147.) London: Institute for the Study of Conflict, 1983.

McBeth, John. "Buildup on the Bay," *Far Eastern Economic Review* [Hong Kong], 122, No. 52, December 29, 1983, 16.

_____. "Vietnam's Reluctant Soldiers," *Far Eastern Economic Review* [Hong Kong], 108, No. 25, June 13, 1980, 43-44.

McGarvey, Patrick J. *Visions of Victory: Selected Vietnamese Communist Military Writings, 1964-68,* Stanford, California: Hoover Institution Press, 1969.

McLane, Charles B. *Soviet Strategies in Southeast Asia: An Exploration of Eastern Policy under Lenin and Stalin.* Princeton, New Jersey: Princeton University Press, 1966.

Nguyen Long (with Harry H. Kendall). *After Saigon Fell: Daily Life under the Vietnamese Communists.* (Research and Policy Studies 4.) Berkeley: Institute of East Asian Studies, University of California, 1981.

Nguyen P. Hung. "Communist Offensive Strategy and the Defense of South Vietnam," *Parameters,* 14, No. 4, Winter 1984, 3-19.

Nguyen Van Canh (with Earle Cooper). *Vietnam under Communism, 1975-82.* Stanford, California: Hoover Institution Press, 1983.

O'Neil, Robert J. *General Giap: Politician and Strategist.* New York: Praeger, 1969.

People's Army of Vietnam General Political Directorate. *The Party Military Committee: Its Organization, Mission, Leadership Principles and Governing Regulations,* Hanoi: Foreign Languages Publishing House, 1972.

Pham Huy Le (ed.). *Our Military Traditions.* (Vietnam Studies No. 55.) Hanoi: Foreign Languages Publishing House, n.d.

Pike, Douglas. "Conceptions of Asian Security: Indochina," *Asian Forum,* 8, Autumn 1976, 77–84.

_____. "Hanoi Looks to the Southwest." Pages 82–92 in Robert A. Scalapino and Jusuf Wanadi (eds.), *Economic, Political and Security Issues in Southeast Asia in the 1980's.* Berkeley: University of California Press, 1982.

_____. "Impact of the Sino-Soviet Dispute on Southeast Asia." Pages 185–205 in Herbert J. Ellison (ed.), *The Sino Soviet Conflict: A Global Perspective.* Seattle: University of Washington Press, 1982.

_____. *Life in North Vietnam, Part Two: The Law.* Berkeley: University of California, January 1973. (Unpublished.)

_____. "The Military Draft and Induction Process in the DRV, 1963–75." Berkeley: University of California. (Unpublished.)

_____. *PAVN: People's Army of Vietnam.* Novato, California: Presidio Press, 1986.

_____. "The Peoples Army of Vietnam." Unpublished paper presented at United States Asian Security Affairs Conference, Naval Postgraduate School, Monterey, California, 1982.

_____. "Soviet Response to an Intra-Communist Crisis: Indochina, 1979." (Unpublished paper read at the Eighteenth Annual Conference on Slavic Studies). October 1979.

_____. "The USSR and Vietnam." Pages 251–66 in Robert H. Donaldson (ed.), *The Soviet Union in the Third World.* Boulder, Colorado: Westview Press, 1981.

_____. *Viet Cong: The Organization and Techniques of the National Liberation Front of South Vietnam.* Cambridge: M.I.T. Press, 1966.

_____. *Vietnam and the USSR: Anatomy of an Alliance.* Boulder, Colorado: Westview Press, 1986.

_____. "Vietnam's Military Assistance," Pages 160–168 in John F. Copper and Daniel S. Papp (eds.), *Communist Nations' Military Assistance.* Boulder, Colorado: Westview Press, 1983.

_____. *War, Peace, and the Viet Cong.* Cambridge: M.I.T. Press, 1969.

Polmar, Norman. *Guide to the Soviet Navy.* (3rd ed.) Annapolis, Maryland: Naval Institute Press, 1983.

Quinn-Judge, Paul. "New Troops for Old," *Far Eastern Economic Review* [Hong Kong], 117, No. 31, July 30, 1982, 18–19.

_____. "Guns over Butter," *Far Eastern Economic Review* [Hong Kong], 127, No. 2, January 17, 1985, 18.

Richardson, Michael. "Hanoi's Nuclear Hand-Me-Down," *Far Eastern Economic Review* [Hong Kong], 100, No. 21, May 26, 1978, 8–9.

Rolph, Hammond. "Vietnamese Communism and the Protracted War," *Asian Survey*, 12, No. 9, September 1972, 783–92.

Rosenberger, Leif. "The Soviet-Vietnamese Alliance and Kampuchea," *Survey* [London], 27, Autumn–Winter 1983, 207–31.

Sagan, Ginetta, and Stephen Denney. *Violations of Human Rights in the SRV, April 30, 1975–April 30, 1983.* Atherton, California: Aurora Foundation, 1983.

Shaplen, Robert. *Bitter Victory.* New York: Harper and Row, 1987.

Song Hao. *Ten Years of Fighting and Building PAVN.* Hanoi: Foreign Languages Publishing House, 1965.

_____. *Discipline in PAVN.* Hanoi: Foreign Languages Publishing House, 1975.

Stetler, Russell (ed.). *The Military Art of People's War: Selected Writings of Vo Nguyen Giap.* New York: Monthly Review Press, 1970.

Tilman, Robert. "The Enemy Beyond: External Threat Perceptions in the ASEAN Region." (*Research Notes and Discussion Papers*, No. 42.) Singapore: Institute of Southwest Asian Studies, 1986.

Tran Van Tra. *A Bitter Dry Season for the Americans.* Hanoi: Foreign Languages Publishing House, 1966.

_____. *Five Lessons of a Great Spring Victory (Winter 1965–Spring 1967).* Hanoi: Foreign Languages Publishing House, 1967.

Turley, William S. "Civil-Military Relations in North Vietnam," *Asian Survey*, 9, No. 12, December 1969, 879–99.

_____. "Origins and Development of Communist Military Leadership in Vietnam," *Armed Forces and Society*, February 3, 1977, 219–47.

_____. *The Second Indochina War: A Short Political and Military History, 1954–75.* Boulder, Colorado: Westview Press, 1986.

_____. "The Vietnamese Army." Pages 63–82 in Jonathan R. Adelman (ed.), *Communist Armies in Politics.* Boulder, Colorado: Westview Press, 1982.

United States. Central Intelligence Agency. Directorate of Intelligence. *Directory of Officials of Vietnam.* Washington, 1985.

_____. Congress. 93rd, 1st Session. Senate. Committee on the Judiciary. Subcommittee to Investigate Administration of the Internal Security Act and Other Internal Security Laws. *The Human Cost of Communism in Vietnam: II, The Myth of No Blood.* (Hearing January 5, 1973.) Washington: GPO, 1973.

_____. Department of Defense. *Soviet Military Power: 1985.* Washington, 1985.

United States Information Service. "The Party in Command: Political Organization and the Viet Cong Armed Forces," (Vietnam Documents and Research Notes, No. 34.) Saigon: 1968.

University of California Indochina Archive Files. The following
materials are from the University of California Indochina Archive
Files, Berkeley, California:
File No. 4, Section 7:
   Part 24—"General Data on Armed Forces."
   Part 25—"Armed Forces Chronology."
   Part 26—"Party-Military Relationship."
   Part 27—"Para-Military and Militia."
   Part 28—"Armed Forces and the Economy."
   Part 29—"Armed Forces Recruitment and Training."
   Part 30—"Veterans and Military Dependents."
File No. 9, Section 7:
   Part 50—"Judicial and Legal Affairs."
   Part 51—"Law Enforcement."
   Part 52—"Internal Security."
Van Tien Dung. *People's War and National Defense*. 2 vols. Hanoi:
Foreign Languages Publishing House, 1979.
Vo Nguyen Giap. *Dien Bien Phu* (rev. ed.). Hanoi: Foreign Languages Publishing House, 1964.
_____. *General Strength of the Revolution*. Hanoi: Su That Publishing House, 1978.
_____. *National Liberation War in Vietnam: General Line, Strategy, and Tactics*. Hanoi: Foreign Languages Publishing House, 1971.
_____. *One Year of Revolutionary Achievement*. Bangkok: Vietnam News Publication, 1946.
_____. *Orders of the Day, Speeches, and Mobilization Letters*. Hanoi: Su That Publishing House, 1963.
_____. *Selected Writings*. Hanoi: Foreign Languages Publishing House, 1977.
_____. *To Arm the Revolutionary Masses to Build the People's Army*. Hanoi: Foreign Languages Publishing House, 1975.
_____. *Unforgettable Days*. Hanoi: Foreign Languages Publishing House, 1975.
_____. *War for National Liberation*. Hanoi: Su That Publishing House, 1979.
Warner, Denis (ed.). *Pacific Defense Reporter, 1983; Annual Reference Edition*. Victoria, Australia: Peter Issacson, 1983.
Wolf, Eric R. *Peasant Wars of the Twentieth Century*. New York: Harper and Row, 1969.
Young, Stephen. "The Legality of Vietnamese Re-education Camps," *Harvard International Law Journal*, 20, No. 3, Fall 1979, 519–38.
Zagoria, Donald. "Soviet Policy and Prospects in East Asia," *International Security*, Fall 1980, 66–78.

———. *Soviet Policy in East Asia.* New Haven: Yale University Press, 1982.

(Various issues of the following Vietnamese language publications published in Hanoi, the Socialist Republic of Vietnam, were also used in the preparation of this chapter: *Giao Duc Ly Luan, Hoc Tap, Lao Dong, Luat Hoc, Nhan Dan, Quan Doi Nhan Dan, Tap Chi Cong San,* and *Tap Chi Quan Doi Nhan Dan.*)

Glossary

Army of the Republic of Vietnam (ARVN)—The military ground
forces of the South Vietnamese government (Republic of Vietnam) until its collapse in April 1975. ARVN originated in the
Vietnamese military units raised by French authorities to defend
the Associated State of Vietnam in the early 1950s. During the
Second Indochina War (*q.v.*), it grew to over 1 million men
and women organized into eleven army divisions (plus specialized units, such as Rangers and Special Forces) deployed in
four Corps Tactical Zones (redesignated as Military Regions
in 1971).

Asian Development Bank (ADB)—Established in 1966, the ADB
assists in economic development and promotes growth and
cooperation in developing member countries. Membership
includes both developed and developing countries in Asia and
developed countries in the West.

Black Flag forces—A band of mostly Chinese adventurers who fled
to northern Vietnam after the collapse of the Taiping Rebellion (1851–64) in China. They eventually placed themselves
at the service of the imperial court in Hue and fought the French
forces in the 1883–84 Tonkin campaign.

boat people—Refugees who fled Vietnam by sea after 1975. Many
fell victim to pirate attacks in the Gulf of Thailand, drowned,
or endured starvation and dehydration as a result of their escape
in ill-equipped and undersized vessels. Those who reached
safety in neighboring Southeast Asian countries were accorded
temporary asylum in refugee camps while awaiting permanent
resettlement in industrialized Western nations willing to accept
them.

bonze—A general term for a Buddhist monk (as opposed to the
more specific *bhikku,* meaning an ordained monk).

Cao Dai—Indigenous Vietnamese religion centered in Tay Ninh
Province, southern Vietnam. It was founded and initially prop-
agated by Ngo Van Chieu, a minor official who, in 1919,
claimed to have had a series of revelations. The faith grew under
the leadership of Le Van Trung, its first "pope" or Supreme
Chief, chosen in 1925. Doctrinally, the religion is a syncretic
blend of Christianity, Buddhism, Taoism, Confuciancism and
Western nineteenth-century romanticism. Before the fall of
Saigon, the Cao Dai had about 1 to 2 million adherents.

chi bo—A party chapter composed of a collection of party cells (*to dang*), the lowest organizational echelon of the Indochinese and later the Vietnamese Communist Party.

chua—A lord or prince. The hereditary title used by the Trinh and Nguyen families, who ruled Vietnam in the name of the emperor during the later Le Dynasty in the sixteenth through the eighteenth centuries.

Colombo Plan—Founded in 1951 and known as the Colombo Plan for Cooperative Economic Development in South and Southeast Asia until it was expanded in 1977 and called the Colombo Plan for Cooperative Economic Development in Asia and the Pacific. It is an arrangement that permits a developing member country to approach a developed member country for assistance on a one-to-one basis. Assistance may be technical or in the form of capital or commodity aid.

Co Mat Vien—An advisory council set up by Emperor Minh Mang following the rebellion of Le Van Khoi in the 1830s.

Committee for Coordination of Investigations of the Lower Mekong Basin—Established in 1957 under the sponsorship of the United Nations Economic and Social Commission for Asia and the Pacific, the Committee aims to develop water resources in the lower Mekong basin through improvements in hydroelectric power, irrigation, flood control, watershed management, and navigation. Its membership is limited to Laos, Thailand, and Vietnam.

Communist International—Also called the Comintern or Third International, it was founded in Moscow in 1919 to coordinate the world communist movement. Officially disbanded in 1943, the Comintern was replaced from 1947 to 1954 by the Cominform (Communist Information Bureau), in which only the Soviet and the ruling East European communist parties (except for Yugoslavia, which was expelled in 1948) and the French and the Italian communist parties were represented. The Cominform was dissolved in 1956.

comprador—Vietnamese communist term (used originally in China to mean purchasing agent) applied disparagingly to the middleman who extracts a profit without engaging in economic production, that is, a "comprador capitalist." The term is also applied to an entrepreneur in Cholon, Ho Chi Minh City's predominantly Chinese sister city.

Council for Mutual Economic Assistance (Comecon)—Also abbreviated CEMA and CMEA, the organization was established in 1949 to promote economic cooperation among socialist bloc countries and is headquartered in Moscow. Its members in the

1980s included the Soviet Union, Bulgaria, Czechoslovakia, East Germany, Hungary, Poland, Romania, Cuba, Mongolia, and Vietnam.

democratic centralism—A basic Marxist-Leninist organizational principle accepted by all communist parties, including the Vietnamese (most recently at the Fourth National Party Congress in December 1976). It prescribes a hierarchical framework of party structures purportedly established through democratic elections.

dong (D)—Vietnam's monetary unit, which in mid-1989 had an exchange rate of US$1 to D4,500.

First Indochina War (1946–54)—The anticolonial conflict, also known as the Viet Minh War, between France and the Viet Minh, a Vietnamese communist-dominated coalition of Indochinese nationalist elements led by veteran revolutionary Ho Chi Minh. The French defeat at Dien Bien Phu in May 1954 marked the final episode of the war. The conflict was brought to an end officially by the Geneva Conference of July 1954 and its resulting agreements.

fiscal year (FY)—January 1 to December 31.

gross domestic product (GDP)—The value of domestic goods and services produced by an economy over a certain period, usually one year. Only output of goods for final consumption and investment is included because the values of primary and intermediate production are assumed to be included in final prices. Reductions for depreciation of physical assets are normally not included.

Group of 77—Founded in 1964 as a forum for developing countries to negotiate with developed countries for development aid, the original 77 developing nations had expanded by the 1980s to include the 127 members of the Nonaligned Movement (*q.v.*).

Hoa—Term applied by the Vietnamese to the ethnic Chinese residents of Vietnam.

Hoa Hao—Indigenous Vietnamese religion centered in An Giang Province, southern Vietnam. It was founded in the 1930s by Huynh Phu So, the son of a village elder in Chau Doc Province. Doctrinally, the faith is a variant of Mahayana Buddhism, but allows no intermediary between man and the Supreme Being. Before the fall of Saigon in 1975, the Hoa Hao had more than 1 million adherents.

Ho Chi Minh Trail—An intricate network of jungle trails, paths, and roads leading from the panhandle of northern Vietnam through Laos and Cambodia into the border provinces of southern Vietnam. At the height of the Second Indochina War (*q.v.*), it was a major resupply artery for Hanoi's armed forces operating in South Vietnam.

Indochina Federation—A political concept, never fully realized, joining the three Indochinese states into a confederation, first proposed at the Indochinese Communist Party Central Committee meeting in October 1930. The government of France resurrected the term in 1946 to describe a limited internal self-government granted to the states of Vietnam (including Cochinchina), Laos, and Cambodia. In the 1980s, the term was used disparagingly by some observers and analysts to categorize Vietnam's military presence in, and influence over, Laos and Cambodia.

International Monetary Fund (IMF)—Established along with the World Bank in 1945, the IMF is a specialized agency affiliated with the United Nations and is responsible for stabilizing international exchange loans to its members (including industrialized and developing countries) when they experience balance of payments difficulties. These loans frequently carry conditions that require substantial internal economic adjustments by the recipients, most of which are developing countries.

International Telecommunications Satellite Organization (INTELSAT)—Established by two international agreements concluded at Washington, D.C. in August 1971, and effective in February 1973, INTELSAT was formed to carry forward the development, construction, operation, and maintenance of the global commercial telecommunications satellite system. In the 1980s, there were 109 signatory member nations and 30 nonsignatory user nations.

Khmer Rouge—The name given to the Cambodian communists by Prince Norodom Sihanouk in the 1960s. Later, the term (although a misnomer) was applied to the insurgents of varying ideological backgrounds who opposed the Khmer Republic regime of Lon Nol. Between 1975 and 1978, it denoted the Democratic Kampuchea regime led by the radical Pol Pot faction of the Kampuchean (or Khmer) Communist Party. After being driven from Phnom Penh by the Vietnamese invasion of Cambodia in December 1978, the Khmer Rouge went back to guerrilla warfare and joined forces with two noncommunist insurgent movements to form the Coalition Government of Democratic Kampuchea.

missing-in-action (MIA)—United States military term for servicemen who remained unaccounted for at the end of the Second Indochina War (*q.v.*). In the 1980s, rumors persisted that some MIAs were still alive and had been detained involuntarily in Vietnam after the war.

National Assembly—The highest organ of government in Vietnam, according to the 1980 Constitution. The National Assembly is empowered with both constitutional and legislative authority. It can, theoretically at least, elect and remove members of upper-echelon government bodies, such as the Council of State and Council of Ministers; it may also pass laws, raise taxes, approve the state budget, and amend the constitution.

new economic zones—Population resettlement scheme undertaken in southern Vietnam after 1975 to increase food production and alleviate population pressure in congested urban areas, especially Ho Chi Minh City (Saigon). The sites selected for resettlement previously had been undeveloped or had been abandoned in the turbulence of war.

Nonaligned Movement (NAM)—Formed as the result of a series of increasingly structured nonaligned conferences, the first of which met at Belgrade, Yugoslavia in September 1961, the NAM's purpose is to insure the sovereignty and territorial integrity of nonaligned nations. In the 1980s, there were 127 member nations.

Parrot's Beak—The part of the Cambodian province of Svay Rieng that juts into the southern Vietnamese provinces of Tay Ninh and Long An. During the South Vietnamese and United States incursion into Cambodia in 1970, and again during the Vietnamese invasion that drove the Khmer Rouge from power in 1978, the area was the scene of heavy fighting.

People's Army of Vietnam (PAVN)—The military forces of the Democratic Republic of Vietnam (until 1976) and, after reunification, of the Socialist Republic of Vietnam. During the Second Indochina War (*q.v.*), PAVN bore the brunt of the fighting against the United States military forces in Vietnam, but was consistently able to recoup its losses and infiltrate units south by means of the Ho Chi Minh Trail (*q.v.*). Failing to topple the Saigon government during the Tet Offensive of 1968, PAVN undertook its first conventional invasion of South Vietnam in the Easter Offensive of 1972. This attempt ended in defeat, but PAVN's next effort, the Spring Offensive of 1975, quickly overran the ineffectual ARVN resistance and toppled the Saigon government, thereby bringing to a close the Second Indochina War.

Produced National Income (PNI)—A measure of an economy's material production that excludes income generated by the service sector and depreciation on capital equipment. It is used to measure controlled or communist economies where accounting procedures may ignore the service sector as "unproductive."

Ruble—Monetary unit of the Soviet Union, which in mid-1989 had an exchange rate of US$1 to Ruble 0.63.

search and destroy missions—Offensive military operations undertaken by United States combat units in Vietnam to find and neutralize the enemy, especially when the enemy's strength and disposition had not been fixed precisely. The capture and holding of territory during such operations was not a priority.

Second Indochina War (1954–75)—Armed conflict that pitted Viet Cong insurgents native to southern Vietnam and regular PAVN (*q.v.*) units with Chinese and Soviet logistical and matériel support on one side against ARVN (*q.v.*), United States, and smaller forces from the Republic of Korea (South Korea), Australia, Thailand and New Zealand on the other. Most of the ground fighting occurred in southern Vietnam. However, part of the conflict also involved an intensive air war over North Vietnam and Laos from 1965–73 and combat between competing indigenous forces in Laos and Cambodia.

to dang—A party cell, the lowest organizational echelon of the Indochinese and later the Vietnamese Communist Party.

Viet Cong—Contraction of the term Viet Nam Cong San (Vietnamese communists), the name applied by the governments of the United States and South Vietnam to the communist insurgents in rebellion against the latter government, beginning around 1957. The Vietnamese communists never used the term themselves, but referred to their movement as the National Front for the Liberation of South Vietnam (also known as the National Liberation Front), formally inaugurated in December 1960.

Viet Minh—Contraction of the term Viet Nam Doc Lap Dong Minh Hoi (Vietnam Independence League), a coalition of nationalist elements dominated by the communists and led by veteran revolutionary Ho Chi Minh. The movement first identified itself in May 1941, when it called for an uprising against the French colonial government. It proclaimed the independence of Vietnam on September 2, 1945, and led the anti-French guerrilla war that followed, until the victory at Dien Bien Phu brought the conflict to an end.

World Bank—The informal name used to designate a group of three affiliated international institutions: the International Bank for Reconstruction and Development (IBRD), the International Development Association (IDA), and the International Finance Corporation (IFC). The IBRD, established in 1945, has the primary purpose of providing loans to developing countries for productive projects. The IDA, a legally separate loan fund administered by the staff of the IBRD, was set up in 1960 to furnish credits to the poorest developing countries on much easier terms than those of conventional IBRD loans. The IFC, founded in 1956, supplements the activities of the IBRD through loans and assistance designed specifically to encourage the growth of productive private enterprises in less developed countries. The president and certain senior officers of the IBRD hold the same positions in the ICF. The three institutions are owned by the governments of the countries that subscribe their capital. To participate in the World Bank group, member states must first belong to the International Monetary Fund (*q.v.*).

Index

Middle Kingdom, 247
military assistance: by Soviet Union, 222–23, 284
military equipment, 278–79
Military Intelligence Department (PAVN), 277
Military Management Commission, 190
Military Obligation Law, 262
military policy-making structure, 275
military relations, 287
military service, 262–63
Militia/Self-Defense Force (PAVN), 274
mineral resources, 146
Ming dynasty (China), 17
Minh Mang, 28
Ministry of Agriculture and Food Industry, 209
Ministry of Culture, 233
Ministry of Defense, 275; organization of, 277; Party Committee within, 275
Ministry of Energy, 209
Ministry of Finance, 168, 178
Ministry of Foreign Trade, xlvii, 164
Ministry of Information, 209
Ministry of Interior, 131, 281, 335; organization of, 292–93
Ministry of Labor, War Invalids, and Social Welfare, 209
Ministry of National Defense, 131, 250, 261
minority peoples: languages and dialects, 98; location of, 96, 98, 100–101; sedentary and nomadic, 96, 98, 100
missionaries, European, 23, 29–30, 31
Mnong people, 100
money supply. *See* inflation
Mongols: invasion by and defeat of, 16–17
Mon-Khmer language, 7, 93
monsoon, 89
Montagnards, 96, 128, 289–90
mountains, 86
Muc Quan, 183
municipalities, autonomous, 211
Muong people, 14, 28, 96, 98

Naforimex, 169
Nam Bo, 4, 43
Nam Viet, 8, 12
Nan-chao, 14
National Assembly, 156, 170, 190, 204, 205, 206–7, 208, 209, 261; changing

goals set by, xli–xlii; role in military policy-making, 275; Standing Committee of, 178, 205, 260
National Committee on Family Planning, 92
National Congress of Red Trade Unions, 42
National Defense Council (NDC), 208, 250, 260–61, 275, 329
National Front for the Liberation of South Vietnam (Viet Cong). *See* National Liberation Front (NLF)
nationalism, 5, 11, 35–40, 204, 211, 213
nationalization, xxxviii, 158, 163; effect on industry of, 190
National Liberation Front (NLF), 61, 62, 99, 197, 226, 251; 326; forms PRG with allies, 72; mission in Moscow of, 65
National Party Congress, 195; Fifth (1982), xxxviii, 151, 166, 228, 332; First (1935), 191, 194; Fourth (1976), xxxvii, xxxviii, 92, 150, 190, 192, 193, 199, 205, 210, 266, 327; Second (1951), 191, 202, 250; Sixth (1986), xxxvii, xl, xli, 111, 112, 137, 143–44, 166, 190, 194, 194–96, 200, 209, 224, 228; Third (1960), 192, 206, 294
National Salvation Army, 49
National Salvation Associations (Cuu Quoc Hoi), 49
national security, 213
NATO. *See* North Atlantic Treaty Organization (NATO)
Natuna Islands, 231
natural gas, 146
natural resources, 146
Navy (PAVN), 278
Navarre, Henri, 56
Nazi-Soviet Non-Agression pact, 45
NDC. *See* National Defense Council (NDC)
the Netherlands, 176
new economic zones, xxxvii, 92, 110–11, 118, 147, 304
New Revolutionary Party (Tan Viet Party), 42
new social order. *See* social structure
ngai (*see also* Hoa), 101
Nghe An Province, 35, 40, 43, 44
Nghe-Tinh revolt, 43–45
Nghia Binh Province, 183

People's Liberation Armed Force (PLAF), 62, 64, 66, 67, 72, 73, 78, 251–52
People's Liberation Army (PLA). *See* People's Liberation Armed Force (PLAF)
People's Organ of Control. *See* Supreme People's Organ of Control
People's Public Security Force (PPSF) (*see also* secret police), 288, 296
People's Republic of Kampuchea (PRK), xliv, 216, 217, 257
People's Revolutionary Committees (VCP), 190
People's Revolutionary Party, 327
People's Security Force (PSF), 288, 293–95
People's Security Service (PSS), 265, 296–98
People's Self-Defense Force Program, 73
People's Supreme Procurate. *See* Supreme People's Organ of Control
people's war, 242
pepper, 104
Pha Lai, 161
Pham Hung, xli, 61, 199, 293, 326, 330
Pham Quynh, 39
Pham The Duyet, 334
Pham Van Dong, 45, 51, 110, 194, 199, 225, 261, 326, 330
Phan Boi Chau, 5, 35–38, 40, 44
Phan Chu Trinh, 5, 36–37
Phan Dinh Phung, 32
Philippines, 229, 230
Phnom Penh, xxxix, 89, 214, 255, 257
Phnom Penh government, 216–17
Pho Hien, 23
Phu Bai, 185
Phu Khanh Province, 183
Phung-nguyen culture, 7
Phuoc Binh, 76
Phuoc Long Province, 76
Phuoc Tuy, 73
Phu Quoc, 185
Phu Xuan, 26
Pike, Douglas, 199
pipeline, 183
PLA. *See* Chinese People's Liberation Army (PLA), *See* People's Liberation Army (PLA)
PLAF. *See* People's Liberation Armed Force (PLAF)
plateaus, 86
Pleiku, 76, 78, 185

police functions (*see also* secret police), 287, 293
Police Protection Regiment, 297
Political Bureau (VCP), xli, 194, 196, 199, 205, 207, 255, 275, 325–32
political commissar, 253, 268–69
political officer in PAVN (*see also* political commissar), 273
political parties, noncommunist, 51, 52
political prisoners, xlvi, 44–45
political struggle, 67
political system (*see also* Confucianism); historical foundation for, 200
Pol Pot, xliv–xlv, 72
Pol Pot regime (*see also* Democratic Kampuchea; Khmer Rouge), 213, 214, 216, 230, 255
polygyny, 114, 118
population: density and growth of, xxxvii, 90–91, 144; displacement by war of, 107–8; redistribution/relocation plan for, 92–93, 100, 110, 117, 304
population control. *See* family planning
ports, 183
Potsdam Conference, 51
Poulo Condore (Con Dao), 30, 37, 45
PPSF. *See* People's Public Security Force (PPSF)
price structure (*see also* contract system; quotas; market system), 157–58, 179; differentials for state and free-market commodities, 180
Prince Canh, 25
prison system, 302–3, 305
private enterprises, xliii
PRK. *See* People's Republic of Kampuchea (PRK)
productivity, 156
Propaganda and Training Department. *See* Central Committee
propaganda teams, 257
Protectorate of Annam, 12
Protestants, 128
Provisional Revolutionary Government of the Republic of South Vietnam (PRG), 72, 189, 226
PSS. *See* People's Security Service (PSS)
publications, 233–34
public health, 134–36

Qin dynasty (China), 8
Qing dynasty (China), 26, 28

Quan Doi Nhan Dan, 137
Quang Nam Province, 25, 36, 37
Quang Ngai Province, 37, 49, 67
Quang Ninh Province, 329
Quang Tri city, 73
Quang Tri Province, 73, 76
Quang Trung, 26, 240
Qui Nhon, 25, 183
quoc ngu, 23–24, 35, 38–39, 49, 95
quotas (*see also* dual quota planning); for production, 180
Quynh Luu uprising, 289

Rach Gia, 185
Raglai people, 100
railroads, 182–83
rationing, 137, 179
Reagan, Ronald, xliv, 227
Red Flag Security, 288
Red River Delta, 3, 4, 7, 8, 85, 92, 119, 120, 153
Red River (Song Hong), 85, 183
Red-Scarf Teenagers' Organization, 197
re-education camps, xlvi, 110, 118, 304–6
reform camps, 111
refugees, 102, 108, 110–11, 257; Indochinese, 227; relaxation of policy concerning, xlvii; from Vietnam to China, 219
Regional Force (PAVN), 274
registration system, 306
Regular Force (PAVN), 274
Religious Affairs Committee, 126
relocation strategy, 92–93, 107–8, 147
remittances, overseas, 177–78
Republic of Vietnam (South Vietnam), 60, 189, 205
reunification of Vietnam, xxxv, 4–5, 189, 190, 205; problems of, xxxvii
revenue, 178
Revolutionary Action Movement (RAM), 298–99
Revolutionary Vigilance Committees, 306
rice cultivation, 7, 86, 104
Rivière, Henri, 32
roads, 182–83
rubber industry, 104, 168, 172–73

Sadang people, 100
Saigon (*see also* Gia Dinh; Saigon-Cholon;

Ho Chi Minh City), 5, 30, 35, 40, 49, 107, 214; in Tet offensive, 70, 72
Saigon government (*see also* Diem regime), 76; recognition of minorities by, 99
salvation associations, 49
San Chay people, 96
satellite-ground stations, 185
scholar-officials, xxxvi, 16, 95, 102, 103, 129, 201, 203
schools, 130; under French colonial rule, 35; state control and reform of, 129–30; vocational, 130–31
search and destroy missions, 66
secret police, 296
security, internal, 287–88; role of youth organizations for, 298; security interzones for, 295–96
shipping, 183, 185
Siam, 31
Sihanouk, Norodom, xliv, 72, 216
silica sand, 146
Singapore, 229; trade with, 170–71
Sinicization (*Han hwa*), xxxvi, 3, 9, 201
Sitthi Sawetsila, xlvii
slash-and-burn farming, 98
social control mechanisms (*see also* re-education camps; surveillance), 110–11, 303–5
socialism, 83; conflict with capitalism of, 83, 109
socialist family, 119
socialist legality concept, 206
Socialist Republic of Vietnam (SRV), 189, 190
social reconstruction, 118
social structure: development and changes in, 102–5; new social order in, 106, 110–12
Song Be Province, 173
Song Da (Black River; Riviere Noire), 85
Song dynasty (China), 14–15
Song Hong (Red River), 85
Song Lo (Clear River; Riviere Claire), 85
Son Sann, 216
South China Sea, 86, 219
Southeast Asia: influence in Vietnam of, 201
sovereignty of people concept, 205–6
Soviet Intersputnik Communication Satellite Organization, 185
soviets (Bolshevik term), 44
Soviet Union, 146, 150; alignment of Vietnam with, 194; economic aid to

Vietnam by, xxxix–xl, 173, 177, 223; educational ties with, 131–32; food and commodity aid to Vietnam, 223; military assistance to Hanoi government by, xxxix–xl, 222–23, 254, 284, 286–87; political influence in Vietnam of, 202; presence in Vietnam of, 286; relations with, xxxix, 190–91, 211; role in Second Indochina War of, 64–65; role in Vietnamese affairs of, 221–22; shipping in Vietnam by, 183; trade treaty with, 166, 172; trade with, 169, 169–70, 171–72

Special Operations Force (PAVN), 278
special zone, 210
Spratly Islands, xlv, 219, 230–31
SRV. *See* Socialist Republic of Vietnam (SRV)
State Bank of Vietnam, 167, 181
State Commission for Cooperation and Investment, xlvii
state enterprises, 178, 180
State Planning Commission, 136, 178
Stieng people, 100
strategic hamlet program, 61
strategic planning (*see also dau tranh*), 242–45
Strategic Rear Force, 274
strikes, 43
student exchange, 131
subsidies, 179; for commodities, 180; for procurement, 168
Sun Yat-sen, 37
supply shortages, xxxvii–xxxviii, 158
Supreme People's Court, 205, 206–7, 208, 209, 300
Supreme People's Organs of Control, 207, 208, 209, 209–10, 303
surveillance, 111, 307
Sweden, 170, 176, 232

Tactical Rear Force, 274
Tai language, 7, 93
Tai people, 14
Taiping Rebellion, 31
Tang dynasty (China), xxxvi, 12, 14
Tan Son Nhut airport, 70, 185, 282
Tan Trao conference, 50
Tan Viet Party, 42
Taoism, 83, 128
Tap Chi Cong San (Communist Review), 234, 329

taxation, 178
Tay Ninh Province, 67, 290
Tay Nung people, 28, 45
Tay people, 96, 98
Tay Son Rebellion, 24–26
tea, 104
Technoimport, 169
telecommunications, 185
telephone system, 185–86
Television Vietnam, 235–36
Ten Circuit Army, 14
Tet offensive, 70–72
Thai-Cambodian border, 220
Thailand, 183, 229, 230, 231; importance to Vietnam of, xlvii
Thai Nguyen Province, 38, 49
Thai people, 96, 98
Thang Long (Hanoi), 16, 26
Thanh Hoa, 183
Thanh Hoa Province, 7
Thanh Nien. *See* Viet Nam Thanh Nien Cach Menh Dong Chi Hoi (Revolutionary Youth League)
Thanh Nien Tien Phong (Vanguard Youth), 49, 50
Thieu. *See* Nguyen Van Thieu
Tho Xuan, 281
Three Cleans movement, 135
Three Exterminations movement, 135
Thuc, 8
tin production, 146, 173
titanium, 146
To Huu, 331
Tong Binh (Hanoi), 14
Tonkin, 4, 31, 33, 35
Tourane (Da Nang), 30
tourism, 168
trade, foreign (*see also* Comecon countries; economic planning; exports; imports), 164, 166–67; decentralization for purposes of, 168–69; volume with Comecon and non-Comecon countries, 169–70, 223
trade boycott, 162, 167, 171
trade deficit, 169–70, 177
trade embargo (*see also* trade boycott), xl, 227
trading companies, 168–69
trading corporations, state, 168–69
Tran dynasty, 16
Tran Hieu, 296
Tran Hung Dao, 16
Tran Kien, 332

Published Country Studies

(Area Handbook Series)

550–65	Afghanistan	550–153	Ghana
550–98	Albania	550–87	Greece
550–44	Algeria	550–78	Guatemala
550–59	Angola	550–174	Guinea
550–73	Argentina	550–82	Guyana
550–169	Australia	550–151	Honduras
550–176	Austria	550–165	Hungary
550–175	Bangladesh	550–21	India
550–170	Belgium	550–154	Indian Ocean
550–66	Bolivia	550–39	Indonesia
550–20	Brazil	550–68	Iran
550–168	Bulgaria	550–31	Iraq
550–61	Burma	550–25	Israel
550–37	Burundi/Rwanda	550–182	Italy
550–50	Cambodia	550–30	Japan
550–166	Cameroon	550–34	Jordan
550–159	Chad	550–56	Kenya
550–77	Chile	550–81	Korea, North
550–60	China	550–41	Korea, South
550–26	Colombia	550–58	Laos
550–33	Commonwealth Caribbean, Islands of the	550–24	Lebanon
550–91	Congo	550–38	Liberia
550–90	Costa Rica	550–85	Libya
550–69	Côte d'Ivoire (Ivory Coast)	550–172	Malawi
550–152	Cuba	550–45	Malaysia
550–22	Cyprus	550–161	Mauritania
550–158	Czechoslovakia	550–79	Mexico
550–36	Dominican Republic/Haiti	550–76	Mongolia
550–52	Ecuador	550–49	Morocco
550–43	Egypt	550–64	Mozambique
550–150	El Salvador	550–88	Nicaragua
550–28	Ethiopia	550–157	Nigeria
550–167	Finland	550–94	Oceania
550–155	Germany, East	550–48	Pakistan
550–173	Germany, Fed. Rep. of	550–46	Panama

550-156	Paraguay	550-89	Tunisia
550-185	Persian Gulf States	550-80	Turkey
550-42	Peru	550-74	Uganda
550-72	Philippines	550-97	Uruguay
550-162	Poland	550-71	Venezuela
550-181	Portugal	550-32	Vietnam
550-160	Romania	550-183	Yemens, The
550-51	Saudi Arabia	550-99	Yugloslavia
550-70	Senegal	550-67	Zaire
550-180	Sierra Leone	550-75	Zambia
550-184	Singapore	550-171	Zimbabwe
550-86	Somalia		
550-93	South Africa		
550-95	Soviet Union		
550-179	Spain		
500-96	Sri Lanka		
550-27	Sudan		
550-47	Syria		
550-62	Tanzania		
550-53	Thailand		

☆U.S. GOVERNMENT PRINTING OFFICE: 1989 -0- 261-866 (00017)